SOCIAL THOUGHTS
and
THEIR IMPLICATIONS
CRITICALLY ANALYSE

KAZI ABDUR ROUF

SOCIAL THOUGHTS AND THEIR IMPLICATIONS: CRITICALLY ANALYSE

iUniverse books may be ordered through booksellers or by contacting:

iUniverse
1663 Liberty Drive
Bloomington, IN 47403
www.iuniverse.com
1-800-Authors (1-800-288-4677)

Because of the dynamic nature of the Internet, any web addresses or links contained in this book may have changed since publication and may no longer be valid. The views expressed in this work are solely those of the author and do not necessarily reflect the views of the publisher, and the publisher hereby disclaims any responsibility for them.

Any people depicted in stock imagery provided by Getty Images are models, and such images are being used for illustrative purposes only. Certain stock imagery © Getty Images.

ISBN: 978-1-5320-5961-2 (sc)
ISBN: 978-1-5320-5962-9 (e)

Print information available on the last page.

iUniverse rev. date: 12/17/2018

Dedication

My great grand father
Late Nasuruddin Sarker
My cousin
Late Quazi Enamul Haque (Danu Vhai)
My brothers
Late Kazi Abdur Rob
Late Kazi Abdul Matin and
My wife Sabina Muzammel

Biography of the Author

Kazi Abdur Rouf has worked in several micro-credit programs, small and medium enterprise (SME) development projects, women's development schemes, community schooling services, community forestry, environmental development and social economy organizations in UNDP Namibia, UNDP Lesotho, UNHCR Afghanistan, UNHCR Pakistan, Red Cross Canada, Good Faith Funds, USA, Toronto Social Services (TSS) and Alterna Savings Community Banking Toronto. Moreover, he woked in community-based different cooperative organizations and facilitated organizational capacity building of many NGOs like Grameen Bank Bangladesh, Grameen Shakti, micro-credit organizations in Philippines, Zimbabwe, Zambia, India, USA and in Canada. He also evaluates many social business organizations like Kasaf Foundation Pakistan, Taraquee Queta Pakistan, COSEDA Namibia, TAKMA Lesotho and Desh Foundation Bangladesh. Rouf has working experience in green micro-financing, community organizing, health and nutrition education, agricultural project management, community education and project management. Currently, he is researching on poverty, social and green business development, community economic development, population problem, and women development.

Researcher Kazi Abdur Rouf completed his Ph. D. from the University of Toronto. Rouf completed his other academic degrees like Masters in Environmental Studies (2008), Post-Graduate in Business and Environment (2008) and BA (2006) with distinction in Women Studies and International Development, York University, Canada; Diploma in Social Work (2005), Centennial College, Canada; MA in Sociology (1980) and BA (Hons.) in Sociology, Chittagong University, Bangladesh in 1978. Moreover, he completed Diploma in Applied Food Science and Nutrition, Dhaka University in 1984. He was a visiting faculty of Chittagong University and a visiting scholar at the University of Toronto. Currently, he is a professor of the Noble International University and founder of Public Welbeing Integrated Services (PWIS) Canada; manager, Noble Institution for Environmental Peace, Research Associate, Center for Learning Social Economy and Work; International Visiting Scholar, School of Education, Indiana University Bloomington USA.

Preface

The book is an attempt to compile author's fifteen essays in a hard copy form that are published in different e-journals in North America, Australia, the Philippines and in India. The essays of the book contain implications of feminist thoughts, social business thoughts, green microfinance and green microenterprise development notions with examples. The essays also contain social economy theories, blue and green economics ideas, ecological theories, environmental theories, community economic development thoughts, citizenry skills development concepts, poverty eradication and good governance approaches, local living economics propositions and their implications in Bangladesh. The last few essays of the book is about different concepts, theories, and approaches to management practices for sustainable business development in the world. The book has its roots analysing social development different thoughts and services to identify gaps and to solve environmental degradation problems, employment generation, poverty reduction, and to identify sustainable 'bottom-up' social development approaches. Moreover, the book explores the process of empowerment of the poor, good governance, and raising community solidarity capital among disadvantaged people in Bangladesh.

In the book, the author writes the essays in a debate form in order to analyse social development different thoughts with examples to explore appropriate initiatives need to be taken for improving disadvantage people livelihoods in Bangladesh and elsewhere. The essays describe how government of Bangladesh and different non-governmental national and international agencies of social development like Asrayan Prokalpa, Grameen Bank, BARC, ASA, Proshika, Nijera Korri, Grameen DANONE, Grameen Health, Grameen Shikka, World Bank

Bangladesh, UNDP Bangladesh, CARE Bangladesh and CIDA etc. are facing challenges to support and implement their development programs in Bangladesh. The author has been working with different NGOs, MFIs, government organizations and international agencies in Bangladesh and abroad since 1978. The author writes the essays and analyses social development different thoughts and programs and discerns their applicability in Bangladesh with his praxis knowledge.

Here the book delighted to note that the author is thankful to Ellie Perkins, Abedin Kusno, Roger Hensall and other dignitaries who have encouraged him for writing the essays. The author acknowledges with thanks his wife, Sabina Muzammel, for writing the essays and publishing the book.

Kazi Abdur Rouf

Contents

Green Microfinance promoting Green Enterprise development

Abstract

The purpose of the research is to examine the possibility of introducing market-based green business development in Canada that would model that of GB and its sister organizations.

Microcredit is a well known tool to address the issue of poverty that is a condition that affects the bottom fifty percent of people. The microeconomic determination program is expanding all over the world to develop economic growth in people's lives; however, if MFI's are not controlled and they are provided to people who practice unsafe and un-ecofriendly businesses, the effect could be a minimalist microcredit approach that is unable to promote sustainable business development. The microcredit programs could not only neglects sustainable development, but also destroys the earth and those who are more closely dependent on it —rural communities if their loan services are not environmentally friendly. Therefore, recent, varied literature is urging for an integrated microfinancing program that has a central socially responsible investment component. This component key feature would be the promotion of socio-cultural, environmental and business development while advancing social capital, human capital, and natural capital with economic growth.

To understand microcredit and renewable energy programs for green development, the researcher visited and studied Grameen Bank Bangladesh, Grameen Shokti's Renewable Energy Project in winter 2008 and had an internship at Alterna Savings' Community Micro Loan Funds program in Toronto in summer 2007 and fall 2007 respectively. This was to gain valuable experience as it relates their green operational microcredit

1

strategies, policies and programs. The researcher stayed in the villages and spoke with GB and GS borrowers. He also read various literatures on green microcredit and sustainable business development. This paper envisions a comparison and contrasting of Grameen Bank and Grameen Shokti credit systems (Bangladesh) with Alterna Savings credit programs (Canada) and its impact on Toronto's local living economics and environmental development. Findings show that within the two sample cases, microcredits are positive to environmental sustainable development.

Grameen Bank green microcredit-programs target microbusiness owners in order to assist them in becoming economically self-sufficient through self-employment. Grameen Bank Bangladesh has accomplished these socio-economic, environmental, sustainable green development features by creating its in-house, sector based institutional collaborative model. Grameen Bank, Grameen Shakti renewable energy (GS) in Bangladesh and Alterna Savings in Canada are examples of green microcredit schemes that implement green business development programs.

Keywords: Green microfinance; green enterprise; Grameen Bank; microfinance institutions (MFIs); solar home system; women empowerment; small and medium enterprises (SME).

Acronyms: Grameen Bank (GB), Grameen Shokti (GS), integrated pest management (IPM), Millennium Development Goals (MDGs), self-employment development initiative (SEDI), green micro-finance institution (GMFI), world center for environmental development (WCED), non-government organizations (NGOs), energy savings company (ESCO), Royal Bank corporation (RBC), Trust Bank (TD), Alterna Savings Community Micro Loan Fund (ACMLF).

1. Introduction

Microcredit is a well known tool to address the issue of poverty that is a condition that affects the bottom fifty percent of people. Microcredit alleviates poverty by engaging communities in microloans and micro-businesses so that they may earn income. This new microeconomic determination program is expanding all over the world to develop economic growth in people's lives; however, if microfinance institutions (MFIs) are not controlled and they are provided to people who practice unsafe and non-eco-friendly businesses, the effect could be a minimalist microcredit approach that is unable to promote sustainable business development. The result will be a microcredit program that is not only neglects sustainable development, but destroys the earth and those who are more closely dependent on it rural communities. Therefore, recent varied literature is urging for an integrated micro-financing program that has a central, socially responsible investment component. The components key feature would be the promotion of socio-cultural, environmental and business development while advancing social capital, human capital, and natural capital with economic growth. Therefore, the matter of sustainable, people-centered environmental developmentis urgent.

To understand microcredit and renewable energy programs for green development, the researcher visited and studied Grameen Bank (GB) Bangladesh; Grameen Shokti's (GS) Renewable Energy Project Bangladesh in winter 2008 and had an internship at the Alterna Savings' Community Micro Loan Fundsprogram in Toronto in the summer and fall of 2007 respectively. This was to gain valuable experience as it relates their green operational microcredit strategies, policies and programs. The researcher stayed in the villages and spoke with GB and GS borrowers. He also read various literatures on green microcredit. This paper envisions a comparison and contrasting of Grameen Bank and Grameen Shokti credit systems (Bangladesh) with Alterna Savings credit programs (Canada) and its impact on Toronto's local living economics and environmental development. The findings are positive to environmental sustainable development.

Green microcredit programs target micro-business owners in order to assist them in becoming economically self-sufficient through self-employment. They also help marginalized women entrepreneurs in their empowerment and promote community-based, local living development.

Grameen Bank Bangladesh has accomplished these socio-economic, environmental, sustainable green development features by creating its in-house, sector-based institutional collaborative model. Contrarily in Canada, people are looking for public funds for poverty-related projects and for socially and environmental responsible investment projects. Grameen Bank, Grameen Shakti (renewable energy) (GS) in Bangladesh and Alterna Savings in Canada are examples of green microcredit schemes that implement green business development programs. The purpose of the study is to examine the possibility of introducing market-based green business development in Canada that would model that of Grameen Bank and its sister organizations.

1.1 Thesis statement

Within a microenterprise development model that has a positive environmental and social focus, microcredit programs can promote and achieve environmental, social and economic gains that are needed for the sustainable development of disadvantaged people.

Microcredit is a well known tool to address the issue of poverty that is a condition that affects the bottom fifty percent of people. Microcredit alleviates poverty by engaging communities in microloans and micro-businesses so that they may earn income. This new microeconomic determination program is expanding all over the world to develop economic growth in people's lives; however, if MFI's are not controlled and they are provided to people who practice unsafe and un-eco friendly businesses, the effect could be a minimalist microcredit approach that is unable to promote sustainable green business development. The result will be a microcredit program that not only neglects sustainable development, but destroys the earth and those who are more closely dependent on it – rural communities. Therefore, recent varied literature is urging for an integrated green social micro financing program that has a central, socially green responsible investment component. This sustainable and people-centered environmental green social development program is urgent. Therefore, the research seeks to explore how microfinance can be structured to create sustainable development through green microenterprise while simultaneously achieving economic, social and environmental goals to address the issue of self-employment.

Green microcredit programs target micro business owners in order to assist them in becoming economically self-sufficient through self-employment. They also help marginalized women entrepreneurs in their empowerment and promote community-based, local living development. Grameen Bank, Bangladesh has accomplished these socio-economic, environmental, sustainable green development features by creating its in-house, sector based institutional collaborative model. Grameen Bank, Grameen Shakti (renewable energy) (GS) in Bangladesh and Alterna Savings in Canada are examples of green microcredit schemes that implement green business development programs.

2. Definitions of microfinance and green microfinance

Microfinance is a program that involves serving the poorest communities in any one area or country, by providing them with soft loans to develop and maintain businesses. The program seeks to provide hands-on support to those who are interested in conducting businesses that better the communities in which they reside without providing harm as a result of their work. Green microfinance is the same sort of program, the difference is that soft loans are provided to individuals or groups of individuals who work directly to support sustainable green and social development, create green jobs and environmentally progressive solutions to practices that are destroying and polluting the earth.

This green microloan service follows the environmental mantra of: recycle, refine and reuse resources. Green businesses are not harmful to the environment, rather they accelerate green social development that is people-centered, fosters human health, promotes social justice, generates income, addresses the issue of poverty and reduces waste in the environment. It not only seeks profit, but it also looks at ecological balance within businesses, resources, the environment and society.

5

Green microbusiness can increase marginalized people's income in order to survive, improve their quality of life as well preserve the environment.

2.1 The importance of green microfinance

Sustainable development and green business development, at the micro-level, need to focus on a goal that encompasses economic, social and environmental concerns. This view is shared by Allen, and Thomas (2000), Anderson (2002), Chambers and Conway (1992), Clerke and Clegg (1998), Colbert (2004), Hick (2004), MacDonald and Oates (2006), Milani (2001), Prahalad and Hamel (2006), Slayter, B. (2003), Torjman (2006), WECD (1987), and Yunus(2002). They all mention that these are necessary elements for sustainable development; one that is able to contribute to the local economy, green development and sustainable livelihood at the local and national levels. There are obviously a number of reasons for the relevance of microfinance to environment:

(1) environmental concerns are very important to increasing the poor's standard of living and quality of life; and

(2) the most transformative green technologies and relationships are ideal for creating sustainable livelihoods as well as improving quality of life; and

(3) microfinance is a decentralized form of investment, totally appropriate for decentralized green forms of production.

Of course, the concern is with the fact that conventional microcredit has not yet become green enough; however, few of them have built-in environmental conservation/development/education programs in their mainstream activities in addition to their focus on economic development practice.

Corporate waste; their toxic products and factory emissions, are spread on the lands, in the air and water. Therefore, corporations hold the major brunt of responsibility for environmental pollution. As a result, it is very important to reduce land pollution, indoor air pollution and water pollution. Grameen Bank and Grameen Shokti (the energy arm of Grameen Bank) are addressing these problems through the provision of microcredit to poor people and installing solar home systems; biogas produced in biogas plants and improved cooking stoves (ICS's) for renewable energy to use at the rural household level. Women cook with bio-gas instead of using wood, animal dung or other bio-fuels. This helps to save energy, use renewable energy and encourages environmental development.

In North America, energy consumption is a central issue. Every day, large amounts of waste are created by individual dwellings, restaurants, hospitals and factories. Packaging waste is also a large problem. Companies make products that end up as garbage, and tax payers become responsible for waste removal and management. Therefore, zero-waste, closed-loop protocols and shifting the responsibility for waste management to the manufacturing industry are vital to environmental protection. This degradable waste economy can be converted into a potential ecological economy through five stages of 'closed-loop production, cyclical alternative economical design': re-use of goods, repair of goods, reconditioning and rebuilding of goods, recycling materials and the production of life extension strategies. Here small and medium enterprises (SME) can play an important role in closed-loop ecological economics that can not only strengthen local living economics(LLE), but also protect the environment.

Integrated pest management (IPM) in agricultural systems reduces pesticide use by giving preference to non-chemical pest management strategies. Green microfinance institutions (MFIs) can support farmers to initiate IPM services in the agricultural sector. Moreover, green social micro credit can play a vital role in attaining the United Nations Millennium Development Goals (MDG's) to eradicate poverty and promote environmental development. The eight Millennium Development Goals (MDGs) were agreed on by world leaders at a UN summit in 2000 and set targets to:

MDG 1 Eradicate Extreme Hunger
MDG 2 Achieve Universal Primary Education
MDG 3 Promote Gender Equality and Empower Women
MDG 4 Reduce Child Mortality
MDG 5 Improve Maternal Health
MDG 6 Combat HIV AIDS Malaria and Other Diseases
MDG 7 Ensure Environmental Sustainability
MDG 8 Develop a Global Partnership for Development

To achieve these goals, poorer countries pledged to improve policies and governance and increase accountability to their own citizens; wealthy countries pledged to provide the resources. The MDGs were built not just as statements of intent, but as achievable objectives.

2.2 Problem statement

While microfinance has emerged as a globally recognized development tool today, there is barely any work being done that looks at the possibility of green microfinance practice through MFI's in Canada. Although several micro financing domestic initiatives have been established in Canada, there is literature that recognizes the lack of public policy as it relates to develop and support of a microfinance industry that would sustain and expand the green action micro lending program for low-income people in Canada (SEDI, 2007); Self-employment in Canada, 1995). However, the public has limited knowledge on the negative effects of chemicals on nature and human health, and corporations completely ignore the negative effects of chemicals on the human body and the environment. Therefore, environmental education on toxic chemicals, petroleum products and waste recycling management to the public through mass media, printed media, and school curricula are of a pressing matter in Canada.

Profit-generating, market-based multi-national corporation (MNC) activities create social inequity and unbalanced social-economic and environmental growth, harming the environment, and affecting climate change (increasing global warming, air pollution, water pollution and other environmental pollutions). Their businesses deplete natural resources through deforestation, river erosion, soil erosion and increased waste in the environment rather than supporting environmental justice. They are over extracting natural resources. They neither maintain, nor reforest nature.

Moreover, the micro green businesses compete with multinational corporations that are solely driven by profit; however, green microcredit and green microenterprises are balancing socio-economic and environmental need with development within society. For example, Grameen Bank puts restrictions on giving polluting business loans to businesses in Bangladesh (Biddimala 1983) that are harmful to human health and the environment. Its sister organizations, like Grameen Shokti, largely work with soft loan credit. In addition to these activities Grameen Shakti supplies solar panels, constructs bio-gas plants, and improves cooking stoves. These help to activate rural energy, rural industries create rural employment and promote microenterprise.

1.4. Rationality of the research

Green micro financing and green micro business development, however, have been underserved in Canada and many other countries. Less attention has been given by various public, private and non-governmental organizations (financial and non-financial) agencies through policies, strategies, and programs. Clearly many businesses are not serious about environmentalism because the values of environmental services are not appearing in business balance sheets. We cannot live without the environment. Moreover, unregulated financial services will undoubtedly result in greater negative environmental impacts and health hazards unless micro financing institution (MFI) practitioners ensure that this does not occur. Therefore, environmental issues are important for microenterprises that are nurtured by MFI's. In Canada, MFI's can support green micro businesses by providing business capital for green businesses, business training, mentoring services, marketing supports, and networking. They can finance environmentally-friendly businesses that produce solar panels, energy saving bulbs, solar water pumps and repair, recycle and reuse waste materials. Although microfinance models exist in some regions, they are neither national in scope nor available to all entrepreneurs in Canada. The researcher explores how both green social and economic components might be linked up within the context of sustainable development. It is expected that this process will contribute to the current knowledge base by identifying and seeking to fill the current gap in the literature.

1.5. Objectives of the study

1. To study the operational practices of Canadian and Bangladeshi microcredit institutions in the area of gender empowerment, poverty alleviation and community organizing.
2. To compare microfinance programs, strategies, implementation and the relative success/failure of the programs in these two countries
3. To explore the extent to which green microfinance is adopted in both countries, and to explore how lessons in microcredit in each of the two countries can inform improvements in the microfinance industry.

3. Methodology

The research methodology employed in this study is primarily through primarily qualitative, quantitative, literature reviews, seminars and field visit experience, interviews and case studies. To understand microcredit and renewable energy programs for green development, the researcher visited and studied Grameen Bank (GB) Bangladesh, Grameen Shokti's (GS) Renewable Energy Project in winter 2008 and had an internship at Alterna Savings' Community Micro Loan Funds program in Toronto in summer and fall 2007 respectively. This was to gain valuable experience as it relates their green operational microcredit strategies, policies and programs. The researcher stayed in the villages and spoke with GB and GS borrowers. He also read various literatures on green microcredit.

This paper envisions a comparison and contrasting of Grameen Bank and Grameen Shakti credit systems (Bangladesh) with Alterna Savings credit programs (Canada) and its impact on Toronto's local living economics and environmental development. The findings are positive to environmental sustainable development.

During the researcher's field visits in Bangladesh and in Toronto, he looked at the following questions to obtain answers from these organizations:

1. Which types of microcredit products, green products and projects are currently available to clients? Where are the projects located?
2. What are the organizational structures, policies, procedures, strategies used to promote green microenterprise and operations in these organizations?
3. How many of the clients/beneficiaries have received gainful employment and/or social and environmental benefit through the projects? How are the micro financing projects contributing to sustainable development?

4. Literature review

The Sustainable Development Approach is not only encompasses income-generation, but it is also a process that has people-centered development, green jobs creation, environmental development and poverty reduction (Allen, & Thomas. (2000); Joan, & Lal, (2006); Habermas (1991); Hopwood (2005); Korten (2003); Milani (2001); Perkins (2005); Sen (1996). Lorenzo Cotula (2002) mentions that the sustainable development approach rests on core principles that are people-centered; multi-level; responsive and participatory, socially, environmentally and economically sustainable business practices, promotion mentorship and stewardship of the social economy. Therefore, it is necessary to examine current scholarly thoughts in the two areas which are currently treated separately.

Grameen Shokti is a renewable energy company established in 1996 with a view of promoting, developing and extending renewable energy technologies in the remote rural areas of Bangladesh. Its market-based renewable energy products are solar power, biogas, organic fertilizer, improved stoves and wind energy for the improvement of the quality life of rural communities. It provides necessary credit facilities for rural communities to access renewable energy technology. In addition, GS builds awareness and motivates rural communities towards adopting environmentally-friendly renewable energy (RE) technology. Its RE services are available all over Bangladesh through providing soft loans to renewable energy users.

Green micro business could be popular in Canada too, but it requires favorable legal frameworks, policies, strategies and a regulatory environment that has strong institutions with strong apex leadership to provide financial and non-financial services (Otero & Rhyne 1994). The Grammen Bank and Shore Bank USA have created millions of self-employment jobs in society. Green social microfinance for self-employment creation, green microenterprise development and for environmental innovations is of an urgent need in Canada, as its scope is broad and has massive demand.

Self-employment, in particular microenterprise development, has been rated by Statistics Canada as the fastest growing segment of the economy, which reduces social expenditures by governments and increases local economic transactions. The federal government has three programs to support self-employed Canadians: the Self-Employment Benefit (SEB), Program in Human Resource and Social Development Canada (HRSDC), and the Community Futures (CF) Program in Industry Canada. In the absence of a national self-employment framework, these programs are not as effective or accessible as they should be. Although some organizations like *Alterna Savings, Vancity,* and the *Coady* International Institute in Canada have started micro financing for micro business funding, they do not focus on green business financing for green micro business promotion.

In Toronto, Riverdale Business Development Corporation and Alterna Savings are centers of excellence within community-based development initiatives that help to create local jobs, develop local enterprises, and provide essential services to low-income people. However, these micro-financing agencies have reduced their services in Toronto. As a starting point, these organizations could extend their loan services to recycling and waste management businesses. Alterna Savings Community Micro-loan Funds has just started its journey from 2000 as a carry forwarded from Calmeadow Foundation. It has now realized and extends its vision and mission to a socio-economic and environmental paradigm in collaboration with other stakeholders to minimize its costs.

5. Green micro business, sustainable development and self-employment

Sustainable development mostly concerns the environment and people's livelihood. Green business is more than clean-up and environmental protection (Milani, 2000). Green business is an alternative environmentally friendly oriented program for community-based ecological economics. Sustainable development promotes people-centered alternative development for social justice, environmental sustainability and is inclusive of everyone (Dale, 2003; Esbcobar, (1992); Hoopwood Mellor, and O'Brien, 2005; Korton, (2000; Rahman, 1997; Sen, 1999, and WCED, 1987).

Grameen Bank provides loans to poor women for the improvement of their household economics as well as to generate social and human capital among them. In San Francisco, 230 investors have formed the New Resource Bank with a focus on financing *"green"* business and community and sustainable development (SEDI, 2007). Canada has not given this strategy sufficient consideration; even the non-profit sector has not considered this strategy significantly as a successful alternative.

Small businesses are less harmful to the environment. However, what cause small businesses to fail in Canada are a lack of to easily accessible credit/bank loans, high interest rates, and a lack training in marketing, sales and business management. This poor access and lack training is more acute for female entrepreneurs. In 1995, women owned 30.3% of the businesses in Canada, and they employed 1.7 million people which are more than the country's 100 largest corporations (Longenceker et al. 1998). Nevertheless, women are having difficulty getting access to credit from banks and other support services. Contrarily Grameen Bank has pioneered collateral-free small loan financing for women with enormous success that has created millions of self-employed in Bangladesh. Therefore, green social small financing programs are essential for the promotion of entrepreneurship in Canada.

5.1 The practice of microfinance - The Bangladeshi and Canadian context

Grameen Bank follows the principle of *Pancha Chakra*. The Pancha Chakra model follows a loan disbursement cycle (2+2+1) cycle- the neediest person receives a loan first followed by two others. The leader is the last one to receive the loan as discussed above. It has a weekly loan repayment system that helps clients to repay their loans in small installments. GB provides loans for activities on the farm, off the farm and non-farm related micro-enterprise in Bangladesh. It has participatory management with a bottom-up planning strategy where borrowers are owners of the bank.

The seventy percent energy crisis in Bangladesh hinders rural socio-economic and environmental development in Bangladesh. In this severe crisis situation, the Grameen Bank Microcredit Program and Grameen Shokti Renewable Energy Program have been appropriately placed in Bangladesh to address the issue of poverty and to fill the energy gap in rural Bangladesh. GB provides loans based on more than 700 hundred items. The top twenty general loans are: milking cows, the fattening of cows, paddy husking, paddy cultivation, grocery shops, seasonal agricultural activities, rice trading, land leasing, irrigated agricultural cultivation, bullock, bamboo works, land management, stationary shops, vegetable cultivation, betel leaf cultivation, vegetable trading, clothing trading, fish farming, poultry farming, and winter crop cultivation. Here, all loans are environmentally-friendly and socially-responsible investments for poor people in rural Bangladesh.

The total number of borrowers of GB, up to December 2007, was 7.41 million. Ninety-seven percent of them were women. It works in 80,678 villages. GB's success is in high-volume lending, a strong loan repayment rate and high profit, which is well liked among development practitioners. Grameen Bank operates nationwide through 2,185 branches. The repayment rate has been ninety-nine percent since 1979. The savings of current borrowers is $2.5 billion. One hundred percent of loans are financed through borrowers' deposits (Grameen Updates, 2007). It runs on its own internal funds and investment income. This makes it economically sustainable.

Table 1

Difference between GB social credit and conventional credit

GB Credit	Conventional Credit
Targets the bottom poor	Not focused on poor people
Greater focus on women	No focus on women
No physical collateral	Required physical collateral
Loan suitable for poor	Loan suitable for rich
Diversified loan portfolios	Fixed loan portfolios
Borrowers are owners of the bank	Borrowers are only clients
Social development opportunity at the grassroots' level	Opportunity open to rich people
Social development is an integral part of MCS	Social development is not first preference
Saving mobilization by members	No saving mobilization by clients
Intensive loan supervision	Causal supervision
Innovative leadership	Stereotypical of conventional leadership
Credit is considered to be a human right	Credit is at the mercy of the lender
Easy lending procedures	Lengthy and cumbersome method of lending

Builds entrepreneurial skills among the poor	No group-based microcredit
Loans for education, health care	No loan for health care, education
Egalitarian system	Isolated/rare integration/ elitist system
Humanitarian	Nonsensical
Mainly concentrated in rural areas	Urbanized
Customized policies and strategies in loan operation, developed in favor of borrowers	Top-down rigid, standardized policies not suitable for all

Practice at Implementation Level	Success Factors in GB
Loan proposal through mutual decision among members	Exclusive focus on disadvantaged rural people
Borrowers are free to select their activities	Manageable size of groups and centers to each worker
Leakage free loan delivery system	Close subversion of loan utilization
Weekly loan instilment with interest	Collective loan accountability
Diversified loan disbursement with housing loan	Transparency in operation
All transitions held in the centre meeting	Decision making decentralized at the field level
Regular monitoring on loan utilization	Staff dedication and mobility in the working area
Proper documentation at all levels.	Disaster management integrated in the process
	Strong support of social development embodied 16 decisions

Features of Implementation	Implementation Strategies
Priority given to rural women	
Credit discipline and close supervision in loan utilization	Extended banking facilities to the poor for self-employment
Bank goes to the borrowers houses	Provide and support credit activities
Proper record keeping and transparency of transitions	Develop programs, policies and implement them based on grass roots information and demand
Peer pressure and peer support in repayment	
Collateral free loans for income generating activities	Recruit local staff
Compulsory regular group savings	Respect local culture and values
Weekly repayment system	

GB Implementation Steps	
GB works at the door step of the borrowers	Projection meeting
Borrowers form group of five men and women	Each group elects a Chair and a Secretary
Each centre selects a Center Chief Peer pressure	Group savings & Individual savings

Figure 1. Grameen Bank Successor Factors and Implementation Strategies

5.2 Grameen Shakti (GS)

Grameen Shakti is a giant in renewable energy market-based action programs in Bangladesh. Only thirty percent of Bangladeshi people have access to grid electricity and most of them live in the cities. Many people cannot afford Solar Home Systems (SHS) individually. This is one of the barriers to scaling up the GS solar program and revitalizing the rural economy through the use solar PV technology. Sustainable energy is a combination of renewable energies like solar energy, energy from biomass and other saved energy. GS is an example of success in the renewable energy market in Bangladesh. Sustainable energy technologies (SETS) contribute to reducing poverty within a market-based integrated approach and providing energy for the poor in Bangladesh.

GS is also able to invest heavily in training for its field staff to develop their capacity to produce SHS accessories locally. The locally made accessories reduce costs of the renewable energy products. GS provides pre-and post-RE services to its clients through its Grameen Technology Centre (GTC) engineers and the trained local technicians from the GTC. Moreover, 25,000 school children from rural schools will receive exposure to RE technologies through 20 existing GTC's. More than 5,000 students have learned about renewable energy technologies through the existing GTC's.

GS has developed an integrated model which uses micro-utility innovatively to make renewable energy technologies affordable for rural people. Instead of being wholly dependable on subsidies, GS emphasizes its institutional strengths, as well as its commitment to borrowers, income-generation, entrepreneurship development, local technology transfer and capacity. Shopkeepers are now able to afford pollution-free, efficient lighting at minimal cost, while keeping their shops open after dusk with reduced health risks and less danger of fire. Kerosene lamps have now been replaced by SHS's.

GS statistics show that, its total employees are 1800 who are mostly engineers. Within its 19-year span, its total unit offices are 365. The number of regional offices is 60 and the amount of divisional offices is 7. The total amount of Grameen Technological Centers is 20. This covers 440 Upzilas (sub-districts) of 64 districts throughout Bangladesh. GS has expanded its activities to 32,000 villages out of 68,000 villages in Bangladesh. The Grameen Shokti report (January 2008) indicates that GS has installed 130,000 SHS's and 5700 ICS's in Bangladesh. It has since installed 5000 SHS's and 700 ICS's and 250 biogas plants throughout Bangladesh. There is a large demand for solar energy in the villages, even in the urbanized areas. Grameen Shakti has developed a link with Grameen Bank which has more than two million live stock farmers who receive loans from Grameen. These GB borrowers can construct biogas plants to meet their energy needs and can generate extra income from the production of biogas.

5.3 Alterna Savings Toronto

MFI's and different environmental, non-government organizations (NGOs) like energy savings companies (ESCO) in Canada can play a great role in basic ecological and environmental education. The Business Alliance for Local Living Economics (BALLE) can advocate for related policies, facilitate partnerships between renewable solar panel suppliers, organic food suppliers, environmental NGO educators and MFI's. Alterna Savings, a community microloan program, offers small loans to small entrepreneurs for sustainable entrepreneurship development. Another objective of this organization is to create a supportive environment for self-employment among low-income people in the Greater Toronto area. It makes socially responsible investments in micro-entrepreneurs in Toronto and Ottawa.

As of December 2007, Alterna Saving's total active loans were 122 and amounted to $567,574; 95 loans were from the Toronto office which amounted to $397,000. The loan repayment rate has been more than 91 percent. The Alterna microloan fund program is an excellent program that promotes green economics in Canada. All of its borrowers invest loans into environmentally-friendly small businesses. Alterna microloan borrowers receive loans for various training and business opportunities like computer training courses, webpage designing, computer repair, children care, ESL learning centers, printing, grass cutting and trimming, cleaning services, restaurants, catering, shoe repair, tailoring, hair cutting and photography. In Bangladesh, microloan borrowers usually receive loans that serve agricultural and livestock rearing needs and tailoring needs.

5.4 Mentor circle networking for Alterna borrowers

In 2007, the Alterna Savings Micro Loan Fund Unit organized a networking Café in its Bay and College Street office and facilitates workshop for its borrowers in the YMCA Central Hall every month. In the mentor circle networking Café, micro-entrepreneurs discuss action plans, marketing plans, goal setting and effective time management. This program facilitates peer support and networking among borrowers for their business growth. Alterna formed an environmentally-sustainable committee in 2008 that reviewed the credit union's footprint, and developed a long–term action plan. Its aim is to continue socially-responsible investing through its on-going membership education.

5.5 Constraints faced by marginalized entrepreneurs in microenterprise development in Canada

Canada has a strong cooperative and credit union movement and other community development initiatives, but they largely ignore the economic plight of marginalized Canadians. According to Self-Employment Development Initiative Canada (SEDI, 2007), the opportunities for green microfinance can be very lucrative to marginalized entrepreneurs in Canada, especially for women. Although Canada is a disposable society, the repair of cell phones, televisions, radios and computers is another way for entrepreneurs to participate in using green micro financing effectively. The opportunities for green micro financing with enough research can be wildly successful. Traditional financial institutions like Royal Bank (RBC) and Toronto Dominion bank (TD) Canada claim that they are unable to economically serve small business loans. Bank regulations are so rigid and tough that they are out of low-income people's range. These financial institutions do not share business risks with micro business owners. However, Alterna Savings' social auditing report 2006-2007 mentions that microenterprise development has proven to have a significant impact on the larger Canadian economy and individual households.

Green social micro financing can open the door for micro entrepreneurs graduating towards small and medium businesses (SME). Here people can start micro businesses with little money and develop their banking behaviors. The graduation process to SME is convenient for both financial institutions and clients, when investing more money into growing green businesses. In Canada, the main setback is the emphasis of MFI's on profit at the outset of the plan. However, Alterna Savings Community Micro Loan Fund in Canada is excellent in incorporating the fundamentals of socially responsible investments (SRI) in their mission and operation. Because they are the SRI green social businesses who avoid markets that are involved in alcohol, tobacco, gambling, weapons and various environmentally-hazardous businesses.

5.6 Alterna savings and its social capital development activities

The Networking Café-Mentors Circle program of Alterna Savings gives an opportunity to clients to network monthly. In the workshop, they discuss their business problems, review their performance, share experiences and get business stewardship training. The attendees of the mentor circle workshop have mentioned that it has helped them to focus on a task at hand and stay on track of their business. They can gradually ascend from small to medium to big business through receiving mentoring support services like access to sufficient business capital; access to public resources; marketing and networking supports from different institutions. Alterna Savings' community loan funds (ACMLF) provides loans to develop new immigrants' professional skills through vocational training to improve employability skills. Alterna supports sustainable and socially responsible goods and service enterprises. Alterna published its first corporate social responsibility accountability report in 2008, which contains social, environmental and financial performance records to its members, clients and communities. However, the Alterna Savings Micro Community Loan Fund and many other MFI's in Canada and (in other countries) do not articulate any clear policies in terms of renewable energy and basic environmental training of its clients. The Young Entrepreneur Financing Program administered by the Business Development Bank of Canada, whose aim is to give start-up entrepreneurs a foundation funds to build new businesses, does not yet have programs that include basic environmental services.

5.7 Social Business Enterprise (SBE)

According to Muhammad Yunus (2008), it is time to move away from the narrow interpretation of business development through the paradigm of capitalist globalization and broaden the concept to include social financing, social economy and Social Business Enterprises (SBE's). In the poverty situations, the Grameen Bank credit program initiates and promotes alternative small business facilities in the villages in an effort to address the poverty and acute, environmental problems.

5.8 Grameen as an example of social business

Grameen Bank is a very good example of an integrative approach to the social economy and social business in Bangladesh. Grameen DANONE is a hybrid SBE project in Bangladesh and went into operation in early 2007. Its share holders are Group DANONE Company, GS, GB, and Grameen Kallayan. Its dividends are not distributed to its shareholders are Group DANONE, GB and GS. GD produces Shokti Doi (Energy Yogurt) that is sold at a low price to rural children. These micro-lending institutions are examples that demonstrate that the concept of microfinance is rooted in local conditions. Green social microfinance promotes culture, heritage, and traditions of society, and promotes business and community networks.

6. Conclusions

Green microfinance and green microenterprise development are interrelated with each other. Grameen Shakti has developed an integrated model that facilitates socio-economic and environmental benefits in society and develops a financial self-sufficiency model for its RE program, instead of subsidies. The link between the RE soft financing model and biodiversity conservation helps fill the energy crisis gap in Bangladesh.

The entire process of a green micro lending program is a very intensive participatory process and requires a lot of capacity building and links with other implementing organizations. If these aspects are lacking, they create constraints on the success of the credit program. Although the financial costs for micro financing are high in Canada, because small amount of loans are given to many people, micro borrowers need more services than those who receive large commercial loans. However, the government, currently, does not put enough resources into this MFI program. These are the barriers in micro financing programs in Canada. However, green micro financing institutions (GMFI's) can support recycling projects through social enterprise funds. Loans can be used to reduce and recycle waste, generate local energy, and work with large institutions to implement better recycling, repairing and reusable projects. NGOs can provide training on recycling waste and renewable energy with targets to 'zero waste'. This is the essence of the ecological economy. This would help in the creation of many good green good jobs, the reduction of waste, and the preservation of our resources.

Metro Credit Unions, the Maytree Foundation and Alterna Savings Community Loan Fund program are aimed at developing financial capital for micro entrepreneurs in Canada; however, they do not streamline enough funds for micro lending to micro businesses in Canada; hence, Environment Canada can allocate resources and budgets to green microfinance institutions for implementing environmental social micro financing projects. Environment Bangladesh could provide supports that are consistent with local ecological demand. Environment Canada and Environment Bangladesh can then help Green micro financing institutions (GMFIs) and other environmental organizations in these two countries. With integrated support from public and private collaboration, green micro finance institutions (GMFI's) together can facilitate people-centered environmental sustainable development.

7. References

Allen, T., & Thomas, A. (Eds.) (2000). *Poverty and development into the 21ˢᵗ century.* Oxford, UK: Oxford University Press

Alterna Savings. (2008). *Atlerna savings annual report.* Retrieved June 7, 2008 from http://www.alterna.ca/Templates/SavingsPersonal.aspx?langtype=1033.

Anderson, R. (2000). Climbing mount sustainability. *Reflections,* 1(4), pp. 6-12

Bangladesh Profile. (2007). *Demography.* Retrieved on January 2008, from http://news.bbc.co.uk/2/hi/south_asia/country_profiles/1160598.stm

Calmeadow Foundation (2005). *Annual report 2005.* Toronto. Self-employment Development Initiativᵉˢ

Canadian Advisory Council on the Status of Women (1998). *Women entrepreneurs: building a stronger Canadian economy.* Ottawa, Canada.

Chambers, R., & Conway, G. (1992). *Sustainable rural livelihoods: Practical concepts for the 21st century.* IDS discussion paper 296. Brighton

Coady International Institute St. Frances Xavier University (2005). *Coady activities.* Retrieved on June 7, 2008 from www.coady.stfx.ca

Colbert, B. (2004). The complex resource-based view: implications for theory and practice in strategic human resource management. *The Academy of Management Review,* Vol. 29(3), pp. 341-358

Cotula, L. (2002). Improving access to natural resources for the rural poor - The experience of FAO and of other key organizations from a sustainable livelihoods perspective. In H.E. Daly (Ed), (2003). *Ecological economics: the concept of sale and its relation to allocation, distribution, and uneconomic growth.* Alberta: CANSEE, Jasper.

Dowla, A. & Barua, D. (2006). *The Poor pay back: The Grameen II story.* Bloomfield: Kumarian Press, Inc.

Drake, C., & Rhyne, E. (Eds.) (2002). *The Commercialization of microfinance: balancing business and development.* Bloomfield: C.T. Kumarian Press, Inc.

Esbcobar, A. (1992). *Encountering development: the making and unmaking of the third world.* Princeton, NJ: Princeton University Press

Grameeen Shakti (2008). *Grameen Shakti report January 2008.* Dhaka: Grameen Shakti

Grameen Bank (2007). *Grameen Updates 2007.* Dhaka: Grameen Bank

Grameen Bank (2008). *Grameen Bank Updates 2008.* Retrieved on June 16, 2008 from http://www.grameen.org

Grameen Bank *Biddimala (1983). Grameen Bank by laws.* Dhaka: Grameen Bank

Grameen *Dialogue (2005). Grameen dialogue #60.* Dhaka: Grameen Trust

Habermas, J. (2002). What does socialism mean today? In I. Kapoor (2002). The devil's in the theory: a critical assessment of Robert Chamber's work on participatory development. *Third World Quarterly,* Vol. 23(1), pp. 101-117

Hart, S. & Milstein, M. (2003). Creating sustainable value. *Academy of Management Executive,* Vol. 17 (2), pp. 56-59

Henry, S. (2006). *How MFI's and their clients can have a positive impact on the environment. Good practices in business development services: How do we enhance entrepreneurial skills in MFIs clients?* Paper presented at the Micro Credit Summit Halifax held in November 2006. Toronto: Alterna Savings.

Hick, S. (2004). *Social Welfare in Canada.* Toronto: Thompson Educational Publishing, Inc.

Hoopwood, B., Mellor, M., & O'Brien, G. (2005). *Sustainable development: mapping different approaches.* University of Nothhumbria, UK. University of Nothhumbria

Hopwood, B. and et al. (2005). Sustainable development, Mapping different approaches, *Sustainable Development,* Vol. 13, pp. 38-52

Human Resource Development Canada (2008). *About Human Resource Development in Canada.* Retrieved May 17, 2008, from http://www.hrdc.gc.ca

Joan, H. & Lal, A. (2006). *How MFI's and their clients can have a positive impact on the environment.* Paper presented in the Micro-credit Summit Campaign. Halifax

Korten, D. (2006). *The great turning from empire to earth community.* Connecticut: Kumarian Press Inc.

Longenceker, J.G., Moore, C.W., Petty, W., & Palich, L. E. (1998). *Small business management.* Toronto: Thomson Publishing

Maytree Foundation (2008). *About us.* Retrieved on June 10, 2008 from http://www.maytree.comMcDonald, S. & Oates, C. (2006). *Sustainability: consumer perceptions and marketing strategies.* Wily Inter-science. Retrieved on June 2008 from WWW.interscience.wiley.com

Milani, B. (2000). *Designing the green economy: The postindustrial alternative to corporate globalization.* Lanham MD: Rowman and Littlefield.

Milani, B. (2001). *From opposition to alternatives:* New productive forces and the post-*materialist redefinition of wealth.* Paper presented at the Environmental Studies Association of Canada (ESAC). Laval Quebec

Otero, M. & Rhyne, E. (1994). *The new world of micro enterprise finance: Building healthy financial institutions for the poor.* West Hartford, Connecticut: Kumarian Press, Inc.

Perkins, E. (2005). *Feminist ecological economics and sustainability.* Paper presented at the conference of the Canadian Society for Ecological Economics (CANSEE). Toronto. York University

Prahalad, K. & Hamel, G. (2006). The core competence of the corporation. *Harvard Business Re*view, Vol. 6 (5), pp. 79-92

Quarter, J., Mook, L., & Richmond, J. (2003). *What is social economy?* Center for Urban and Community Studies, Research Bulletin #13

Rahman, A.I. (1997). Poverty, profitability of micro enterprises and the role of Credit, in G. Goeffrey Wood & I. Sharif (Eds.). *Who needs credit: Poverty and finance in Bangladesh* London: Zed Books,

Rouf, A. K. (2011). Green enterprise, development through green micro financing. (Master's thesis) *The International Journal of Research Studies in Management*, Vol. 1(1). 85-96

Rouf, K. A. (2012). Green Microfinance Promoting Green Enterprise Development. *Humanomics, Green Innovation Management: theory and practice.* Bingley UK: *Emerald Group of Publishing limited. Vol.* 28(2), pp.148 – 161.

Self-Employment Development Initiative (SEDI) 2007. *Self-employment development initiative.* Retrieved on June 7, 2008 from http://www.sedi.org/html

Sen, A. (1999). *Development from freedom.* New York: Anchor House

Sherri T. (1998) Strategies for carrying society. *Caledon Institute of Social Policy Presentation.* Vol. 23 (3), pp. 1-20

Slayter, B. (2003). *Southern exposure: International development and the global south in the twenty-first century.* Bloomfield: Kumarian Press, Inc.

Small Business Quarterly (2007). Financing of some exporters: Barriers do exist. *Small Business Quarterly,* Vol. 9(1), pp. 1-8.

Statistics Canada. (2007). *Number of children at home (8) and census family structure (7) for the census families in private households of Canada, provinces, territories, census metropolitan areas and census agglomerations, 2001 and 2006 Censuses - 20% Sample Data (table). Topic-based tabulation.* 2006 Census of population. Statistics Canada catalogue no. 97-553-XCB2006007. Ottawa

Vancity (2008). *Vancity my money.* Retrieved on July 15, 2008 from https://www.vancity.com

Women Task Force Committee (2003). *Prime Minister's task force on women enterprises.* Ottawa. Oct. 2003

World Bank (1995). *Grameen Bank: Performance and sustainability.* Washington: The World Bank

World Bank. (2002). *Bangladesh financial services for the poorest.* Report number PID 10990, Washington

World Commission on Environment and Development (1987). *Our common future (The Brundtland Report).* Oxford: Oxford University Press.

Yunus, M. (2002). *Grameen Bank-II: Designed to open new possibilities.* Dhaka: Grameen Bank.

Yunus, M. (2006). *Grameen Bank at a glance.* Chittagong: Packages Corporation Limited.

Yunus, M. (2006). *Social business entrepreneurs are the solution.* Chittagong: Packages Corporation Limited

Yunus, M. (2008). *Creating a world without poverty: Social business and the future of capitalism.* Dhaka: Subarna Publishers Ltd.

Peasants' Socio-Economic Scenarios and Technology Use Dynamics in Bangladesh

Abstract

Capitalistic profit motive economy forced traditional agriculture move toward commercialization of agriculture in Bangladesh. However, Bangladeshi traditional peasants are suffering from getting their crop duly prices in commercialized market relations. These peasants are unable to fulfill their basic needs; hence they cannot cross the poverty line. The objectives of the paper are (1) to acquaint readers with the issues and conditions of life that Bangladeshi peasants are facing from crop marketing and to environmental degradation in Bangladesh and (2) to understand the causes and consequences of peasants' poverty. This paper is written by the author from his own experience. The paper uses secondary data from different studies conducted in Bangladesh.

Peasants' social organizations, traditional cultures, cultivation technologies and peasant economics (agro economics) are changing and moving toward mechanized capital intensive agriculture that creates inequality and injustice in the society among poor peasants by rich peasants in Bangladesh. Peasant joint family structure is changing to single family. Peasant festivals, customs and cultures are decaying. Chemical agricultural green revolutionis oriented to economic profit that totally ignored ecological and social factors. Westerguard (1978) finds in his Bangladesh research that rich peasants' loss their lands because of population increase. For example, density of population was 668 in 1942, it was 1066 in 1957. First average peasant farm size was 6.2 acres, and then declined to 4.9 acres. Landless population was 4% in 1942; it increases to 30% in 1975. More than 10 acres of land household were 16% in 1942, but it stands 9% in 1975. The above statistics show land fragmentation is increasing that affects peasant socio-economic life.

Moreover, in Bangladesh, land tenure system has created exploitative and uneven power structure and patron-client relations (Hall, 1973) between Zamindars (Landlords) and Ryots (tenants). Bangladesh Institute of Development Studies (BIDS) study shows that marginalized peasants and landless people have risen. The market economy alarmingly defeated peasant subsistence economy. Although the commercialized peasants' economy becomes dominant in the capitalist market relations, marginalized peasants are in the periphery of the market economy. Hence they are exploited in the capitalistic market relations in Bangladesh. Many peasants and their children have been trying to co-opt with the commercial market relations. However, marginalized peasants are victims of pauperization (forced sale) process. They use modern agriculture technology to get benefits from the market since 1970s; however, competitive capitalist market put them out from the privilege of commercial market. Hence state should come forward to support the peasant economy and peasant culture in Bangladesh.

This paper helps readers to know the patterns and scenarios of peasants' socioeconomic life, dynamics of technology use and peasants' different issues that they are sufferings from undergoing sustained deprivation in Bangladesh. Hence the peasants' salient aspects of the paper wish to draw the attention of Bangladeshi peasant economists, researchers and policy makers to address the issues that they are suffering from and thus to redress their distress as much as possible.

Keywords: Commercial market relations; green revolution; land tenure system; peasant culture; peasant economy; poverty; Rayotis; subsistence production; surplus production; and Zamindars.

1. Introduction and Importance of the Study

Bangladesh's main economy is agriculture. Peasants of Bangladesh have their own distinct agricultural economy, social organizations, land tenure system, cultures, cultivation technology, economy and life styles which have been changing drastically for the last few decades. Capitalistic consumer economy hugely forced traditional agriculture to commercializing agriculture. Few rich peasants are able to invest capitals to agriculture, co-opt with mechanized cultivation, commercial agriculture market and make profit from their agriculture production. However, maximum peasants are unable to fulfill their basic needs from their substance economy and hence they are suffering from absolute poverty in Bangladesh.

2. Objectives of the Study

The objectives of the paper are (1) to introduce the readers with the issues and conditions of life that Bangladeshi peasants are suffering from crop cultivation, modern technology use and crop marketing in rural Bangladesh and (2) to understand the causes and consequences of peasants' poverty.

3. Methodology of the study

This paper is written by the authors from their own experience in Bangladesh. The paper uses secondary source information and data of different studies conducted in Bangladesh. The paper also contains peasant economists and social scientists (Anawarullah, 1978; Areefen, 1986; Atiar Rahman, 1986; Chynov, 1986; Humphrey, 2014; B. K. Jahangir, 1978; Mahabub, 1987; Patnaiak, 1976; Shannin, 1984; Wood, 1978; etc) thoughts on peasants' socio-economic life.

4. Peasant and Peasant Society

In Bangladesh, a peasant is a member of a traditional class of cultivators and farmers, either laborers or owners of small lands and cultivating them. Peasants have their distinct society which is different from urban social life. Anthropologist Caroline Humphrey (2014) says, "Peasant society has plantation economy (A plantation economy is an economy based on agricultural mass production, usually of a few commodity crops grown on large farms called plantations. Plantation economies rely on the export of cash crops as a source of income. In short, peasants are rural people involves in cultivating land for crop production and their livelihood based on crop production economy).

Many researchers classify peasants into several classes in Bangladesh. For example, Hashmi, Taj Ul-Islam (1994) classifies peasants into four groups- landless poor, poor peasants, middle class tenants and land lords. B. K. Jahangir (1978) considers peasant society as a "little community". Peasant society is relatively widespread entity which contains peasant family, clan, group, kinship, household or home, and maintained them through their different relations, activities events and festivals.

Peasant society means a collection of group of families, clans and a collective feeling where different households of neighborhood connected. Peasant society is the combination of many family units (farms). Peasants have intensive relations and create social solidarity among them. Humphry (2014) says, "Peasant society is a moral institution which includes peasants and different craftsmen mainly involved in land cultivation and making household crafts." Peasant society maintains its social solidarity through different festivals, events, customs and traditions. Peasants orally transmit their agriculture technology to their neighbors, relatives and to their next generations. Caroline Humphry (2014) emphasizes on influence of nature on agricultural production. Areefen (1986) describes, "It is beyond kinship relational organization that has social collectivity and political bondage (civil rights) and its members have mutual bondage relationships. The plantation agriculture (sowing) uses land as subject labor which is opposite to industrial labor.

5. Peasant Social Organizations

Peasant society is a mixed social organization entity in a social structure because peasant society has many relationships with different social organizations. Family, clan, group, kinships, household and home etc. are elements of peasant society. Traditional peasant society characteristics are using manual labor; individual means of production, unplanned labor division, easy available land from the family and use natural raw materials and attain self-sufficiency. Traditional agricultural system is based on clan and lineage relationship among peasant family members. Traditional peasant economy is self-consumed subsistence agriculture. However, in the materialist society, mechanical agricultural production and accumulation of agricultural resources are important than self-consumed biological reproduction. Recently market relations takes place oriented role instead lineage relations in Bangladesh. However, Bangladeshi peasants are in halfway (transition) in the use of modern agricultural technology. However, Bangladeshi peasants are suffering from the following issues and challenges that need to be addressed at micro level, mezzo level and macro level by local and national organizations.

6. Issues of peasants in Bangladesh

- Integration and attachment of traditional peasants with capitalistic market relations and the peasant economy;
- Accessibility of agricultural inputs, access to credit facilities, access to agricultural technological knowhow and access to improved technology and poor peasants' involvement in the process of modernization of agriculture;
- Relationships between the land tenure system and the problems of improved agricultural practices;
- Pattern of unequal income rise and unequal economic income distribution among different classes of peasants ;
- Emerging unequal power and authority of leadership structural development in villages and its impact on ordinary peasants' life;
- Agricultural development or agricultural productivity structure increases influenced by population growth and population diversity;
- Modernized agriculture destroys ecological balance.

Eric Wolf (1966) finds peasant society varies according to geography. He finds peasant society has two different families: Nuclear family and extended family. This dyadic relations occurred by husband, wife, children mother and father. It depends on influence of gender relation in the family. Dyadic relations have importance to agricultural production and social, economic and biological reproduction. Both single family and extended family are integral part of production strategy for peasants' survival in the traditional peasant society. However, joint family uses more its family members to agriculture production. Eric Wolf (1966) considers extended family contributes to peasant development cycle-the structure of extended family continues when parents, children, husband wife and grand children live together and work together. The leadership of father ended after his death and then it passes to brothers which creates tendency to build single family. In single family, family labor demand is different from extended family members' demand. Aziz (1983) mentions this is a *family development cycle* that continues, but reverse is rare. However, through this cycle, single family system is increasing.

7. Peasant social stratification in Bangladesh

Social stratification and social class division can be seen in peasant society in Bangladesh based on religious traditions, social class division, land tenure system and occupation. Social stratification and social class division can be seen in Hindu religion; aristocracy status can be seen also in Muslim families, but now social status is determined by ownership of wealth in Bangladesh in addition to above sociality. Anawarullah (1978) finds four types of social stratification in Muslim family: Sayed, Sheik, Moghul and Pathan. However, contemporary social stratification structure is Khanda, peasant cultivators, day labors, weavers, doctors (Baiddi). Khandanis in first row, they have less participation in agriculture although they have enough lands. However, cultivators' basic features are they use labor in their agriculture. Day labor has no land, but they sell their manual labor to other places for their livelihoods. Weavers and doctors are in lower strata. Monirul Islam Khan (1991) mentions Khandan and cultivators have separate relationship in marriage. Khandan people usually do not marry cultivator families. In Hindu religion, there is no marriage between higher cast and lower caste. In Hindu religion, Brahminis the higher caste; Shaha, Dhopa and Napit are lower caste. Fishermen, blacksmith and masons are scheduled caste. Higher castes people have land. They get crops from share croppers. Now lower caste people have good economic condition in the village. However, this ascribed generational family status, occupation, and economic situation of villagers is changing in Bangladesh.

Non-agriculture occupational mobility rapidly changes among peasants in Bangladesh. For example, a study was conducted in Hathazari UpZilla by Fatimatu-Zohra (2013), a student of Sociology, Chittagong University, Bangladesh on peasant occupational mobility. The study finds 92% peasant family members expressed they like to involve in non-agricultural jobs (driving, auto mechanics, plumbing, electricians, constructions, typists etc jobs) in their life. This study respondent thinks income from agriculture is less than income from non-agriculture occupations in their area. Moreover, the study also finds second generation of peasants has less land than their first generation because of fragmentation of land ownership.

Many Indian sociologists and economists put contribution to Indian agriculture system analysis. Ram Krishana Mukhrjee, Daniel Throner, and Utshe Pat Nayek are prominent researchers who studied Indian peasant society. Mukherjee (1978) studied six villages in Bogra six decades ago. He divided peasants into five classes: Jotdar, rich peasant, Rayot, unproductive land owner and Rayot sharecropper. Throner mentions three classes: land owners, peasants and labors. Some lands are fertile and some are not. Hence peasant class categories are not fair according to land ownership.

Arefin classifies marginal farmer if he has .01-.99 acres of land, but Westerguard (1978) mentioned .1-2.99 acres. Siddiqui, Kamal (1978) and Wood (1978) gives importance to land tenure system for identifying peasant class position that determined by land owning, land leasing and share cropping criteria. Wood did not label peasant classification although he categorized peasants on the basis of land size-group; however, he agrees that land owners can produce surplus those have 2.4 acres of land. Patnaik (1976) divided peasants according to land ownerships which are based on Indian survey. His peasant class classification is based on how much labors they receive from outside labor or not receive labor from outside or they themselves provide labor in agriculture. Patnaik class divisions are: Land lord, rich peasant, middle class peasant, small peasant, poor peasant, and landless labor. However, petty cultivators' number is increasing; therefore, Patniak's peasant class classification based on land ownership is not 100% accurate in Bangladesh. He finds land lords receive tax from their tenants and buy cheap labor from the society; however, he himself is not directly involved in agriculture work. Patnaiak's (1976) study shows rich peasants exploit labor wages by giving peasants less wage for their job.

Many scholars divided peasant society into different categories. Eric Wolf (1966) makes three types of society: primitive society, peasant society and industrial urban society. In Europe, peasants were divided into three classes according to their personal status: slave, serf, and freeman. Vilen Van Scandal emphasizes class analysis based on economic categorization. His class classification based on food purchasing capacity and standard of living. (A) class of people is unable to collect full year food and their standard of living is poor, (B) class of people are able to purchase food but standard of living is poor, (C) the middle class people who is able to produce little surplus. (D) Rich people are able to maintain their family with scarcity. Rich peasant, middle class peasant, poor peasant are results of peasant economic class division that is encouraged by land tenure system and modern commercial agricultural system.

Recently the class division emerges through market competition success and failure and cumulative resource accumulation in Bangladesh.

Marxism calls it the process of power dynamism and differentiation. This process becomes strong in the capitalistic society. This economic inequality exists in peasant society, but polarization process starts when capitalistic relations are wide spreading. Atiar Rahman and Borhanuddin Jahangir (1978) find differentiated socio-economic polarization process happens in the advanced villages in Bangladesh based on land ownership. For example, Borhanuddin (1978) finds in the studied village it has 34% land was owned by top 10 families in 1951, but in 1981 it increases to 50.28%. On the other hand, bottom level peasants were 60% which was 24% in 1951, but now they own only 10% land. It means rich become richer and poor become poorer in Bangladesh. However, Atiar Rahman study (1986) shows these economic differentiations include non-crop production other elements. For example, the cattle farm owners are the non-crop production group in Bangladesh. The authors find cattle ownerships are less among the peasants than it was before 1970s in Bangladesh.

Anawarullah Choudhury (1978) analyzes Bangladesh village social stratification and his analyses are related to agriculture structure. His analysis of social stratification based on three elements: (1). Strengthening of production ownership ability, (2) Social status and (3) Power. He divided household members based on agriculture occupation and non-agriculture occupations. His main three classes of peasant are based on agriculture system (1) Land owners, (2) Share croppers or tenants, (3) Landless labors. Non-agriculture occupations are petty traders, paid employed, craftsmen, blacksmiths, fishermen, barbers etc. in the villages, but agriculture and non-agriculture occupants have relationships with each other because many businessmen have lands in villages. Business people earn money from both lands and other business.

Class division also exists among landowners. For example, some peasants own 80 bighas land; some own 20 bighas of land. Again Anawarullah (1978) divides peasants based on labor relations: (1) one class never involve in agriculture cultivation even they do not supervise agricultural activities. They leased their lands to other cultivators and collect leased money. Small peasants cultivate their own lands for their livelihoods. In the village, he finds 48 people are share cropper peasants. These sharecroppers have little lands, but they cultivate lands by paying tax to other land owners. Here Anawarullah's (1978) social stratification and social classification based on persons main occupation as well as main source of income. However, poor landless people exist in villages which he does not include in his peasant agriculture stratification and peasant classification.

8. Peasant economics

According to Danial Thorner (1984) peasant economics is an area of economics that have a wide variety of economics used in peasant society. The traditional peasants are partly integrated into the market economy. Modern peasant economic assumptions are about the maximization of profits, risk aversion and drudgery (hard work); however, they have subsistence agriculture production and consumption. Chayanov argues that peasants would work in order to meet their subsistence needs, but they have no incentive beyond those needs and therefore, traditional peasants would slow and stop working once their need meet. However, in consumerism society, peasant family members are surrounded by non-subsistence demand which is totally different and opposite to corporate agricultural economy. Peasants are satisfied if they can feed and meet their basic needs from subsistence crop production; however, corporate consumption economyis greedy of maximizing profit by exploiting peasants' market relations. Moreover, the consumer economy does not care for environmentalism.

There are two types of peasant economy: peasant agricultural economics and commercialization of capitalist agriculture. Now traditional economy is treated as peripheral economy that neglects universal rationality' of the neo-classical economy. However, in Bangladesh context peasant economy needs to be considered within the major main economy.

A.V. Chaynov (1986) peasant theory is based on demographic economy. According to A. V. Chynov peasant reduce his hired labor because his family has more capable labors. Fragmentation of land size and fragmentation of land ownerships is acute in Bangladesh because of increasing family members in the peasant society in Bangladesh. Moreover, industrial plants, housings and public works capture huge lands in Bangladesh.

T. Shanan (1973) says that agriculture enterprises are (ferme) and the household is the basic economy unit (menge) of the peasant society. He also highlights the capitalist peasant entrepreneurs lack the freedom action; commercial entrepreneurs regulate the peasant labor force. It is inhuman. However, traditional peasant family is trying to maximize the labor input rather than profit. A.V. Chaynov's (1986) thinks the intensity factor in agriculture is depending on the availability of labors and technological level is determined for the reproduction of the family and the unit of production. However, Chaynov is unable to retain distinct agricultural economy through agricultural production in Bangladesh.

8.1. Peasants' subsistence production economy and commercial production economy

Eric Wolf (1966) says, "Peasants are those who are involved with cultivation." However, in capitalistic society polarization is going on in peasant society–the landless poor and the rich commercialized peasants. Big farmers run their agriculture commercially, they are selling their products in the commercial market. However, the traditional peasants aim is to feed the family (subsistence agriculture). Peasant produces agriculture for his family need and his primary aim is to fulfill his own family need and the secondary target is to sell surplus products in market. However, the traditional peasants have intra-family agri-cultivation system that lacks of surplus production. Their agricultural productions are for self-consumption and family consumption. They do not produce agriculture for-profit. There is no absentee landlordism in peasant society. In peasant society, peasants need to produce crops for his family and to continue his agricultural production. If he fails subsistence agricultural products, he might be in challenge to survive himself and his family. Therefore, there is no sharp class differentiation, economic exploitation and to influence to other weak people. Moreover, no social dependents and no economic exploitation observe in traditional peasant society. They have no bindings for industrial production and ownership. Their ownership pattern is local and familial.

Agricultural food production is essential for peasants' physical survival and for the continuation of his agriculture (seed, plough and cattle). A portion of his agriculture production is used for his future agriculture. According to Eric Wolf, the excessive agriculture production is surplus. Peasant involved in surplus production for carrying their expenses of ceremonial fund where all need to contribute fund for it. Wolf (1966) says, "As farms are not only an economic unit rather it is a house which has a big role in peasant family. It is a place not only for production, but also consumption unit of agriculture products. All family members contribute to labor. However, division of class exists in peasant and it is influenced by capitalism. A.V. Chaynov (1986) thinks traditional peasant society is static because they are not aware of social dynamic.

Eric Wolf (1966) mentions society has dualism-traditionalistic and modern society. Traditional society's main character is uniformity, static and firm integrity. On the other side, modern society main character is labor division. Clover finds peasant societyis in between two societies. Shannon (1984) talks about the peasant familial farm characteristics. This family farm has both production and consumption relationships. Although family head is the owner of the land, but all the family members have rights to the family land. Family members have gender division of labor and they have gender identity. Similarly male/female has specific responsibility in the family. Father has the highest status in the family. Usually children raise cattle and youths involve in agriculture labor. Here his economic status is high in the family. Moreover, father's opinion/decision is final in the family economic sphere.

9. Commercial agriculture

The capitalistic and feudal peasant economy becomes remnant/rapidly disappear because of rapid growth of commercial agricultural and manufacturing. The commercial agriculture encourages modernization. What, how and how much to produce and what to do with the product obtained to move to substantial agriculture or commercial agriculture. However, traditional agriculture contradicts how much to produce for maximizing rates of profits and accumulations. Hence it is necessary to think about distinct forms of social organization of production. Moreover, traditional and commercial agriculture classified by scale of production for securing/sustaining means of production-'factor cost'-market price of inputs, land rent, wages of family wages and value of input purchased from market.

Commercial agriculture is about a simple 'mercantile economy'. This market economy is –on- the- spot consumption economy or self-sufficient economy transfer to material requirement for its reproduction economy inputs or final consumption goods must be acquired from the market by using money. For this purpose, the family unit is formed to join the market for goods and services as a supplier of product or for labor power. Here the decision what to produce is based on the marketability of the product. Selling products what has produced is part of peasant economy.

One of the special features of the peasant society is that it makes use of labor force which would not create value in other production sector-the children, old people, women and the head of the family and his adult children- all are working unsystematically. This is one reason for the ability of the family unit to bring product to the market at lower prices than communal production and prices. Marginal labor force is using in the traditional agriculture, but they are not regarded labor force in the commercial sector, but these marginal labor force contributing to net increase in the family income. However, traditional peasant society risk internalization is occurring to co-opt with entrepreneurial behavior of profit making in Bangladesh. Entrepreneurs have risk or uncertainty in their profits that can be derived from alternative applications of their capital, but these uncertainty views as probability functions (Shanin, 1984). They calculate this risk and profit probability that might zero game by adverse situations. Lipton views it "survival algorithim", which lead them to avoid risks despite the potential profits. They internalize this risk and uncertainty through they generate lower incomes and lessen expected outputs. For example, many peasants do not cultivate certain high yielding crops to avoid complex technology use and buy high yielding variety (HYV) seeds from complex distance marketing mechanism.

In the commercial society, there is a clear separation between capital and labor power, between owners of means of production, land owners and labor power. The commercial society principal aim is to secure at least average profit. Here peasants articulate with the market economy by linking them with the rest of the economy-exchange of goods and services (or values) between sectors: exchanges ad transfer of surpluses from the peasant sector to the rest of the economy-the capitalist agriculture and the urban industrial complex.

10. Commercializing Peasant Economy

In commercial agriculture production society, land ownership is the prime, but lands are concentrated to few people hands. In peasant society, peasants are not specialization in mechanized agriculture production. Children informally learn agriculture from their families. However, traditional cultivation is changing and peasants are using chemical fertilizers, pesticides, and mechanics for plough and for irrigation. Many whole buyers and middleman traders buy products at cheap prices from peasants. Hence peasants are not able to get their crop production costs by selling their crops in the market.

Shanin (1973) comments peasant economy has relation with the village community in addition to family farming. Family is not a separate entity in peasant society rather family is a part of village community and work for it. Peasant labor relation has link with village. They exchange their labor receiving money or in kinds. Family tree (Lineage), clan and group has active role in peasant economy and social control. Shanin (1984) uses the term market in two different ways (1) market is a place where people meet and exchange their products with mutual bargaining, and (2) market is an economic institution where people supply, demand and sell products. However, market social context should consider for peasant economics in Bangladesh.

Village market is social gathering for peasants. For example, rural peasants gather in the market, chat, discuss and exchange information there. However, now peasants also have connections with external world through market. Competition, opportunity and individuality are market relations (Scott, 1985) which are rare among traditional peasants. In capitalistic society, production universality and profit are market principle. Shanin (1984) says, "Peasant society power structure control ownership of land." Land owners and land users are always not one individual. Land users are subordinate of land owners, but this relation is a process of exploitative system. This exploitation system continues through tax system. In this way peasant society becomes stratified and people (serfs) are exploited and subordinated through land lords. According to Shannon (1984), "It is about patron-client relations. Robert Redclif (1973) says, "Currently peasant society emerged for the need of urban society and economy. He treats peasants as rural natives. These two rural and urban societies have mutual relationships and they are dependent on each other. It is because peasant uses many urban industrial products (chemical fertilizers, pesticides, hybrid seeds) for their crop production. Urban dwellers also use peasant products. However, urban society controls peasants' socio-economic life through different economic agencies, social organizations political institutions. For example, Bangladesh has *Shalish* (informal arbitration, justice system) performed by *Mattabo*rs (informal village arbitrators) in villages in addition to Union Parishad and Upzilla Parishad who control the villages.

11. Peasants market relations

Peasant produces crops for his family need and the surplus (if any) for market for buying non-agricultural family necessary goods. However, rich farmers produce cash crop products which have market relations.

Peasant economy is treated *'petty commodity produce'* (Scott, 1985). However, peasant products go to urban merchants. Merchants processed agricultural products and sell them at higher prices in the market. Currently peasant economy is saturated and integrated in the world market. The capitalist society forced middle class peasant or marginal peasant to produce products for market because these peasants are dependent on market in various ways. Marginal peasants are compelled to repay his dues or livelihoods costs from investors' loans. Through capital economy, capital accumulated by market production system. However, in Bangladesh many peasants' loss their production cost in the competitive market.

Peasant economy market relations expand with the expansion of new technology. Bangladesh and India peasant economy market relations expanded by agricultural technology development through green revolution. Mahbub Hossain finds (19870 that agricultural labor market increases with the expansion of production. As a result labor market becomes active. But labor demand increases with expansion of production. Rich peasant hires labor from outside market. Lower middle class peasants also depend on labor. Peasant economy is intensively (closely) related to commodity production. Hence agriculture labor demand and use is increased in rural area. However, very few peasant families use their own family members' labor; so many crop producers find agriculture production as capital intensive than before. Therefore, rich peasants lease lands to petty peasants for cultivating their lands.

Recently it is observed that there are many intermediate organizations existing in capitalist production process among producers and consumers For example, the Gold Leaf cigarette company reaches its products through its many wholesalers and retailers in Bangladesh. However, these market agents wholesalers and retailers rarely influenced the Gold Leaf production company. However, the non-agriculture occupation people has huge role to link peasant society with market. In this way, market interlock relationships develop between peasants and intermediate marketing group.

Rich peasant has control over two market sources. (1) Land market and (2) Capital market. As profit gain from these two sources of markets, their controls over share croppers also become powerful. Wholesalers and brokers exist in villages that control crop products and capital market. In Bangladesh, peasants consume surplus agricultural production. Wholesalers and brokers are businessmen and capital investors. Peasants sell their crops in advance to wholesalers and brokers before starting crop harvesting seasons. Even poor peasants receive advance loans for spending family expenditure. Small peasants repay these loans after crop harvesting.

Peasants get fewer prices from selling their crops to Mahajons and loan investors because peasants are forced to repay their crop loans that they received from money lenders and loan agencies. Wholesalers and brokers make profits through this catch. Wholesalers and brokers are widespread in cities and villages across Bangladesh. Whole buyers control peasants by providing advance capital to them. Loaned peasants are bound to repay their loans immediately after crop harvesting, but the crops price is low when peasant sell their products in market and repay their loans. This '*forced commercialization and forced loan repaying*' process cannot give peasants economic relief/ salvation. The reason is *distress sale*-crop sell is immediately done after harvesting for peasant family need. Recently micro finance institutions (MFIs) in Bangladesh provide crop loans to poor farmers, but MFIs put pressure to borrowers to repay loans immediately after crop harvesting. MFIs think loan receivers shall not be able to repay loans or divert the agriculture loans if MFIs are not brisk to collect crop loans immediately after crop harvesting.

12. Peasant culture

Cultural changes and moral changes occur in peasant society. Peasant moral values are different from capitalistic norms and values. According to Chyanov (1986) and Dobrowolski, Kazimierz (1984) peasants have one kind of static mentality and that static mentality is responsible for subsistence production and they become happy with this limited agricultural production; hence progressive capitalist economy does not exist among majority peasants in Bangladesh. Peasant society is described as static-unchanging or slowly changing society, but now peasant society ties peasants with urban peoples, ties cities and villages. Moreover, there exists a cultural lag among peasants because peasants need time to catch up or adjust cultural innovation and to solve social problems and social conflicts that is happening within their spheres. However, it needs time to adapt urban culture. So the cultural lag keeps peasant old-fashioned. However, through socio-religious and economic networks, Bangladeshi peasants maintain close contact with their neighbors that results peasant community which is again a part of wider rural unity. However, traditional economy is voluntary economy that has risk for modern commercial sustainability.

Usually traditional culture receives superstitions knowledge, values, customs from past. For example, many peasants do not like to pay or get money at night. Traditional culture appreciates colorful past. So there is an objection to follow modern culture, norms, values and customs. Traditional culture continues without barriers transmitting to next generations. However, when past tradition become unpopular or irrelevant then it creates a certain situation where change is inevitable. It is seen that the poor women come out from their home for employment or for work outside home by breaking traditional Purda (seclusion) system in villages in Bangladesh. Purda system is related to economic need, economic ability (congruity) or economic inability. Hence it is not correct that peasant culture is always stagnant in Bangladesh which is applicable only in primitive society.

Peasant society has many cultures. By market relation with other society, cultural interaction is occurring in society. By using improved technology, many peasants of Bangladesh have exposed themselves to new outlooks, developed new attitudes and create a new social relationship that weakens the old traditions. Lower technology weakens total economy that also weakens social mobility that favors to continue traditional culture.

If a leader/Matabbar is leading a society from a rich family or from the same class it becomes an informal tradition, customs/practices in the society. However, if there is an opportunity a leader can come from different families at different periods, then the society could be dynamic and can be changing. In a dynamic society, the culture and the social mobility could be varied and increased. New view-point/outlook is necessary for a new leadership development and for emerging dynamic social mobility.

13. Pauperization and Polarization of Peasants in Bangladesh

Westeguard (1978) discusses pauperization/impoverishment (going out, flowing out, escape) process in rural Bangladesh. He researches pauperization process in Bogura, Bangladesh. Westergard (1978) compared contemporary social structure (1970s) and social system with 1940s social structure; he observed pauperization process happened more than polarization. Westergard (1978) finds rich peasants loss their lands because of population increase. Density of population was 668 in 1942, it was 1066 in 1957. First average peasant farm size was 6.2 acres, then decline to 4.9 acres. Land less population was 4% in 1942; it increases to 30% in 1975. More than 10 acres of land household were 16% in 1942, but it stands 9% in 1975. However, middle class peasant family increases. In such situation, Westergard does not support polarization process that affects peasants in Bogura.

14. Power and authority structure of peasants in Bangladesh

The term 'peasant class alignment' uses to explain peasants acceptance of others' leadership to revolt against Zamindars and Jotdars. However, in Bangladesh context, factionalism (division), patron-client relation (service providers and receivers relationships) ideas are more important to analyze rural power structure and political relations (Wood, 1978). Lower class people are unable to organize and unite themselves for fulfilling their own needs and interest rather they make difference among them. They accept others' leadership, but there are no relations with leaders with their materialistic interest. Poor peasants, landless labors become aware of their own rights and revolts against Zamindars and Jotdars. Many people think that Bangladesh peasant class awareness emerges because of agriculture modernization. Villagers are aware of many public rights (Rouf, 2012). Although currently Zamindars and Jotdars groups are not prominent in Bangladesh; however, peasants are exploited by money lenders. Alavi and Bayers Scott (1973) observed class based group solidarity among marginalized peasant. They predicted marginalized people realize that politically unite/group has no significance if material interest is different from upper class people.

Power and authority is unequally distributed in almost all society, but distribution pattern is changing based on social type. The power and authority vary mainly on economy. Power and authority is closely related to politics. Max Weber mentions power and authority in society influence other social institutions. It is about imposing ones will upon the behavior of other persons." Powerful person authority is like a lord. Atiar, Rahman (1986), Gazi Saleh Uddin (1996) finds that during British period, influential Zamindars, and Jotdars have gangster forces for protecting them and forcibly collect land tax from tenants if any peasants don't pay tax. Likewise European Vassals or tributary lords created in feudalism for maintaining land lords authority. However, in Bangladesh, village powerful elites forced marginal peasants to have subordination relations with them. However, subordination relations become a tool of exploitation to marginalized peasants by the rural elites.

Hamza Alvi(1973) comments on power and authority of peasant society. He thinks peasant society is not a separate entity like primitive society rather it is a part of state society. It has links with urban society. Now in Bangladesh, peasant politics are active and they are not separate entity rather class division and economic inequality are obvious/explicit in Bangladesh. However, in order to understand village power and authority structure, it is important to realize the peasant encapsulation (inclusion) system and factionalism (division) process, patron-client relations patterns and class relations in rural Bangladesh. Moreover, it needs analyzed them to know the peasant society power structure and political structure in Bangladesh.

15. Use of modern technology in agriculture

In modern agriculture total planning is important which is absent in traditional peasant agriculture society, but peasants run their family lands in a traditional way. However, modern economic system depends on expert farm management that is lacking in traditional agriculture. Here capital investment risks do not exist. Agriculture family consumption is the main features of the traditional peasant economy, but accumulation of capital is slow.

The traditional agriculture inputs per unit land are lower. Ramkrishna Mukerjee study finds advanced technology uses village incomes have increased than backward/underdeveloped villages.

Table 1: Farm size and productivity of land in rice cultivation in technology advanced and backward villages, results of a farm survey, 1982, Paddy yield in tons per hector

Farm size	Backward villages	Advanced villages	Percent difference (advanced over backward)
Small farm	1.80	2.72	51
Medium farm	1.43	2.32	62
Large fram	1.32	2.13	61
All farm	1.59	2.55	60

Source: Hossain, M. Nature and Impact of Modern Rice Technology in Bangladesh, International Food Policy and Research Institute, Washington DC, 1988, cited from Khan, A. R. and Hossain, M. 1989

Bangladesh Institute of Development Studies (BIDS) surveys villages and it finds technology advanced village per head income is TK. 3304 which is higher than 29% than technologically less advanced village. The survey finds rich farmers' incomes have increased 34%, but marginal peasant incomes have increased 22%. The study finds small peasants are expert in using green revolution technology. They cultivated HYV rice more than average users. Intensive farming or intensive agriculture is characterized by generally the high use of inputs such as capital, labor, or heavy use of pesticides and fertilizers http://en.wikipedia.org/wiki/Fertilizersto agriculture production. Intensive crop farming is a modern form of intensive farming that refers to the industrialized production of crops. Intensive crop farming's methods include innovation in agricultural machinery, farming methods, genetic engineering technology, techniques for achieving economies of scale in production, and the creation of new markets for consumption and patent protection of genetic information.

With intensification, energy use typically goes up provided by humans, or supplemented with animals, or replaced with machines. The intensive crop intensity increased based on agriculture irrigation in dry seasons since 1960s in Bangladesh. The following table shows modern irrigation increases over time.

Table-2: Land use in irrigation

System	1981	1984	1987
Modern irrigation	2,496	3,355	8,549
Traditional irrigation	1,555	1,449	890

Source: The agriculture sector I Bangladesh – a data base, USAID/Bangladesh, 1989, p. 64.

The use of high inputs of fertilizers, plant growth regulators or pesticides, and mechanization is increasing in Bangladesh. However, rich farmers or rich business men have capital for modern intensive farming by using agricultural machinery; they can afford modern farming methods and genetic technology. They are able to manage techniques for achieving economics of scale in production and the creation of new markets for consumption.

However, use of technology by marginalized peasants is an issue in Bangladesh. The reason is that technology use is expensive. Therefore, marginalized peasants are not able to manage the use modern technologies in their crop cultivations. Moreover, technology is not safe. For example, spraying pesticide in the crop fields is unhealthy and environmentally unfriendly. Many birds, animals and marine resources are destroyed because of spraying pesticide in the crop fields. Chemical fertilizers pollute soil and water. For example, by using chemical fertilizers the micro-nutrient values of soil have been destroyed in many places in Bangladesh. However, subsistence agriculture uses traditional eco-friendly technologies and these traditional rural agricultural technologies are transmitting to post-generations by orally and informally in Bangladesh.

16. Consequences of Green Revolution

After the green revolution, when the technology and the notion of chemical agriculture were introduced, it seems that the gross production of main grain rice has increased. However, it has created a large negative impact on rural farmers and the environment. Chemical agriculture is only oriented to economic profit; however, ecological and social factors are totally ignored. Chemical agriculture is totally anti-natural and destructive. Consequently this agricultural chemical technology creates many problems in the environment. Prominent problems among these are topsoil depletion and degradation, and groundwater contamination; moreover, it declines of family farms, continued neglect of the living and working conditions for farm laborers, increasing costs of production, and the disintegration of economic and social conditions in rural communities. Chemical use green evolution creates health hazards due to food degradation and environment (soil, air and water) pollution because of agricultural poisons.

17. Modern agriculture and ecological problem

Modern agriculture creates ecological problems in Bangladesh. The uses of inorganic fertilizer and pesticides cause a lot of problems to the soil, water and air. Soil become hard and degraded, water holding capacity reduced, soil PH become imbalanced that cause some micro-nutrient deficiency, reduce soil microbial activities result in less availability of plant nutrients. Increasing pest use in agriculture in Bangladesh that degraded soil becomes unhealthy. Unhealthy soil grows unhealthy plants. The products grown with excessive chemical fertilizers and pesticides are low in quality resulted degradation of food quality. This low food quality has become of less taste and has less nutrition food value of the food products. Chemically grown products have less nutrient contents (protein, vitamins and minerals) and higher water content. The high water content may be one of the main reasons for lack of taste and low preserving capacity of chemically grown product.

Use of chemical pesticides results pollution of the environment as they are chemical poison. They are very much effective in killing living things and have long term residual effect (some cases more than 10 years). The poison pollute the product first and then soil, air and water consequently. This pollution results in poisoned product, soil degradation, and the extinction of fish, birds and other animals. However, use of the organic fertilizer enriches organic matter supply to soil and can produce healthy food.

18. Land Tenure System and History of Land Tenure System of Bangladesh

The Mughul Raj had introduced land tax through Mughul Land Tenure System. Tenants have no land ownership during Moghul period. The Moghul Raj collected land tax through village Mattabors in India who had contact with Moghul Raj. After Mughul Raj, East India Dewani Prarti land tenure system had been introduced by the British East India Company in 1765. The East India Company got Bengal land tax collection attorney from Moghul Raj in 1765. In a memorandum, it was mentioned Rayots shall not increase by British company rather it'll protect Raiyats from tax exploitations and injustice. However, British East India Company exploited Krishok (peasants) much more than it was during in Moghul Raj. The land tenure system was not developed although land tax increased. British introduced the Land Tenure Permanent Settlement Actin 1793. Before permanent Settlement Acts, Zaminders were the agents of land collectors of the Moghul Raj and for the East India Company. Peasants have no land occupying rights; however, after Permanent Settlement Act, Zamindars got land occupying rights and they were the owner of lands. Previously they are the agent of land collectors from independent Krishoks (peasants) for the Moghul Raj. Afterword, Zaminders got rights to collect land tax from Krishok and control Prajas (tenants). The British Settlement Actmade provision for 90% of the land tax should send to Company by Zamindars.

Sher-E-Bangla A K Fazlul Hoque is a non-official pioneer in Krishak Praja Party activities and a starting point of Krashak Rajniti (peasant politics), but it was risky to relate peasants great leaders political and official activities to rural development and to peasant development in Bengal. Fazlul Hoque had contributed to the welfare of Bengal peasantry and to the welfare of the Bengal educated class. Fazlul Hoque was famous for passing the Bengal agriculture debtors Acts of 1935; Bengal Tenancy Act of 1938, the Act of 1885, 1929 and 1938 are all amending Acts of the Permanent Settlement Act of 1793. All these acts are about rights of Ryots (tenants), under-Ryots and occupancy-Ryots. Occupancy-Ryots exempted from payment of a transfer fee. The right of pre-emption was taken away from the landlord and given to the co-sharer tenants. Moreover, provision of rent increase was suspended for a period of ten years. However, there was no improvement occurred in agriculture and that effect without securing the tenures of the peasant on his land.

Sriniketan: establishes the Pally Mongal Samitty (Village Development Committee) by Tagore. It is a cooperative provided by the adult education centers to serve health care services. Tagore introduced training camps (Look Shava) for village workers and landless people. It organizes folk festivals as part of rural reconstructions.

Several peasants revolted against land tenure tax imposed by British Raj (regime) and other rulers in Bengal. Followings are descriptions of different Movements in Bengal.

Krishak was not involved in politics until Khilafat movement and non-cooperation movement and emerging of communalists in the nineteenth century. Baserkillah (bamboo) Fort was organized by Sariatullah during British is a historical event in Bengal. There was a movement against Nell cultivation by Bengal peasants. However, Krishak issues were not visible in Indo-Pak mainstream politics. Politics were limited to feudal elites. In 1935, the tax payers of six areas voters organized against British during Macdonald Rayadad period. This movement was against Jotdars and land lord elites who exploited and were unjust to Krishak. Muslim Bourgeois politicians used Krishoks for their own interest. Therefore, many local peasant leaders' revolts and campaigns against British tax system. However, Indian Congress National Party was mute to avoid Hindu Muslim communal sensitivity issues.

19. Fazlul Hoque Movements and Abolition of Mohajoni Pratha

In 1935 a new Act (1937 Election Act) introduced where Fazlul Hoque talked about Krishok rights through his Krishok Praja Party. This act and campaign was for the competition with Muslim League. In 1929-31, Bengali Krishok citizens were suffering from economic crisis and suffering from loss of their lands. The reason was money lenders forcibly collecting loans and cumulating interest from Krishoks. Fazlul Hoque campaigned against the British Permanent Settlement Acts. In the election, Fazlul Hoque was unable to get majority votes; however, he made a cabinet in collaboration with Muslim League. However, the cabinet was unable to fulfill the demands/rights of the Krishok. Although he changed some laws of Muhajongs (Money Landers), there was no radical change in Krishok life. Unfortunately later Fazlul Hoque was ousted by Muslim League.

Krishok Shava was another Indian peasants' platform that changed few clauses of the peasant land tenure acts through communist influence. Many Krishoks were organized under the leadership of Krishok Shova.

There was an alliance among Krishok and labors of Bengal under the Krishok Shava banner.

20. Tevaga Movement

Tevaga Movement becomes alive against Permanent Settlement Act before and after Indo-Pak partisan. After 1947, the Communist Party politics and Tevaga movement were inactive. However, then increased bourgeois politics that impacted negatively to the Krishok rights in Bengal. Mowlana Vasani was a spokesperson for the peasants' rights and peasant socio-economic development in Bangladesh. Many places Krishoks had organized under Krishok Samitty leaded by Vashani. Vashani conducted many meetings; processions for the rights of Krishok, but he did not use Krishok for voting him or for his party. However, it was his personal strategy and it was against pretty bourgeois exploitations and injustices. However, organizationally Krishak Samiltty was not successful to achieve its manifesto.

21. Nankar Movement

There was another Krishok revolt and movement against Nankar (payment of tax against agriculture products and labors) and it is called Nankar movement in Bengal history. *Nankar* was the name of a type of land tenure characterized by payment of rent in produces or labours during the *Zamindari* period. This system prevailed in Sylhet/Assam areas. The term Nankar is derived from *Nan* (bread) and *Kar* (tax or rent). Nankar may not be confused with *Malikana (ownership)* rather it is an allowance usually ten per cent payable to the state on the gross revenue demand for ownership right for peasants/labors subsistence. The Nankar system of land tenure has a relationship with the modes of production and payment. Zamindar collects the Nankar allowance for maintaining his establishment. Moreover, since Zamindar did not pay his officials in cash, he gives them Nankar or a land assignment in lieu of salary to officials. In return, the officers engaged people as laborers, bearers, cleaners, servants, lathials (clubmen), etc. on Nankar term. These people were paid for in nankar assignment of land. Landholders give *raiyati* rights to the Nankar peasants. At the end of the British colonial rule, the Nankar peasants began to assert their rights on the land they had been cultivating from generation to generation. They demanded that Zamindars must recognize their rights on land as normal Rayots. The reason is Zamindars abused Nankar people was common practice of Zamindars. The conflicts between the landlords and Nankar Raiyats came to surface in 1922-23. Series of uprisings took place later included the Shukhair rising, Kulaura uprising (1931-32), and Bhanubil uprising (1933-35). Under pressure, many Zamindars recognized the rights of nankar raiyats. The nankar rebellion continued even after the Partition of Bengal (1947). Finally, the movement died down when the Zamindari system was abolished in 1950.

22. Krishoks after liberation of Bangladesh

After Bangladesh, land tenure system amended two times. During Majib period, the highest land ceiling was 100 bigha and Ershad time 50 bigha. Last land tenure adornment committed Khas land will distributed to landless people. Sharecropper dead should be at least 5 years. The share cropping system should be one share for land owner, one portion to share copper ad one share to that provides inputs. Many researchers think the sharecroppers are exploited by the Tevagha system.

After 1971, Bangladeshi people organized under a new dimension. Different organizations and political parties were trying to organize Krishoks. However, many divisions happened in contemporary politics, but there was a need for new strategy to activate Krishoks. According to Badaruddin Omar (1974), Krishok must be aware of bourgeois politics and correcting political leadership, but they (Krishoks) should not be involved in direct confrontation with them. The politics need to be aligning with Krishok and they must be away from feudal and bourgeois politics. He suggests labor leaders must know Bangladesh land tenure system, its nature and structure if they want to act politically. Omar

(1974) suggests politicians should know Krishok past history, present situation, their current issues and demand. If not, Krishok movements will not be successful.

23. Peasant poverty and way forward

Absolute poverty is seen in Bangladesh everywhere. Bangladeshi poor peasants are suffering from absolute/acute poverty, deprivation of resources and subsistence-the basic conditions that are not fulfilled. Marginalized peasants spend miserable life in their livelihoods, they are suffering from malnourishment and clothing, become illiterate and homeless etc. problems. Hence many peasants are unable to fulfill their basic needs-food, housing, cloths, education, health and other fundamental essentials. As a result, increases social, economic and environmental inequalities and injustice among peasants in Bangladesh.

Moreover, their life is suffering from threat of physical unhealthy existence. Peasants live below standard life. Social inequalities, mildistribution of resources, deprivation of resources, injustice and unethical human accumulation of resources, lack of food security and lack of social safety nets are responsible for acute poverty among marginalized peasants in Bangladesh. Lack of total socio-economic and political planning is responsible for peasant poverty. Sometimes natural disasters, draughts, flood, earthquakes, cyclones, hurricanes, climate change, water pollution, environmental pollution, epidemic diseases, soil erosion etc. destroy crops, destroy resources and peasants are unable to recover their resources that are destroyed.

Usually widower, divorced, separated women, older people and children do not have enough land for cultivation; they do not have enough scope for income for their livelihoods in Bangladesh. Usually they depend on other members of the family for their livelihoods. State does not support them enough. Peasants are suffering from lack of social safety net, food security and other support services from the state because capitalistic profit motive exploitative market mechanism and commercialization of agriculture lead them to deprivation of fulfilling their basic need.

Agricultural production inputs costs and outputs prices in market forced peasant to buy and sell their products at less prices then it should be. Peasants are unable to buy their household necessities and services from market. Therefore, they are suffering from earning low income and suffering from shortage of resources for fulfilling their necessities. Hence this is a societal problem instead a social problem in Bangladesh.

Capitalism thinks poor peasants are lazy and unskilled in crop cultivation, which is one kind of stereotyping to them. Hence it is vital to emphasis on the marginalized peasant economic sphere. Some sociologists' remark that peasant is unable to co-opt with the modern agricultural production system and marketing system, capitalist trading and commercialization process, and hence they are unable to survive in the modern agricultural market mechanisms. Moreover, existing exploitative land tenure system, lack of technology of genetically modified innovation (GMI) agriculture, high yielding variety (HIV) crop production, and green revolution excluded marginalized peasant from mainstream agriculture. They are unable to fulfill their household necessities by selling their agricultural products in the market; hence they are suffering from buying household necessities (health services, education services, housing, food, and clothing etc.) from private market. Hence they are suffering from poverty, malnutrition, education, food, clothing and housing. Even they do not get proper justice from the society because rural elites, political chieftains, and religious leaders play injustice to poor peasants in Bangladesh.

Landlessness and homelessness is the most extreme forms of social exclusion in society. Capitalist society blames individual fault is responsible for poor poverty. Poor people have less effort, less skills and potentials to earn more income and to overcome their miserable life. Lacks of agricultural processing industries in the villages resulted high rate of joblessness among marginalized peasants. Children of peasants are born into poverty and they suffer from the vicious cycle of poverty and retransfer it to their descendent family and society.

Government fiscal budget contributes more to urban development in Bangladesh; however, remote villagers get less physical and social infrastructural facilities from the state. Peasants are excluded from the industrial labor market as they are not skillful of machines and information technology (IT); hence peasants' are exposed to loss of non-agricultural job market in Bangladesh. Moreover, landlessness people are suffering from lacking of cultivable lands for food production. River erosion, flood, cyclone, hurricane, fire, social exploitations, and capitalistic market structure lead peasants to poor poverty in Bangladesh. The cause-effect consequences can be seen among homeless/landless people in rural and urban areas in Bangladesh.

Agriculture welfare services is absent for the poor peasants although the agricultural subsidy system exist in the fiscal policy in Bangladesh; however, the fiscal policy has few positive impact on them. Government should play a central role in reducing inequalities among peasants through the provision of subsidization of certain goods and services. The reason is poor peasant families are unable to get education, healthcare, housing, income support, and unemployment and pension facilities. Hence they are outside of the state service benefit.

Maloney, Clarence and Ahmed, A. B. Sharfuddin (1988) conducted a survey in 1991 on peasant wage and savings status in Bangladesh. The survey finds daily wage workers save and reinvest 9%, marginal and middle farmers save 12%, salaried people 14% farmers who have trading business 22% and local rich 30-45% (Maloney, 1991). It shows from the statistics that marginal and middle farmers are sufferings from savings and invest money for crop cultivation. Hence it is necessary to develop a mechanism to save and invest money for more production and develop their food security systems. Simultaneously promote and develop the spirit of peasant entrepreneurship in rural Bangladesh. Furthermore, assist peasant social organizations like family, clan and household to develop cooperation among them and articulate their culture and values for producing high yielding crops. Moreover, provide agricultural knowhow knowledge to peasants through popular adult education. Rural peasants are living close to agricultural lands. So it is urgent decentralized agricultural and non-agricultural manufacturing plants across Bangladesh instead Dhaka based and or setup them few cities in Bangladesh.

Implication of the study: The paper discusses the fundamental concepts, principles of peasant and peasants' socioeconomic life and their different issues and sufferings in Bangladesh. This paper gives readers to know and understand the patterns and scenarios of peasants' socioeconomic life and their different issues that they are sufferings from. Peasants' salient facets of the paper could draw attention of Bangladeshi peasant economists, researchers and policy makers to address the issues of the peasants in Bangladesh and thus to mitigate their suffering and to break the vicious poverty ring.

24. Conclusion

Agriculture labors are isolated and their wages are little. Peasant cooperatives are few. Manirul Islam Khan (1991) and Bailey, F. G. (1984) therefore, recommends it is necessary to increase agricultural labor wages and enhance forming peasant cooperatives in the villages. Support peasant cooperatives. Receiving loan for agriculture is difficult for peasants in Bangladesh. Grameen Bank has been providing agricultural seasonal loans to its borrowers for buying agricultural inputs since its inception. Stuart Rutherford (2009) finds microcredit is helpful to marginalized peasants for cultivating their small lands, leased lands and sharecropping lands. Hence, revival and revitalization Samabay (cooperative) Bank is a must for peasants' for their access to agricultural loan.

The paper also recommends strengthening of local government agencies and opens their activities to poor peasants for their access to local resources in Bangladesh. Moreover, develop physical infrastructures and social infrastructures at the village level. Simultaneously peasants' entrepreneurship development is very crucial for reviving rural economy. Women household activities and their agricultural processing activities are not count in the Bangladesh national economics. However, their contributions to household economy and national economy are important. Therefore, it is necessary to count women domestic and agricultural processing activities that have economic value to the household economy and to the national economy. Many rural agricultural labors are unemployed for many months round the year in villages, so develop alternative income generating activities for utilizing their labors during lean periods in Bangladesh.

Huge population growth causes collapse of development; however, Bengali peasant life can support the greatest population density on the land without destroying the resource base. Therefore, design a village development plan and implement these plans by mobilizing village natural resources instead borrowing outside resources. Hence, a socio-economic reform should put in place for the benefit of peasants that can raise their class consciousness, improve rural land holding, and retain the cultural system of beliefs that support the structure of the peasants' economy and culture. Traditional peasant means of production is neither threat to environment nor destructive to the natural process of genetic selections; hence the agricultural extension education should promote natural agriculture that is eco-friendly in Bangladesh.

25. References

Alavi, Hamza (1973). Peasant classes and primordial loyalties. *Journal of Peasant Studies,* Vol. 1(1), pp. 23-62

Anawarullah Chowdhury (1978). *A Bangladesh village: A study of social stratification.* Dhaka: CSS.

Arefeen, H.K. (1986). *Changing agrarian structure in Bangladesh, Shimulia-a study of a peri-urban village.* Dhaka: CSS.

Atiar, Rahman (1986). *Peasants and classes: A study in differentiation in Bangladesh.* Dhaka; UPL.

Aziz, K. M. Ashraful (1983). Kinship in Bangladesh. *Monograph Series 1.* Dhaka: ICCDRB.

Bailey, F. G. (1984). The peasant view of the bad life, (Ed.) T. Shannin, *Peasants and peasant societies*. England; Penguin Books

Byres, T. J. 1982). The new technology, class formation and the class action in the Indian countryside. *Journal of Peasant Studies,* Vol. 8 (4), pp. 405-454.

Chaynov, A. V. (1986). *The theory of peasant economy*. UK, Manchester University

Dobrowolski, Kazimierz (1984). Peasant traditional culture, (Ed.) T. Shanin in *Peasants and peasant societies*. England: Penguin Books

Eric, R. Wolf (1966). *Peasants*. New Jessi: Prentice Hall

Fatema-Tu-Zohra (2013). *Peasants' occupational mobility in Bangladesh* (Unpublished). A survey conducted in the Hathazari UpZilla in Bangladesh by a student of the Department of Sociology, University of Chittagong, Bangladesh.

Hall, Anthony (1973). Patron-Client relations. *Journal of Peasant Studies*, Vol. 1 (3), pp. 506-509

Hashmi, Taj Ul-Islam (1994). *Peasant Utopia: The communalization of class politics in East Bengal, 1920-1947)*. Dhaka: University Press Limited

Humphrey, Caroline (2014). *Remoteness and alternative spatial concepts at the Russian-Mongolian boarder*. Director of Miasu: Cambridge University

Hussain, Mahbub (1978). Nature of tenancy market in Bangladesh agriculture. *Bangladesh Developmenty Studies*, No. 5(2), pp. 139-162

Hussain, Mahbub (1987). *Green revolution in Bangladesh: Its nature and impact on income distribution*. Dhaka: BIDS

Jahangir, B. K. (1978). *Differentiation, polarization ad confrontation in rural Bangladesh*. Dhaka: CSS.

Maloney, Clarence and Ahmed, A. B. Sharfuddin (1988). *Rural Savings and credit in Bangladesh*. Dhaka: University Press Limited

Monirul I. Khan (1991). The process of technological change in the agriculture of a Bangladesh village: its relevance to mode of production. *The Journal of Social Studies*, Vol. 53, pp. 38-67

Monirul Islam Khan (1991). *Kishok Samaj: Prathagoto Samikha (Peasant Society: Conceptual survey)*. Dhaka: Samaj Nirikhan.

Monirul Islam Khan (1991). Landless irrigation and social relations: A study on the social impact of a BRAC program. *Journal of Social Studies, Vol. VI.*

Mukherjee, Ramkrishna (1971). *Six villages of Bengal.* Bombay: Popular Prakashan

Omar, Badaruddin (1974). *Bangladeshi Krishok (Peasants) in Chirosthae Bondobstho (Permanent Settlement).* Dhaka: Maowla Brothers

Patnaik, Utsa (1976). Class differentiation within the peasantry: An approach to the analysis of Indian agriculture. *Economic and Political Weekly,* Vol. 11(39), pp. A82-A85+A87-A101

Rouf, K. A. (2012). Green microfinance promoting green enterprisedevelopment, *Humanomics,* Vol. 28 (2), pp.148 – 161

Rouf, K. A. (2015). Revenue-generating social and economic mission-entwined organizations. *Global Journal of Human Social Sciences* (E), Vol. 15(3), pp. 77-97.

Rutherford, Stuart (2009). *The Pledge: ASA, peasant politics and microfinance in the development of Bangladesh.* Dhaka: Oxford University Press

Saleh Uddin, Gazi (1996). *Bangladesh land tenure, land reform and rural development.* Chittagong: Mimitta.

Scott, James (1985). *Weapons of the weak: Everyday forms of peasant resistance.* Massachusetts: Yale University Press

Shanin, T. (1973). The nature and logic of the peasant economy-a generalization. *Journal of Peasant Studies,* Vol. 1(1).

Shanin, T. (1984). *Peasants and peasant societies.* England: Penguin Books

Siddiqui, Kamal (1978). *Land reform legislation in the '50s' and '60s' in Land reform in Bangladesh.* (Ed), M. K. Alamgir. Dhaka: CSS.

Thorner, Danial (1984). *Peasant economy as a category in economic history in peasants and peasant societies.* (Ed.) Teodor Shanin). England: Penguin

Westergaard Kirsten (1985). *State and Rural Society in Bangladesh: A Study in Relationships.* London: Curzon

Wood, G. (1978). *Exploitation and rural poor: A working paper on the rural power structure in Bangladesh.* Comilla: BARD.

Community Communal Capacity Building for Swiping Out the Individualistic Norms and Values in Socio-Economic Divide Polarizing Trap Society

Abstract

Capitalism, consumerism, industrialization, globalization and corporations are promoting individualism, sexism, classism, racism, privatization, competition, urbanization, and socio-economic division between rich and poor, increasing social polarization gap, inequalities, injustice, and discriminations in the society at the expense of human face. They are not promoting environmentalism, Cinderella economy and people-centered green economics among majority people. The socio-economic divide polarizing society has anti-community communal altruistic values and norms. However, alternatively community organizing, community capacity buildings, community planning process and social networking are excel in building a sense of community belonging, caring and supportive each other and cooperative exchange (social capital), and altruistic local living sustainable economy. Community development approach addresses the issues of unemployment, poverty and gender discrimination in the society.

The objectives of the paper are to explore the contributions of community development, and to familiarize readers about successful different community initiatives in different communities in Canada and in Bangladesh as oppose to individualism. The paper explores why community development work is essential in the society? The paper questions what are the means and strategies could be developed for developing altruistic communal values and norms in the community? The paper contains author's own academic scholarships, working experiences working with the community agencies Noble Institute for Environmental Peace (NIEP), Ahamodhya Society, MCC in Canada and Grameen Bank (GB), Grameen Motsho & Poshosampd Foundation (GMPF) in Bangladesh. The paper contains literature reviews on community organizing and community development.

Community development is a living process that strives for creating communal identity and changing the dominating power structure of the society. Community communal values can minimize power struggle and develop trust among community people instead create competition and conflict among people in the society. Hence promotion of community communal norms, values and practices of caring each other and helping each other is essential and important in the socio-economic cultural divide modern society. However, it is required to understand meaning of community and community development; know about strategies of community organizing, community capacity building and community planning steps/process. This knowledge can help community people organize themselves to use their community resources, create opportunities for local initiatives, feeling of "We" instead "I". These processes assist people engaging in community development activities and uphold deepening community solidarity communal values in their life. The paper provides implications of effective community buildings, methods of community organizing and community social capital development with examples from Canada and Bangladesh. The paper finds it is possible to build the conditions for mutual aid and prosperity among community members even in the giant cities. The paper generates new knowledge of community organizing where people can generate green jobs; protest against bad governance, address their poverty and environmental degradation issues in their neighbourhoods.

Key Words: Altrustratic communal values, capitalism, community development; community organizing; community planning, consumerism, deepening community; globalization, individuaslism, industrialization, social capital, social network, virtual community, and urbanization.

1.0. Introduction

Canadian community builder Paul Born (2014) asserts that taking care of one another and looking out for one another had been an evolutionary prerequisite. It is why we have survived. However, capitalistic society creates walls around people that separate people from one another. However, the "survival of the kindest" states that evolution is more a cooperative process than competitive one. Species that have been able to collaborate and learn from one another are much more adaptable to their environments and able to respond to the changing circumstances. Caring for one another and working together are at the heart of community. It is how community people build a sense of belonging and prompting cooperative exchange. It is necessary because in the capitalistic modern society and individualistic value oriented urbanized society people are increasingly suffering from socio-economic divide, which creates miseries, injustice, discrimination, exploitation, competition, poverty, unemployment and many other socio-economic and environmental problems in the community. Hence promotion of community communal norms, values and practices of caring each other and helping each other is important in the socio-economic cultural divide society. Therefore, this thematic paper is emphasizing the understanding of different community types, possibilities of developing different means and strategies for community organizing and community capacity social capital building for the betterment of human wellbeing and community development because community builders can enhance happy and joyful life in the community. The paper narrates some community agencies like Mennonite Central Committee (MCC), Ahamodhya, Noble Institution for Environmental Peace (NIEP) in Canada and Grameen Bank (GB) and Grameen Motssho and Pashusampd Foundation (GMPF) in Bangladesh are examples of community development that create community communal values in these two countries.

2.0. Research questions

What does mean by community, neighbourhoods, virtual community, community organizing, community development, social capital development and deepening community? Is there a difference between a community and social network? Why community development work is essential in the society? How do people make the connection from self to others? What are the means and strategies could be developed for developing altruistic communal values and norms in the society?

3.0. Objectives of the study

This paper is to identify the meanings and characteristics of community, virtual community, neighbourhood, community development, and deepening community; to explore the contributions of social network in community organizing, and community development; and discover the role of local or geographical boundaries and the role and challenges of communication technologies, social capital (social network) in community development.

4.0. Methodologies

The paper used author's own academic scholarships, personal working experiences with Noble Institution for Environmental Peace (NIEP), Ahamodhya, Menonnite Central Committee (MCC) in Canada and Grameen Bank (GB) and Grameen Bank Motshu and Pashusampad Foundation (GMPF) in Bangladesh. The paper uses MCC, Ahamodhya, GB and GMPF secondary data and reviews their literatures. This paper enlarges readers about these agencies community development strategies and knowledge. The study also contains literature review and short history of the declining the value of community communal values in the current society.

5.0. Significance of the study/ statement of the problems

Individualistic norms and values have started from the pre-industrial and industrial capitalistic society, but individualistic economic divide polarization process increases in the post- industrial period through emerging giant cities and globalization. This socio-economic and cultural polarization process creates community divide, uneven rural-urban divide, socio-economic divide, cultural divide, and environmental destructions in the society. Giant cities and globalization over exploited natural resources and human resources without giving return to earth and community. Cities have become so large that comparatively simple services and agencies have posed problems. Even technology unable to solve social and economic problems rather technology increasingly create socio-economic gap, injustice, anti-altruism unethical individualistic values and norms in the unsatisfactorily. The financial crisis of 2008-2009 grows from the same root-a fundamental flaw in the theoretical construct of capitalism (Yunus, 2013). This new capitalistic industrialised urbanizing society not only looks for profits at the expense of human exploitation, social, economic, cultural and environmental exploitation and injustice in the society, but also swipes community communal altruistic values, cooperative norms, principles, human common wellbeing. As a result, increase poverty, unemployment, financial artificial crisis; exploit human cheap labour, gender discrimination, racism and stereotyping individual capability in the society. Consequently resources and power concentrated in the hands of few dominating people. Mass people of the society are less wealthy and suffering from miseries across the world.

The modern large city, the giant metropolis, has been viewed by scholars as an indication of the disintegration of community civilization (Barker, 1999; Korten, 2006; Koening, 1957; MacIver (1955). People are exhausted of expenditure of money and somehow make life livable without comfort, joy and happiness. Capitalists, industrialists, bankers' force people to be robot labourers, having no voice and choice in their workplace and social life. According to Samuel Koenig (1957) there is extreme concentration of wealth and power under a merciless economic and cultural regime. Even spiritual and intellectual things are appraised in monetary terms. Now rich and poor neighbourhoods' separatism and polarisation, exploitation, and extremes of wealth and poverty reach maximum heights (Quarter, 2014). The capitalist regimes think village community with its substance agricultural economy and primary relationships are dating back as far as the Neolithic age. In such situation, majority people are socially, economically, culturally sick living in environmentally polluted world. Mass people are suffering from economic and social unjust in the society. Because capitalistic society puts importance to individual competition, market competition and distance traveling commodity consumers instead of creating community communal altruistic feelings among people.

Moreover, there are increasingly concerned with the relations of animals and plants to neighbours and environment upon plants, weather, water, air, lands, animals and human beings. Now people become job slavers instead developing community communal carrying beliefs, norms, values and activities in the neighbourhoods to help each other and to mobilize local resources. However, alternatively community development is a way to enhance the resources (both human resources and non-human resources) of a community can increase quality of life of community people and acquiring access to resources. CD approaches and addresses the problem of poverty in a sustainable way (Yunus, 2013). This phenomenon helps each other, able to develop solutions to the issues and opportunities within the community members in their own ability to take action. Therefore, community development communal services, community capacity building, neighbourhoods link and cooperation, community development planning are essential in the contemporary society in order to develop civic wellbeing, economic wellbeing, cultural and environmental restorations and justice in the neighbourhoods.

6.0. Defining Community

According to Christenson, Fendley & Robinson (1994), a community is defined as people that live within a geographically bounded area who interact socially, have one or more ties with each other and the place in which they live (p.8). This is done while maintaining social networks through intense ties, social interaction and an identification with the community. However, there are many communities that interact with and network among themselves without living in a particular geographical area. For example, Muslims may interact about issues from different places via the Internet. The lesbian gay bisexual transsexual community (LBGT) commune to celebrate different festivals in different places along the lines of acknowledging and celebrating their sexual diversity. The author believes that in a community there are features such as people, place/territory and purpose.

According to Robert M. MacIver (1955) in his book *Society: Its Structure and Change* mentions that a community is a group of people "who live together", who belongs together, so that they share, not this or that particular interest, but a whole set of interests wide enough and complete enough to include their lives." He includes community as villages, cities, tribes and nations. Kingsley Davis, in *Human Society*, defined community as "the smallest territorial groups that can embrace all aspects of social life." Other sociologists usually conceive of it as a local aggregation of people, i.e., village, town, or city, but some sociologists referred to as societies. So it is a local area over which people are using the same language, conforming to the same mores, feeling more or less the same sentiments, and acting upon the same attitudes. However, now people restrict a community to the village, cities or nations rather claiming that community needs close relationships, which are essential characteristics of the community, prevail only in such smaller areas. Defining communities in terms of geography is only one way of looking at them. Communities can also be defined by common cultural heritage, language and beliefs or shared interest. These are called communities of interest. Aboriginal communities not confined to geography rather they are larger part of non-Aboriginal geography.

Community can also be defined as a group of individuals or families that share specific values, services, institutions, interests and/or geographic proximity (Barker, 1999, p. 89). Another definition of community or a sense of community exists when two or more people work together toward the accomplishment of mutually desirable goals (Lofquist, 1993. p. 8). It can also be defined as a number of people who share a distinct location, belief, interest, activity or other characteristics that clearly identifies their commonality and differentiates them from those not sharing it (Homer 2004, p. 150).

Community shapes our identity and quenches our thirst for belonging. In the community, people's personal identity becomes part of the collective identity. It has the power to unite people all in a common bond as community people work together for a better world. For example, people feel a sense of connection by joining a church, yoga class, community gardening, shared food preparation, sports clubs, and music clubs.

7.0. Community Characteristics

- In a broad sense, a community has its own physical features, people, locale, values and spirit. It includes the formation of identity, cooperation, interaction and networks amongst its members.
- Physical features (the size, gathering locations, key points of reference, natural features that include: flood, draught, abundance of water, forestation, dwelling types, mosquitoes, etc.)
- People (population size, length of time living there, demographic breakdown: age, density, family make up, marital status, income, education, ethnic background)
- Place/ geography/territory/ natural resources/physical features

- Common interest/feelings/beliefs/goals/lifestyles/needs/activities
- Values/spirit/customs/practice/rituals/ habit/conduct
- Identity/common attachment/ psychological identification
- Cooperation/solidarity versus competition
- Networks/communication
- Action, interaction, reaction (regularly/casually), printed/ electronic media (email/Internet/ face book, etc., and
- Neighbourhoods (specific physical area/location/ where people live). It is used more in urban housing settings.

According to Paul Born (2014) there are five simple principles of community: seeking community is natural; people all have many communities in their lives; people can choose to deepen their experience of community; seeking community is part of their spiritual journey; and healthy community leads to individual and collective altruism. Here the key qualities of community people are either lead or participate in a community development initiative: respect for the individual, group and community, strong sense of responsibility and commitment, empathy, openness to look at alternate solutions, new opportunities, and ways to improve, patience, perseverance and endurance, creativity, innovation, and institution, willingness to participate without always having to lead, trust others and self-confidence.

8.0. Types of Communities

In ancient time, village community was preceded by a nomadic economy and the latter by a collective economy, which was the most primitive. Villages developed into towns when a class of traders settled permanently in the villages and began trading from their homes. Latter towns developed metropolises, or large cities, which appeared with the rise of empires and of national states (Korten, 2006). The smallest living clusters are community people live together. Primary community refeered as intimate relationship community like fishing, lumbering community, and secondary community-main function is to collect the basic, materials produced in the surrounding area and to distribute them throughout the region, manufacturing community involved in producing finished products and sent their products to commercial centers where commercial communities are living. Communities are commonly divided into two generic types- rural and urban. Now many other communities exists such as agricultural community, trading community, professional community, music groups, sports group, arts group, dance group, and manufacturing group etc.

9.0. Benefits of community

In the community, people can learn from sharing stories. In fact, this sharing benefits community people, individually and collectively. Community belonging shape people identity more broadly. Community builds the conditions for mutual aid and prosperity. Community improves over all human well-being. It can help us to engage in and embrace a communal approach that benefits many and approached from many directions. Here community people become involved in agriculture, renewable energy, information technology, spirituality, education, health, employment services and many similar areas and sub areas. For example, Ahamedhya Muslim community and Mennonite community aids its members in Canada. They feel that their community and their faith in God are insurance enough. When there is a medical emergency, personal need, these community people takes up a collection to pay the hospital bill. They are one another's insurance. This is their definition of "Mutual Aid." Ahamedhya faiths beliefs service is part of their worship. Many people have joined credit unions and cooperatives. GB and GMLF Bangladesh organize poor people to be involved in community livestock, community fisheries, and community agriculture and community informal adult education. By joining others, people have a better chance of being successful. This allows people to support one another. These community people trust success of one becomes the success of all.

10.0. Virtual Community

Virtual/Cyber-communities are usually created through online interaction. They exchange and share information with certain goals and aims. Contemporary technologies, primarily digitalization and the Internet, have shrunk our world, making all events and all problems omnipresent to us. People can be smarter and more effective in community. Facebook, Twitter, LinkedIn, Flicker, Printerest, Instagram, Bookmark, Skype Confrence, and Telephone Conference etc. are great virtual tool help people understand others and find patterns to follow. The virtual community trend is increasing across the world because accessing the Internet has become relatively easy. Computers, Tabulate, Smart phones and Internet-mediated communication connect people globally. The advantages of the Internet in terms of community, learning and networking are that members are able to gain information with a wide range of possibilities available. The Internet may be used to develop supports where there were once weak ties. Here, the virtual community fulfills the definition of community, although they are not meeting the geographical criterion.

As a result, the traditional definition of community may become problematic as information technology has allowed for this definition to be expanded through developed and maintained relationships via email, online networking sites, and cellular communication. Barry Wellman and Milena Gulia (1999) have raised the question: *are virtual communities 'real' communities?* They fear that the virtual community is a zero-sum game where more time is spent interacting online and less time is spent interacting in real life. According to them, the Internet is especially suited to people who cannot see each other frequently. Online relationships are based more on shared interests (p. 353). Its architecture supports the maintenance of a large number of community ties.

Although, key facets in the definition of community should include having real-world interaction and face-to face communication, modern communication technology (IT) and the challenge of the 'digital divide' help people to retain their relationships and communication while sharing information, values and ideas among interested parties. KNET in Canada blurred community *informatics* (the application of information and communications technologies) to enable community process and the achievement of community objectives (Stoecker p.14). Many young people are building connections through the Internet, cleverly and determinedly findings ways to connect cybernetic community. Social media can be used to bring people together to celebrate or work on a common cause. However, this virtual capability is ever danger because of people emphasis on individualism at the cost of community.

11.0. Neighbourhood

In larger urban centers, communities are often defined in terms of particular neighbourhoods. Most people belong to more than one community, but people belong to particular neighbourhood. Many scholars refer community as neighbourhoods. Neighbourhood is similar to a community, but it is a smaller area in which relationships tend to be primary, or more or less intimate. The neighbourhood, in other words, is a section in which live a number of families among whom close relationships exist. It is a group in which no introductions are needed. Neighbourhood as an area in which the residents are personally well acquainted with each other, and are in the habit of visiting one another, of exchanging articles and services, and in general, of doing things together. Neighbourhood has a geographical area characterized by both a physical individuality and by cultural characteristics of people who live in it. People living in such an area posses a common set of institutions, customs, traditions, beliefs, attitudes, and ways of life, they constitute a more or less distinct culture unit within a wider culture. The Ahamadhya community neighbourhood, MCC neighbourhoods in the town houses Mable and Cambridge in Ontario is an example neighbourhood where they have close intimacy each other. They celebrate religious, cultural, music, theatres, sports events in their community religious centers, community recreational center around the mosque.

The question is as a community worker, how to get to know neighbours in the neighbourhood. The tip is go door-to door. It will help meet people face-to-face, which is very best organizing approach. Collect their email and other contact information to make things much easier. Consider changing front yard for sitting and enjoy the fullness of front yard flowers, shrubs, fruits and vegetables- and greet neighbours as they pass by. Get out and play. Children can bring a neighbourhood together, and dogs (in some cases) are also great building relationships. Stop and talk while people are walking in the community. It is surprising people have no interactions living together in the neighbourhoods many years especially in giant cities. Hence consider forming a neighbourhood or apartment association, take the initiative to visit neighbours, talk with them and greet them. Do not wait everyone come when organizing meetings or events. Take a risk to organize an event, many will join the event. This can facilitate the organization of community events, socials and programs that will support neighbourhood cohesiveness.

12.0. Association

People who are associated with particular goals and objectives, meet to discuss issues, has a leader, abide by certain rules and procedures that are usually formal. However, a community is usually developed naturally whereas members of an association become a community through interaction that are both formal and informal. In a neighbourhood, dwellers live in certain regions and may or may not interact among themselves. Also, they may or may not have homogenous characteristics as it relates to class, interest, beliefs and lifestyle. Community by associations can cross many boundaries. Most often they are not restricted by geography; rather they provide a context for identifying with others like oneself or with a cause about which one cares deeply. An association can provide a sense of solidarity and brings feelings of belonging. Communities of association are formed by those who feel outside or on margins of the mainstream, who are struggling together for broader acceptance in society.

13.0. Community social capital

A social network is a collection of nodes (people, organisms, institutions) connected by a variety of ties, relationships, directions, and reciprocity that are based on the exchange of resources (emotional, social, financial and informational). People create social networks through their interaction of similar interests, shared values, visions, ideas, financial exchange and friendship. For example, the Toronto Bengali Cultural Club (TBCC), MCC members, NIEP members, GB, Udichi Theater, and GMPF members have a network/circle where they share, exchange Bengali culture, music, dance, theatre and food. They also exchange Bengali books, movies and teach English to newcomers, teach English and Math to school children in Toronto. They maintain community activities through their connections, networking and shared interests. Social networking is an essential element for community formation and maintains community solidarity.

Social capital refers to connections among individuals for creating social cohesion value, better health, education and security. Bonding social capital facilitates in developing social relationships within the framework of community and development. Here, social capital can create close bonds within the community without bridging other groups; an example may be that of church-based women's reading groups, books circle group. For example, bridging social capital includes the civil rights movement and many youth service groups. Bonding social capitalis good for mobilizing solidarity and bridging networks in the community, and is also better for linking external assets and information diffusion.

Social networking involves mutual communication and exchanging of information among members; it is one of the essential ties of a community. Social networking includes building relationships and loyalty to a community and neighborhood. It has strong ties and weak ties depending on the relationship and interaction among persons. The services in a social network are usually specific, while those of communities are usually more general. A social network is based on shared interests for the wellbeing of the community. For example, Winnipeg Mondragon Cafe and Book Club creates a social network among Winnipeg downtown neighborhoods which at the same time can be termed as a Winnipeg Mondragon Cafe and Book club community too. MCC volunteers, NIEP volunteers, Grameen Bank and GMPF field workers build networks among marginalized people in Canada and in Bangladesh. Therefore a community can be analyzed using a social network approach.

Robert Putnam is particularly concerned with the loss of social capitalin modern communities and what might be done to rebuild it. He describes two kinds of social networks. The first and more common kind is created by bonding with people who are like us. The second involves bridging by connecting and engaging with people who are not like us-people who have different belief systems or skin color or socio economic status. Though people are different; citizens can bridge these differences and build cohesiveness. This physical place of gathering becomes a tremendous source of personal and community identity. For example, the design of walk able communities is to facilitate connection by making it more a part of everyday life, meeting a neighbour while walking to the grocery store. Social networks are the way people get to know one another better over time.

14.0. Role of local or geographic boundaries and the role of communication technologies and social capital in community development

A community of practice may be more relevant for people rather than a geographically place-based community. However, to do community development work, organizers need to initially use on-the-ground techniques in organizing the people and then have an online presence or vice versa. A community or neighborhood can exist with close links to the larger society and still retain it's identify and viability because it provides a basis for the local population to engage in community actions (Christenson, Fendley & Robinson 1994, p. 7). Hence nowadays place is becoming less relevant and is being replaced by mutual networks. For example, automobiles and Internet have made it possible for people to live farther from where they work within metropolitan areas as compared to fifty years ago. Still, space affects our access to jobs and public services (especially education); our access to shopping and culture and the availability of medical services. The Internet, email, skype conference, telephone conference, and other digital technology make social networking and space creation easier for people to be together without physically being together. However, poor and working-class families are less likely to own instruments of eliminating or reducing the 'digital divide'such as a computer that has Internet access including an e-mail exchange.

15.0. Community development

Community development (CD) is not imposing solutions from top or from outside, it is a community democratic decision making process that requires the active participation of a variety of people. According to Christenson, Fendley and Robinson (1994) Community Development (CD) would be driven not by competition and deprivation, but by cooperation and affluence for the wellbeing of people (p.15). From this point of view, the author prefer the CD definition by the Centre for Urban and Community Studies, University of Toronto, Action Aid Bangladesh is working for poverty reduction in Costal areas of Bangladesh that asserts that community development is positive change in the social, economic, organizational or physical structures of a community that improves both the welfare of the community members, reduce poverty of community members, and the community's ability to control its future. It entails a variety of citizen-led efforts carried out within or on behalf of a community, to define problems, develop solutions, and attract the resources necessary to implement activities that address the identified problems. For example, Bangladesh Red Cresent Society, Dritipat, MCC, Ahamodhya, Grameen Bank (GB) and Grameen Motsha and Pashu Shampatt Foundation GMPF), Action Aid Bangladesh, Care Bangladesh ect. are about to help poor and working class citizens improve their socio-economic status.

MCC, Ahamodhya Group, NIEP, GB and GMPF, Dristipat, Care Bangladesh, BRAC, Proshika, ASA, BRDB, and Milk Vita etc. are community development (CD) agencies who are fundamentally about building partnerships, collaborations and information sharing and helping people that they need where community people and community builders develop integrated actions and services to improve conditions of people's lives in the society in Bangladesh. Community development approach is built upon the belief in people's need, freedom of choice and voices, ability, knowledge and interactions and relationship development. It is about mutual cooperation, altruism, not for competition to one another. Community development aim is for its members to work with together for improving quality of life, green development among the community people, particularly poverty reduction for marginalized people of the community. It is about integration of people towards community belonging, not social, economic and environmental dividing among community people. CD promotes the development of common knowledge and critical awareness among community members. CD provides community both formal and informal adult learning, children transformative learning and promotes popular culture in the society. Thengamara Mohila Samitty, BRAC. Gano Shikka and Grameen Shikka etc. organizations have adult learning services in addition to their other programs in Bangladesh. Moreover, community mutual learning and mutual helping among community members is central to common wellbeing of human life. Community development is not one time token service in the community, rather community development is a continuous process for the belonging, engaging and connecting each other for creating opportunity of socio-economic and green wellbeing and to eradicate poverty from the community. Deepening relationships and empathetic feeling, community identity among community members is the key to community engagement and development.

The strength of CD is to bring diverse interests together to achieve a common purpose. CD is a continuous process where organizations can work hands to hands with people and mobilise resources for the interest of the community disadvantaged people. Grameen Shikka, BRAC, Noble Institution for Environmental Peace (NIEP), Gono Shasta, Nagar Health, Green Peace Bangladesh, Oxfam Bangladesh and PROSHIKA and Nijara Kori etc. have campaigns for community awareness is one of the beginning steps of community green actions for green community capacity building in Bangladesh.

Community development activities usually serve people to improve their socio-economic status, health, political-civic engagement, cultural activities, religious observances and educational outlets. It also empowers them to be self-managing. State macro-policies, mezzo and micro community development policies and their support services that are based around online virtual communities can serve only those who are using the Internet. Marginalized poor people may be left out of online community development activities especially in developing countries. However, the Kuh-Ke-Nah Network (K-Net), a regional network of more than 60 aboriginal communities around northern Ontario and Quebec, is used for health, education and other social services. Grameen Phone and other mobile companies in Bangladesh send different types of messages by mobile phones to their clients to inform them about weather, temparatures, cyclones, flood information and other information for alerting them about natural disasters. This is an excellent CD scheme to serve Bangladesh mobile clients and to northern marginalized First Nations people in Canada through modern communication technologies. Community informatics may be used to achieve CD objectives. However, information and communication technologies (ICT) have eclipsed the traditional concept of CD.

16.0. Components of Community Development

The CD has four components: building support, making plan, implementing and adjusting the plan, and maintaining momentum.

Building support creates awareness, understanding and support for the community development process. CD is an inclusive process. Community members shared vision and a sense of belonging to their community initiate the community development process. It includes economic, social, environmental, organizations, (government, labour, business, social services- all are part of CD. However, Frank and Smith (2005) assert the following diagram that has nine agencies community planning participants.

Diagram 1: Agencies involved in the CD capacity building process (Frank & Smith 2005).

However, there are some mistakes made when a wide cross section of interest are present by outsiders or insiders of the community members/agencies-misunderstanding silence or the tone of voice of the community members responses, presenting ideas instead of asking for input, assuming needs, treating interactions as competitions instead of learning opportunities, inappropriate framework of thinking patterns, judging or stereotyping by their gender, appearance or past and giving more attention to officially recognized leaders. Soil Development Banglasdesh officials casually visit farmers and advise them as an outsiders how to retain soil micro-nutrients for their crop lands and how to prepare compost in their lands. However, regular followup is necessary to get feedback from the farmers are farmers do compost properly. The diversity of community members' farming interests, political interests, organizational mandates and existing structures are factors that must be recognized and built into the community development process.

17.0. Community Economic Development and Grameen Bank, Grameen Motsho and Pashusampad Foundation (GMPF) Bangladesh experience

In Grameen Bank and in Grameen Motsho and Pashusampad Foundation (GMPF) local communities work together at setting up businesses and promoting their own interests through economic expansion. Here the definition of economy serves all community economic development (CED) approaches (Ced, cEd, and ceD) can be given as a system of human activity directed to meeting human basic needs that is determined by deliberate allocations of scarce resources" (Boothroyd, P. and Davis, H. 1993: 230). Micro financing is a small business financing system, whereby, interested private entrepreneurs borrow money for running their own sustainable small business ventures. Micro financing is run by NGOs all over the world. For example, micro financing everywhere is working with local currency to provide for the poor create self-employment through income generating schemes; helps meet basic needs and build the local economy.

Micro-financing institutions also mobilize small deposits and community savings which are used to invest in community planning. Bangladesh is a non-welfare state and a largely rural society where these programs are needed. The Government of Bangladesh has been implementing a 'Cooperative Village' approach as a means to achieve integrated rural development through the Bangladesh Rural Development Board (BRDB). Grameen Bank (GB) sixteen decisions provide the poorest rural women with a ray of hope of total socio-economic improve life. It provides them with the opportunity, through microfinance, to start and run their own businesses and to be social and economic actors in their community. This is the notion of the ceD approach that has implication to the theme of integrated rural development approach in Bangladesh.

Grameen Bank operates nationwide through 2185 branches. The repayment rate has been highly satisfactory (99%) since 1979. The majority of them (97.9%) of them are women borrowers. The Bank serves a total of 8.5 million borrowers through 130, 000 rural landless associations in 70,370 villages in Bangladesh. Total loan disbursement is $15.65 billion since its inception. Of them $10.00 billion has been repaid. Current borrower savings are $7.5 billion. To date, its monthly loan disbursement is $58.00 million and 100% loans financed from borrowers deposits. It has 21, 500 staffs working at the village level nationwide (GB Updates, 2016). GB never receives any grants from outside sources since 1996. It is run based on its own borrower's savings, an internal fund mobilization, which makes it economically sustainable.

The Grameen Bank (GB) and GMPF, MCC are shining examples of a locally and democratically run organization CED organization) designed to serve the poor people by being run by them. GB is responsive to the people and engages with them on regular bases which are all features of good Ced. Every year GB officials, at all levels, face an election. This process of electing a leader helps to develop democratic norms and facilitates networking among members, especially poor women. All centre chiefs and group chairmen gather at a monthly workshop organized by each branch where they discuss and exchange new strategies and concerns. Women organize independent associations to receive loans from GB. Borrowers receive loans and save money, repay loans individually and collectively participate in the local association or centre weekly meeting. They receive loans from the grameen bank and run their businesses in their locality. They earn money and gradually create personal and collective (community) assets. As part of the monthly meetings, they discuss their status of the business, family matters, community problems, children's education, health and other social agenda. GB and GMPF borrowers perform community development as well as community economic development activities in which GB officials act as a catalysts and help them to reach their goals eradicating of poverty and to empower their societies.

Like Grameen Bank and GMPF, there are many community economic development organizations- Bangladesh Rural Advancement Committee (BRAC), Asocciation for Social Advancement (ASA) in Bangladesh that includes poor rural women in its cEd program, and provides small loans to rural poor women through group formation and business initiatives. These organizations give preference to female empowerment because they feel that women suffer more from poverty than men, and women are much more active to escape poverty than men. The Bank focuses its attention on female community organizing, because it explores and promotes female empowerment both economically and socially. These businesses built up savings and help them find dignified livelihoods by increasing income providing education, creating material assets and developing social and human capitalto overcome poverty. One of the prime objectives of the Grameen Bank is to promote female entrepreneurships and to create self-employment. This empowers women economically and socially by increasing their income and creating leadership and networking among them In addition, clients of the GB gain access to better nutrition, housing, and social activities which help them acquire new skills and coping strategies. This is typical CED -using economics to improve the community in non-economic ways.

Beginning in 2003, Grameen Bank expanded and began to directly tackle homelessness. Approximately 79,000 beggars have already joined the 'Struggling Members Program' setup to deal with their unique situation. $1.2 million has been lent to street people so far; of that $0.53 million has already been paid off. The poor commonly live in isolation, trapped in their homes. The objective of microfinance and the Grameen Bank is to create an environment under which people can develop the confidence to survive on their own. Again, this is quintessential ceD service in Bangladesh. Although Boothroyd, P. and

Davis, H. says," the limitation of ceD is that it is out of step with the mainstream attachment to unlimited growth." p. 235); however, GB activities contributed to Bangladesh poverty eradication.

Grameen Bank community development program does not only maximize local economic activity in the locality, but also creates the kind of social and emotional environment in which people connect with each other to strengthen mutual aid norms and practices through GB landless women associations. Social cohesion and solidarity among them crystallizes through making associations. They discuss their business problems, family problems, and other social problem and how to solve them, and exchange business ideas.

18.0. Community organizing

Community organizing is essential for community development and community wellbeing of its members, which creates opportunities for group formation and address community issues collectively. The value of mutual cooperation, participations, mutual aid, and mutual actions, mutual voices create autonomy, collective affords, develop and solve local problems by using local resources. These are the valuable components of community organizing. Influence, imposition, exploitations, injustice, competitions, top-down decisions and top-down executions are anti-community organizing phenomenon. Community builders need to be successful motivators and selflessness. In Toronto, many community agencies are successful in making networks among its community members and to provide community services to their services. Examples are: Food Share, Regent Park Community Services, MCC, Islamic Social Services and Rehabilitation Services (ISSRA), NIEP, Ahamodhya Association, Scott Mission and Red Cross Programs of Toronto etc. However, in Bangladesh, religious institutions are serving the notion of community organizing both in rural and urban areas. Communitty people go to their prayer centers everyday or weekly for praying and meet there, greet there. Prayer centers are fulfilling people's spiritual and social wellbeing everywhere in the world.

These organizations are able to make networking, bridges across age, gender and ethnicity. Several members of these agencies have able to make strong connections to each other in terms of personal and familial ties. Scarborough Village Center is able to develop strong ties among its senior's members in Scarborough, Toronto. However, there is a weak tie among Canadian born immigrants and first generation new immigrants. It is because new immigrants take time to familiar with the new country social economic, cultural, political values and norms, and technological system. Therefore, bridging program- one-o-one counselling services and new immigrant family link with new immigrants with Canadian family service agencies and Canadian in-born families could help the new immigrants to know the Canadian existing values, norms, customs and systems. Community builders could look into these features for new immigrants' adaptation with the community. However, new immigrants feel comfortable to get services from their country of origin citizens in Canada. They have more connections and interactions from their country inmates. In Bangladesh, Praveen Samity Houses are places for young, adults, and seniors where they meet, greet and interact each other, discuss their community issues in their neighborhood.

BRAC, Proshika, Nijera Kori, Grameen Bank and GMPF in Bangladesh are community organizing schemes in the sense that landless poor women organize themselves in the centre, develop leadership qualities, and are involved in decision making process, resolve problems through mutual dialogues for improvement of lifestyle, children's education and health in Bangladesh. They help other poor people and work with them. They work together towards improving hygiene and sanitation in their village, resolve neighbourhood conflicts, violence, dowry problems, vote, and participate in other human rights issues. They involve themselves in public awareness and act for their class consciousness and social uplift. They become interconnected with each other. Today, they are no longer socially isolated. Many of them use their credit for home-based businesses. All their activities create an impact on local businesses and economy. Thus people play a collective role in local economic development. In Canada, Scarborough Storefront and Bangladesh

Business Trade Fairs and other business centers organize small business fairs, community picnic, volunteer gathering, and homemade food selling fairs, farmers market, street festivals, community storytelling, community gardening, and community music festivals. These events help neighbours to gather in these events and selling their products, exchange greetings and acquainted each other, share ideas and skills etc. These activities, events have allowed community members participate in these community organizing events to engage with other neighbours and organization employees, volunteers that may have previously unrelated to neighbourhood-specific community activity participations. Through these events, community organizing new immigrants, community people get a scope to of informal learning with other local community members, organizations, and built connection, network among each other and relief loneliness life, and discuss and exchange their neighbourhood various issues and solutions.

19.0. Community capacity building and community development

Problem-solving, conflict resolution skills and team building skills are important in the community capacity building process. To be effective in problem solving, community builders need to have the ability to identify the issue, or problem; look at options and alternatives, help individuals understand the views of others, break the impasse if discussion get bogged down, manage conflict when it occurs, help find common ground, assist members to recognize, make agreement when it happens and ensure that everyone understands the agreement. Both community development and community capacity building are being viewed as community-based participatory model of development. Principles and values are key part of both community development and capacity building when they are being considered as participatory or inclusive processes (Frank & Smith, 2005). They are about respecting people, improving the quality of living, caring one another, appreciating and supporting cultural and individual differences and being good stewards of the land, water and wildlife.

Community development process takes changes of the conditions and factors that influence a community and changes the quality of life of its members.

It is a tool for managing change and therefore, it is not a quick fix to a specific issue within the community. It is a process that seeks to exclude community members from participating and an initiative that occurs in isolation from other related community activity (Frank & Smith, 2005). However, one of the primary challenges of community development is to balance the need for long term solutions with day-to-day realities that require immediate decision and short-term action. According to Flo Frank and Anne Smith (2005) effective community development has a long- term endeavour, well planned, inclusive and equitable principle. It has a holistic and integrated approach, initiated and supported by community members. As a result it enhances mutual benefit to the community members, facilitates shared responsibilities among community members, and connections between social, cultural, environmental and economic matters. Moreover, it respects diversity of interest and grounded in experience that leads to best practices.

20.0. Community planning process (CPP)

Roles of the community and relationships are not always clear-cut at the beginning of the community building process, but it needs to be adjusted to the local context and situations. In the CPP, there could be some common mistakes: failure up-front need to develop support for CD, imposing a vision on community members, failing to involve all the interests and sectors of the community in the visioning process; designing processes that are not inclusive or open to all, failing to inform members about the community plans and programs, and involve the community, leaders fails to build community ownership. To overcome these mistakes, Frank and Smith (2005) suggest seven steps in a community planning process: The following diagram provides an illustration of the community planning process.

In the CPP, it is important to create a community vision could help a picture what the community builder wants. Assessing the current situation involves factors outside the community and within the factors. The process involves identifying strengths, weakness, opportunities and challenges.

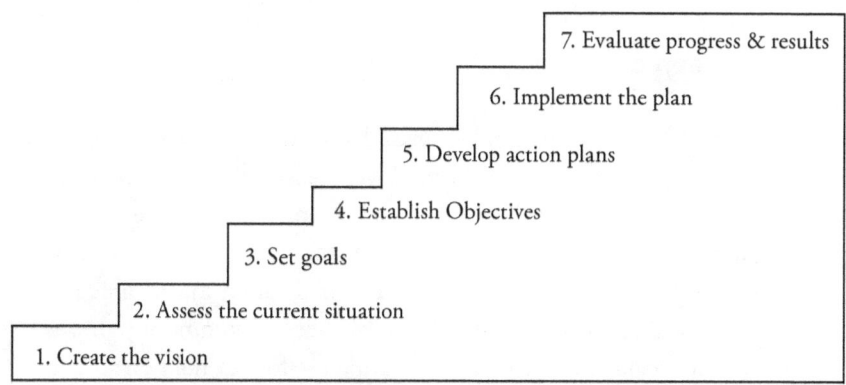

Diagram 2: Community planning steps (Frank and Smith, 2005).

Here community planning needs develop action plan includes who, what, when and how around the plan. After implementation of the plan, it is CD.

Factors that contribute to successful community planning are: shared vision, long-term commitment, leadership, resources-financial, physical and human, support-community and political commitments. Other factors are a realistic appraisal of the current situation, a desire to build on the accomplishments and efforts of the past, an inclusive process and the ability to work as a team. Most importantly a commitment to use the plan as a tool and to modify and make adjustments as needed at the implementation level. Therefore, designing a local community development process involves: understanding the community, learning from other community, development success stories, and learning from past efforts that have not worked well, recognizing the efforts. Knowledge, skills and abilities of all involved in the CPP are very important. CPP is bringing a responsive and flexible CD process to community people. However, the community members also need valued the CPP activities that suit the community. Community development and community building are processes that increase the ability of people to prepare for and respond to opportunities and challenges in their communities. It develops community based accountability and responsibility for the future.

21.0. Deep community

The term "deep community" is used by Paul Born in Canada. If society care poverty, safety, or human well-being, then the experience of community is essential. Because capitalism worships the idea of competition and winning that raised the status of competition to be a defining part of our nature. Moreover, cooperation and democracy are discounted as inefficient in capitalism. Deepen community means to make consciousness, proactive, intentional effort to hold on to and build on the connections between us, connections that will help us resist the pull of the often-neurotic social responses to the complexity of our times Born (2014). Paul Born mentions two other community- shallow community and fear-based community (p. 34)). However, the deepening community creates the opportunity for people to care for and about others that builds a sense of belonging. This makes people more resilient and it makes community people healthier. Moreover, it improves our economic opportunities, networking and makes people happier.

Through community activities children have not only develop a positive self-identity, but also a positive community identity. Our culture's individualistic approach does not bring deep satisfaction. Children, youth, adult and seniors all enjoy community weddings. However, here the challenge is to understand self own sense of isolation and the cultures of individualism, acting in ways that astern cultures would see as selfish (Born 2014).

Paul Born, Director of Tamarack Institute, Canada believes that seeking deeper connection, and relearning the skills of community engagement and collaboration, could reach the goal of reducing poverty for one million families in Ontario. Through community engagement and collaborations; Canada, Bangladesh and other countries can create a positive vision, organize community people to achieve it, and realize better future for all. The deeper the community, the easier and better the outcome people can receive. Paul Born gives his life experience on MCC Canada. Paul Born grew up in the Mennonite farming community in Ukraine and member of the Mennonite Central Committee (MCC) Canada. MCC has community bondage in Waterloo and Cambridge in Canada where MCC members helping each other, fest together, and kept close to one another. The immigrated Ukraine people are a community that are trying to heal and establish itself (MCC) in Canada. Born mentions (2014) that in MCC people grew up feeling a tremendous sense of warmth, identity and belonging, which is the foundation of MCC members understanding of deep community. The following chart made by Paul Born (2014) that distinguish shallow community, fear-based community and deep community.

Diagram 3: Types of community described, (Paul Born 2014)

Shallow community	Fear-based community	Deep community
This is my story. Entertained, no emotional bond	I am not one of them	To open doors between us, Stories unite us.
Hedonism. Friends see once a month, family at Charismas, people has association but lack bonding	Join others against others. We are right and they are wrong. We must stop them.	Knowing one another by spending repeated time together. Celebrate together in person, children know and trust us.
Take care of yourself-no one else will. Send a get-well card, phone on their birthday; post a birthday message on Facebook. Our doctor cares for us when we are sick	Believe that "we" have a greater right to life (happiness) than "they" do. We are stronger when they are weak	Mutual acts of caring build a sense of belonging. We know and act when neighbours and friends and family are sick. Mutual acts of caring occur often.

Shallow community	Fear-based community	Deep community
I am alone in this world. Send in a donation, click "Like" on Facebook, sponsor a child in Africa, and yet do not know names of children next door.	Share a belief that we are right and they are wrong, and work together to realize that belief. If we work together, we can win and they will lose. Will do whatever it takes for my "tribe," or people, to win and defeat the other.	Share a belief that creates a benefit for all, act together for the benefit of all. An absence of "they" or "them." As we care for others, our caring for each other deepens.

In the shallow community, people do not require ongoing connection and mutual caring. Here personal peace may be doomed; pursuit of pleasure can create a vacuum or have abusing pleasure–alcohol, drugs or sex. In this shallow community, consumerism waste natural resources, create inequality among those who produce what we consume, and distance people from the real nature of people. Shallow community could be an attempt to deny innate desire for deep community or to avoid making the effort to deepen community. According to Paul Born (2014) the shallow community is a turning away from the challenge of building deep community, and fear-community is a misguided attempt to build deep community.

22.0. Fear-based community

A community based on fear is a dangerous place. These community people position themselves against the other to feel safe or hopeful. They do not accept people for who they are, but required them to unite against someone or something as the price of belonging. This fear can grow out of control quickly when groups start to organize against the other side. Islamophea exist among Muslim people in the Western World. Poverty-stricken neighbourhoods become places of fear after dark, when gangs, drugs/prostitution come to life.

However, deepen community is a place where people find opportunities for ongoing connection with those they care about and those who care about them. It builds an emotional resilience within and between people that, in turn, builds mutually and reciprocity. Examples are MCC, Ahamodhya sharing potluck meals after their worship services, mourning together at funerals, opening their hearts to one another, building reciprocity and a sense of belonging. Here people have warmth commitment to do and share each other. People share altruism and express collectively, causes a form of connection that makes people commitment strong and the work light.

When people develop deep community, they can overcome their loneliness and challenge their fear; they can come together to make sense of destruction around them; they can reach out together and actually do something about it. There are four acts in the deep community: sharing their stories, enjoying one another, taking care of one another and working together for a better world. Deep community comes from a commitment to be in relationship with others. Deepening community involves creating places and opportunities where people can care for others: community people expect something of us. Paul Born thinks that hope needs to be based on a mutual understanding of what people want, of what they hope, together. People have choice, they can make a difference. They can build deep community together. People also prosper together.

Paul Born (2014) identified five broad categories of basic understandings of deepening community: community as identity, community as place, community as spiritual, communityas intentional, and community as a natural living system. For example, Ubuntu, an African term, describing the interconnection between people; Human is defined as individual and social, but preciously as belonging to one another. It is not "I" rather "We."

A community of faith helps people to strengthen their spiritual understanding and discipline their spiritual practice. A sorting of ideas, both supportive and challenging of lifestyles, reaffirms the importance of a common bond and understanding. Healthy spiritual practice, however, allows for "creative seeking" and for challenging belief, both personal and collective. This helps the community to grow in understanding and strengthens the overall belief system. Personal belief system indicates an important source of identity. The deepen spiritual community, when open, can help us to deepen peoples' commitment to each other and in turn, be a wonderful place for joy together.

Places of worship, service clubs, and community centers, which create trusting communities over time, can provide an environment of belonging that provokes mutual acts of caring. Helping one another during illness, supporting one another through celebrations and tragedies, knowing what is going on in one another's lives, and caring and acting collectively are all part of communities of belonging. Corporations such as Disney, Apple, and Ben & Jerry's have created international cultures committed to corporate social responsibility. Moreover, the cultural bonding among immigrants provides a sense of connection bonding among immigrants provides a sense of connection and promotes acts of mutual caring, creating a community of belonging in a new country.

To move from fear-based community to deep community most likely is a process and is requires transcending people desires and responses. Paul Born (2014) provided the following chart of the community transcending process:

Diagram 4: Moving from fear community to deepening community (Paul Born, 2014)

Community building	No community	Shallow community	Fear-based community	Deep c community
Share story	This is my story	Entertained, no emotional bond	I am not one of them	To open doors between us, stories unite us
Enjoy one another	What's in it for me?	Time-limited connection	Join against others. We must stop them.	Shared identity. This draws us together. Seeking deeper connection.

Community building	No community	Shallow community	Fear-based community	Deep c community
Care for one another. (Build social capital)	Hedonism (pleasure seeking)	Friends we see once a month, family at Christmas. We have association but lack bonding	Bond together against others or something is right and they are wrong.	Knowing one another by repeatedly spending time together. Mutual acts of caring build a sense of belonging.
Take care of one another (empathy and belonging)	Take care of yourself- no one else will.	Send a get-well card, phone on their birthday, Facebook birthday, post Our doctor cares for us when we are sick.	Believe that "we" have a greater right to life (happiness) than "they" do. We are stronger when they are weaker.	Celebrate together in person, children know and trust us, we know and act when neighbours and friends and family members are sick, mutual acts of caring occur often.
Work together for a better world (collective altruism)	I am alone in this world	End in a donation, click "Like" on Facebook, sponsor children in Africa yet do not know names of children next door.	Share a belief that we are right and they are wrong work together to realize that belief. If we work together, we can win and they will lodes.	Share a belief that creates a benefit for all; act together for the benefit of all. An absence of "they" or "them." As we care for others, our caring for each other deepens.
Giving your full identity	Delusional	Born into this community. These are my people.	I will do whatever it takes for my "tribe" or people to win and defeat the other.	I believe in this so much that I will give my whole self to this.

Helping one another is the key to the survival of all living things. People are working together to build a better world. This may mean improving a neighbourhood near their work or church. It can be starting a recycling program in a neighbourhood. It may mean cleaning up a park, feeling the hungry or visiting prisons together. When people do these together, with collaborative intention, they create the power of collective altruism (Yunus, 2013).

Collective awareness of group and transcendent knowing contribute to "collective wisdom." Paul Born says, "This collective wisdom is the hope for people's future in the chaotic times." Groups have the potential to be sources of extraordinary creative power are the incubators of innovative ideas, and instruments of social healing. Through gather together, learning together, working forward, people are able to find the solutions they need for a more effective world. For example, GB groups have the potential to be sources of extraordinary creative power, incubators of innovative ideas, and instruments of social healing. The MCC, Ahamodhya, GB and GMPF members learn to identify with a group (social identity) and, in turn, shape their sense of self within the context of the group. The collective act seemed to deepen the resolve of the many. Working together is a powerful testament to the aphorism (saying) "many hands make light work," it is like when everyone gets involved in something, the work gets done quickly. When people work together with purpose, the work feels light and the accomplishment extraordinary, resulting in joy. The giving and receiving relationship provides a form of mutuality and takes the work beyond charity. Paul Born called it "restoring our humanity."

23.0. Community development is necessary as a grass roots phenomenon and or need the external assistance

Christenson, Fendley and J Robinson (1994) say community development impacts localities because it stimulates local initiatives by involving people in the process of social and economic change. However, state planners' emphasis on economic development without people development doesn't fulfill the concept of community development. Community development is concerned with public policy, governmental action and other types of action that affect people. This is because outsider influence can disturb community self-help efforts. State community planners have worked extensively to meet the needs of governmental decisions. It is sometimes difficult to depend on the government for policies, programs and monies to deal with local problems. Community development activities can have more impact through communication-building among local people, which promotes solidarity and improved social, economic, and cultural well-being of community residents. Therefore, self-help efforts are put first before taking assistance from outside. Governmental support could be used in the construction of bridges, roads, Internet connections, post offices, police stations, schools and hospital/health centers in communities. Governments can allocate public resources to the community for its socio-economic programs to assist the community to achieve its mission, vision and goals. Therefore, I strongly believe both the self-help approach and external supports (without influence) is essential for the development of community. There should be; however, equal distribution of resources within society; otherwise, poor and working class citizens will be deprived of opportunities that others will not be deprived of.

24.0. Implication of the paper

The end product of this paper would encourage community development builders, community organizers to know different initiatives of community development activities in Canada and in Bangladesh. The paper provides new knowledge of Canadian community organizers initiatives, activities and the women borrowers of Grameen Bank, and GMPF are to be able to use the knowledge for the improvement of their personal life and citizenry development in their communities. This paper also discovers GB non-declared community development learning system and its implication to borrowers' social life.

25.0. Limitations of the study

The study is not an analytical paper rather it is a thematic paper and narrates author's own experience on community development work in Canada and in Bangladesh, but the paper does not measure their socio economic development that is also significant. Moreover, the paper does not have primary survey data on the impact of community development in community members' life. The study only reviews community development literatures, community organizing process and community planning process.

26.0. Validity

This paper has intrinsic validity in the rich and poor socio-economic divide process because it defines and reviews community communal values and norms, community organizing, community capacity building skills from the point of view community communal altruistic value and norms creation perspectives and contexts. The paper has external validity too through careful review and analysis of MCC, Ahamodhya society and GB community capacity development learning strategies and implementations.

27.0. Conclusion

Community development is a living process. It brings about change, forges new relationships and shifts power, but power struggle can arise in the community development process. Some community members may perceive a loss of power or be threaten by the new relationships that they see being developed. The community builders can minimize power struggle issues by aware their community people about community development involves change and change with those who will be affected. The community builders also need assess the community situation, confusion and power struggles are likely to occur and indentify action. MCC, Ahamodhya, and NIEP in Canada and GB and GMPF in Bangladesh are community builders/ agencies can take to minimize these social ambiguities, work to develop trust and promote two-way communication, develop open dialogues who are resistant to change and to know what is happening and why it is happening in the society. Moreover, the community builders/agencies need to promote the vision and goals of community development plan to create a common purpose and focus. Therefore, add it is necessary to invite and encourage those most likely to be affected by the community development process to take leadership roles and actively participate in group participation in finding solutions or creating opportunities. To maintain interest and support over time, inclusion and local participation of the community people should be built into the very nature of the community organizing process.

28.0. Reference

Barker, R. L. (1999). *The social work dictionary* (4th ed.). Washington, DC: NASW Press

Christension, James, Fendley, Kim, & Robinson, Jerry. (19940. Community Development. *In Community development perspective*, (eds). Christenson & Robinson. Ames, Iowa; Iowa State University, pp. 3-25.

Christension, James. (1994). Themes of community development. In *Community development perspective.*, eds. Christenson & Robinson. Ames, Iowa; Iowa State University, pp. 26-47

Dreier, Peter, Mollenkopf, John, & Swanstrom, Todd. (2001). *Place matters: Metropolitics for twenty-first century.* Lawrence, Kansas: University Press of Kansas, pp. 1-27

Durkheim, Emile (1897). *Suicide: A study in Sociology.* Robin Buss, translate. New York: Penguin Books

Fenwick, T. J. (2006). Work, learning and adult education in Canada. In *Contexts of adult education: Canadian Perspectives* (Eds.), Tara Fenwick, Tom Nesbit, Bruce Spencer. (2006). Toronto: Thompson Educational Publishing, Inc.

Frank, Flo and Smith, Anne (2005). *The community development handbook: A tool builds community capacity.* Quebec: Human resource Development Canada

Freire, P. (1973). *Education for Critical Consciousness.* London: Sheed and Ward

Grace, A. P. (2006). Critical Adult Education: Engaging the social in theory and practice. In *Contexts of adult education: Canadian perspectives* (Eds.), Tara Fenwick, Tom Nesbit, Bruce Spencer, (2006). Toronto: Thompson Educational Publishing, Inc.

Homer, M. S. 92004). *Promoting Community Change: Making it Happen in the Real World:* Arizona State University: Chicago

Koenig, Samuel (1957). *Sociology: an Introduction to the Science of Society.* New York: Barnes & Noble Inc.

Kretzmann, J. P. and McKnight J. L. (1993). *Building Communities from the Inside Out.* Chicago: ACTA Publications

Lee, B. (1999*). Pragmatics of community organization.* Mississauga: Common Act Press.

Lofquist, W. A. (1996). *The technology of development: A framework for transforming commun*ity *cultures.* Tucson, AZ: Development Public*ations*

Lotz, J. (1987). Community Development- A Short History. *Journal of Community Development,* May/June, pp 40-46

MacLeod, Greg. (1997). *From Mondragon to Am*erica: *Experiments in community economic development.* Sydney, N.: UCCB Press

Martin, Samuel. (1985). *An essential grace.* Toronto: McClelland and Stewart

Mook, L., Quarter, J., & Ryan, S. (2014). *Manages business differently.* Toronto: University of Toronto Press

Ornish, Dean (1998). *Love and Survival: The Scientific Basis for the Healing Power of Intimacy.* New York: Harper Collins

Paul Born (2014). *Deepening Community: Finding together in chaotic times.* San Franciesco: Berret-Koehier Publishers, Inc.

Putnam, Robert D. ((2000). *Bowling alone: The collapse and revival of American community.* New York: Simon & Schuster

Quarter, J., Mook, L., and Armstrong, A. (2009). *Understanding social economy: A Canadian perspectives.* Toronto: University of Toronto Press

Results Canada (2006) *Action Sheet,* September 2006

Rouf, K. A. (2014).Community capacity building for eliminating the individualistic norms and values in a society polarized by a socio-economic divide. *Global Journal of Human Social Sciences (GJHSS),* Vol. 14(3), pp.1-15.

Rouf, K. A. (2014). Earth Community - Green Women and People-centered Altruistic Economies, Politics and Cultures: A Book Summary and Review of 'The Great Turning from Empire to Earth Community' (2006). *Global Journal of Management and Business Research (GJMBR)*, Vol. 15(2), Version1.0. pp. 1-12.

Shragge, E. (1997). *Community Economic Development-in search of empowerment*. Montreal: Black Rose Books

Stocker, R. (2005). Is community informatics good for communities? Questions confronting an emerging field. *Journal of Community Informatics*, 1(3), pp. 13-26.

Tutu, Desmond (2000). *No future without Forgiveness*. New York: Imagine

Wellman, B., & Gulias, M. (1999). Net surfers don't ride alone. In B. William (ed.), *Networks in the global village*. Boulder, CO: Westview Press, pp. 331-366

Wilkinson, P., & Quarter, J. (1996*). Building a community-controlled economy: The Evangeline Co-operative Experience*. Toronto: University of Toronto Press

Yunus, M. (2008). *Creating a World without Poverty*. Dhaka: Subarna Publications Ltd.

Yunus, M. (2013). Concept of Social Business. *Grameen Dialouge-89*. Dhaka: Grameen Trust

Eradication of Poverty Through Community Economic Development Using Micro Financing: Lessons Learned from Bangladesh

Abstract

Community Economic Development (CED) model is an alternative socio-economic development approach that provokes for the local economic development in order to eradicate poverty among the disadvantaged people in the community. P. Boothroyd and H. Davis (1993) in their article talk about the "Community Economic Development: Three Approaches" where they narrates three different frameworks of community economic development. Although these three frameworks of CED emphasis on the holistic economic community development, each CED approach/framework has a special feature that emphasizes on particular socio-economic elements pointed by capital letters Ced, cEd, and ceD based on each community development project's nature and type. This paper is an effort to explore the application of CED- three approaches in the contexts of Canada and Bangladesh. The paper also deeply looks at Grameen Bank activities in Bangladesh, K-Net Canada as case studies; and analyzes GB activities and K-Net Canada activities in the lens of the CED- Three approaches designed by P. Boothroyd and H. Davis (1993).

Key terms: Community development; community economic development (CED); community organizing; feminization of poverty; Grameen Bank micro-credit.

1.0. Introduction

Micro-credit plays a vital role in attaining the Millennium Development Goals (MDGs) to eradicate povertyin many countries. The Grameen Bank (literally 'village bank') of Bangladesh is a notable example of using micro-credit to facilitate community economic development in Bangladesh. The Grameen America group-based micro-credit program is even successful in USA. It has a significant impact on poverty alleviation as well as fostering local citizen empowerment in Bangladesh and many other countries in the world. The micro-credit institutions (MFIs) have managed to both increase local economic activity and build community savings through their highly successful and world-renowned projects. This essay reflects upon a number of experiences, as a result of the author's hands-on exposure to micro-finance management through his years of work at the Grameen Bank and many other micro-credit projects in different countries. The paper also explores the various concepts of poverty, feminization of poverty, community economic development and micro financing in the context of Bangladesh. Finally, it will explore how Grameen Bank fits the concept of Community Economic Development (CED) formulated by Boothroyd, P. and Davis, H. (1993) in their article "Community Economic Development: Three Approaches".

According to the World Bank (2010), poverty is a shortage of income that makes people vulnerable to chronic hunger and disease. Cheston, S., and Kuhn, L. (2002) and Yunus (2007) mention that poverty victims are suffering from to feed them three meals a day. Poor people are victims of living in decent house; they do not have money to buy health care.

Most dictionaries define poverty as having 'inferior quality or insufficient amount' of resources for fulfilling the basic needs of people. This definition is inadequate. Poverty must be experienced to be understood. Walk in the shoes of the poor and you understand that: Poverty is an unmet need and an unfulfilled belonging. Poverty is lack of food, shelter, and everything good. Poverty is being sick and unable to see a doctor. Poverty is never having an opportunity to go to school. Poverty means not knowing how to read and write. Poverty is clothes that don't fit. Poverty is standing on the outside looking in. Poverty is dirty water you must drink. Poverty is a man without a job and a family without a home.

Poverty is a long walk without shoes. Poverty is illness without treatment. Poverty is pain in the stomach. Poverty is vulnerability to every scheme, lie, and cheat. Poverty is an empty refrigerator. Poverty is no refrigerator, no stove, and no electricity. Poverty is one toilet for one hundred neighbors. Poverty is a thief in the night. Five talents termed it 'poverty is a drunken father'.

Poverty is a child lost to preventable disease. Poverty is a mother weeping. Poverty is injustice without appeal. Poverty is cruel. Poverty is stress. Poverty is shame. Poverty is famine. Poverty is war. Poverty is pain. Poverty is life without life. Poverty marginalizes, poverty suffocates, and poverty kills. More than 3 billion people live in poverty in the world. Among them, more than 1.3 billion people live in extreme poverty.

While on the surface poverty is often defined as a lack of income or assets, in the day-to-day lives of the very poor, poverty becomes a network of disadvantages, each one exacerbating the others. The result is generation after generation of people who lack access to education, health care, adequate housing, proper sanitation and good nutrition. They are the most vulnerable to disasters, armed conflict and systems of political and economic oppression and they are powerless to improve their circumstances. These conditions often carry with them dysfunctional family and societal relationships, paralyzing low self-esteem, and spiritual darkness. Poverty is a lack of hope.

It's clear that handouts and traditional aid are not enough to solve the problem of poverty and its many entanglements. Many organizations like End Poverty seeks to equip the poor to free themselves from poverty in a holistic way.

Borgen Project thinks "Issues like hunger, illness, and thirst are all causes and effects of poverty. That is to say, that not having food means being poor, but being poor also means being unable to afford food or clean water. The effects of poverty are often interrelated so that one problem rarely occurs alone. Bad sanitation makes one susceptible to diseases, and hunger and lack of clean water makes one even more vulnerable to diseases. Impoverished countries and communities often suffer from discrimination and end up caught in a cycle of poverty."

J. Mack (2013) says that definitions of poverty really matter. They set the standards by which we determine whether the incomes and living conditions of the poorest in society are acceptable or not and are essential for determining questions of fairness.

Amartya Sen (2004) thinks poverty is more appropriately viewed in terms of the absence or limited access to opportunities for human development rather than merely as low income which is the standard identification of poverty. He asserts that Poverty is the deprivation of freedoms and lack of opportunities, including: Work, medical coverage, public health care, sanitation (clean water, good sewage system), education, law and order, protection from violence (including domestic violence), and safe work environment.

Over 1.3 billion people have an income of less than $1 (US) per day, and more than 3 billion people are below the poverty line. This is a massive tragedy of human suffering and loss of potential. Seventy percent of rural women in Bangladesh live below the poverty line, which is significantly higher than the overall national average of fifty-one percent. The rate of unemployment in Bangladesh is a staggering 52.5% (Human Rights Report, 2005). However, now poverty rate is 22% in Bangladesh. The United Nations Human Development Index (HDI) identifies a lack of health care, education and social involvement of poor people in Bangladesh. Furthermore, there are serious inadequacies with respect to environmental conditions, religious and political freedom and basic human needs there, although situation economic is improving gradually.

2.0. The Situation in Bangladesh

Currently, Bangladesh has 156 million people in an area of 147,570 square kilometers. Half of the population is female (Bangladesh Profile, 2014). The density of the population is 763 per square kilometer and individual's per capita income is $2100 (US). Only 30% of the population has access to basic health services and 76% of all households are deficient in calorie intake (CIDA, 2001: Gender profile Bangladesh). There is a strong link between extreme poverty and women as a result of a lack of basic human rights for women in Bangladesh.

The feminization of poverty is increasing day by day at an alarming rate in the world (Human Right Report, 2013). Women are regularly objectified and treated as commodities. Female labor force participation in paid employment is limited. They are forbidden to work outside of the home due to prevailing social norms. Wives are not to travel far from the home and are restricted to performing stereotypically acceptable female labor such as agriculture and seed preservation. The most significant human rights problems were arbitrary arrests, regulation of online speech, and poor working conditions and labor rights (Human Rights Report Bangladesh, 2013). This feminization of poverty in Bangladesh has strong historical roots. For 200 years, the country was under misogynistic British rule. Later under Pakistani rule, the exploitation continued. Governments discouraged eradication of poverty through community economic development using micro financing female egalitarianism and worked actively to destroy self-sufficient communities resulting in reduced literacy. Natural calamities, capitalism, globalization and structural adjustment policies (SAP) have all had a negative impact on rural women in Bangladesh. However, several individual NGO initiatives and cooperatives were found to have rescued these vulnerable women from their predicament. Nonetheless, many of these initiatives failed to address poverty directly, due to a lack of support from the state.

People resented a lifestyle which only focused on hard labor and despair. Access to formal credit from financial institutions, to improve their situation, was impossible since such institutions required collateral, which an extremely poor person could not provide (Yunus, 2007). All through their lifetime, they have learned only to work for others, which contributed to low self-esteem and left no hope for future. In such deprivation of banking facilities, the Grameen Bank group-based micro-credit services at the door step of poor has provided a great ray of hope to rural marginalized people in Bangladesh.

3.0. Significance of the study

Individualistic norms and values have started from the pre-industrial and industrial capitalistic society, but individualistic economic divide polarization process increases in the post- industrial period through emerging giant cities and globalization. This socioeconomic and cultural polarization process creates community divide, uneven rural-urban divide, socioeconomic divide, cultural divide, and environmental destructions in the society. Giant cities and globalization over exploited natural resources and human resources without giving return to earth and community. Cities have become so large that comparatively simple services and agencies have posed problems. Even technology unable to solve social and economic problems rather technology increasingly create socio-economic gap, injustice, anti-altruism unethical individualistic values and norms in the unsatisfactorily. The financial crisis of 2008-2009 grows from the same root-a fundamental flaw in the theoretical construct of capitalism (Yunus, 2013).

This new capitalistic industrialized urbanizing society not only looks for profits at the expense of human exploitation, social, economic, cultural and environmental exploitation and injustice in the society, but also swipes community communal altruistic values, cooperative norms, principles, human common wellbeing. As a result, increase poverty, unemployment, financial artificial crisis; exploit human chief labor, gender discrimination, racism and stereotyping individual capability in the society. Consequently resources and power concentrated in the hands of few dominating people. Mass people of the society are less wealthy and suffering from miseries across the world particularly in Bangladesh. However, the community micro-credit Grameen Bank banking services is a community economic program (CED) in Bangladesh that assists poor people to engage in small businesses to earn income and make networking among them. Now the Grameen Bank group-based micro-credit is popular and effective all over the world even in the developed countries.

4.0. Definition of Community and Community Economic Development (CED)

Before discussing the relationship between micro finance and community economic development (CED), it is important to define community and community economic development. A community is a group of people who know each other personally and who plan together towards a common goal, and work to overcome adversity (Shragge, 1997). It is an alternative economic program that is working for to solve problems that community people ate facing-unemployment, poverty, job loss, and environmental degradation. According to Christenson, Fendley, and Robinson (1994), a community is defined as people that live within a geographically bounded area who interact socially, have one or more ties with each other and the place in which they live (p.8). This is done while maintaining social networks through intense ties, social interaction and an identification with the community. However, there are many communities that interact with and network among themselves without living in a particular geographical area. For example, Muslims may interact about issues from different places via the Internet.

Community development is a living process that strives for creating communal identity and changing the dominating power structure of the society. Community communal values can minimize power struggle and develop trust among community people instead create competition and conflict among people in the society. Hence promotion of community communal norms, values and practices of caring each other and helping each other is essential and important in the socioeconomic cultural divide modern society. It is required to understand meaning of community and community development; know about strategies of community organizing, community capacity building and community planning steps/process. The promotion of community communal norms, values and practices of caring each other and helping each other is important in the socioeconomic cultural divide society. This knowledge can help community people organize themselves to use their community resources, create opportunities for local initiatives, feeling of "We" instead "I". These processes assist people engaging in community development activities and uphold deepening community solidarity communal values in their life.

Community means a group of people living in the same place or having a particular characteristic in common. Community is a feeling of fellowship with others, as a result of sharing common attitudes, interests, and goals. Merriam –Webster dictionary defines community it is a unified body of individuals: such as state, commonwealth and the people with common interests living in a particular area; broadly: the area itself. It is a social group of any size whose members reside in a specific locality, share government, and often have a common cultural and historical heritage.

A community is a small or large social unit (a group of human living things) who have something in common, such as norms, religion, values, or identity. Communities often share a sense of place that is situated in a given geographical area (e.g. a country, village, town, or neighborhood) or in virtual space through communication platforms. Durable relations that extend beyond immediate genealogical ties also define a sense of community. People tend to define those social ties as important to their identity, practice, and roles in social institutions like family, home, work, government, society, or humanity, at large. Although communities are usually small relative to personal social ties (micro-level), "community" may also refer to large group affiliations (or macro-level), such as national communities, international communities, and recently developed virtual communities (internet based face book, twitter etc. The word "community" derives from the Old French *comuneté*, which comes from the Latin Communitas "community", "public spirit" (from Latin communis, "shared in common").

Human communities may share intent, beliefs, resources, preferences, needs, and risks in common, affecting the identity of the participants and their degree of cohesiveness. From ecological point of view in ecology, a community is an assemblage of populations of different species, interacting with one another. Community ecology is the branch of ecology that studies interactions between and among species. It considers how such interactions, along with interactions between species and the biotic environment, affect community structure and species richness, diversity and patterns of abundance. Species interact in three ways: competition, predation, and mutualism. Competition typically results in a double negative—that is both species lose in the interaction. Predation is a win/lose situation with one species winning. Mutualism, on the other hand, involves both species cooperating in some way, with both winning. The two main types of communities are major which are self-sustaining and self-regulating (such as a forest or a lake) and minor communities which rely on other communities (like fungi decomposing a log) and are the building blocks of major communities.

Groups of people are complex, in ways that make those groups hard to form and hard to sustain; much of the shape of traditional institutions is a response to those difficulties. New social tools relieve some of those burdens, allowing for new kinds of group-forming, like using simple sharing to anchor the creation of new groups.

One simple form of cooperation, almost universal with social tools, is conversation; when people are in one another's company, even virtually, they like to talk. Conversation creates more of a sense of community than sharing does.

Collaborative production is a more involved form of cooperation, as it increases the tension between individual and group goals. The litmus test for collaborative production is simple: no one person can take credit for what gets created, and the project could not come into being without the participation of many.

An online community builds weaker bonds if allows users to be anonymous. It is an audience isn't just a big community; it can be more anonymous, with many fewer ties among users. A community isn't just a small audience either; it has a social density that audiences lack." The sites that offer online communities, like MySpace, Twitter, Facebbok, Instagram, Tumbler and Printerest allow users to "talk" their community and act anonymously.

McMillan and Chavis identify four elements of "sense of community":

1. membership,
2. influence,
3. integration and fulfillment of needs,
4. shared emotional connection.

They give the following example of the interplay between these factors:

Someone puts an announcement on the dormitory bulletin board about the formation of an intramural dormitory basketball team. People attend the organizational meeting as strangers out of their individual needs (integration and fulfillment of needs). The team is bound by place of residence (membership boundaries are set) and spends time together in practice (the contact hypothesis). They play a game and win (successful shared event). While playing, members exert energy on behalf of the team (personal investment in the group). As the team continues to win, team members become recognized and congratulated (gaining honor and status for being members), Influencing new members to join and continue to do the same. Someone suggests that they all buy matching shirts and shoes (common symbols) and they do so (influence).

Neighborhood members are the participants in joint activities experience that built a sense of community. A *Sense of Community* has been developed in neighborhoods, in schools, in the workplace, and a variety of types of communities. Community development is a socialization process of learning to adopt the behavior patterns of the community. Here neighborhood individuals develop the skills and knowledge and learn the roles necessary to function within their culture and social environment. Socialization is influenced primarily by the family, through which children first learn community norms. Other important influences include schools, peer groups, people, mass media, the workplace, and government. The degree to which the norms of a particular society or community are adopted determines one's willingness to engage with others. The norms of tolerance, reciprocity, and trust are important "habits of the heart."

Community development is often linked with community work or community planning, and may involve stakeholders, foundations, governments, or contracted entities including non-government organizations (NGOs), universities or government agencies to progress the social well-being of local, regional and, sometimes, national communities. More grassroots efforts, called community building or community organizing, seek to empower individuals and groups of people by providing them with the skills they need to effect change in their own communities. These skills often assist in building political power through the formation of large social groups working for a common agenda. Community development practitioners must understand both how to work with individuals and how to affect communities' positions within the context of larger social institutions. Public administrators, in contrast, need to understand community development in the context of rural and urban development, housing and economic development, and community, organizational and business development.

5. Community building and community organizing

Scott Peck (1987) argues that the almost accidental sense of community that exists at times of crisis can be consciously built. Peck believes that conscious community building is a process of deliberate design based on the knowledge and application of certain rules. He states that this process goes through four stages:

1. **Pseudo community**: The beginning stage when people first come together. This is the stage where people try to be *nice*, and present what they feel are their most personable and friendly characteristics.

2. **Chaos**: When people move beyond the in authenticity of pseudo-community and feel safe enough to present their "shadow" selves. This stage places great demands upon the facilitator for greater leadership and organization, but Peck believes that "organizations are not communities" and this pressure should be resisted.

3. **Emptiness**: This stage moves beyond the attempts to fix, heal and convert of the chaos stage, when all people become capable of acknowledging their own woundedness and brokenness, common to us all as human beings. Out of this emptiness comesto think fixing the neighbors' unmet needs.

4. **True community**: the process of deep respect and true listening for the needs of the other people in this community. This stage peck believes can only be described as "glory" and reflects a deep yearning in every human soul for compassionate understanding from one's fellows.

More recently Peck remarked that building a sense of community is easy, but maintaining this sense of community is difficult in the modern world. Community building can use a wide variety of practices, ranging from simple events such as potlucks and small book clubs to larger-scale efforts such as mass festivals and construction projects that involve local participants rather than outside contractors.

Community building that is geared toward citizen action is usually termed "community organizing." In these cases, organized community groups seek accountability from elected officials and increased direct representation within decision-making bodies. Where good-faith negotiations fail, these constituency-led organizations seek to pressure the decision-makers through a variety of means, including picketing, boycotting, sit-ins, petitioning, and electoral politics.

Community organizing is sometimes focused on more than just resolving specific issues. Community organizing often means building a widely accessible power structure, often with the end goal of distributing power equally throughout the community. Community organizers generally seek to build groups that are open and democratic in governance. Such groups facilitate and encourage concuss decision-making with a focus on the general health of the community rather than a specific interest group. The three basic types of community organizing are grassroots organizing, coalition building, and "institution-based community organizing," (also called "broad-based community organizing," an example of which is faith-based community organizing, or congressional-based community organizing. If communities are developed based on something they share in common, whether that is location or values, then one challenge for developing communities is how to incorporate individuality and differences.

Community services are a wide range of community institutions, governmental and non-governmental services, voluntary, third sector organizations, and grassroots and neighborhood efforts in local communities, towns, cities, and suburban-exurban areas. In line with governmental and community thinking, volunteering and unpaid services are often preferred (e.g., altruism, beneficence) to large and continued investments in infrastructure and community services personnel, with private-public partnerships often common.

Non-profit organizations from youth services, to family and neighborhood centers, recreation facilities, civic clubs, and employment, housing and poverty agencies are often the foundation of community services programs, but it may also be undertaken under the auspices of government (which funds all NGOs), one or more businesses, or by individuals or newly formed collaborative. Community services is also the broad term given to health and the human services in local communities and was specifically used as the framework for deinstitutionalization and community integration to homes, families and local communities (e.g., community residential services).

In a broad discussion of community services, schools, hospitals, clinics, rehabilitation and criminal justice institutions also view themselves as community planners and decision makers together with governmental leadership (e.g., city and county offices, state-regional offices). However, while many community services are voluntary, some may be part of alternative sentencing approaches in a justice system and it can be required by educational institutions as part of internships, employment training, and post-graduation plans.

Community services may be paid for through different revenue streams which include targeted federal funds, taxpayer contributions, state and local grants and contracts, voluntary donations, Medicaid or health care funds, community development block grants, targeted education funds, and so forth. In the 2000s, the business sector began to contract with government, and also consult on government policies, and has shifted the framework of community services to the for-profit domains.

However, by the 1990s, the call was to return to community and to go beyond community services to belonging, relationships, community building and welcoming new population groups and diversity in community life.

Bangladesh Community in Canada is a rapidly expanding and extending community in Canada with its professionals, students and families. In Alberta, Bangladesh Heritage and Ethnic Society (BHESA), a not-for-profit socio-cultural & heritage association known to lead to greater understanding of culture and heritage of Bangladesh, and characterized by planning, action and mobilization of community, the promotion of multicultural changes and, ultimately, influence within larger systems. It is establishing its link to the larger or more extended communities with national, international, and virtual community.

5.1. Types of Community

A number of ways to categorize types of community have been proposed. One such breakdown is as follows:

1. Location-based Communities: range from the local neighbourhood, suburb, village or city, region, nation or even the planetas a whole. These are also called communities of place.
2. Identity-based Communities: range from the local clique, sub-culture, ethnic group, religious, multicultural or pluralistic civilization, or the global community cultures of today. They may be included as *communities of need* or *identity*, such as disabled persons, or frail aged people.
3. Organizationally based Communities: range from communities organized informally around family or network-based guilds and associations to more formal incorporated associations, political decision making structures, economic enterprises, or professional associations at a small, national or international scale.

The usual categorizations of community relations have a number of problems: 1) they tend to give the impression that a particular community can be defined as just this kind or another; 2) they tend to conflate modern and customary community relations; and 3) they tend to take sociological categories such as ethnicity or race as given, forgetting that different ethnically defined persons live in different kinds of communities — grounded, interest-based, diasporas, etc.

In response to these problems, Paul James and his colleagues have developed a taxonomy that maps community relations, and recognizes that actual communities can be characterized by different kinds of relations at the same time:

1. Grounded community relations: This involves enduring attachment to particular places and particular people. It is the dominant form taken by customary and tribal

communities. In these kinds of communities, the land is fundamental to identity.

2. Life-style community relations: This involves giving give primacy to communities coming together around particular chosen ways of life, such as morally charged or interest-based relations or just living or working in the same location. Hence the following sub-forms:

- Community-life as morally bounded, a form taken by many traditional faith-based communities.
- Community-life as interest-based, including sporting, leisure-based and business communities which come together for regular moments of engagement
- Community-life as proximately-related, where neighborhood or commonality of association forms a community of convenience, or a community of place.

5.0. Community economic development

The paper below talks about the meaning of community economic development (CED). Eric Shragge (1997) defines CED the in following way: "CED is a cooperative attempt by local people to take control of the socioeconomic destiny of the community to respond to local needs" (p. 12). It is an attempt is to democratize the economic lifestyle of the neighboring communities (p. 103).

Community Economic Development (CED) is action by people locally to create economic opportunities that improve social conditions, particularly for those who are most disadvantaged. CED is an approach that recognizes that economic, environmental and social challenges are interdependent, complex and ever-changing. CED projects have triple bottom line impact in society. Community Economic Development (CED) is an action by people locally to create economic opportunities that improve social conditions, particularly for those who are most disadvantaged in community. CED is an approach that recognizes that economic, environmental and social challenges are interdependent, complex and ever-changing. To be effective, solutions must be rooted in local knowledge and led by community members. CED promotes holistic approaches, addressing individual, community and regional levels, recognizing that these levels are interconnected. It is an approach creating vibrant, resilient and sustainable local economies in community development. CED activities often focus on three strategies to improve local well-being:

- Supporting individuals
- Building enterprises
- Strengthening communities (click on any of the images below to see a larger version)

Angel Gurria, Secretary-General of the Organization for Economic Co-operation and Development, in his address to ECONOUS 2016, the National CED Conference says, "*The only way we can promote inclusive and more sustainable growth is by working with our local communities. Development is always a bottom up process. Taking an integrated approach that cuts across employment, skills, economic development, the social economy, and entrepreneurship is absolutely crucial.*"

Many scholars define community economic development (CED) is a field of study that actively elicits community involvement when working with government, and private sectors to build strong communities, industries, and markets.

Community economic development is deeply connected with community economic growth because community economic growth (CEG) involves economic development initiatives that support communities to advance their economies, as well as adjust to changing and challenging economic circumstances. By using knowledge and resources resident in the community, CEG identifies and capitalizes on local opportunities to stimulate economic growth and employment. This includes strengthening the infrastructure and capacity of communities to achieve their full economic potential. Communities have increased economic opportunities and capacity to respond to challenges, as well as the necessary investments in public infrastructure. Western Economic Diversification Canada (WD) contributes to community economic development in urban centres and rural areas through initiatives that capitalize on opportunities for growth and development, and enable communities to adjust to challenges that hinder competitiveness and quality of life. A significant proportion of the WD community economic development funding program stems from the Western Canada National Program offered by the Federal Government of Canada usually for infrastructure programs. Bangladesh Government has huge funding for infrastructure development specially for constructing bridges, roads, culverts, primary school buildings and public housings for low income people etc.

Mihailo Temali (2002) defines community economic development as actions taken by an organization to improve the economic situation of local residents (income and assets) and local businesses (profitability and growth); and enhance the community's quality of life as a whole (appearance, safety, gathering places, and sense of positive momentum.

Shaffer, Deller and Marcouiller (2004) define community economic development is determining economic development needs and opportunities, deciding what can and should be done to improve the economic condition in that community, and then moving to achieve agreed-upon economic goals and objectives. Moreover, they think it is a comprehensive concept for changing the economic situation within the community. So from their point of view community economic development is about how economic forces and theory explain community change and how policies and actions can affect that change. So community economic development is sustained progressive change to attain individual and group interests through expanding, intensifying, and adjusting the use of resources; identifying new or expanding markets, altering rules of economic activities to facilitated adjustments to changing conditions or altering the distribution of rewards; and improving insights into the choices available. Therefore this community economic development decision-making capacity is the ability of a community to initiate and sustain activities that promote local economic and social welfare. According to Shaffer, Deller and Marcouiller (2004) community economic development is dynamic; it is concerned with movement and change, with overcoming obstacles and capturing opportunities. Their CED definition also extend to it is about producing wealth, opening economic opportunities, and facilitating adjustment (monetized and no monetized wealth).

Phillips and Pittman in Deller (2014) mentions in his PowerPoint that most practitioners think of community [economic] development as an outcome – physical, social, and economic improvement in a community – while most academicians think of community [economic] development as a process – the ability of communities to act collectively and enhancing the ability to do so. CED works for local economic development because Blakely and Bradshaw think the central thesis for local economic development is that locally based economic development and employment generation is more likely to be successful if initiated at the community and local level than elsewhere.

Blakely and Bradshaw (2002) think here community leaders can assess their community's situation and place it in a larger context. Similarly, they can assess affected groups to determine how these will respond to different courses of action. In this way, local solutions can be found for national problems. They think CED is local organizations who have the potential, through partnerships, to identify their assets and use them to build a better local economy. Therefore, Blakely and Bradshaw identify local economic development has one primary goal: to increase the number and variety of job opportunities available to local people. To perform these activities, local governments and community groups need to assume an initiating rather than a passive role because the goal of (economic development) capacity-building involves a complex, multitasked process featuring many actors. Moreover, the (economic development) process affects the entire environment of the community physical, regulatory, and attitudinal factors and determines the nature and quality of economic products. Therefore, local economic development (LED) requires the ability to facilitate interaction, to mobilize stakeholders, and to reconcile different goals and values among key development actors. Moreover, LED roles are asset building (e.g., skills and capacities of individuals, associations and institutions within a locality) lays the foundation upon which economic development is built (Deller, 2014).

In other words, CED is a socially directed approach in which individual groups devote their efforts towards meeting the basic needs of the others in the community. These necessities are determined by deliberate allocation of scarce resources. Here local communities work together at setting up businesses and promoting their own interests through economic expansion. Here the definition of economy serves all CED approaches (Ced, cEd, and ceD) can be given as a system of human activity directed to meeting human basic needs that is determined by deliberate allocations of scarce resources"(Boothroyd & Davis, 1993, p. 230). Community Economic Development (CED) is a field of study that actively elicits community involvement when working with government, and private sectors to build strong communities, industries, and markets.

In both the practice and the literature of community economic development, conceptions of the process differ markedly. Boothroyd, P. and Davis, H. (1993) in Table 1 grouped these various conceptualizations into three general approaches that are respectively oriented to growth (cEd), structural change (ceD), and communalization (Ced). Each approach implies a particular role for the CED planner. Table 1 summarizes our differentiations of the three approaches. cEd pre-dates the term CED itself and has appeared in two major phases: smokestack chasing and planned growth. The former and earlier phase involves community boosterism to attract government attention and major private investors. The latter phase involves coordinated strategic planning by a wide range of community institutions using sophisticated financial, legal, and promotional tools. The cEd planner is a networker, deal-facilitator, and provider of information on markets, technology, and funding opportunities.

The planning process which the cEd planner serves may be broadly based within the community, but it is frequently one in which dominant roles are played by community leaders (or even outsiders) from business, labor, professional, government, or educational sectors.

Table 1: A comparison of the three approaches to CED

Descriptions	cEd	ceD	Ced
Concept of economy	Monetary transactions	Monetary and nonmonetary transactions	Market and production distribution based on market and nonmarket principles
Concept of community	Localities	Home	Mutual commitments
Primary goal	Growth jobs, income	Stability and sustainability	Sharing and caring
Primary strategies	Increase monetary inflows	Increase local control through structural change	Integrate social and economic development

5.1. Ced Assumptions

Ced is based on the following assumptions:

The local economy encompasses market transactions (monetary and nonmonetary), but also includes production and distribution based on nonmarket principles of common ownership, sharing, mutual aid, and improving productive life even at the expense of efficiency. The distinction between economic and social issues is not clearly drawn and, as in the case of the family, social and economic relationships are intertwined. The purpose of CED is to increase community solidarity, distributive justice, and broadly defined quality of life. Economic institutions should be organized to promote cooperation rather than competition (i.e., they should combine social development with economic development). All community members must be empowered to participate in planning and decision- making processes that shape the community's economy.

5.2. Ced Strategies

Boothroyd, P. and Davis, H. (1993) developed three categories of Ced strategies that are describing below:

Working through local and senior governments to eliminate marginalization or exploitation of particular people within the community: Ced practitioners can urge governments to encourage work sharing, prevent discriminatory lending-policies, monitor work conditions, facilitate unionization, etc. They can 'fight city hall' to establish fairer distributions of community services and development impacts and to make planning processes more participatory. Structuring ceD institutions (such as co-ops, land trusts, and community development corporations [CDC]) to favor those most in need. Co-ops, for instance, can be organized not only to buffer individuals from the market, increase collective bargaining power, and retain earnings in the community-all ceD objectives-but also to promote social justice. Worker cooperatives in particular often design their salary scales, working conditions, and profit distributions to meet Ced goals within the firm and the larger community (Melnyk 1985). Some credit unions give special assistance to enterprises initiated by low-income people.

CDCs in particular lend themselves to serving the goal of economic justice (MacLeod 1986); Zdenek 1987). Because they are owned by the whole community, they potentially can be more communalistic than co-ops, which focus their own members and often exclude the very poor. As employers, all Ced institutions can strive to make work more meaningful by encouraging worker participation in decision making.

CDCs are strengthening noncash mutual aid norms and practices: Traditionally, these have enabled weaker members of a community to survive (e.g., through distributions of food or caring for children at risk) and households, regardless of their relative financial situations, to accomplish tasks beyond their individual powers (e.g., through barn-raising bees). Such practices also increase the sociability of the community and make work more enjoyable. While greatly weakened by modernization, the ethic of mutual aid survives, particularly in aboriginal communities. Elsewhere, mutual aid survives as 'volunteerism'. In some economic sectors (such as organized recreation for children) volunteers play major roles in planning and delivering services.

Another form of mutual aid involves collaborative activity by diverse associations (e.g., worshippers, musicians, athletes, or hobbyists). Ced points out the importance of mutual aid to the community economy and promotes its expansion.

Community Economic Development is a multifaceted comprehensive approach to community change that is not limited to just poverty programs, nor is it synonymous with industrial recruitment. Community Economic Development is not an attempt to exploit resources to yield the maximum economic return (Schaffer, Deller, & Marcouiller (2004). Community Economic Development is often involved in a process of building social enterprises that are the component of social economy. CED organizations sometimes called the NGOS, third sector; a community-based social enterprise is a partnership between government agencies, small to medium enterprises, large national or transnational corporations and the not-for-profit sector, and aims for social, economic and/or environmental outcomes that none of these agencies could achieve for and by themselves.

6.0. Examples of Community Economic Programs

K-Net Canada is a CED program in Canada is providing healthcare information services Northern Canada. The Toronto Community Housing Corporation (TCHC) is housing for the low-income people in Toronto build by the Government of Canada now managed by private sector in Toronto. Grameen Bank Bangladesh, Asrayon Prokalpa (housing for landless) is a CED program in Bangladesh supported by the Government of Bangladesh and managed by Habitat, an NGO in Bangladesh. The grameen bank community banking is a CED program in Bangladesh that works for poor people to make them an economic actor and a social actor in the community in Bangladesh.

Micro financing is a small financing system, whereby, interested private micro-entrepreneurs borrow money for running their own sustainable small business ventures. Micro financing is run by NGOs all over the world.

7.0. Achievement of three approaches of Community Economic Development (Ced, CEd, and cED) through Grameen Bank group-based microcredit services in Bangladesh

Micro financing is working with local currency to provide banking services for the poor to create self-employment among them through involving them in income generating schemes; this CED micro-financing service helps poor earn income for meeting their basic needs and building the community local economy. It also mobilizes small deposits and community savings which are used to invest in community planning. Bangladesh is a non-welfare state and a largely rural society where social safety nets programs and services are needed. The Government of Bangladesh has been implementing a 'Cooperative Village' approach as a means to achieve integrated rural development through the establishment of the Bangladesh Rural Development Board (BRDB). In 1972, it established the Mahilla Samitty (Women's Cooperatives) to encourage women to work eradication of poverty through community economic development using micro financing independently from men, acquire literacy skills and engage in planned family planning as well as to develop leadership skills for their representation in the local community. However, the programs tend to exclude the poorest women in Bangladesh, as they are unable to pay the weekly membership fees, the equivalent to one Canadian penny.

Naila Kabeer, a social scientist of Bangladesh, also mentions the systemic denial of women's autonomy in Bangladesh (Kabeer, 1983, p. 6). In this situation Grameen Bank (GB) provides group-based mini-cooperative micro financing services to the poorest rural women that generate a ray of hope to them. GB provides them with the opportunity, through microfinance, to start and run their own businesses. Grameen Bank operates nationwide through 2185 branches. The repayment rate has been highly satisfactory (97%) since 1979. The majority of them (97.9%) are women borrowers. The Bank serves a total of 8.6 million borrowers through 130, 000 rural landless associations in 70,370 villages in Bangladesh. Total loan disbursement is $16.65 billion since its inception. Of them $14.00 billion has been repaid. Current borrower savings are $5.2 billion. To date, its monthly loan disbursement is $58.00 million and 100% loans financed from borrowers deposits (Grameen Bank Updates, 2014). It has 22,000 staffs working at the village level nationwide. GB has not been receiving grants from outside sources since 1990. It runs its microcredit program based on its own internal fund mobilization, which makes it economically viable and sustainable.

The Grameen Bank (GB) is a shining example of a locally and democratically run CED organization designed to serve the poor people by being run by them. GB is responsive to the people and engages with them on regular bases which are all features of good Ced approach meaning emphasis on community values. Poor women organize independent associations to receive loans from GB. Borrowers receive loans and save money, repay loans individually and collectively participate in the local association or center weekly meeting. They receive loans from grameen bank and run their businesses in their locality. They earn money and gradually create personal and collective (community) assets. Every year GB officials, at all levels, face an election. This process of electing a leader helps to develop democratic norms. This system facilitates networking among group members of GB especially poor women.

All center chiefs and group chairmen of GB gather at a weekly meeting organized by each center where they discuss and exchange new strategies and concerns. As part of the weekly and monthly meetings, center members discuss their status of the business, family matters, community problems, children's education, environmental hazards, health and other social agenda. In this way, GB borrowers perform both community development and community economic development activities in which GB officials act as a catalysts and help them to reach their goals eradicating of poverty and to empower them in their communities. Grameen Bank, Grameen Shakti and ASA etc. are few community economic development organizations in Bangladesh that include poor rural women in its cEd program. They provide small loans to rural poor women through group formation and business initiatives. Grameen Bank gives preference to poor female empowerment because it feels that poor women suffer more from poverty than men; and women are much more active to escape poverty than men. Grameen Bank focuses its attention on female community organizing, because it explores and promotes female empowerment both economically and socially. These businesses built up savings that help them find dignified livelihoods by increasing income, providing education to their children, creating material assets and developing social and human capitalto overcome their poverty.

One of the prime objectives of the Grameen Bank is to promote female entrepreneurships and to create self-employment. This empowers women economically and socially by increasing their income and creating leadership and networking among them. Now women borrowers of GB become more valuable to their households and they act as catalysts of development in their families. In addition, clients of the GB gain access to better nutrition, housing, student loans and social activities which help them acquire new skills and coping strategies. Women, who are income earners, are empowered to promote their own well-being as well as their families and neighborhoods. This is typical an example of all CED-using economics to improve the community in non-economic ways.

Beginning in 2003, Grameen Bank expanded and began to directly tackle homelessness. Approximately 79,000 beggars have already joined the 'Struggling Members Program' setup to deal with their unique situation. $1.2 million has been lent to street people so far; of that $0.53 million has already been paid off (Impact of Grameen Bank on local society (2007) from http://www.rdc.com.au/grameen/impact/htm). The poor commonly live in isolation, trapped in their homes because they have no means to make associations with their neighbors. In this circumstance, GB group-based community banking for the ultra-poor is a milestone initiative for them to make association among them and earn income for their livelihood using micro-business model. The objective of microfinance and the aims of Grameen Bank are to create an environment under which poor people can develop the confidence to survive on their own.

Again, this is quintessential ceD. Although Boothroyd & Davis (1993) say," the limitation of ceD is that it is out of step with the mainstream attachment to unlimited growth" (p. 235); however, GB activities contributed to Bangladesh poverty eradication with wide scale. Although there are critics of CED approach, arguing that it is out of step with the mainstream economy and certain political ideologies, Grameen Bank succeeds in contributing to both the local and the national economy in Bangladesh. In 1998, the World Bank found that extreme poverty among GB borrowers in Bangladesh was cut by over 70% making Grameen micro finance a powerful tool in combating poverty and female empowerment.

Many borrowers of GB are progressing as smart and sustainable business people. The resulting businesses are closely tied into the local neighborhoods, providing an opportunity for development for all the members of the community. Landless women are directed, by the bank, to setup their facilities, relying on the local market and focusing on building strong bonds with the community (bridging bonds among poor people in the community) and other members of the bank. This promotes a sense of responsibility among the members as well as local entrepreneurships, self-employment and a steady flow of income. It reduces dependence on external investments and outside decision making for the family and for the community. The community itself manages its own resources in the tradition of CED. The Grameen Bank community development program does not only maximize local economic activity in the locality but also creates the kind of social and emotional environment in which people connect with each other to strengthen mutual aid norms, values, customs and practices through GB landless women associations.

Micro financing is working with local currency to provide for the poor create self-employment through income generating schemes; helps meet basic needs and build the local economy. It also mobilizes small deposits and community savings which are used to invest in community planning. Micro financing is a small financing system, whereby, interested private entrepreneurs borrow money for running their own sustainable small business ventures. Micro financing is run by NGOs all over the world. So the microfinancing model is working in Bangladesh and elsewhere in the world.

All centre chiefs and group chairmen of Grameen Bank gather at a monthly workshop organized by each branch where they discuss and exchange new strategies and concerns. Women form independent associations to receive loans from GB. Borrowers receive loans and save money, repay loans individually and collectively participate in the local association or centre weekly meeting. They receive loans from the bank and run their businesses in their locality. They earn money and gradually create personal and collective (community) assets. As part of the monthly meetings, they discuss their status of the business, family matters, community problems, children's education, health and other social agenda. GB borrowers perform community development as well as community economic development activities in which GB officials act as a catalysts and help them to reach their goals eradicating of poverty and to empower their societies.

Grameen Bank is one of the few community economic development organizations in Bangladesh that includes poor rural women in its cEd program, and provides small loans to rural poor women through group formation and business initiatives. Grameen Bank gives preference to female empowerment because Grameen Bank feels that women suffer more from poverty than men, and women are much more active to escape poverty than men. The Bank focuses its attention on female community organizing, because it explores and promotes female empowerment both economically and socially. These businesses built up savings and help them find dignified livelihoods by increasing income providing education, creating material assets and developing social and human capitalto overcome poverty. One of the prime objectives of the Grameen Bank is to promote female entrepreneurships and to create self-employment in Bangladesh. Grameen micro-enterprise program provides loans to the educated children of GB borrowers for running micro enterprises in Bangladesh. The Grameen Bank micro enterprise loan services to young entrepreneuers promote micro enterprise development in rural Bangladesh.

This empowers women and young entrepreneurs economically and socially by increasing their income and creating leadership and networking among them. Women become more valuable to their households and act as catalysts. In addition, clients of the GB gain access to better nutrition, housing, and social activities which help them acquire new skills and coping strategies. Women, who are income earners, are empowered to promote their own well-being as well as their families and neighbourhoods. This is typical CED -using economics to improve the community in non-economic ways.

Social cohesion and solidarity among them crystallizes through making associations. The borrowers of GB discuss their business problems, family problems, and other social problem and how to solve them, and exchange business ideas. This is the theme of community economic development where "CED organizations help to enhance local initiatives that are proactive economic and servicing ventures that invite energetic commitments in the community" (Burman, 1996, p. 139). Moreover, Grameen Bank is a community economic development scheme in the sense that landless poor women organize themselves in the center, develop leadership qualities, are involved in decision making process, resolve problems through mutual dialogues for improvement of their lifestyle, enhance their children's education and health. These poor women help other poor people and work with them for their development.

The borrowers of GB are working together towards improving their hygiene and sanitation in their village, resolve neighborhood conflicts, violence, and dowry problems, develop their voting behaviors, and participate in other human rights issues. They involve themselves in public awareness and act for their class consciousness and social uplift. They become interconnected with each other. Today, they are no longer socially isolated rather they interconnected with their community people. In addition, GB members are involved in CED activities as it is a place and tool for them for involvement in business for income generation. They use their credit for home-based businesses or run businesses locally. They are not involved in distance businesses. Therefore, all their activities create an impact on local businesses and local economy. Poor people now play a collective role in local economic development, which is the impact of Grameen Bank group-based community banking in the villages in Bangladesh.

The Grameen Bank actively provides more than just a source of money to the poor in Bangladesh. It provides help with socio-economic development and simply with the skills of life. Grameen Bank teaches its clients signing their names, basic hygiene, nutrition, family planning and motivates borrowers growing vegetables, animal husbandry, and profitable ways of investment. It assists borrowers to develop their business marketing strategies and cope with disasters. Grameen Bank sixteen decisions create borrowers' attention to develop their leaderships, take care of their children, collective duties and responsibilities as citizens; learns people on how to develop healthy social values, campaign for effective anti-dowry debates and disputes and other such feelings. At the beginning of group trainings, borrowers are organized into small homogeneous groups. Such training facilitates group solidarity and cohesiveness as well as participatory interaction among GB group members in their community. Organizing the borrowers into primary groups and associations has been the building blocks of GB's operating system. Emphasis from the very outset is to organizationally strengthen the Grameen Bank client so that they can acquire the capacity for business planning and implementing CED theme at the micro level development decisions.

Grameen Bank community organizing activities include economic activities through micro financing and businesses to increase their income, developing their businesses along with improving social status. GB staffs interactions with its borrowers on regular basis is enhancing borrowers' expose to psychological mobility, social mobility, local economic activities; this two way communications are focusing on developing the local poor women communities, empowering local citizens and fostering community control and management.

Grameen Bank is free from bureaucracy. Rather, its officials and clients are like mutual partners in the businesses because loan repayments depend on their mutual goodwill and responsibilities. The bank constantly monitoring and adjusts its policies from grassroots feedback. Therefore, it can be called a community economic development process for the poor that empowers GB women borrowers' family space and public space development in their community. Different types of clients' workshops at the grass root level, organized by GB, help them to open their mind and to develop socially, while adding to human capital.

Grameen Bank breaks the traditional office-based and mortgaged-based loan financing system. For example, the bank goes to people's houses. Loans are delivered to poor women without collateral and loans are collected from their doorsteps. The borrowers do not need to come to the branch, to collect or repay their loans. They do not incur any extra expenditure to get loans. So the GB borrowers appreciate the Bank's economic and social responsibilities concerning their well-being, and reciprocate with a satisfactory performance in their own interest.

8.0. Women borrowers of Grameen Bank is suffering from Patriarchal value domination

Grameen Bank operates and provides loans to poor people with a 20% interest rate. Although GB is a specialised bank, it is operating much like other commercial banks with the aim of profit. In 2005, GB made a profit of US$680,000. Although it is an example of totally self-reliant poverty eradication initiative, its interest rate is the same as loans given to much richer people. Although there have been many success stories of women borrowers of GB who have been emancipated through Grameen micro-credit, Robin Isserles (2003) cautions that many women are still dominated by their husbands and they do not actually enjoy the benefits from their financial gains or loan investments. In many cases, their husbands take the credit, and use the money to their own personal advantage (Rouf, 2011).

Since patriarchy is still dominant in Bangladesh, it results in the exploitation of borrowers' rights, choices and voice. Grameen Bank borrowers are highly renowned for their smooth repayment of loans, before they are overdue. However, high repayment rates always do not indicate high efficiency and quality of women's lives. Isserales, in his study mentions, that 57% of women saw a rise of verbal aggression after they received loans from their households. 16% experienced verbal and physical abuse from their husbands if they (women borrowers) refused to hand over the money to their husbands (Isserales, p. 49). Therefore, Grameen Bank could include an agenda for gender equality rights for its woman borrowers in Bangladesh.

9.0. Recommendations to improve Grameen Bank services in Bangladesh

The Government of Bangladesh supports to NGOs, micro financing and female entrepreneurship can mentor the bottom 50% of the disadvantaged women and empower them economically, socially and politically in the society both collectively and independently in Bangladesh. Howeever, national strategies are needed in Bangladesh for other micro financing institutions (MFIs) to improve and make easy micro financing and savings systems available to disadvantaged women. Because there is a lack of funding for women centered initiatives and CED activities as well as heavy administrative costs which burden CED clients.

Therefore, NGOs need some subsidies to cover their organizational overhead costs so that clients should not be required to cover those costs. Advocacy on public subsidy to CED is important for a certain period until NGOs can reach a sustainable situation. It should not seek community development through charity because charity destroys people's initiatives. Burman (1996) rightly says that charities are offensive as they organize the poor in the best way to serve their way of helping (p. 149). Micro financing economic institutions, business promotion institutions and business training institutions both at local and national level should be organized and tailored and linked with the community to promote cooperation among beneficial rather than competition, but public national organizations should not be coercive to CED NGOs.

Bangladesh Rural Development Board's (BRDB) many cooperatives are running where both men and women are members of the same cooperative. Many cooperatives in many countries are also running same way where men and women belong to one cooperative. However, women can get more benefits if CED cooperatives are formed exclusively for women, where they can help each other, feel free to organize, discuss problems, make decisions and exchange ideas without male dominance.

10.0. Conclusion

Micro financing institutions (MFIs) and the number of their clients are increasing all over the world. For example, in 2011, more than 150 million and in 2004, more than 66 million of the world's poorest people, of whom 83% of them women, received small loans to start or to expand small businesses compared to 7.6 million in 1997 (Microcredit Summit 2011 and Results Canada Action Sheet, September 2006). In Bangladesh, Grameen Bank's contribution to Bangladesh socio-economic development proves that they contribute to small enterprises and to eradicate poverty locally. From the above discussion and analysis, it is found that Grameen Bank has implemented Boothroyd and Davis's three approaches to community economic development (CED) theme. Canadian CED organizations and government organizations can take lessons from Bangladesh MFIs and mentor the CED NGOs to promote micro-financing in Canada for revitalizing marginalized people local economy and to empower the bottom 50% of the disadvantaged women in Canada and move forward to eradicate their poverty.

11.0. Bibliography

Angel Gurria (2016). Community economic development. *Addressing to ECONOUS2016, the National CED Conference 2016, OECD*, Retrieved from https://ccednet-rcdec.ca/en/what_is_ced, dated October 21, 2017

Blakely, E.J. (1989). *Planning Local Economic Development,* Newbury Park, California: Sage Publications

Blakely, Edward J. and Bradshaw, Ted K. (2002). *Planning Local Economic Development. Third Edition.* Thousand Oaks, California: Sage Publications

Boothroyd, P. (1991b). Community development: The missing link in welfare policy. In *Ideology, Development and Social Welfare: Canadian Perspectives* (ed.) B. Kirwin. Second edition. Toronto, Ontario: Canada Scholars' Press

Boothroyd, P. and Davis, H. (1993). Community Economic Development: Three approaches in *Journal of Planning Education and Research*, Vol. 12, pp. 230-240

Borgen Project(2017). *Poverty thought.* borgenproject.org

Bruyn, S.T. (1987). Beyond the market and the state In *Beyond the Market and the State*, (eds.) S T Bruyn and J. Meehan Philadelphia, Pennsylvania. Temple University Press

Burman, P. (1996). *Poverty's bonds- power and agency in the social relations of welfare*, Toronto: Thompson Educational Publishing, Inc.

Calmeadow Foundation. (2005). *Annual report 2005.* Toronto: Calmaedow Foundation

Chekki, D.A. (1979). *Community Development Theory and Method of Planned Change*, New Delhi: Vikas Publishing House

Cheston, S., & Kuhn, L. (2002). *Empowering women through microfinance.* In S. Daley-Harris (Ed.), Pathways out of poverty: Innovations in micro-finance for the poorest families (pp. 167–228). Blomington: Kumarian Press Inc.

Christension, J., Fendley, K., & Robinson, J. (1994). Community development, in J. A. Christension, J. & J.W. Robinson (Eds.), *Community development perspective* (pp. 3-25). Ames, Iowa: Iowa State University

CIDA. (2001). *Human rights report.* Dhaka: CIDA

Coady International Institute. (2015). *Themes.* Retrieved from http://WWW.coady.stfx.ca

Cruikshank, B. (1994). The will to empower: Technologies of citizenship and the war on poverty. *Socialist Review*, Vol. 23(4), pp. 29-55

Daly, H.E., and J.B. Cobb Jr. (1989). *For the Common Good Redirecting the Economy Toward Community, the Environment, and a Sustainable Future Boston*, Massachusetts. Beacon Press

Davis, H.C., and Davis, L.E. (1987). Local exchange trading systems: Wealth creation within the informal economy, *Plan Canada*, Vol. 27, pp. 238-248

Deller, Steve (2014). Community Development, Economic Development, or Community Economic Development? An Introduction. *PowerPoint presentation at the Deller, UW Madison/Extension Symposium.*

Gardner, J., and M. Roseland (1989). Acting locally Community strategies for equitable sustainable development, *Alternatives*, Vol. 16, pp. 36-48

Gershuny, J.I. (1979). The informal economy: Its role in post-industrial society, *Futures*, Vol. 10, pp. 135-148

Grameen Bank (2015). *Impact of Grameen Bank on local society.* Retrieved from http://www.rdc.com.au/grameen/impact/htm dated June 15, 2006

Grameen Dialogue. (2006). *SME and microcredit.* Newsletter #63, April 2006. Dhaka: Grameen Trust

Grameen Bank Updates. (2014). *Grameen Bank at a glance.* Dhaka: Grameen Bank

Henderson, H. (1990). Making sense of economics, *Common Ground,* Vol. 31(8), G0-G1

Hick, S. (2004). *Social welfare in Canada-understanding income security.* Toronto: Thomson Educational Publishing, Inc.

Human Right Report. (2013). *Executive summary, Bangladesh.* Dhaka: Bangladesh Manobadhikar Samonnoy Parishad (BMSP)

Isserles, R. G. (2003). Microcredit: The rhetoric of empowerment, the reality of development as usual. *Women's Studies Quarterly,* 3(4), pp. 38-57

Kabeer, N. (1983). *Minus lives–Women in Bangladesh.* Dhaka: University Press

Kretzmann, J. P., & McKnight J. L. (1993). *Building communities from the inside out,* Chicago: ACTA Publications

Lee, B. (1999). *Pragmatics of community organization.* Mississauga: Common Act Press

Lotz, J. (1987). Community development- A short history. *Journal of Community Development,* Vol. 1, May/June, pp. 40-46.

Luke, J.S., C. Ventriss, B.J. Reed, and C.M. Reed. (1988). *Managing Economic Development,* San Francisco, California: Jossey-Bass Publishers

Mack, J. (2013). *Definition of poverty. Poverty and social exclusion.* Retrieved from http://www.poverty.ac.uk/definitions-poverty dated October 21, 2017

MacLeod, G. (1986). *New age business community corporations that work*, Ottawa, Ontario: Canadian Council on Social Development

Mahzia, E. (1985). *Local Economic Development*, New York: Irwin.

McMillan, D.W., and Chavis, D.M. 1986. *Sense of community: A definition and theory*, p. 16.

Melnyk, G. (1985). *The Search for community from utopia to a cooperatzve society*, Montreal, Quebec. Blackrose Books

Morehouse, W. (ed.). (1989). *Building Sustainable Communities Tools and Concepts for Self-Reliant Economic Change*. New York: Bootstrap Press

Nicholls, W.M., and W.A. Dyson (1983). *The informal economy where people are the bottom line:* Ottawa, Ontario: VIF Publications

Paul James (2006). *Globalism, nationalism, tribalism, in bringing theory back*, Volume 2 of Towards a Theory of Abstract Community. London: Sage Publications

Results Canada (2006). *Results Canada Action Sheet*, September 2006

Rouf, K. A. (2011). Grameen Bank women borrowers familial and community relationships development in patriarchal Bangladesh. *International Journal of Research Studies in Psychology*, Vol. 1(1), pp. 17-26

Rouf, K. A. (2016). Eradication of povertythrough community economic development using micro financing: Lessons learned from Grameen Bank Bangladesh, *International Journal of Research Studies in Managemen*t, Vol. 5(2), pp. 3-11

Schaffer, R., Deller, S., and Marcouiller, D. (2004). *Community economics: linking theory and practice.* Iowa: Iowa State University Press

Scott Peck, M. (1987). *The different drum: Community-making and peace*, pp. 83-85.

Sen. Amartya (2004). *Definitions of poverty*, Washington: World Bank

Shaffer, Ron; Deller, Steve; and Marcouiller, Dave (2004). *Community economics: Linking theory and practice.* Ames: Blackwell Publishing

Shragge, E. (1997). *Community economic development-in search of empowerment.* Montreal: Black Rose Books

South Asian Foundation (2014). *Bangladesh statistical profile.* Retrieved on from http://www.southasiafoundation.org/saf/bangladesh/banglastats.asp

Temali, Mihailo (2002). *The community economic development Handbook*. St. Paul: Amherst H. Wilder Foundation

The Canadian CED Network (2017). *Community economic development*, Toronto

Western Economic Diversification Canada (2017). *Community economic growth*, retrieved from www.wd-deo.gc.cadated October 22, 2017

Wong, W. A. (2002). *The poor women- a critical analysis of Asian theology and contemporary Chinese fiction by women*. New York: Peter Lang

World Bank. (2010). *World development report*. Washington DC: World Bank

Yunus, M. (2007). *Creating a world without poverty*. New York: BBS Public Affairs

Zdenek, R. (1987). Community development corporations, in *Beyond the Market and the State*, (eds.) S. T. Bruyn and J. Meehan. Philadelphia, Pennsylvania: Temple University Press.

Appendix-1

Sixteen Decisions of Grameen Bank

1. The four principles of Grameen Bank-discipline, unity, courage and hard work-we shall follow and advance in all walks of our lives.
2. Prosperity we shall bring to our families.
3. We shall not live in dilapidated houses. We shall repair our houses and work towards constructing new houses at the earliest.
4. We shall grow vegetables all the year round. We shall eat plenty of it and sell the surplus.
5. During the plantation seasons, we shall plants as many seedlings as possible.
6. We shall plan to keep our families small. We shall minimize our expenditures. We shall look after our health.
7. We shall educate our children and ensure that they can earn to pay for their education.
8. We shall always keep our children and environment clean.
9. We shall build and use pit-latrine/sanitary latrine.
10. We shall drink tube well water. If it is not available, we shall boil water or use alum.
11. We shall not take dowry in our son's wedding; neither shall we give any dowry in our daughters' wedding. We shall keep the Centre free from the curse of dowry. We shall not practice child marriage.
12. We shall not inflict any injustice on anyone neither shall we allow anyone to do so.
13. For higher income we shall collectively undertake bigger investments.
14. We shall always be ready to help each other. If anyone is in difficulty, we shall all help him/her.
15. If we come to know of any breach of discipline in any Centre, we shall go there and help restore discipline.
16. We shall introduce physical exercise in all Centers. We shall take part in all social activities collectively.

Feminization of Poverty and Gender Development Policy

Abstract

Gender development policy and women development different socio-economic programs, approaches, strategies, services and measurements are important components for eradicating feminization of poverty. A holistic development approach with women's issues as a priority is important for women's empowerment. Naila Kabeer, a feminist economist, talks in her book Reversed Realities how women are suffering from exploitations patriarchal male domination and injustice both in private sphere and public spheres. This paper is the chapter wise overview and analysis of the book Reversed Realities. Moreover, this paper discusses how women are exploited by the institutions both at the micro level and macro level with examples in terms of formulating policies and planning, strategies, providing services to women, devaluating women through measuring their works both at family label and community label; and marginalizing them to feminization of poverty.

Key terms: Capabilities approach,; feminization of poverty; gender roles framework (GRF); gross national product (GNP); human development index (HDI); participatory poverty assessment (PPA); social roles framework (SRF); social benefit cost analysis; triple roles framework (TRF); women in development.

1.0. Introduction

Poverty may be defined as the deprivation of either the ability to fulfill basic human needs or gain access to resources to meet these needs (Kabeer, p.137). The concept of poverty is highly feminized in that gender sex-role stereotypes affect how an individual experiences poverty and how policies are developed to address the destitute situation based on the gender of the sufferer. This is especially true in regards to Bangladesh as women are over represented in the ranks of the poor. Unfortunately, planning efforts to alleviate poverty are usually targeted towards men as they are assumed to dominate productive, economic roles while women (categorized mainly in reproductive roles) are relegated to secondary welfare considerations. Women are also exploited through different socioeconomic and political processes. Naila Kabeer, in her book *Reversed Realities* points out these crucial issues throughout and explains micro-economical feminism. This paper initially presents a chapter-wise summary of the book and secondly, goes on to examine an analysis of the economic and social perspectives of measuring poverty and how these methodologies affect how policies are developed to address the issue. Recommendations are then made for promoting training methods that will be more gender inclusive for poverty alleviation and development.

2.0. Overview of the book *Revised Realities*

In chapter one of the text, Naila Kabeer presents the historical background of the introduction of women into the arena of development policy and planning and examines the establishment of the ideology of women in development. Up until around 1980, women were excluded in state policy, and were underrepresented in development agencies. A woman's place was even more decidedly seen to be in the home while men dominated in the outside home productive roles. Policy makers encouraged male based programs in state policy. Nevertheless, women were not only involved in producing babies and taking care of them but also contributed economically to their families and society; but many of these active ties were ignored by or invisible to planners and the society at large. For those who were members of the workforce, they were subject to unfair and unequal conditions. Even international organizations like the United Nations (UN) did not regard women's issues as essential in development. Ester Boserup who wrote *Women's role in economic development* in 1970 who is credited with drawing the attention of develop mentalists to include women's issues in the UN's agenda. After 1980, policy shifts were made to include and focus more on women's issues such as their treatment in the work force and in education. Here; however, Kabeer introduces the permeating argument of the ongoing biases inherent in planning agencies both national and international.

The second chapter deals with the theoretical foundations of the issue of Women in Development (WID). Naila Kabeer examines the contribution of these theories to the debates on policy making. The discussion shows that the overall operating mindset of the institution must be changed before any real progress may be made in changing the process of gender equityin policy development. Efforts of WID advocates and scholars played a major role in the overall shifts in policy maker's views of women in the development process and in the new policies that were constructed. There was a major distinction made between productive and reproductive work (women were viewed solely in the reproductive aspect while men mainly in the productive roles).

Policy making generally favors men in the area of production. There is a general neglect of interconnections between production and reproduction. This failure to promote gender equitymay be a result of the struggle to maintain the status quo of class and gender from planners in development agencies as well as members of other organizations and society itself. More accurate data is needed in order to examine the situations of gender and development in different regions of the world especially in the Third World countries. However, still more radical revisions are necessary to change policy making and planning procedures. International development agencies need to be transformed into more accountable and democratic structures in order to help with the efforts of WID advocacy.

Chapter three highlights the structural perspective in the ongoing discussion on Women in Development (WID). Here Kabeer begins with an analysis of Marxist theory as a foundation, but moves beyond to examine other theoretical perspectives that grew out of Marxism.

She attempts to apply a Marxist analysis to the study of women in development planning has helped to produce a deeper and more questioning area of analysis within which the structural questions of class and gender (questions missing from the WID analysis) can be located. Feminist theorists have revised Marxist theory to include the marginalized status of women in the economic arena and to address the weaknesses in its concepts.

A focus on gender relations extends the Marxist preoccupation with production of things to the production of human life and well being. A use of gender relations as a category of analysis also shifts the focus away from the earlier one on women and extends instead to the broader arena of interconnecting relationships through which women are positioned as a subordinate group. This takes away from the notion that women are the cause or the solution to issues of gender. Gender must be analyzed from a holistic point of view as it is often interconnected to other social interactive, economic and political issues. This will help us to understand the issues facing members of both genders and how to deal with those issues.

The fourth chapter revisits the issue of development, but uses this new holistic and integrative gender perspective to examine how this new aspect of development might look. A reanalysis of development impacts on both the production of knowledge and the distribution of resources. Current methods have favored economic growth in development over meeting basic human needs. This has continued to serve the interests of privileged groups (mainly men), and helped to produce the skewed development practices of the past decades. Knowledge generated by excluded groups would help to transform development thought, extending it to take account of what has been previously excluded, deepening it to uncover the inter-connections which have been previously overlooked and concealed through divided analyses of development. This will also contribute to a revising of priorities so that individuals' rights and responsibilities and claims and obligations may be properly situated.

Households and household decision-making notions are the subjects of chapter five. Economic models of households are based on the assumption that family members have shared and collective interests and that decision-making takes place with the interests of all members of the family by the kind head of the household. When the predictions of this model are compared to actual research in real household structures worldwide, it reveals the errors in the reasoning of economists who tend to attribute altruism overwhelming kindness to the member who controls the most assets, food, luxury items and leisure time (men). By their privileging of individuals to the exclusion of structures, of the economy over the cultural, and of objective quantitative predictions over qualitative explanations, neo-classical economists have succeeded in drawing a veil over the power dimension of intra-household relations.

Chapter six focuses on poverty. It first presents some methods of measuring poverty and some limitations to these methods. Kabeer says that there are two challenges in poverty measurement: (1) Relevance of importance and (2) Practicality of measurement. Secondly, it looks at how individuals may become poor and illustrates that this is a process that is usually different for men and women. Kabeer specifically discusses cause and effects of feminization of poverty in Bangladesh although she does not mention all. Poverty may result from either one or a combination of the following: no resources in the entire family and break ups in the family unit (divorce, separation, death, and female headed household). Women who are abandoned may migrate from rural areas to urban areas in search of work. It is risk for them to be in the urban area because there is limited housing, hygiene, health care facilities, security, and employment opportunities for women. As a result, women and children suffer from malnutrition. The female mortality rate tends to be higher because of pregnancy, abortion, physical violence and male dependence. Women stay poor because they do not have access to credit and employment.

The chapter seven is about the assumptions behind cost-benefit analysis is examined. This is an important tool in measuring development interventions. Social Benefit Cost Analysis (SCBA) is a method for assessing both cash profit and loss of public project as well as includes intangible social costs and benefits. The problem lies in that economists view the market as the assigner of value and only costs and benefits that can be given a market price are recognized. As a result, increases in productivity will count as a benefit, but increases in autonomy will not; increases in the wage component of the project will count as a cost but the increase in the workloads of women as a result the project will not. SCBA would be a significant cost benefit analysis tool of public sector planning that includes all kinds of public objectives than private profit driven objectives.

Chapter eight presents an overview of population policy. Population control has been a major issue on the development agenda since 1960 in India and Bangladesh. From then they established Family Planning Department. Population pressure is determined as a major cause of poverty where women are held almost entirely responsible for controlling population growth. Although focuses were given to primary health care in Bangladesh and India; however, women received disproportionate amount in population control program. Women bodies and social experiences differ in reproduction significantly from those of men. The proliferation of contraceptive technology has given greater control to women over their own bodies. On a more theoretical note, the arguments presented here gives credibility to point of view that choice – reproductive or otherwise – will not become an actuality unless it is backed up by information, resources, accountability and enfranchisement.

Chapter nine tackles the issues of power and empowerment. Empowerment is a combination from the grassroots works. It is the result of rhetoric of participatory development despite the fact that power remains in the hands of a minority at the top. Women empowerment is always a key goal of feminist grassroots organizations that want to move beyond the WID focus on formal equality with men. Kabeer mentions that the notion of empowerment always rooted in the notion of power, it is the reverse of powerlessness or the absence of women power (Kabeer, p. 224). The chapter emphasizes the point that more conventional approaches to the design and evaluation of development interventions, which privilege certain world views over others, are unlikely to give rise to projects of enfranchisement and empowerment.

The concluding chapter of the book is about training methods. Gender training is important to feminist advocates because through training they can de-institutionalize male privilege in development planning and policy. The chapter compares three approaches to gender issues in development planning which have been extracted from gender training efforts over the past decade and draws out what they have to say about gender inequalities in production, labour, resources and power within the official and unofficial institutions of development. These training approaches are namely the Gender Roles Framework (GRF), the Triple Roles Framework (TRF) and Social Roles Framework (SRF).

3.0. Organizing the paper

Now below the paper is going to analyze three issues related to women impoverishments: (1) economic poverty measures, (2) social theoretical approaches to poverty, and (3) recommendations for frameworks for measuring and dealing with poverty based on a combination of economic and social dimensions.

4.0. Analysis of how women are suffering from feminization of poverty

4.0.1. Different methods to address the issue feminization of poverty

Poverty is viewed by economists as the lack of money or capital resources to provide for oneself and one's family. The poverty line and the GNP are a few of the major elements used to measure poverty from an economic perspective. The Poverty Line Approach identifies poverty as limitation in earnings and purchasing power; while the GNP equates the value of goods and services in an economy with the prices that they could get in the marketplace. Although Naila Kabeer says that "the assessment of poverty must make space for considering the extent to which the tangible and intangible basic needs of the poor women and men are met" (p. 140), she only mentions and explains the economic poverty line approach. However, I am going to discuss some other poverty approaches that are applicable to poverty in Bangladesh.

The poverty line approach can separate the poor from the non-poor (cut-off point) and focuses on (a) national per capita income at the micro level, and (b) per capita household income. It focuses more on economic growth and places emphasis on daily income as a minimum requirement for the survival of household members. The advantages of this approach are that it provides empirical data which enables the planners to map the extent of poverty. For example, 3 billion people (50%) survive on a $2 a day income while more than half of the world's population lives on under $1 per day (absolute poverty). 67% of the world's women live below the poverty line. Asian women have only 1% of the wealth in the world although they carry out 66% of the work that is needed for human survival (Wong, 2002: 47).

In Bangladesh, 57% of the population exists below the poverty line; 36% in absolute poverty (Bangladesh Profile, 2001). Currently (2017) only 24% population of Bangladesh are living below poverty line. Within this huge rank of poor people, women are the most affected and children the worst victims (Hick, 2004: 147). While the poverty line gives a relatively clear picture of the levels of economic depravity; it is a fact that survival extends far beyond monetary income to include social facilities such as access to safe water, sanitation, education, health services and reasonable nutrition; and access to community and state resources. By extension, human well-being depends on developing purchasing energy power as well as a sense of dignity and self-respect. The poverty line approach says little about women's experience of poverty in comparison to men, and it also can not differentiate between abject and acute poverty.

Another renowned method for expressing the wealth or poverty of nations is the Gross National Product (GNP), which is the sum of the value of a nation's output of goods and services. This is calculated by adding up the amount of money spent on a country's output of goods and services or by totaling the income of all citizens, including income from factors of production used abroad. The shortfalls of the GNP are similar to that of the Poverty Line measure. It only covers marketable goods and services which excludes women's household labour and any other work that does not make it to the market. The process of ascribing value to products and services is also open to extensive biases depending on the subjective ideologies of the individuals or agencies. Women's domestic work and reproductive values are thus grossly devalued.

The GNP would appear to be a relatively inaccurate tool for measuring poverty in its entirety. In the film "If Women Counted" Marilyn Waring states that "national income achievement is not enough without counting women's work in the national economic census and GNP calculations" (Waring, 1984). The major economy of Bangladesh is agriculture and women are involved in many aspects of agricultural work like seed and crop processing, seed storage, food processing, homestead gardening and backyard poultry rearing. In addition, they are also involved in fetching water, collecting firewood, cleaning, and clothing, child bearing and rearing, supporting the husband and even in providing basic health care to family members. On average, rural Bangladeshi women work 16-17 hours per day at home, but these are not recorded in GNP Bangladesh calculation (Appendix A).

Half of the women population of Bangladesh (66.5 million) is left out from GNP estimates, which is reflective of a failure to recognize gender in societies and to achieve efficient economic performance. The invisibility of women in the GNP translates into their invisibility in national and international economies. This may also be a factor in the minimal attention accorded to women's issues by planners and policy makers' in development organizations. Marilyn goes on ask that if male farmers' works are included in the market economy then why is it not the same for the female producer (Marilyn, 1984). Despite recent changes to the GNP calculation to include some housework carried out by females, women's reproductive and food processing work continues to be excluded (Economic Census, Bangladesh: 2000).

Economic measures of poverty and the policies that are developed based on this methodology present an empirical picture of the global poverty situation. However, the image they provide is incomplete in light of the multi-faceted structure of this issue. Economic theorists focus on economic development as a critical element in the overall development initiative. However, this leads one to question the extent to which improvements in economic rates reflect greater prosperity for the general population. Marylin says, "When income-generating activities were provided they generally coincided with sex-role differentiation" (p. 7). It emphasizing economics and down playing the social repercussions of poverty will not serve to efficiently remedy and make life better for the poor.

Human needs go beyond the ability to afford daily nutritional provisions, but can be extended to living a healthy and active life and participating in community activities (Maryling, p. 139). There are several schools of thought in support of the social theoretical perspective of poverty measurement and alleviation. Some measures used are: the capabilities approach, participatory poverty assessment and the theory of 'hierarchy of needs'.

These poverty approaches go beyond human economic needs and are more inclusive of other aspects of human life. For example, the Capabilities Approach developed by Amarta Sen (1984) explores the endowments and entitlements (means) of functioning achievements (ends), especially in relation to women. This approach adds up income and commodities, community participation and achieving self-respect as important elements of human well-being. Functional capabilities approach is not only include people's choice, but also personal achievements and social constraints. Therefore, the focus of this approach extends to gender social inclusion and responds to the failure of economic growth to benefit the poor (not even in a trickle-down effect). Health and education are functioning achievements and are measured at the community and national level. The advantages of the human capabilities approach are to monitor basic achievements across country borders, gender relations and make gender inequalities visible. Although the approach defines and is inclusive of social aspects, those that are intangible are not quantifiable.

An extension of the Capabilities Approach, an actual operating example, is the Human Development Index (HDI). Recently, the Human Development Index (HDI) of UNDP has added income, life expectancy and educational attainment. The Human Development Report in 2000 of Bangladesh made recommendations for massive literacy public policies as essential for eradicating poverty and for developing human capabilities for the disadvantaged rural poor and for vulnerable women in Bangladesh. This method is advantageous seeing that the destitute situation in Bangladesh extends beyond economic concerns to include low achievement in education (43%), health, nutrition, political participation and other areas of human development.

Another multidimensional poverty measurement tool is the Participatory Poverty Assessment (PPA) which explores cause and effects of poverty in a specific context. It looks at the experience of poverty from poor people's perspective. The advantages of PPA are: it is not only concerned with basic needs, but also issues of security, accumulation, social standing, and self respect, along with using a variety of subsistence means of surviving. It also includes unskilled labor and the extent of the social network. PPA also discusses a different form of gender discrimination like dowry, domestic violence, unequal decision making power and disproportionate workloads; connects production and reproduction. Hence, the Capabilities Approach, HDI and Participatory Poverty Assessment methods would seem to be more applicable for addressing the feminization of poverty and to tackle gender discrimination in Bangladesh than a simply economic measure such as the Poverty Line approach.

The model of "Hierarchy of Needs" was proposed by Chambers (1988) to examine the importance of achieving high self-esteem through providing for one's family. An opposing view point points to the overriding necessity to secure basic necessities over "feeling good" or "proud" of one's accomplishments. The question is how will a high self esteem substantially benefit the poor?

Moreover, Chambers (1988) says, "Human need is more than physiological survival; it is also about living a healthy active life and participating in the community" (p. 139). Chambers' viewpoint extends the categories of basic human needs from strong social participation and healthy active lives to include intangible aspects of deprivation – "powerlessness, dependence and isolation" (pp 139). Although this is not a direct measurement tool for poverty, this ideology provides just another social theoretical framework from which sociologists examine the issue of poverty. It is important to illustrate the psychological deprivations associated with poverty adding to a more holistic picture of deprivation. The poor not only suffer from lack of money, access to resources, deprived social and community participation, but also deprived mental health. It is difficult to feel good about oneself when you live in a deficit.

Both the economic and the social theoretical view points affect how policies are developed in recognition of poverty. The economic perspectives forces policy makers to focus on the development of sustainable economic institutions, such as job creation, training and credit programs; while social theorists stress overall well being and social inclusion. Due to the fact that males are seen as the major breadwinners in households, these policies tend to favor them instead of women. Women are continuously marginalized even within international and national bureaucratic agencies. Therefore, gender training policy is important for gender equity. Gender awareness in policy and planning requires analysis of social relations of production within the family, community, market and state to understand gender inequality.

Naila Kabeer mentions, "Gender equity goals would be more effectively addressed through gender training if it could be used to encourage more critical self-examination among planners as to how exclusionary structures work within their own institutions, through their hierarchies of authority and knowledge, rules of recruitment and divisions of resources and responsibilities" (p. 303). So Gender training and its related policies can play a great role to change and to de-institutionalize male privilege in development planning and policy. Training is a particular method which may change present institutional practices. So gender training can help policy makers to include gender in their work. The author mentions three training frameworks: the Gender Roles Framework (GRF), Triple Roles Framework (TRF), and the Social Relations Framework (SRF). The GRF mainly focuses on efficiency of resources, but is limited in its dealings with gender relations. The TRF enables policy makers to analyze their roles in gender inequality and transforming women's self development, but it fails to differentiate between gender divisions of labor.

The Social Relations Framework (SRF) as presented by Kabeer (1994) provides an ideal example of an integrative model for reeducating both planners and those being planned for alike. Training courses run in the third world country and bring different people together to receive training that can develop sustaining interrelations among them. The great advantage of this training is that it addresses personal dimensions of social change and recognizes women's tangible needs like assets, monies, commodities and human wellbeing; as well as intangible resources such as solidarity, information, and contacts, security and autonomy. Intangible resources are used to improve women's material resources and it is important where social security is absent. SRF infiltrates the whole system of male power and privileges, and presents all forms of inequalities, producing knowledge on alternative gender perspectives and assists in the rethinking of existing gender conventions and norms, and allocation of resources. Therefore, the end result of the SRF is the achievement of human well-being which is important for strategies to empower women. This framework of training seeks to achieve a shift from gender-blind to gender aware policy making through rethinking of assumptions and practices.

5.0. How Grameen Bank Bangladesh address the issue of feminization of poverty

Alternatively, decision makers who hold the social theoretical viewpoint recognize the importance of the female counterparts in households and tend to develop strategies that will be as beneficial to them as well as the whole family. It appears to be true that neither economic nor social viewpoints are enough to address poverty, but rather, a combination of the two. Another ideal example of an integrative measuring tool and developmental approach is evident in the Grameen Bank and its credit delivery system to the poorest of the poor in Bangladesh. The Bank provides credit to 8.6 million rural landless women in Bangladesh without collateral through cooperatives (Grameen Dialogue, 2016). Through credit programs it mobilizes the poor women in a self-sustaining process and gives its members reasonable strength both individually and collectively to move up the social and economic tier. Grameen Bank narrows down its poverty measurement to its borrower's level. It uses ten indicators to measure poverty for its members. The measuring parameters are: (1) ability to have three meals per day, (2) ability to send children to school, (3) live in their own house (4) have winter clothes, (5) can afford health services and buy necessary medicine (6) use safe drinking water (7) have no land mortgage (8) use mosquito nets, (9) regularly repay Grameen loans and pension schemes unless affected by natural disasters, and (10) ability to count. Here the holistic development approach drives Bangladeshi rural poor women to be self-employed, independent, able to make decisions in family affairs, and to alleviate poverty from their lives. Grameen Bank Statistics 2005 says 52% of its borrowers graduated from poverty by using Grameen loans and they were associated with other social programs as mentioned before.

6.0. Conclusion

The book *Revised Realities* presents a strong critique of the economic perspective and some issues related to the social perspective; however, the author examination falls short in regards to making strong recommendations for ideal frameworks and a reevaluation of mindsets which are necessary for planning that considers the different gender roles and experiences of poverty. A more comprehensive analysis of an integrated approach to women in development is urgently needed to address the feminization of poverty in Bangladesh. A holistic development approach with women's issues as a priority is important for women's empowerment. Therefore, "more radical revisions are necessary to change policy making and planning procedures" for women in development (p. 303).

Productive, Reproductive and Invisible Work of Rural Poor Women

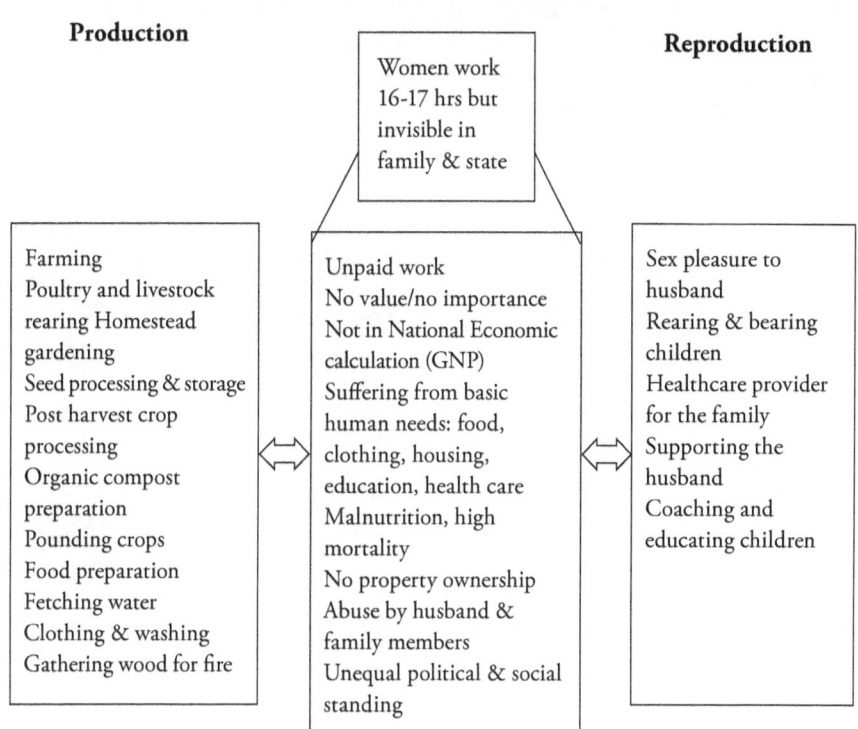

Production

Reproduction

Women work 16-17 hrs but invisible in family & state

Farming
Poultry and livestock rearing Homestead gardening
Seed processing & storage
Post harvest crop processing
Organic compost preparation
Pounding crops
Food preparation
Fetching water
Clothing & washing
Gathering wood for fire

Unpaid work
No value/no importance
Not in National Economic calculation (GNP)
Suffering from basic human needs: food, clothing, housing, education, health care
Malnutrition, high mortality
No property ownership
Abuse by husband & family members
Unequal political & social standing

Sex pleasure to husband
Rearing & bearing children
Healthcare provider for the family
Supporting the husband
Coaching and educating children

Cause and effects of women's exploitation

Cause	Effect
Son preference (patriarchy)	Not included in National Economy
Market economy (price calculation)	Invisible in the society
Religious customary laws	No property rights, no access to property
Private and public realm	Violence against women
Traditional, norms against women	Malnutrition, high mortality rate
Globalization/SAP	No power, no voice no choice
Male dominance in institutions & in state policy	Exploit women's body
	No reproductive rights
Natural disaster (flood, river erosion, cyclone, hurricane)	Internalize patriarchal value (socialize patriarchy)
Family breakdown	Scarcity of resource like female hostel
Migration crisis rural to urban	No housing and hygienic facilities for women
Unequal wage, certain job fix in the line of gender, no work safety	No access to credit & other financial and social opportunity like health, education, job etc.
No education, no access to credit	
No reproductive rights	Suffering from feminization poverty
Gender blind	

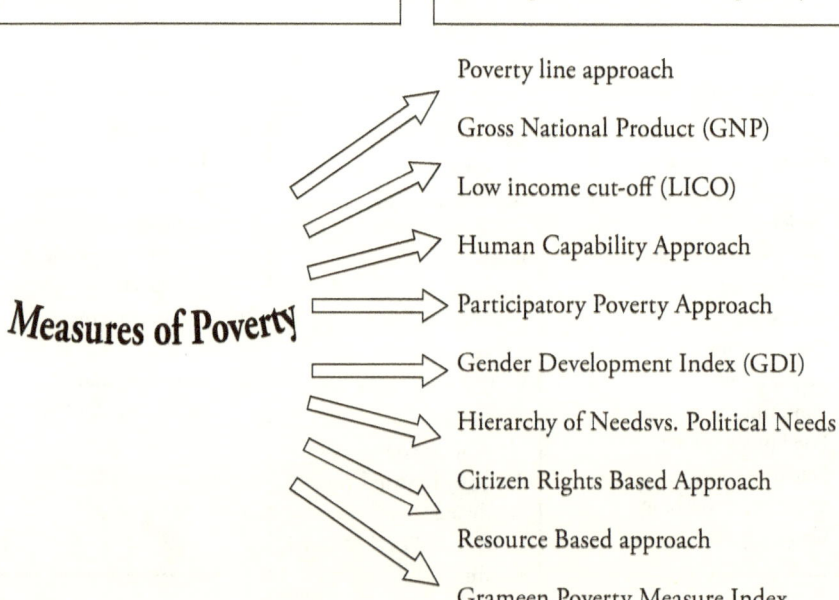

Measures of Poverty

Poverty line approach

Gross National Product (GNP)

Low income cut-off (LICO)

Human Capability Approach

Participatory Poverty Approach

Gender Development Index (GDI)

Hierarchy of Needsvs. Political Needs

Citizen Rights Based Approach

Resource Based approach

Grameen Poverty Measure Index

7.0. Bibliography

Boserup, E. (1970). *Women's role in economic development*. London: Earthscan Publications

CIDA (2001). *CIDA: Bangladesh profile*. Retrieved from http://www.southasiafoundation.org/saf/bngladesh/banglastats.aspdated June 08, 2005

Grameen Dialogue (2016). *Social business,* Newsletter #63, April 2006. Dhaka, Bangladesh: Grameen Trust

Hick, S. (2004) *Social welfare in Canada-understanding income security.* Thomson Educational Publishing, Inc, Toronto

Kabeer, N. (1995). *Reserved Realities-Gender hierarchies in development thought.* London, Great Britain, Biddles Ltd.

Marilyn Waring. (2001). *If Women Counted.* Film

Rouf, K. A. (2015). Against all odds: Socio-economic and political factors related to female labor force participation and decision making power in Bangladesh. *International Journal of Research Studies in Management,* Vol.5 (1), pp. 53-63.

Sen, A. (1984). *Poverty and famines: an essay in entitlement and deprivation,* Oxford: Clarendon Press

Wong, W. A. (2002). *The poor women- A critical analysis of Asian theology and contemporary Chinese fiction by women.* New York: Peter Lang.

Against All Odds: Socio-Economic and Political Factors Related to Female Labour Force Participation and Decision Making Power in Bangladesh ·

Abstract

Gender inequality and discrimination is persistent in different socio-economic and political institutions. Women are mainly treated as second sex, sex objects, reproductive agent and their economic contributions to the family, market and state are largely ignored. These discriminations are transferred through the institution of patriarchy, labor force participation and different national and international programs and policy processes. The rigidity and confinement of women within households is experiencing minimal change. A majority of women continue to experience inequalities in different sectors of the society; both in developed and developing countries. However, in terms of gender inequality, female labor force participation is a major factor. This paper reviewes feminist literatures and author personal experiences working with women particularly marginalized women in many countries. The paper examines the interrelating issues of female labour force participation, patriarchy, differential household structures and development policies as they exist in Bangladesh.

Key Words: Grameen Bank; gender inequality; Gender Responsive Budget (GRB); Millennium Development Goals (MDGs); patriarchy; Participatory Poverty Index (PPI); Poverty Reduction Strategy Paper (PRSP); poverty; social reproduction; and women commoditization.

1. Introduction

The institution of patriarchy is a pervading factor which affects almost all aspects of society including the state, market, community and the family. The continued discrimination of females is maintained by the biases brought about by patriarchy. Examining and making recommendations for changing the operations of this institution, especially as it affects women's economic lives, should contribute towards the overall empowerment of women and gender equalityin the context of Bangladesh and in other regions as well. This paper will incorporate the analysis of two books. The first section describes the summaries of two books: (1) *Eradication and the Millennium Development Goals* by Naila Kabeer and (2) *In Quest of Empowerment: The Grameen Bank Impact on Women's Power and the Status* by Ainon Nahar Mizan, and analyse Marylin Wayne book. The second part of the paper presents the issues mentioned above.

2. Part A: Summaries of the Books

2.1 *Gender mainstreaming in poverty eradication and the millennium development goals* by Naila Kabeer (2003).

There are eight chapters in *'Gender mainstreaming in poverty eradication and the millennium development goals* by Naila Kabeer. The first chapter talks about gender in poverty and the development policies initiated by different international agencies like the World Bank and the United Nations. The reports produced by these two organizations did not place significant emphasis on gender equalityand poverty until the Millennium Development Goals (MDGs) 2000. MDGs of 2000 are focused on eradicating extreme poverty and hunger, promoting universal primary education, and promoting gender equality and environmental sustainability. Women were identified as the poorest of the poor in the world and they were usually found to be the majority of the victims of globalization.

Chapter Two focuses on integrating gender into macro economic analysis. Here the author describes neo-classical economic frameworks in comparison to political frameworks in order to get an understanding of gender and poverty. Before 2000, macroeconomic policies were not gender neutral. Macro economists treated human resources as natural resources. Reproductive work was considered natural to women and regarded as their main goal. Therefore, goods and services produced by women go relatively unnoticed in the economic sector. Women's domestic and reproductive labour is not priced in the market. Naila Kabeer mentions (2003) that there is also an assumption from the macroeconomic perspective that a reduction of men's poverty would automatically help women.

Chapter Three narrates the geography of gender inequality. Institutions play a powerful role in shaping human behavior and give rise to regional patterns in labor force participation and the economic activity of men and women (Kabeer, 1995). Social reproduction creates gender discrimination. Regional differences create various types of kinship relationships, household patterns and gender division of resources. These combine to produce differences in production and reproduction, paid and unpaid wages and domestic and public domains (Ibid, 1993). However, due to patriarchy there are lower rates of female labour force participation and wage differentials between women and men in Bangladesh (Ibid, 1993).

Chapter Four discusses approaches to poverty analysis and its gender dimension. There are several approaches to measuring: the poverty line approach, capabilities approach and the participatory poverty approach. The poverty line approach separates the poor from the non-poor (Kabeer, 2003). Through the capabilities approach individuals can explore their personal circumstances and overcome social constraints. Participatory Poverty Index (PPI) emphasizes visual techniques, metrics, mapping, and diagrams to analyze poverty. It assumes that gender discrimination is innate and biologically driven.

Chapter Five relates gender inequality with poverty and its effects on household livelihoods. In South Asia (India, Bangladesh) male farming systems is a major means of livelihood; whereas in Sub-Saharan countries female farming systems are the main components of the economy. Regions with male farming systems usually have more patriarchal households while those dominated by female farming systems have more egalitarian households. Rural poverty in South Asia is connected with landlessness, rural wage labour and the caste system (Kabeer, 1995). Many poor women are forced to migrate to urban areas in search of employment. This makes them vulnerable to exploitation in terms of wage differentials and abusive, and live in unsanitary conditions.

Chapter Six of the book deals with 'gender equality and human development outcomes; that is, enhancing capabilities'. Human capabilities are associated with education. Female education reduces women's fertility rates as women are more aware of and have access to contraceptives. Gender equality is the achievement of equivalent well-being between women and men, boys and girls. This equality rationale is the issue of mainstream social justice. Higher levels of maternal mortality rates are found in the lower income groups. This chapter indicates that there is a strong relationship between mothers' level of education and child mortality, contraceptive use and health care.

Chapter Seven of the book focuses on gender equality and women's empowerment, which is the third millennium development goal. Naila Kabeer (1995) mentions the ways to achieve these goals are: closing the gender gap in education, equalizing wages and increasing women's participation in politics. The combination of these factors should contribute to women's agency and independence. It is well accepted that women's empowerment is possible through education, paid work and political participation.

Chapter Eight talks about institutionalizing gender equality goals in the policy process. There are several policy strategies developed such as the Poverty Reduction Strategy Paper (PRSP) which addresses gender equality and poverty reduction by national and international actors. Another strategy is the Gender Responsive Budget (GRB) which promotes greater transparency in the policy process for interests of gender equality. These strategies are important in gender equality analyses because in extreme patriarchy, economic growth fails to address gender discrimination; and even women's working conditions continue to deteriorate and remain insecure to women workers.

2.2 Book Summary: In Quest of empowerment: the Grameen Bank's impact on women's power and status by Ainon Nahar Mizan (1994)

The study presented in *In Quest of empowerment: the Grameen Bank's impact on women's power and status* by Ainon Nahar Mizan (1994) documents the result of an investigation into the effects of women's economic participation and earnings on their marital decision making power, that was carried out in rural Bangladesh. The author researches the Grameen Bank (GB). This Bank extends credit without collaterals to rural landless women in order to generate cash income and improve their economic conditions. It helps to create self-employment and contributes to the empowerment of women. The research examined the effects of rural work and income of Bangladeshi woman on her marital decision making power from the theoretical perspective of family sociology.

Chapter Two of Mizan's book deals with the demographic, socio-economic and cultural patterns of women's status in Bangladesh. In 1994, Bangladesh had a population 113.9 million people. More than half of the rural population was female. Of the 28.5 million civilian labour forces only 2.3 million were women. The majority of the population in Bangladesh is Muslim. Sons are highly valued in Bangladesh because they perpetuate the lineage and provide labour and income for the family. Rural women are confined to household work and have no decision making power in the family. Their work is invisible in the society.

Chapter Three reviews the sociological literature on women's economic participation and family decision making power to identify the gaps and problems between the two social aspects. Mizan analyses the concept of power, and its dynamic power relationship in the family decision making process from both an ideological and pragmatic point of view. She analyses these concepts pulling views from some sociologists like Max Weber, Blau and Szinovacz. To draw a concrete conclusion on the impact of the GB on its female borrowers, Mizan incorporated Blood and Wolf's Resource Theory which examined how resources of the spouses became effective in determining their levels of power in the family.

The actual design, methodology is described in chapter four. The study was conducted in 1988 in two villages of Bangladesh. 100 female borrowers of Grameen Bank have interviewed, 50 women from each villagen (one is controlled village and the other one is experimental village). For comparison, an equal number of non-GB women borrowers were interviewed from the same village. This was done in order to compare the differences in families of those not working and those engaged in income generating activities.

Chapter Five presents the major findings on household decision making power, fertility control, health care and political participation. The findings indicate that household decision making power by GB borrowers was significantly higher than non-borrowers of GB. The fidings indicate that GB loans were successful in creating income generating activities for women in the informal sectors of the economy in the experimental village.

The final chapter examines the theoretical and policy implications of the factors determining women's power. The two major implications of the findings in this study are that they are related to either family or to social policies of Bangladesh. Norms and social context essentially define what a wife's resource is and what it is not. In this sense, Blood and Wolf's theory is not enough to account for marital power in different social contexts. In rural Bangladesh, norms and role expectations determine the position one holds in the family and society. So resource theory alone does not provide a full expectation of women's marital power.

3. Part B: Analysis of the three books' themes

Institutional rules, norms, and conventions have powerful material effects on people's life (Kabeer, 1995). These are varied based upon standards of the family, community and society, influence gender division of labour (productive versus reproductive) and participation in economic activities by women and men. The influence of patriarchy results in lower rates of female labour force participation outside home in society. **Annexure: 1** Women are forced to operate their families silently with male authority both in the home and outside (Kabeer, 1995; Mizan, 1994).

Different institutions like states, markets, civil society/community and kinship/family determine the processes of production and reproduction, distribution of resources within a society and are influenced by patriarchy (Kabeer, 1995). For example, the state is responsible for the general leadership of society and different gender rules are determined and executed by it. Markets are based on the idea of "maximization of profit" and resources are exchanged through contractual entitlements. Maryling Waying (2001) asserts that kinship/ families are the forms of social organization that includes clans that are based on descent, marriage and various forms of adoption. These institutions do not often work in egalitarian ways; instead they support hierarchical relationships which are dominated by patriarchy. There are biases and preconceptions in the household and community to allocate resources (Kabeer, 1995; Waying 2001).

These biases result in inequalities of ownership or access to the means of production (land, capital, finance, and equipment) between men and women (Waying, 2001). Therefore, gender inequality is constructed through both formal laws and unwritten norms. In the words of Naila Kabeer (1995), "[The] different rules, norms and values [that] govern the gender division of labour and the gender distribution of resources are critical elements for understanding the nature of gender inequality in different societies" (p. 51). Instead of being directly involved in gender stereotyping, state or market institutions become *'bearers of gender'*. They position women and men unequally in access to resources and assign them unequal value in the public domain (Kabeer 1995 & 2003). For example, in Seguino's study, findings show that gender inequalities in wages contribute to positive economic growth in patriarchal societies because social and political institutions support male power (Kabeer, 2003, p. 78). This positive synergy between economic growth and gender inequities in wages can be found in Hindu and Muslim dominated areas like India and Bangladesh, not excluding other regions

According to Naila Kabeer (2003) gender is one of the key organizing principles upon which the distribution of labour, property and other valued resources in society are based. It exists everywhere in patriarchal society. Even NGOs treat women as dependent clients than active clients and banks refuse to lend to women entrepreneurs. The state treats women as second class citizens. That is why Naila Kabeer (1995) says, 'While institutional norms, beliefs, customs and practices help to explain the distribution of gender resources and responsibilities in different social groups" (p. 77). Patriarchy reinforces the interrelation of social norms that favor men and they create gender discrimination. For example, employers refuse to recruit women, discourage membership in trade unions and professional association.

Within the region of South Asia especially Bangladesh, which is this paper's main focus, religion is a major factor in creating and maintaining gender inequalities. **Annexure 2.** As seen in Mizan's book, the country is mainly divided between the Hindu and Muslim sects and these two systems serve to sub-serve some category of women. Hinduism is based on a caste system, which discriminates against women of lower and poorer castes. Islam on the other hand, relegates women into the private sphere, in light of the practice of *purdah* which states that the woman's place is in the home or extends so far as her husband or male superior approves. As a result of these practices, these women are either confined to household reproductive labour or to the limited informal sector where they are more prone to exploitations.

Mizan's (1994) research findings on the Resource Theory shows that loans and other financial resource has positive impact on poor women's self-employment and income as well as productivity-whatever little they earn contributes to the increasing household and per capita income (Mizan, p. 79). Resource opportunities for women lead to an emphasis on competence and achievement. In this context, achieved resources of the spouses become effective in determining their levels of power in the family. In addition, to decrease Islamic religion's depressing effect on women's decision-making power, some local practices of Islam that have negative impact on women's status should be dispelled.

Women in Bangladesh have different experiences from men in regards to labour force participation. There are two major factors connected to this issue: (1) the under-representation of females in economic sector (market economy) and (2) the over representation of women in the informal labour market

The impact of patriarchy extends into inequalities in labour force participation by members of both genders. Gender inequalities in the market means that women's labour is not calculated accurately or not recognized. The market and state do not provide resources to women for their equal participation in the labor market. Women are doubly disadvantaged in terms of their sex as well as that they have two main areas of responsibility while men have only one. Their time is divided between the household and the workplace. Women must carry out many tasks ranging from child care, food preparation, agricultural works, cleaning, and services to husband and all other domestic chores. In Bangladesh women work 10% longer than men, but only 35% of their work is counted in National Accounts (Kabeer, 2003; p. 74). 50% of women's work time goes into unpaid family labour in agricultural production among middle income families (Kabeer, 2003). These informal aspects of female labor are excluded from the national economy.

Despite their exclusion from income calculations, rural women in Bangladesh have always been active in both *'income generating'* and *'income conserving'* production. Naila Kabeer (2003) gives the example of a myriad of agricultural activities such as reaping and crop preparation that is carried out by these rural women which is a major contribution to the agricultural economy in their regions as well as to the whole country. These activities unfortunately also remain invisible.

Women's pattern of works in recent decades has experienced change. There has been a rise in the percentage of women in the labor force and an accompanying increase in their share of overall employment (Kabeer, 2003; Marying, 2001). For example, women's participation in manufacturing and service industries like tourism, garment, plastic industries and other manufacturing works have increased more rapidly than men's in India and Bangladesh. Women are also becoming increasingly involved in export sectors of market economies. In some regions women comprise 60% of this sector of the economy (Kabeer, 2003, p. 69)

Unfortunately, the characteristics of the new forms of labour (garment, fruits, vegetables and flowers packaging) in the formal employment results in different forms of exploitation from outworking, contract work, casual labor, part time work and home-based work (Kabeer, 2003). Women in these areas are usually grossly underpaid, forced to work for very long hours with forced overtime, have poor living conditions and often exposed to hazardous work environments leading to sickness. According to the MSN Resource Centre, women comprise 85% of the workforce in the garment sector, earning an average of US$1.54 per day. This industry is very age restrictive as employers tend to favor women up to the age of 35. Women outside of this group face severe discrimination, and are liable to lose their jobs. Within these areas of production women's jobs are highly insecure, devoid of pensions, no household or health benefits and there is almost no possibility of advancement.

The situation for men in the economic sector is the adverse of women. Men generally make more than the women in the market. They have more opportunities available to them. They are able to travel as the rules of *purdah* do not apply to them but are rather controlled by them. They usually have higher levels of education, and therefore are not restricted finding work in the informal or the agricultural sector. For example, in the factories men are the overseers and the supervisors while the women are the main labour force.

Another aspect of exploitation of female labour comes in the form of structural adjustment policies (SAPs) which are used by the IMF and the World Bank. This export oriented market through globalization and SAP has negative effects on the female labor market because of changes in the technology of transportation, telecommunication and dismantling of the regulatory frameworks of national and local markets for labor and capital. SAPs create *newly poor* in developing countries and increase the invisibility of women's involvement. Women are concentrated in lower skilled and lower paid jobs because of fast changing technology (Kabeer, 2003). SAPs put pressure on women to work more in factory related industries for minimal earnings. Therefore, women are victims in this globalization processes because society continues to invest less in women's skills development.

The migration of poor women to urban areas in search of employment has been increasing in Bangladesh. This is in response to the limited availability of both agricultural and off-farm paid work. However, this move to urban areas requires some mobility skills, financial capital and other technical skills. **Annexure-3**. These unskilled poor women are at an extreme disadvantage as they do domestic work, often living in with employers and have very low wage, work long hours which may be detrimental to their health.

Family wage is another example of inequality that continues to be a reality for women today because women continue to receive lower wages for the same work. The original idea behind this was that men would support the family and women would not work outside the house. If they did work, it is argued that they would receive lower wages because they do not have the responsibility of supporting the children.

In Bangladesh, women may receive as little as half the wage that a man receives for doing the same job. Patriarchy has positive relationship between gender inequities in wages and rates of economic growth.

Furthermore, women and men may have different hierarchical positions in the marketplace. There are large numbers of women in the formal economy although they are underrepresented at the higher levels and over-represented in those lower down. For example, women in South Asia, a region with extreme patriarchy continue to be concentrated in unpaid family work (over 60 percent of the female work force) while in sub-Saharan Africa percentages of women in unpaid family work is generally below 60 percent" (Kabeer, 2003; p. 72). So it is indeed a tragedy for women who have unequal access to economic opportunities in the labor market.

The household structure to which a woman is exposed may affect the extent to which she participates in the labour market and how this participation may in turn impact her power and position in her household. There are four types of household structures to be considered: joint families, nuclear families, corporate households and segmented households. **Annexture-4.**

Family structure places men at the head of the household in decision making and providing for the family. In Bangladesh, *male farming systems* are prevalent. Therefore, men make up the majority of the agricultural labour force. These households would then tend to be completely dominated by the husbands who would make most of the important decisions, and would control all the resources. In comparison female farming systems, which are found mainly in regions of Sub-Saharan Africa, are those systems in which the females dominate in the agricultural sector and have much more egalitarian and self-sufficient positions within their households (Kabeer, 2003).

The corporate and segmented households are connected to these two types of agricultural systems. In the corporate family structure men own most of the household's material assets control the labor of women and children and determine women's relationship with non-familial world. On the other hand, in the fragmented family structure men and women have separate but interdependent responsibilities in production, and separate, but interdependent objectives to their families. Within segmented households men and women combine their income and an egalitarian household structure exists. Corporate households are related to regions such as Bangladesh where men are the absolute heads, who are involved in the formal market economy; while segmented structures are found mainly in Sub Saharan Africa where both spouses contribute towards household income.

Joint and nuclear family settings exist in Bangladesh, but the nuclear family is increasing. In the nuclear family, specific gender roles are assigned to the husband and wife. It is not a natural organization. In the '*ideal*' nuclear family, the women are the caregivers, breeders and domestics; while men are the breadwinner. It is the source of gender inequality. Here men and women are differentiated by the division of labor. The emergence of the nuclear family is a consequence of complex interactions between male power and a capitalistic society. Gender division of labor creates a power difference between women and men. It adds to the subordination of women. As a result, women are dependent on men for economic support. However, in the joint/extended family women have more egalitarian positions in the agricultural society although men and women have some responsibility both inside and outside the home. This egalitarian extended family values has changed by introduction plantation and cash crop economy. Men have more power and privileges in the labor market in the nuclear family.

Different findings show that increasing the wage of wives has significant positive impact on their economic status as well as the whole household. In addition, wife's income contribution enhances her position in the family and increases her power in decision making. It especially in the areas of fertility control decision about how many children to have. Mizan's study findings (1994) acknowledged a wife's income gives her leverage in power relations in the family due to her breaking away from the traditional roles of housewife and child bearer to enter the provider role.

Anon Nahar Mizan (1994) studies on Grameen Bank finds that women's dependency on male members is getting reduced and there is emerging a new pattern of relationship in their households and in the society as they are growing earning members. They are not only gaining economic independence, but are also emerging as a social force to fight away all prejudices and obstacles (Mizan, p. 23). Orthodox economic thinkers still have biases that produce constraints to policy makers in developing effective poverty reduction strategies through the concepts of price stability, marketization, commoditization, and the male bread winner (Kabeer, p. 212). They never think gender equality in labor force participation in the market. So in macroeconomic there is no gender equality rather more discrimination exists against women in employment, gender specific role. For example, women do secretarial jobs, men do construction jobs.

Conservative policy makers treat human resources as natural resources. They generally think that a reduction of men's poverty would automatically reduce poverty in women. Women's earnings are considered secondary and so priority is given to the primary breadwinner, men. However, households are not egalitarian and there major inequalities in the distribution of basic needs (Waying, 2001). Therefore, women and children may not benefit from an improvement in the improvement in the man's economic condition. To make macro-economic policies more gender aware, it needs to understand women's contribution in production and reproduction. Therefore, more attention needs to be paid to the microeconomic sector of the family which is the key institution of the reproductive economy; and where women make major contributions.

Although in Millennium development goals poverty reduction has taken a central place in development effort and pro-poor growth; however, gender equalityis still not the first priority in MDGs (Kabeer, 2003). Although there are several development polices and strategies that have been developed with the help of international agencies to address gender and poverty; this paper will pay special attention to Poverty Reduction strategy Papers (PRSP), Gender Responsive Budgets (GRB), Sectoral Strategy for Poverty Policy (SSPP)and Gender Management System (GMS) that are used in macroeconomic policy. **Annexture-5.**

The poverty reduction strategy paper (PRSP) audits the gender activities and reviews the role of gender responsive budgets (GRB). PRSP deals with a country's macro-economic structural and social policies and programs to promote economic growth and reduce poverty and to identify external financial needs of a country (Kabeer, 2003). It examines the role of the institutionalization of gender competences in the policy process. However, it does not consider gender inequality which has negative effects on household livelihood. Although PRSP explore opportunity for gender mainstreaming and poverty reduction, it has not; however, become an integral component of aid-cooperation agencies but rather, is heavily influenced by the World Bankand IMF and grown reliant on external technical advice. Although the gender issue in PRSP is better integrated in health, nutrition, population and education sector, it is vague because if gender issues not brought up at the diagnostic stage, it is unlikely appear in the action or monitoring stages (Kabeer, 2003).

PRSP policy design was studied in Burkina Faso, Gambia, Vietnam and Kenya. The studies identified low levels of productivity in farm and off-farm activities where there was an imperfect market for goods and services which contributes to rural poverty. Unequal educational opportunities held back women's employment in the modern labour market (Kabeer, 2003). It expands global rules of trade and global market expansion regulated by bi-lateral and multilateral trading agreement, tariffs and non-tariffs barriers. These barriers cost $100 billion a year, twice as much as they receive in international aid (Kabeer, 2003, p. 211). PRSP pays little attention to women's role in reproductive economy, voice and influence on macroeconomic policies. Issues like domestic violence and political education are not considered to be relevant to poverty reduction strategies.

The Sectoral Strategies for Poverty Policy (SSPP) are used by macroeconomic policy makers. This strategy emphasizes key opportunities and constraints within and across sectors because there are interconnections between mezzo and micro level analyses of household strategies with macro level analysis. However, it is a question of sectoral priority for resource allocation to poor, disadvantaged women because women are at a greater disadvantage in their reproductive well-being which is culturally discounted within the family.

The Gender Responsive Budget (GRB) is also called the gender sensitive budget (Kabeer, 2003). It aims to assess the impact of government budgets mainly at the national level for different groups of men and women. It analyzes gender-targeted allocations, expenditures across all sectors and services and reviews equal allocations of expenditure within government services (Ibid, 2003). GRB analysis plays a number of different roles in promoting greater transparency in the policy development process and strengthening accountability. It intends for government expenditures to target women and to promote gender equality. However, gender commitments are backed by financial resources and are tied to PRSP technical cooperation aid. GRB does not interfere with location-specific variations on gender inequalityissues at the micro level.

Although gender equality exists in MGD; however, still some barriers exist in the mainstream society. For example, lack of political will, under funding and marginalization in women affairs, and institutionalization of patriarchal intent and deep rooted resistance in budgetary allocations. To avoid the above barriers on policies of gender equality the Common Wealth Secretariat developed Gender Management System (GMS) tools for maintaining gender in policy making. GMS is a set of concepts and methodologies built to develop network structures, mechanisms and processes that are intended to develop policies, plans and programs for women and to provide comprehensive gender inequality analysis. However, the success of gender mainstreaming requires a review of national development plans. GMS is intended to bring fundamental and lasting change in society but it starts organizational change at the government level; which is a shortcoming because change requires gender awareness strategies at the grass roots level to change the formal and informal norms, rules and attitudes that institutionalize inequalities. However, government agencies are working at the macro and mezzo levels that are far from grass-roots.

Lack of gender expertise in policy making bodies adds to a lack of consultation with primary stakeholders. This can be effectively addressed by building up active and organized constituencies at the grass root levels through consciousness raising to exercise pressure for gender equality goals and to hold governments and states accountable for their action or inaction (Kabeer, 2003). In Bangladesh some NGOS like *Narri Pakka* and *Nijera Korri* started to monitor government services delivery at the local level despite their minimal influence. United Funds for Women (UNIFEM) played an important role to bring civil society together to promote GRB analysis. It seeks to empower women and women's organization to influence budget decisions and advocate for women's equality by building their technical budget expertise (Kabeer, 2003). However, UNIFEM is an international external resource organization that is not always available to support all countries. Therefore, national gender budget experts are necessary for mobilizing gender equality goals and national gender action plan through collective action by women advocacy group.

Gender equality in labour markets, access to services, household economics and in policy process is not a linear one because patrilineal oppression and dominance is still very much embedded in every aspect of society. It is the achievement of women's movement and other activities in different countries. All these activisms have positive implication in closing the gender gap in women's health services and education. It starts to count women's role as visible in the national economy; however, the concern still remains to engage institutions more directly with the policy process through gender activism. Therefore, the major challenge is for gender advocates and activists in the 21st Century to form alliances with others for seeing equitable international order to ensure that gender equality interests remain at the forefront of the struggle (Kabeer, 2003, p. 233).

Another recommendation involves increasing women's waged employment in the non-agricultural sector and to secure land tenure because a working wife bringing valued resources and income into the family is expected to gain a significant increase in decision making power relative to her husband and have more power than non-working wife. It is hoped that with the change in women's income, employment and education there will be other opportunities to change the extremity of patriarchal influence over women. Anion Nahar Mizan says (1994) that when both partners (husband and wife) contribute equally to their mutual satisfaction then they have egalitarian power in the family.

The Grameen Bank has also been extremely instrumental in providing income generating opportunities to women and in their overall empowerment through the extension of collateral free banking to rural poor women in Bangladesh. Women's participation in Grameen Bank results in their increased outside participation which increases their physical and social mobility. This will positively affect their role and position in society. However, there is still a great need for the government to reform labor market policy and introduce affirmative actions to promote labor market equality and ensure women's access to productive resources, mobilize efforts to break the patriarchal dominance in the labor market and alter economic and institutional arrangements to promote more choices to women (Kabeer, 2003; and Waying, 2001).

4. Conclusion

In three books, by Kabeer, Marying and Mizan, they critically examined Bengali disadvantaged women situation in Bangladesh. These females are doubly disadvantaged in both poverty and gender. The writers also agree, as it has been presented in this paper that these women may be empowered and their socio-economic and political conditions improved through the continued and increased work of NGOs and the restructuring of decision-making, policy development and increased opportunities are necessary for formal labour market participation. One concrete example can be found in Mizan's study where she concludes from her findings that the creation of social welfare mechanisms especially micro-lending seems to be a highly successful means of bettering the conditions of the rural poor and overriding the conditions that create poverty. However, gender equality is threatened by male power and privilege of policy makers. Therefore, the opinion of this author is that it is imperative that the elements of patriarchy be dismantled through rethinking and restructuring of policy making before any major changes towards gender neutrality can occur in Bangladesh.

5. Annexure

Annexure 1

Institutions related to female labor market

Market	State	Family	Patriarchy
Rural agricultural and Off-farm activities Urban domestic work Cash crop and plantation economy World Trade Organization (WTO) Globalization, Capitalism Service Industries (Hospitality and Tourism) Manufacturing (garment, plastic and their processing works Export Promotion Zone	Macroeconomic policy National Planning Commission Man power Bureau Structural Adjustment Policy National Budget Multinational Corporations Bilateral agencies and Multilateral International organizations (World Bank, IMF and UN) Bureaucrats NGOs	Production & reproduction Asraf & Atraf Muslim family Economic & Social values of girl Agricultural and off-farm activities Microeconomic households Kinship- patrialinial & patrilocal Exogamy & Endogamy Polygamy	Private & Public realm Masculinity &femininity Religion: Hindu & Muslim Caste system (Social Stratification) Rural elites Money lender & rich farmer Police and Courts Parliament Traditional Customary law Norms and Values Media

Annexure 2

Gender Inequality in Bangladesh

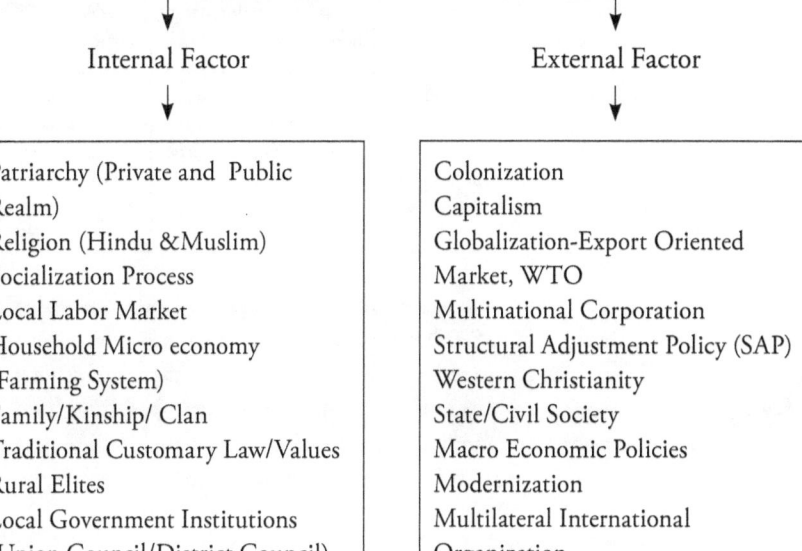

Internal Factor	External Factor
Patriarchy (Private and Public Realm)	Colonization
Religion (Hindu &Muslim)	Capitalism
Socialization Process	Globalization-Export Oriented Market, WTO
Local Labor Market	Multinational Corporation
Household Micro economy (Farming System)	Structural Adjustment Policy (SAP)
Family/Kinship/ Clan	Western Christianity
Traditional Customary Law/Values	State/Civil Society
Rural Elites	Macro Economic Policies
Local Government Institutions (Union Council/District Council)	Modernization
Nationalism/Tribalism	Multilateral International Organization
	Private and Public Sector Organization

Annexure 3

Gender inequality, women labor and household povertyin South Asia

Country	The gender distribution of work in rural areas	Household poverty & women's paid work in rural areas	Gender & work in urban areas	Household povertyand women's work in urban areas
India	Landless poor in lower cast in both off-farm activities such as non-agricultural wage labor and high female labor force participation in agricultural waged labor.	Women from landless and land-poor households have the highest participation in paid work -women combine paid and unpaid work with domestic chores	-Workers in the organized sector are mainly high caste, skilled male workers -poor women are in the informal economy -women's participation in the urban labor force is lower than men's and that also exist in rural areas.	-women are involved in low paying, low skilled jobs -lowest paying home worker and the informal economy which is most women are involve in

Country	The gender distribution of work in rural areas	Household poverty & women's paid work in rural areas	Gender & work in urban areas	Household povertyand women's work in urban areas
Bangladesh	growing landless, declining farm size -off farm activity such as construction, trade, transport Female labor force participation remains low	-Greater poverty in households with female wage earners because their husband's income is in sufficient or due to death, sickness etc.	-A rise in females living in urban areas -poor women migrate to the city to earn a living mainly in exports such as the garment industry	-gender segmentation in the informal economy -women worked in the garment factories while men worked in skilled crafts, transport and service (Kabeer, 2003)

Note: This graph illustrates and agrees with Nalia Kabeer's (2003) study that female seclusion in regions like South Asia of extreme patriarchy explains women's low levels of labor force participation. Work in the public sector demonstrates women's loss of work and status in the domestic sphere. Rural poverty is lined with caste rural wage labor and landlessness in India and Bangladesh. Urban poverty is linked with an attempt for the rural poor to search for employment.

Annexure 4: *Family Structure*

Family Structure   Extended family
                          Nuclear Family
                          Corporate Family (Male Farming)
                          Segmented Family (Female Headed Farming)
                          De-Jure Female Headed Household
                          De-facto Female Headed Household

Annexure 5: *Gender Poverty Policies/Strategies*

Gender Poverty Policies/Strategies : Basic Needs Approach (BNA)
                          : Poverty Reduction Strategy Paper (PPRS)
                          : Gender Responsive Budget (GRB)
                          : Sectoral Strategy Poverty Policy (SPP)
                          : Gender Management System (GMS)
                          : Bargaining Model
                          : United Nations Institution of Feminism (UNIFEM)

6. References

Kabeer, N. (1995). *Reserved Realities-Gender Hierarchies in Development Thought.* London, Great Britain, Biddles Ltd.

Kabeer, N. (2003) *Gender mainstreaming in poverty eradication and the millennium development goals.* Ottawa: International Development Research Center (CIDA)

Mizan, A. N. (1994). *In Quest of empowerment: the Grameen Bank's impact on women's power and status.* Dhaka: The University Press.

Rouf, K. A. (2015). Against all odds: Socio-economic and political factors related to female labor force participation and decision making power in Bangladesh. *International Journal of Research Studies in Management,* Vol.5 (1), pp. 53-63.

Rouf, K. A. (2015). Micro financing implementation and expansion strategies of Grameen Bank in Bangladesh. *Global Journal of Management and Business Research* (C), Vol. 15 (10), pp. 7-14.

Waring, M. (2001). *If Women Counted (Film). Ottawa:* National Film Board of Canada (NFBC)

Wong, W. A. (2002). *The Poor Women- A Critical Analysis of Asian Theology and Contemporary Chinese Fiction by Women.* New York: Peter Lang.

Green Economics and Bio-diversity Through Green Micro-Financing

Abstract

In the industrialized and the globalised capitalist world, market consumption is rapidly expanding and creating needless hyper consumption wishes among people, increasing waste that pollutes the environment. Hegemonic globalization destroys local initiatives and the local economy. This paper discusses the importance of waste reduction to preserving a healthy environment, and the use of micro financing to promote small green enterprises that focus on reuse, recycling and re-building. These green small enterprises can foster a sense of community organizing and build local economies.

Global enterprises are weakening and even destroying local economies. Modern capitalistic industries are producing wastes, produces carbon emissions, deforestation, loss of biodiversity and rangeland, soil degradation, air and water pollution. Hegemonic globalization destroys diversified green local initiatives and the local economy. To counter this hegemonic economic power, it is vital to create alternative green economic biodiversity forces, where green micro financing to green social small businesses can play an active role in green biodiversity socio-economic development, address the issue of poverty and environmental development. Green micro-finance institutions could finance to green small entrepreneurs to involve in biodiversity businesses, agricultural food productions, and other pro-environmental social enterprises.

In Bangladesh, solar panels, solar water pumps and solar cookers, energy savings stoves, bio-gas plants are promoting and serving to people through Grameen Shakti, a green micro-financing organization in Bangladesh. This organization also supplies green energy products and environmental education in the villages in Bangladesh, but it is not involve in organizing training workshops on biodiversity education. However, green microfinance program can include organizing training workshops on bio-diversity education (nursery, homestead gardening, renewable energy, biogas plant among MFIs officials, and clients in Bangladesh.

Key words: Bio-diversity; climate change; environmental development, globalization; green businesses, green economy; green micro-financing; and local living economics.

Acronyms: Grameen Bank (GB) Grameen Shakti (GS), Integrated Pest Management (IPM), Micro finance institutions (MFIs), and Non-government Organizations (NGOs).

Thesis statement: This paper discusses the importance of waste reduction to preserving a healthy environment, and the use of micro financing to promote small green enterprises that focus on reuse, recycling and re-building. These small enterprises can foster a sense of community and build local economies.

1.0. Introduction

In the industrialized capitalist world, market consumption is rapidly expanding, increasing waste that pollutes the environment. Hegemonic globalization of capitalism destroys local initiatives and the local economy everywhere in the world. The world has become an increasingly unequal place- the gap between the haves and have-nots has widened. For example, over fifty countries are now poorer than they were ten years ago. Access to basic services such as clean drinking water is getting worse in some countries. Corporations are over-extracting natural resources, depleting the earth's richness and creating huge waste in their production processes. Global enterprises are weakening and even destroying local economies.

Marx calls it the tyranny of nature. It creates poverty among disadvantaged people and brings excessive wealth to the rich. However, our natural resources are limited. Global warming is increasing, and it negatively affects nature, people, and communities. This is while corporations are making large profits without an appropriate level of social and environmental responsibility. Brian Milani (2000) says, "Modern capitalism maintained material scarcity through waste production" (p. 23). Hence, there is no turning point from this process, unless there is an alternative development strategy- a green economic movement. This movement needs people-centered communities managing their energy and water needs locally and focusing on the reduction of waste and environmental renewal. Through increased corporate responsibility and a service-based economy, communities can grow stronger. In this paper, describes concepts that define and measure green economics: sustainable development, waste management and community economic development. In the paper, I first explain environmental degradation through waste and its management. Secondly, the paper discusses the role of micro financing in green economics, and finally, it narrates a conclusion with some recommendations for Bangladesh and for North American society.

2.0. Description of concepts

2.1.0. Green business

For the author, the green business can be explained: (1) business that involves in manufacturing and waste management (2) Local vs. global energy and economics. In Milani's words, *it is more than clean up and environmental protection.* He says, "Green economics is capital, material and energy savings, and people intensive" (p. 75). Green businesses are necessary for human being, wildlife and marine livings and for the Mother Earth long-lasting services to pollution free ecology and anthropogrenee. Therefore, scholars termed green business as sustainable business, which is an enterprise that has minimal negative impact on the global or local environment, community, society, or economy-a business that strives to meet the triple bottom line. Often, sustainable businesses have progressive environmental and human rights policies. Green business is functioning in a capacity where no negative impact is made on the local or global environment, the community, or the economy. A *green business* will also engage in forward-thinking policies for environmental concerns and policies affecting human rights. People coined green business with green economy. The green economy aims at reducing environmental risks and ecological scarcities, and that aims for sustainable development without degrading the environment. It is closely related with ecological economics, but has a more politically applied focus. The 2011 UNEP Green Economy Report argues "that to be green, an economy must not only be efficient, but also fair. Fairness implies recognising global and country level equity dimensions, particularly in assuring a just transition to an economy that is low-carbon, resource efficient, and socially inclusive."

Green economics is different from traditional economics. Green economics is the direct valuation of natural capital and ecological services as having economic value. However, general economics see everything in terms of money, and products have contributed to GDP. General traditional economics has quantitative values, but green economics has both quantitative and qualitative values are stainable in the community and in the state.

2.2.0. Waste

Waste is any substance which is discarded after primary use, or it is worthless, defective and of no use. Bodily waste synonymous are garbage, rubbish, trash, refuse, litter, debris, flotsam and jetsam, dross, junk, detritus, scrap materials through in the landfills, forest, mountains, rivers, lacks, seas, and oceans. Every day huge amounts of waste/garbage are created by individual dwellings, restaurants, hospitals and factories. They are throughing and using or expending wastes carelessly, extravagantly, or to no purpose; materials that are not wanted; the unusable remains or by-products of something. Wastes are material, substance, or by-product that are eliminated or discarded as no longer useful or not required after the completion of a process. *Waste* and *wastes* are unwanted or unusable materials. Examples include municipal solid waste, (household trash/refuse), hazardous waste, waste water (such as sewage, which contains bodily wastes (feces and urine) and surface runoff), radioactive waste, and others.

Carbon emissions, waste and corporate businesses have negative environmental impacts include deforestation, loss of biodiversity and range land, soil degradation, air and water pollution that are responsible for corporate economics. Environmental issues are becoming more pressing to corporate economics due to accelerated GDP economic development, natural resource depletion, and rapid population growth. In North America, energy consumption is a big issue which is threat to ecological sustainable development. Because human petro mobile energy love affair with the automobile is costing us more than fill-ups at the gas pump. Huge areas of Western communities are eaten up by parking lots, the emissions are polluting our air, and we get less exercise.

Companies are producing 94% waste materials that degrade the environment (Milani, 2000, p-144). In North America, most people prefer not to pay attention to the negative effects of emissions on the Earth. Packaging waste is also a huge problem. Energy consumption from USA is 21% (Myers & Kent, 1998).

One of the main messages of the paper is that we cannot continue to disregard the environment as we have for the past several hundred years. The paper shows how the industrialized economies based on capital growth and over-use of natural resources have created waste that is harming the environment badly.

Companies make products that end up as garbage, and tax payers are responsible for the waste removal and management. Therefore, zero waste/closed loops and shifting the responsibility for waste management to the manufacturing companies is vital to environmental protection.

In Germany, they banned disposable plastic cutlery in favour of washable cutlery. In addition, to reducing plastic waste, this move actually created new businesses that washed and sterilized metal cutlery. Neil Seldman (2003), in his article *The New Recycling Movement-Part-1*, documented the great success of the recycling movement. For example, recycled materials increased from 5% in 1968 to 30% in 2003. By 2000, there were 56,000 recycling companies employing 1.1 million, with annual sales of $236 billion.

However, there are still today huge amounts of broken and outdated products creating waste in the environment when they could be repaired and/or recycled. Waste from hospitals could be reduced by sterilizing reusable instruments rather than using disposable instruments.

2.3.0. Extended producer responsibility (EPR) for disposal of manufacturers' products

Transition to a service economy with manufacturers being responsible for final disposal of their products (extended producer responsibility (EPR) would motivate manufacturers to build better products with a longer life. Extended Producer Responsibility (EPR) is a policy approach under which producers are given a significant responsibility–financial and/or physical–for the treatment or disposal of post-consumer products. In the field of waste management, *extended producer responsibility (EPR)* is an important strategy designed to promote the integration of environmental costs associated with goods throughout their life cycles into the market price of the products. Extended producer responsibility (EPR) is an environmental policy approach in which a producer's responsibility for a product is extended to the post-consumer stage of a product's life cycle.

Manufacturers would also build products to be upgradeable and to be disassembled easily. Not only would this help to reduce waste but would help manufacturers build long and loyal relationships with customers. In North America, environmentalists are trying to move to zero waste/closed loop productionand promote a service economy. Today municipalities manage the disposal of garbage using taxpayers' money.

In North America, the transition from a waste economy to a service economy will not be an easy one to make. It will be a challenging transition because companies today focus so much of their effort on minimizing labor costs as labor is the most expensive component of manufacturing in an economy that undervalues natural resources. Companies save money by reducing staff. For example, General Motors (GM) is reducing staff to minimize production costs. Many corporations exploit cheap labor by relocating their manufacturing plants to third world countries. Today's corporate obsession with growth and selling more things are difficult sickness to cure. And, until this sickness is under control, waste will continue to be one of our toughest challenges. Manufacturers have honed technology to a point where it is cheaper to throw away most products and buy new rather than repair. The only way to break this cycle is to make either the consumer or the manufacturer pay for the cost of disposal.

The best way to motivate manufacturers to design products for long life is to extend their responsibility to the end of the product life cycle and make them pay for disposal. Most consumers hate the thought of throwing away an item such as a phone, microwave, computer, refrigerator, television, or camera, but getting repairs and/or upgrades is more difficult, and in many cases more expensive, than buying new. If companies can make it easier and affordable to repair or upgrade products, that would be the choice of many consumers. We need to take advantage of consumers' desire to waste less.

Largely in response to pressure from the public, Sony has begun taking back their products in certain areas, while Kodak and Fuji are taking back disposable cameras. Milani identifies Xerox as a good example of a 'document service' company that leases the majority of its equipment and takes it back. They are looking at ways to upgrade and recycle as much as possible.

As learned from many readings, it is found that consumers have been quite successful in lobbying and applying pressure to companies to improve their environmental record. Their efforts, however, must be organized and long term.

Micro financing is a type of banking service that is provided to unemployed or low-income individuals or groups who otherwise have no other access to financial services, is another tool that can help in this transition to a service economy. Banks and government agencies could develop a loan product called 'green loans' for individuals and small companies looking for financing to start businesses that are focused on repairing and recycling existing products. Brawngart (1994) suggests building waste 'supermarkets' and recycling centers. Large manufacturers could 'outsource' their disassembly and recycling responsibilities to small companies or franchises located in cities and smaller towns where consumers can return broken or outdated products. This would help in the creation of good jobs, reduce waste, and preserve our resources.

A group of individuals could start a small businesses coming to people's homes to fix small appliances. Now that the world has gone wireless and digital, could someone find a way to recycle the materials used in cassette tapes, and soon CDs that will no longer be used?

In the textile area, some interesting new developments are taking place, such as Honeywell developing a recyclable nylon fibre. Garment industries fabrics wastes are called 'Jottes' that are using for manufacturing household matt products and other household usable products in Bangladesh. As we have read, carpeting is a very good area for transition to a 'service' business, where consumers 'lease' carpets or at least return used carpeting for recycling (Braungut 1994).

NGOs can help by advocating for policy change regarding responsibility for waste management. They could lobby for a shift in responsibility to private companies, ideally through some kind of incentive program, but failing that, through penalties. Governments need to do their part by creating tough but realistic policy and legislation that other third parties such as insurance companies, banks, and consumers can hold companies accountable to. N. Gunningham, M. Phillipson and P. Grabosky (1999) in their article *Harnessing Third Parties as Surrogate Regulators: Achieving Environmental Outcomes by Alternative Means* suggest that government would do better to support self-regulatory efforts of private enterprise, and work with them to define performance benchmarks. If the benchmarks are not met, that's when penalties or the influence of third parties can be more effective. Policing and monitoring is very expensive, so other tactics are preferable.

Dare O'Rourke in his article *Market Movements -NGO Strategies to Influence Global Production and Consumption* (2005) suggests NGOs should also get involved in setting standards and monitoring compliance with regulations.

How can we educate North American society about the damage that has been done to the environment through waste, and how we need to adopt new behaviour in order to restore our planet to better health?

The issue is particularly directed at North Americans, as it is evident that our European and far Eastern neighbours are not the environment offenders that we are. A European study found in 1997 that the per capita material throughput was 80 tons per American, 51 tons per citizen of the European Union, and 45 tons per Japanese. These numbers indicate that terrible waste is taking place in the manufacturing processes, particularly in North America

Jacquelyn Ottman, in her article *Green Marketing- Opportunity for Innovation (1998),* says that 8% of consumers' claims to know a lot about environment issues, leaving 92% who do not understand the state of our environmental problems and the threat to human and wild life. An environmental sensitization program built into our education system and communicated via the media is clearly needed.

Micro finance can contribute as one of the tools not only to finance small businesses and provide employment, but also to contribute to environmental development, including educational programs. How can a micro financing program help deliver a green economy? Micro financing institutions (MFIs) can enable loans for recycling and service economyprojects. Loans can be used to reduce and recycle waste, generate local energy, and work with large institutions to implement better recycling and reuse projects. Government can provide incentives to companies for waste reduction and recycle projects. Government can make available soft loans to these business people. NGOs can provide training in this transition to a service economy. Targets for 'zero waste' and progress on meeting those targets is urgent. This is the essence of the green economy and the course.

Brain Milani's book *Designing the Green Economy: the Post-industrial Alternative to Corporate Globalization* speaks on behalf of green businesses and opposes transnational corporations and chain stores. However, green business is not popular in North America. Rather it is struggling to survive and compete with big, consumer-hungry businesses. The growth and penetration of chain stores is substantial, and local governments typically welcome these new stores to their towns, not sufficiently aware of the negative impact potential on local retailers.

Local Economies, is a peer-reviewed journal operating as an interdisciplinary forum for the critical review of policy developments in the broad area of local economic development and urban regeneration. It seeks not only to publish analysis and critique papers, but also to disseminate innovative practice. However, local economy for the most part, is getting weaker, and every town is starting to look the same as Wal-Mart and Dunkin' Donuts dominate the landscape in North America. Even many other MNCs business locations occupied huge landscape in their business primacies all over the world. Moreover, due to MNCs businesses diversity, biodiversity is disappearing everywhere in the world.

3.0. Corporate World's businesses in the world and their destructions

Wal-Mart doesn't care about local communities and local businesses. They treat all people the same, and they put local retailers out of business.

Local economies usually lose out as well when it comes to government subsidies. Corporate world overriding small businesses even they are mushroomed by perverse subsidies. Corporate means relating to business corporations or to a particular business corporation. Corporate world is synonym with corporate capitalism is a term used in to describe a capitalist market place characterized by the dominance of hierarchical, bureaucratic corporations.

A large proportion of the economy of the Bangladesh even every country corporate world labour market falls within corporate control. In the developed world, corporations dominate the market place, comprising 50% or more of all businesses. Those businesses which are not corporations contain the same bureaucratic structure of corporations, but there is usually a sole owner or group of owners who are liable to bankruptcy and criminal charges relating to their business. Corporations have limited liability and remain less regulated and accountable than sole proprietorships.

Norman Myers (1998) in his article *"Perverse Subsidies: Tax $$ Undercutting our Economics and Environments Alike"* estimates, "there are over $1.5 trillion in perverse subsidies paid out by the governments worldwide." These are subsidies that the author believes have a negative effect on the economy and the environment in the long run. Coal subsidies are costing Germany $6.7 billion. Removing these perverse subsidies has the potential to decrease the rate of biodiversity loss, promote sustainable resource use, and create further revenue generating capacities that can be targeted toward activities that promote conservation (James et al.,1999). In the paper discussions, there are a concerns raised about the huge subsidies offered each year to big businesses at the federal, state and local levels. Subsidies are not a right, and need to be re-evaluated carefully. This amount of money, properly channeled into environmental programs, could have a tremendously positive effect.

Bangladesh has reduced fertilizer subsidies dramatically. The Environmental Summit in South America discussed how governments could redirect perverse subsidies into positive initiatives in support of sustainable development. Gary Gardner and Erick Assadourian in their article *Rethinking the Goodlife* strongly advocates eliminating perverse subsidies and adopting pollution taxes to create a cleaner environment. However, today's tax approach does not encourage pro-social behavior. (Roberts 2005).

Stacy Mitchell in her article *Rebuilding Community-Rooted Enterprise* says that corporate chains are damaging the environment, undermining the social and civic fabric of communities, and weakening local economies. Expansion of chain stores needs to stop because chain stores are: consuming land at a staggering pace, creating major problems through storm water runoff, and increasing air pollution through the entire automobile and truck traffic they generate huge air pollution in nature. Mitchell suggests having a size limit on chain stores, steering business downtown, and doing thorough impact reviews when chain stores try to come to town. She also suggests for stoping subsidizing and offering incentives to local businesses.

4.0. Role of microfinance institutions (MFIs) and community organizations to environmentalism

Grameen Bank (GB) micro financing and other MFIs and community organizations in Bangladesh are not only address the issue of poverty, but also work for environmental development. Environmental sustainability is sustainable development, which means sustainable economic growth, which is an oxymoron. No form of economic growth can be continued indefinitely. Furthermore, all economic growth today is terribly environmentally degrading. Herman Daly, one of the early pioneers of ecological sustainability, looked at the problem from maintenance of natural capital viewpoint. It is using renewable resources, produce no pollution, zero carbon emissions businesses and away from depletion of the non-renewable resources.

Grameen Bank and its sister organizations in Bangladesh provide loans to farmers for organic production, agro forestry, ecologically sound crop intensification, fisheries, livestock, aquaculture, integrated pest management, rickshaws, bicycles, solar panel installation businesses, biogas plants, recycling businesses, and many other ecologically sound small businesses. GB does not provide loans for alcohol, tobacco or narcotics businesses, puppy cultivation or other rural industries that create health hazards to rural areas.

Micro Financing Institutions (MFIs) should adopt environmental principles: reduce, re-use and recycle waste, but how can the policy be implemented and internalized within the institution? To start, they can create lists of business types that negatively impact the environment and ensure that loans are not provided to those kinds of businesses. These lists can give micro-entrepreneurs a clear idea of the types of businesses that will not receive loans. The Business Alliance for Local Living Economics (BALLE) can advocate for such a policies, and facilitate partnerships between solar energy suppliers and MFIs. *Micro credit plus programs* could include environmental training programs, tree planting, seed supply and nursery programs.

4.1.0. Positive impact of small enterprises

From my experience in Bangladesh, I can say micro enterprises definitely have a positive impact on the environment. Small entrepreneurs are involved in organic seed businesses, backyard poultry raising, homestead gardening, preparing compost organic fertilizer, hand weaving fabrics, and rickshaws and bicycles for peddling transport. All of these businesses contribute to a healthier environment. Sustainable production techniques such as reforestation, controlled water usage, enhance natural pesticide applications (integrated pest management, IPM), wood working, promote environmentally-friendly micro drip irrigation, facilitate solar panel businesses, and bio-digester plants all conserve environmental resources. Recycling micro enterprises are also helping the environment. MFI staffs need to understand the negative impact of certain industries on the environment in order to ensure that these businesses do not receive financial support, unless they provide proof that they will not be adding to our planet's waste problem.

4.2.0. Negative impact of micro enterprises on the environment?

Usually micro enterprises income generating activities include agricultural activities such as farming, fishing, raising livestock, agricultural processing, and food processing. Some micro enterprises could have a negative impact on the environment. Cultivating tobacco or narcotics, or using pesticides in farming can create problems for the greater community. Respiratory sickness, diarrhea, cancer and other health hazards are some of the problems that could result. Diesel and kerosene selling businesses create more carbon in the environment. Sale of endangered species is unethical. These enterprises create air and water pollution, damage the earth, ruin the soil, and reduce forests and wildlife. Some small enterprises like soap making, charcoal production, timber harvesting, tanneries, textile dying, open animal slaughter, and small mining operations have negative consequences on environment. A clause could be inserted in all loan applications, "I certify that I will do my best to do business that will not harm the environment". This can raise consciousness about environment among both clients and staff.

We have to remember that poor people are more 'exposed' to the environment, and they are more dependent on natural resources. Artisans, farmers, food vendors, textile producers, charcoal sellers and many others use natural resources for their livelihood. The depletion of these resources reduces the sustainability of their businesses, and could jeopardize the supply or the quality of the resources if there is no program to re-plant and restore. Grameen Bank and its sister organizations are examples of organizations that given careful consideration to environmental impacts. Socially and environmentally responsible micro financing is very important. So MFIs should develop an environmental criterion for lending.

5.0. Grameen Shakti renewable energy program

Grameen Shakti (GS) renewable energy program is a popular and successful venture in Bangladesh. Renewable energy services make villages more prosperous and strengthen the local economy. This program increasingly creates new opportunities for micro finance to support the environment because in Bangladesh only 30% people have access to the national electricity grid. In this situation, Grameen Bank, through its sister organization Grameen Shakti (GS) is promoting, developing and extending renewable energy technology like solar panel power, biogas plants, organic fertilizer, improved stoves and wind energy in remote rural Bangladesh. GB has extended credit support to install 77,000 solar power systems in Bangladesh. This program is employs 1,135 engineers and 2,075 trained technicians in 25,000 villages across Bangladesh. Total beneficiaries are 500,000. (Grameen Shakti, November 2006). With this solar power system, GB clients are able to light their homes, shops, rural offices, mosques and fishing boats. They also operate TVs and cell phones. People do not pay monthly electricity bills. It is pollution free.

Through the above-stated Grameen energy program, local communities get easier access to environment-friendly renewable energy at lower costs to meet their socio-economic needs, increase technology transfer at the grassroots level, and create new businesses and employment opportunities in the community. It protects people from the affects of the kerosene carbons. It creates new income opportunities including manufacture of accessories for the solar home system and local repair shops in the rural Bangladesh.

Although GB solar panels, solar chargers for cell phones, solar water pumps and solar cookers, etc. are enhancing renewable businesses in Bangladesh, these alternative energy technologies/materials are not manufactured in Bangladesh. Therefore, GS is dependent on importing solar panels from other countries. Biogas, an alternative energy to firewood, saves cutting and using wood for fire. So it prevents deforestation. This biogas technology makes slurry which is a high quality organic fertilizer used for crop and fish production. It protects air pollution too. This organic fertilizer removes acidity of the soil and reduces toxicity. However, liquid cow dunks producing methane gas and this gas is spreading, creates germs, bacteria and bed smelling in the neighborhoods that effects human body and environment. Grameen Bank and GS provides credit for biogas plant construction. Recently, GS installed wind pumps in the cyclone centers of coastal areas of Bangladesh to produce electricity which is used in the centers.

In Canada, there are many community economic development organizations and credit unions which are investing money and providing capital to local entrepreneurs. There are 57 community investment funds (NGOs) and 54 Aboriginal financial institutions in Canada, but only a few community micro loan funds exist in Canada. (Calmeadow report 1999). In Toronto, Riverdale Business Development Corporation and Alterna Savings are centers of excellence within community-based development initiatives that help create local jobs, develop local enterprises, and provide essential services to low income people. These organizations could extend their loan services to recycling and waste management businesses. However, these cooperative organizations are struggling to cover their operating costs. Without subsidies, these CED organizations cannot be sustained.

In Canada, most levels of government have developed purchasing policies and criteria to give preference to 'green' and environmentally friendly products and services. This mandate encourages all companies that want to do business with the government to be attentive to providing environmentally friendly products and solutions.

Below the paper is focusing on how the concept of micro lending can be employed in North America to assist people to make their communities healthier and more self sufficient. Why is local business important in North American communities? David Korten (2002) suggests that local businesses encourage living economies which are economies for life. Global corporations and financial speculators engaged in the single-minded pursuit of money are destroying communities, cultures, and natural systems everywhere on the planet. Major corporations today are legally structured to allow virtually unlimited concentration of power to the exclusive financial benefit of absentee shareholders who have no knowledge of or liability for the social and environmental consequences of the actions taken on their behalf. According to Korten, this process can be referred to as a type of suicide economy that is dominated by human choice and motivated by a love of money, rather than a love for life; this in turn, creates monumental negative consequences.

Korten emphasizes the need for government regulation to ensure that the true cost of energy and natural resources is incorporated in the cost of manufactured products—including environmental impact costs and waste management. Local living economies benefit locally rooted enterprises, and locally-owned enterprises recycle money in the community. They strive to save energy and provide increased educational opportunities and services to drop crime rates. This economy shifts from *creating demand* to *responding to demands and reducing pollution*. We need to get rid of the suicide economy by displacing transnational corporations.

Michael Shuman, an economist from Washington DC, studied 500 local businesses which were involved with what is known as 'Sustainable Connections' shopping for Thanks giving and Christmas. The study highlights how local businesses 'give back' to the community through things such as community culture, ecology, architecture, music and art. Every local purchase has a *multiplier effect* on a particular society and its environment. For instance a dollar spent on rent might be spent again by the landlord at the local grocery store, who in turn pays an employee, who then buys a movie ticket. The more times a dollar circulates within a defined geographic area, the more benefit to the community.

How can these suggestions be done? All Maximum literature materials are full of theories, but how do we put them to practice when our culture seems to be addicted to shopping at WalMart? We need to break down these high consumption habits. Korten says, "It is monumental mess".

An interesting experiment would be to include micro lending with the concept of 'community currency'. If a community did create its own currency, then small business loans could be offered in community currency with an extremely low interest rate.

It's obvious that life in Bangladesh and life in North American have very little in common. So can micro credit have the same success in North America as it has enjoyed in poorer countries like Bangladesh. The answer is yes. The Grameen America has been working in American eleven cities and it has been providing micro loans to 97, 750 low income micro entrepreneurs in America. Its services are expanding to more cities in America. The Grameen America micro loan program is very polular and successful in USA. This is an example of local living economic program in America. Canada needs the green micro financing program for green enterprise development in Canada.

The Bangladesh unemployment rate is 57%. 67% of the rural people live below the poverty line and would not qualify for credit at a regular bank (Bangladesh Profile, 1982). A huge number of people are unable to fulfill their basic needs now in 2018, Bangladesh poverty rate has reduced to 22% (Bangladesh Planning Commission), but in North America, there is a larger safety net that poor people can tap into. Our culture is totally different from that of Bangladesh. In North America, 80% of people work in giant corporations. Entrepreneurs are getting scarce, but during Abraham Lincoln's time entrepreneurship was strong. After 200 years entrepreneurship is relatively depleted in

North America. People are scared to take on the risk and challenge of operating a small business. They believe in unions, and worship money significantly more than they worship community. Milani says that people do not understand the suffering associated with absolute scarcity. Therefore, micro credit is not popular in North America. The majority of people are able to get credit at a local bank.

6.0. Why micro finance has succeeded in Bangladesh. Is it possible in North America?

In Bangladesh, the Grameen Bank (GB) micro lending concept has become so successful, as it is tailored to Bangladeshi culture. Grameen Bank has researched Bangladeshi local cultures and has come up with a system that helps poor people start their own small business and eventually escape poverty. Its lending policy is different from the commercial bank. GB is carrying the community; however, in Canada, banks are not carrying the communities. Rather, they are profit driven. GB adopts the local culture and has developed a simple lending operation.

How do we re-kindle (re-build) the entrepreneurial spirit within North American culture? It's difficult when global corporations want to sell everything to people. Their 'one stop shop' principles are displacing small businesses by undercutting their prices until small businesses die.

Micro credit could be a very useful tactic for creating a vibrant community where people are focused on helping one another. Hopefully more wealthy people will follow the lead of billionaires Bill Gates and Warren Buffet who have both realized their social responsibility later in life. The self-employment culture is not popular here largely due to the domination of big business. Municipalities can initiate pilot projects focused on energy self-sufficiency, recycling and waste management. From these projects, small businesses should emerge. We need to educate our young about the green economy and start recycling renewable business, return to local artisans, which may help keep out WalMart and promote community values of caring.

In Bangladesh, micro financing not only reduces poverty but also create biodiversity, improves drinking water, sanitation, and the health of the environment. For example, they educate rural poor people not to litter in open places, to grow vegetables year round, crop-diversification and to have smaller families. They also provide loans for low cost housing that promotes use of local materials. GB has come to see a poor woman, in contrast to a poor man, as a "natural and better fighter of poverty" and this is why they have targeted primarily women. In North America, women and men enjoy equality on most things. For example, here men and women are equal in their property rights.

Small business initiated by local people that respond to local needs. Moreover, small entrepreneurs attempt to create biodiversity and democratize the economic lifestyle of the neighboring communities (Shragge 1997, p. 103). Grameen Bank helps community people find dignified livelihood through increasing income, education, creating material assets and developing social and human capital. This empowers them economically and socially by increasing their income and creating leadership and networking among them.

7.0. Conclusions

We have to remember that poor people are more 'exposed' to the environment, and they are more dependent on natural resources. Artisans, farmers, food vendors, textile producers, charcoal sellers and many others use natural resources for their livelihood. The depletion of these resources reduces the sustainability of their businesses, and could jeopardize the supply or the quality of the resources if there is no program to re-plant and restore. Grameen Bank and its sister organizations are examples of organizations that given careful consideration to environmental impacts. Socially and environmentally responsible micro financing is very important. So MFIs should develop environmental criteria for lending.

From the previous discussion, it shows that green small businesses can offer biodiversity in the community and can an alternative to corporate globalization, but green small enterprises need appropriate strategy and support from the government and other agencies. Lending to appropriate environmental technologies like solar electric systems and solar ovens needs to be a priority. National strategies are needed to encourage the recycling of manufacturing waste. All these green social small businesses contribute to the local economy without harming the local environment. It is advisable for national MFI regulation to deny loans to those sectors that are harmful to environment.

Green social microfinance practitioners can work to improve the environment by providing loans for green micro enterprises and businesses that are not harmful to environment. Green microfinance activities can include organizing training workshops among MFIs officials, and clients. Sustainable agriculture needs to be a priority, so loans for nursery, homestead gardening, renewable energy, biogas plant and biodiversity should be easy to get. Making crafts and renting out cell phones makes poor people self-reliant and confident.

Today, economic power and wealth is increasingly becoming concentrated within a small number of multinational corporations and squeezing the biodiversity in the world. To counter this hegemonic economic power, it is vital to create alternative green economic biodiversity forces, where green micro financing to green social small businesses can play an active role in green biodiversity socioeconomic development, address the issue of poverty and environmental degradation and development. The idea of corporate responsibility can be shifted by a green economics movement and biodiversity movement that are to become the heart of its very value system, which is crucial in developed and developing countries.

8.0. References

Anielski, M. (2004). *Genuine wealth accounting: measuring the sustainability of communities*, BC: New Society *Publishers*

Anielski Alberta (2006). *Management Inc.,* Retrieved from www. anjelski.com dated 9/11/2006

Bangladesh Planning Commission (2018). *Bangladesh Poverty Status*, Dhaka: Bangladesh Planning Commission

Bangladesh Statistics (1982). *Bangladesh Profile 1982.* Bangladesh Bureau of Statistics, Dhaka

Barua, D. (2006). *An integrated approach to rural energy service.* Dhaka, Grameen Shakti

Bauce, W. (2006). *Capitalism at the crossroads: The unlimited business opportunities in solving the world's most difficult problems* at http:// www.truthforce.info/index.php?qdated November 09, 2006

Boothroyd, P. & Davis, H. (1993). Community Economic Development: Three approaches, *Journal of Planning Education and Research* Vol. 12, pp. 230-240. Association of Collegiate Schools

Braungart, M. (1994). *Product life cycle management to replace waste management.* Cambridge: Cambridge University Press

Burman, P. (1996). *Poverty's bonds- power and agency in the social relations of welfare.* Toronto: Thompson Educational Publishing, Inc.

Calmeadow Foundation (2005). *Calmeadow Annual Report 2005.* Toronto

Coady International. (2006). *About Coady.* Retrieved from WWW. coady.stfx.cadated June 01, 2006

Commoner, B. (2005). *Pollution prevention: The source of an ethical foundation for sustainable development.* New York: Queen College. Downloaded from http://www.czp.couni.cz/values/citanka/ dobris/barry_commoner.htm dated June, 05 2006 Downloaded retrieved from h*ttp://ilsr.org/recycling/newmovement2.html dated October 26, 2006.*

EPR Working Group. (2003). *A prescription for clean Production pollution prevention and Zero waste.* Downloaded from *www. GRRN.org/epr/epr_pri*nciples.html dated 9/11/2006

Feldman, I. (2006). Microfinance institutions and the environment. Paper presented at the *Micro Credit Summit, Halifax* 2006. Green Track strategies Environment. USA

Fishman, C. (2003). *The WalMart you don't know.* Downloaded from ht*tp://www.fastcompany.com/mazagine/77/walmart*.html dated October 9, 2006

Grameen Bank (2006). *Impact of Grameen Bank on local society.* Retrieved from http://www.rdc.com.au/grameen/impact/htm dated May 23, 2006

Grameen Shakti (2006). *Renewable energy in Bangladesh,* Grameen Bank, Mirpur Two, Dhaka, Bangladesh

Gunningham, N., Phillipson, M. and Grabosky, P. (1999). *Harnessing third parties as surrogate regulations: Achieving environmental outcomes by alternative means. Canberra,* The Australian National University

Jackson, W. (2001). *Natural systems agriculture: A radical alternative.* Salina: The Land Institute. http://www.landinstitute.org/vnews/display.v/Art/2001/04/ dated October, 09, 2006

James, Alexander N., Gaston, Kevin J. and Balmford, Andrew (1994). 'Balancing the Earth's Accounts' in *Nature,* Vol. 401, 23 September 1994.

Korten, D. (2002). *Living Economics: Economics for Life.* YES in http://www.futurenet.org/article.asp?id=533dated 9/11/2006

Manning, R. (2004). *The oil we eat: Following the food chain back to Iraq.* North point Press. Downloaded from ht*tp://*www.greeneconomics.net/OilWeEat.htm. dated 9/27/2006

Milani, B. (2000). *Designing the Green Economy: the Post-industrial alternative to corporate globalization.* Lanham MD: Rowman and Littlefield

Milani, B. (2000) *Mindful Markets, Values Revolution and the Green Economy: EPR, Certification and the New Regulation*

Millennium Development Goals (2000). *Millennium Development Goals.* Retrieved from http://www.un.org/millenniumgoals dated October 11, 2006

Mitchell, S. (2005). *Rebuilding Community-Rooted Enterprise, Institute for local Self-Reliance Minneapolis* downloaded retrieved from http://www.newrules.org/hta/index.htm dated October 09, 2006

Myers, N. & Kent, J. ((1998). *Perverse Subsidies: Tax $s undercutting our economics and environments alike.* Winnipeg: The International Institute for Sustainable Development

Ottoman, J.A. (1998). *Green Marketing: Opportunity for Innovation,* NTC-McGrew Hill. Retrieved from http://www.greenmarketing.com/green_Marketing_Book/Chapter 02.htm, dated October 09, 2006

O'Rourke, D (2005). Market movements-NGOs strategies to influence global production and consumption. *Journal of Industrial Ecology,* Vol. 9(1–2), pp. 115–128

Roberts, W. (2005). *Making sexy: Green Gurus say we should use city taxes to punish ugliness and reward sustainability.* Toronto: Now Communication Inc.

Rouf, K. A. (2012). Green economics and biodiversity through green micro financing. *Prime Journal of Business Administration and Management.* Vol. 2(4), pp. 513-520.

Rowe, J. (2001). *Is the corporation obsolete? in the Washington Monthly-Online.* Downloaded Retrieved from http://www.washingtonmonthly.com/books/2001/0107.rowe.html, dated October 09, 2006

Seldman, N. (2003). *The new Recycling Movement part-1.* Washington: Waste to Wealth

Shragge, E. (1997). *Community Economic Development-in search of empowerment.* Montreal: Black Rose Books

Shuman, M. (2006). *An open letter to Bellingham.* Buckspot, Maine. Downloaded retrieved from www.smallmart.org, dated October 09, 2006

Shuman, M. H. (1998). *Going local: Creating self-reliant communities in a global age.* New York and London: The Free Press

The Daily Toronto Star (2006). *Green development,* September 22, 2006. Toronto.

Grameen Bank as a Bank for the Poor and as NGO is Successful or Not?

Abstract

The paper discusses the origin of Grameen Bank (GB) and other MFIs and NGOs in Bangladesh, and their impact on social development. Secondly, it examines the extent to which credit helps women to be empowered; free from their male partners' dominance and violence; and is able protest/fight against fundamentalism in Bangladesh. Thirdly, it discusses GB's management system, participatory rural approach (PRA), democracy, and accountability to citizenship. Fourthly, the essay looks at the commercialization of Grameen-Phase-2 and its effects on advocacy for citizenship development. Lastly, it discusses the replication of the Grameen Bank model, and its future dimensions.

From the research, it appears that the Grameen Bank and other NGOs are playing a very important role in socioeconomic development in Bangladesh although many of them have credit programs. Even though there are some criticisms about the controversial roles of Grameen Bank and MFIs/NGOs, the widespread existence of GB and other MFIs/NGOs involved in social development programs cannot be ignored. They are well able to improve many people's living standards and eradicate poverty of many poor people in Bangladesh. Although the Grameen Bank is firm to its credit delivery program, it could initiate a pilot project for lobbying for women's equality rights. This initiative can be achieved through involving people in civic engagement programs.

Key words: Building community capacity; citizenry; Grameen Bank; Grameen Shakti; group lending; microfinance institutions (MFIs);

mission growth; non-governmental organizations (NGOs); poverty; sixteen decisions, social development and women empowerment.

1.0. Introduction

Poverty, unemployment, hunger, malnutrition, illiteracy, social inequality, gender wage inequity, gender discrimination and diseases are major concerns in Bangladesh. It is a densely populated country, and therefore, it is difficult for the government to provide adequate food, clothes, shelter, healthcare, and education for its all citizens. There is no social safety net like Canada in Bangladesh. This failing has resulted in the emergence of the Grameen Bank (GB) as a bank for the poor in Bangladesh in late 1970s. The Bank's high performance in poverty eradication has attracted donor agencies and caused them to shift their programs from the government to the non-governmental organizations (NGOs) due of the failure of the former to provide sufficient services and input to the countries destitute situation during 1970s and onward. Development through Grameen Bank and other micro finance institutions (MFIs) and NGOs is the new orthodoxy in Bangladesh. However, GB's main programs involve economic determination and it has recently become more profit driven. Hence, the question is how much are they actually contributing to the social and economic development of the country? Therefore, this paper examines and analyzes the Grameen Bank to discover what it does well and where it needs to improve. The paper examines which lessons can be taken from Grameen Bank and applied elsewhere. This paper also relates with NGOs and examines the plan and actions taken by NGOs for social development in Bangladesh. Finally, it proposes solutions to the problems that the Grameen Bank faces.

2.0. Organization of the paper

First, the paper discusses the origin of GB and other MFIs/NGOs in Bangladesh, and their impact on social development. Secondly, it examines the extent to which credit helps women to be empowered; free from their male partners' dominance/violence; and whether they are able to protest/fight against fundamentalism in Bangladesh. Thirdly, it discusses GB's management system, participatory rural approach (PRA), democracy, and accountability to citizenship. Fourthly, the essay looks at the commercialization of Grameen Bank Phase-2 and its effects on advocacy for citizenship development. Lastly, it discusses the replication of the Grameen Bank model, and its future dimensions.

3.0. Concept of non-governmental organization (NGO) and micro-finance institution (MFI)

A non-governmental organization (NGO) is any non-profit, voluntary citizens' group which is organized on a local, national or international level. Task-oriented and driven by people with a common interest, NGOs perform a variety of service and humanitarian functions, bring citizen concerns to Governments, advocate and monitor policies and encourage political participation through provision of information. A non-governmental organization (NGO) is a non-profit, citizen-based group that functions independently of government. NGOs are organized on local, national and international levels to serve specific social or political purposes. Some are organized around specific issues, such as human rights, environment or health. They provide expertise and the situation and serve as early warning mechanisms and help monitor and implement international agreements. Their relationship with offices and agencies of the United Nations system differs depending on their goals, their venue and the mandate of a particular institution. The primary purpose of an Advocacy NGO is to defend or promote a specific cause. As opposed to operational project management, these organizations typically try to raise awareness, acceptance and knowledge by lobbying, press work and activist event. Service NGOs are providing, delivering different types of services in the field of education, health, infrastructure development, relief distribution, housing, clothing, rehabilitating the victims of war and victims of natural disasters etc.

Non-governmental organizations play an increasingly important role in international development. They serve as a funnel for development funds both from individual donors in wealthy countries and from bilateral aid agencies. At the same time, NGOs are frequently idealized as organizations committed to "doing good" while setting aside profit or politics—a romantic view that is too starry-eyed. Development-oriented NGOs, which have existed for centuries, have played a growing role in development since the end of World War II; there are currently 20,000 international NGOs. This paper argues that the strengths of NGOs and their weaknesses easily fit into economists' conceptualization of not-for-profit contractors. Key concepts of NGOs include:

- Strengths of the NGO model produce corresponding weaknesses in agenda-setting, decision-making, and resource allocation.
- The increased presence of NGOs can be explained by 3 factors: a trend to outsource government services; new ventures by would-be not-for-profit "entrepreneurs"; and the increasing professionalization of existing NGOs.
- As NGOs increasingly produce their own funding and develop their own professionalized class, it is appropriate to expose them to greater market forces beyond donor preferences.
- The use of aid vouchers allowing beneficiaries to purchase private goods and services is one tool for introducing more market forces.

Some examples of international NGOs are business-friendly international (BINGO), Shining Hope, Oxfam nternational, Red Cross); environmental NGO (ENGO); Greenpeace and World Wildlife Fund; international NGO (INGO), example Oxfam); QUANGO; quasi-autonomous NGO; and International Organization for Standardization (ISO). Bangladeshi NGOs are BRAC, ASA, Proshika, Nijera Kori, Grameen Kallayan, Grameen Shikka etc.

NGOs are involving various types of social, economic, environmental and infrastructural development and rehabilitation in society particularly for serving to disadvantaged people in community in different countries. According to Global Concern Classroom, the following activities are performing by NGOs in the world:

1. They are neither a part of government nor the private sector. There is no focus on power over people or becoming wealthy through working at an NGO.

2. NGOs are humanitarian groups. People and the community are the priority of the organization. NGOs strive to better the world and help the less fortunate.

3. NGOs range from International to National to Local. There are approximately 40,000 NGOs in the world in addition to the community-based organizations according to the United Nations Development Program. An NGO can be a domestic organization and reach those in their community or they can be international and help those thousands of miles away.

4. NGOs are non-profit. This means all surplus money will be placed back into the organization's work and will not be a profit to owners, staff or donors. There is no interest in money for NGOs. The mission is often to relive suffering and protect the people. These NGOs are depending on either government funding or other sources of funding to run their programs in society.

5. There is a passion and desire to help: NGOs consist of people who volunteer to aid development; there is no mandatory requirement to join an NGO. All NGOs share the common principle of humanity and those committed to NGO activities support this principle in interest of bettering the world.

6. Every little bit counts. NGOs are funded by various ways. There are government grants, grants from foundations and corporate businesses, small donors and even large donors. You don't have to be a billionaire; anyone can donate. Every donor is appreciated and aids the cause, no matter how big or how small.

7. NGOs work to make a difference. The work of an NGO may vary from healthcare, livelihood, poverty, child mortality, education, emergency response, water & sanitation and other

needs of the people. If there's an issue or need, there's most likely an NGO working on it.

8. NGOs do not use aid to further religious, political or military standpoints. NGOs are independent and do not work for governments or partner with armed forces. Neutrality is a must to access all areas in need of aid and relief. Working for a government or partnering with an armed force might portray an NGO as a threat rather than a source of safety and help.

9. NGOs do not use armed forces. This means guns are not allowed in offices or project sites. They do not exchange information with the military or use armed or military escorts. NGOs do not support violence and conflict. NGOs value peace, tolerance and the people.

10. NGOs believe in the rights of the people. NGOs are a force in the global civil society and aim to provide access to basic human rights to those in need. Development is not a gift or privilege; it's a process that NGOs push for.

Banelle Mana, Global Concern Classroom, commented that it's obvious NGOs are awesome! They're like superheroes donating effort and time to make people's lives better.

According to Erwin A. J. Dressen (2000) non-profit/non-government organizations, micro-finance institutions and volunteer sectors are those who are registered under the Charity Acts, but the profits are returned to the organization. Michael Hall and Keith G. Banting (2000) mention that different scholars use various terminologies for the nonprofits sector. For example, *Nonprofits* is the language of economists that view nonprofits organizations as a residual category; sociologists call it the *Voluntary Sector*; and political scientists, the *Third Sector*. According to Aditee Nag Chowdhury (1989) NGOs have been described as associations formed on personal initiative by a few committed people dedicated to implementing development projects at the grassroots level. They work outside the government structures but function within the legal framework of the country. Grameen

Bank is a specialized bank designed for providing microcredit to poor people in Bangladesh. It is a non-governmental organization, but it is not registered under Charity Act. Here, in the paper, Grameen Bank is considered a bank for the poor, but analyse its activities as a non-goverrnmental micro-finance institution. The paper also compares and contrasts GB activities with NGOs in Bangladesh.

4.0. Funding sources of NGOs

As non-profit organizations, NGOs rely on a variety of sources for funding projects, operations, salaries and other overhead costs. Because the annual budget of an NGO can be in the hundreds of millions (or even billions) of dollars, fundraising efforts are important for the NGO's existence and success. Funding sources include membership dues, the sale of goods and services, private sectorfor-profit companies, philanthropic foundations, grants from local, state and international agencies and private donations. However, Grameen Bank run its activities and covers its costs from its own resource mobilization.

Individual private donors comprise a significant portion of NGO funding. Some of these donations come from wealthy individuals-such as Ted Turner's $1 billion donation to the United Nations, or Warren Buffett's pledge to give 10 million, the Bill and Melinda Gates Foundation (valued at more than $31 billion in June 2006). Many NGOs; however, rely on a large number of small donations (rather than a small number of large donations). However, in Bangladesh private donors for NGOs funding or MFIs funding is rare. In developed countries, private donations are common for philanthropic agencies or NGOs.

Despite their independence from government, many NGOs rely heavily on government funding in order to function. Some governmental NGO funding may be viewed as controversial because the funding may support certain political goals rather than a nation's development goals.

5.0. Grameen Bank activities in Bangladesh

In the 1970's Bangladesh faced severe famine, hunger, starvation and poverty due to various economic, social and political crises. The rural poor in need of credit could not receive loans from the banks. They were outside the orbit of the banking system. In 1979, Muhammad Yunus initiated the Grameen micro credit pilot project designed to address the economic crisis aiming to (1) extend banking facilities to poor people, especially women, and create self-employment opportunities; (2) eliminate the exploitation of the moneylenders; and (3) empower women through engaging them in income-generating activities. In October 1983, the Grameen Bank project was transformed into an independent bank by a Government Ordinance (P.O. No. 26, 1972). Grameen Bank was registered under special ordinance in Bangladesh in 1983 as a specialized bank for the poor, but it has to follow central bank policies in Bangladesh. Usually many literatures categorised Grameen Bank as an NGO; however, its legal structure is positioned with the specialised bank Act that mentioned earlier in the paper. There were several other NGOs which were officially recognized in the 1970s as well.

The first NGO activities started through Christian missionary groups. By 1793, the famous British missionary, William Carey, had arrived in Calcutta, India and began social welfare activities through the missionary-run school setup all over Bengal (Nurruzaman, 1994); Khan, 1981). In the post 1971 period; however, there has been a mushrooming of NGOs in Bangladesh. Initially they rebuilt, provided relief, and rehabilitated the war-ravaged country. In the late 70s many NGOs were involved in eradicating poverty, malnutrition, illiteracy and setting up health programs. There has also been a tremendous increase in the number of NGOs in Bangladesh. Presently, there are 22,000 local and international NGOs registered in Bangladesh (Rahman, 2006). According to Chowdhury (2005) they provide services to nearly one-fifth of a population of 130 million in Bangladesh.

There are some NGOs which have been successful in the development of Bangladesh since the 1980s; such as the Bangladesh Rural

Advancement Committee (BRAC), Proshika Manobik Unnayan Kendra (PROSHIKA), Nijera Kori, Association of Social Advancement (ASA), and CARE Bangladesh etc. They are best known for their multi-purpose development activities related to socioeconomic development in rural Bangladesh. For example, BRAC covers a range of activities for the rural poor, such as education, income-generation through poultry and livestock rearing, fisheries, forestry and handicrafts, just to name a few (Haque, 2002). Proshika is working in Bangladesh. However, it has been facing a whole lot of coercion and conditionality from the national government. Additionally these NGOs, including BRAC are severely dependent upon donor funds. In contrast, Grameen Bank gained popularity partly because it has become a self-sustainable organization as it works to alleviate poverty. The Bank began its nationwide micro credit program to provide collateral free small loans to the landless poor. Hoever, the question is how much it now contributes to social development which is not only concerned with economic enhancement.

6.0. Micro finance Institutions (MFIs)

Microcredit and microfinance are separate, but related concepts. The debate over microcredit vs. microfinance has been going on for decades, but our experience has shown that microcredit loans that depend on external loan capital are less sustainable and less impactful than the form of savings-led microfinance. In simple terms, microfinance or microcredit or micro loan gives those in need a means to lift them out of poverty.

Microfinance is often defined as financial services for poor and low-income clients offered by different types of service providers. The term is often used more narrowly to refer to loans and other services from providers that identify themselves as "microfinance institutions" (MFIs). These institutions commonly tend to use new methods developed over the last 35 years to deliver very small loans to micro borrowers, taking little or no collateral. These methods include group lending and liability, pre-loan savings requirements, gradually increasing loan sizes, and an implicit guarantee of ready access to future loans if present loans are repaid fully and promptly. From a global perspective, microfinance organizations envision a world in which low-income households have permanent accesses to a range of high quality and affordable financial services offered by a range of retail MFIs providers to finance income-producing activities, build assets, stabilize consumption, and protect against risks.

The purpose of microfinance is to meet the needs of the 50% of poor households worldwide who are 'unbanked'. In practical terms, this means providing a community with a safe place to save, the means to take small loans from a communal pot, and access to basic business training (Five Talents). MFIs provide/supply small amount of business loans to poor people to invest in their micro-enterprises. MFIs are grass-root organization working with low income people who are looking for business capital for running their business in the community. Usually MFIs cover their operation cost from their credit investments and savings interest of their clients deposited in respective MFIs.

Each microfinance programme is based on a model that is designed and operated by community organization either independently or partnering with local, state or international partners. They know their communities best and they try to the model builds sustainable development groups for supporting more to disadvantaged low income people in the communities. Many Philanthropic organizations add micro-financing products in their program. Even many NGOs turn to MFIs agencies in order to survive their program or to cover their operational costs.

MFIs have increased in dignity of the poor rather than being given a handout each entrepreneur is provided with the tools to lift themselves out of poverty. The benefits of microfinance include:

- Growing a safety net of savings: A central benefit of microfinance program is that poor can develop his or her savings behaviours.
- Building and expanding business and incomes: The main microfinance benefits are the investments made by poor from

receiving micro loans which enable them to establish and grow their small businesses. And this is a long-term impact.

- Many studies show that the receivers of micro loans are able to run successful businesses after receiving MFIs training.

- Being able to meet basic household needs like invest income for clients' schooling, diets, and improve the quality of the family's healthcare.

- Women empowerment: Empowering women through microfinance is at the heart of MFIs services. Many studies indicate that disadvantaged women borrowers of micro loan are empowered to make decisions about how to save and invest their incomes and earn money for themselves, which increases their decision-making power in their households and communities more widely. Women's empowerment through sustainable microfinance is important, not only because it offers a route out of poverty, but also because it addresses problems of inequality. However, microfinance success is always achieved when the model is designed with the client in mind and adjusts with local culture and values.

- There are many ways to reduce poverty, but in the rural area in which MFIs work, microfinance and development go hand-in-hand. Many studies show poverty alleviation through microfinance is highly efficient. Microloans for women increase decision-making power in the household and improve their socio-economic status in the community (Rouf, 2011).

According to the United Nations (1995), social development means the integration of economic growth with social welfare policies leading to a higher standard of living for all. According to David Hollister (1982) social development is "the process of planned institutional change to bring about a better fit between human needs, social policies and programs. Based on the above definition, social development has several components including the eradication of poverty, expansion of education, healthcare for all, and the assurance of fairly equitable distribution of income. However, here the question is to what extent the Grameen Bank has, as a micro financing Institution (MFI) in Bangladesh, affected changes of the level of social development?

Although Grameen bank has no direct health care services for its clients, its sister organization Grameen Kallayan has health care services like eye clinic, pathological clinics, health care centers etc. that are serving to Grameen Bank borrowers at different locations across Bangladesh. Borrowers buy Grameen health insurance package and receive health care services with cheap rate from these Grameen Kallayan health centers in Bangladesh. Grameen Shakti Doi is popular for fortified Yougurt that serves malnutrition problem in rural Bangladesh. Shakti Doi is nutricious but cheap in villages, so it is affordable to villagers and to children.

7.0. Debates on Grameen Bank and other MFIs activities in Bangladesh

Grameen Bank has an intensive socioeconomic and environmental campaigning program called the Sixteen Decisions, established in 1983, that helps to promote a peer support lending system among women. This creates social collateral which can be used by the Bank in lieu of material collateral (Kabeer, 1987; Karim, 2001; Mahamud, 2004; and Rahman, 1999). The Sixteen Decisions provide women with an opportunity to meet with each other and discuss various social development issues like healthcare, education, environment, agriculture, and village events as well as pay installments. The Sixteen Decisions represent the social, economic and green development agenda. Grameen centres are places for creating social solidarity among women. Muhammad Yunus says, "each center tries to ensure that all its members are guided by the Sixteen Decisions in their daily life" (Yunus, 1997, p.19). However, Aminur Rahman (1999) interprets this collective social collateral which should enhance social solidarity, as a strategy for ensuring high repayment rates, and which actually escalates violence against female borrowers. While it is true that the Grameen Bank targets women more than men; it is with this strategy that GB directly channels loans to the poorest thus helping to improve their living standards. Along with providing credit, GB offers guidelines to members for codes of conduct and activities aimed at improving their social and financial conditions. It provides information to women concerning maternal health, nutrition, and childcare to generate a demand for basic health care services in Bangladesh.

There is a pervading evidence to be found in different credit review and NGO literature that GB has an overall positive impact on the lives of the poor in terms of creating higher income and self-employment opportunities as well as poverty alleviation. For example, a World Bank study (1998) indicates that 5 percent of Grameen Bank households rose above poverty each year. This GB micro credit system has had a great impact on extreme poverty (Khondaker, 2003). It can play a vital role in attaining Millennium Development Goals (MDGs). In the words of Kofi Anan, UN Secretary General, "microfinance has proved its value, in many countries, as a weapon agains poverty and hunger. It is recognized as a development model for income generation, self-employment and empowers disadvantaged women" (Grameen Dialouge-60, p. 1, 2005). However, there is still an overwhelming amount of negativity surrounding the effects of NGOs and MFIs like the Grameen Bank. Grameen bank is one of the agenda of neo-liberalism. It is doing business with the poor people in Bangladesh and charge interest to its micro-loan investments to poor in Bangladesh.

GB's special feature is that 94% of its borrowers are women and they are in first place. The Bank encourages borrowers' participation in the decision making process. It has easy policy guidelines for the staff. It uses local language, adjust with local culture, values and disburses loans in a very simply way. It has gained some concrete experience in its more than three decades of operation such as: micro credit being a very effective instrument to increase poor people's income. Muhammad Yunus (2002) argues that welfare or handouts cannot help poor people. The Grameen Bank's credit creates opportunities for poor women in Bangladesh to increase their income and overcome poverty.

Despite the activities of GB in Bangladesh with its main agenda of poverty alleviation, poverty still persists as a major problem in Bangladesh. According to the Asian Development Bank (ADB) report, Bangladesh remains one of the poorest countries in the world with a per capita income of approximately US$ 337 in 1998 and with nearly one half of the population living below the poverty line (*The New Nation*, 1999). The pace of poverty reduction has been very slow. Another study shows that "at least 67.5 million rural people live in absolute poverty and of these 30 to 46 million exist in extreme, hard core poverty" (Lovell, 1992; p. 11). There is no doubt that currently there has been a significant decline in poverty which has decreased to below 25% (GoB Report, 2017. For example, Bangladesh poverty rate is 22.45%. Many studies recognized that reduction of poverty in Bangladesh is due to the contribution of intensive micro financing activates by many MFIs in Bangladesh.

My research uncovered two opposing views on MFIs/NGOs. One is the pro-MFIs/NGOs and the other, the anti-MFIs/NGOs. The pro-MFIs/NGOs view holds that MFIs/NGOs are more effective than the government agencies because they operate at the grassroots level and work closely with the target groups that make them known to each other. Hence, they can easily identify the root of the problems, which could help them to take accurate action. They also argue that MFIs/NGOs not only work for social development, but help people by providing access to modern technology, and education that contributes to social development (World Bank, 1994). However, there is also evidence to show that MFIs are exploiting the poor while doing business with them. MFIs are charging high interst to their micro-borrowers. They put pressure and coercive to repay loans even during financial crisis of borrowers.

Although MFIs/NGOs are non-profit organizations, the majority are exploiting the rural people (and especially women) through micro credit programs. *The Daily Independent* newspaper in Bangladesh (1999) published an article that revealed an analysis of micro finance data collected from 495 MFIs/NGOs in the country. The results showed that about 95% of MFIs/NGOs are directly involved in such suppression. It was also noticed that 95% of MFIs charge interest rates within the range of 12 and 25 per cent. In contrast, even the largest MFIs – ASA, Proshika and Grameen Bank– only charge 15 per cent, 12.5 per cent, 18 per cent and 20 per cent respectively (The Independent, 1999).

With the anti-MFIs/NGOs view, scholars assert that although MFIs/NGOs are non-political and non-profitable organizations, their main aim seems to be political and profit driven rather than towards social development. According to Aditee Nag Chowdhury (1989) NGOs have cultivated a self-image that they are "development partners" working for removing poverty. Most MFIs/NGOs do not properly use their funds. In fact, 70% of the MFIs/NGOs funds and resources are spent on the salary and allowances of foreign employees, experts and consultants. According to Khaliquzzaman (1994), "These NGOs fashionably named projects: poverty elimination projects, target group project etc. have not brought about any changes in the economic structure in Bangladesh". Thus the conclusion drawn was that MFIs/NGOs have done very little for eradicating poverty from the country. In such situations GB is exceptional because its various studies provide affirmative information about poverty eradication, but there is still conflicting information found in the research regarding women's empowerment.

Women's empowerment is the process of gaining power over their lives, in terms of increasing welfare and reducing subordination to men through the expansion of their choice and voice in the decision making process. According to Lamiya Karim (2001) the Grameen Bank has provided the world's financial community with the seductive information that the poor are credit worthy and the Bank goes to the doors of the poor. However, the high repayment rate of 99% does not tell the reader how money is recovered from its poor borrowers. She finds that money is often recovered through intimidation, force and violence against poor female members. Simeen Mahamud (2004) asserts that although women have good access to credit, the norms and practices put them at a definite subordinate position to men, which means they have little power in the decisions that shape and render them vulnerable in the society. In this situation advocacy/lobbying programs of MFIs/NGOs can play an important part in fighting against patriarchy in the society.

Now below the essay discusses how GB's credit provisions perpetuate violence against women. GB believes that income-generating activities by women could create the potential to enhance their power and status at home. However, several studies indicate that although GB has contributed to poverty eradication and created self-employment, its activities have not yet been able to empower women to fight against patriarchy (Goetz and Sengupta, 1996; Isseriles, 2003; Karim, 2001; Mahamud, 2004; and Rahman, 1999).

Many studies assert instead, a loan liability raises tension and anxiety within borrowers' households and increases violence against women. For example, Rahman's (1999) study reports that 70% of borrowers confessed to increased violence and aggressive behavior in their household because of their involvement with the Bank. "Men are users of more than 60% of women's loans (Ibid, p. 75). Karim (2001) finds that 90% of the loaned money went to men. She remarks that women are the bearers of the credit although not its users. The NGOs use women's social vulnerability and powerlessness but do not support them in the fight against patriarchy (Karim, 2001). The same conclusion was reached by Isserles (2003) where he mentions that although GB has seen many success stories of women who have been emancipated through micro credit, he cautions that many women are still dominated by their husbands and do not actually reap the benefits of the financial gains of their investments. In many cases their husbands receive the credit. However, Rouf's study (2011) shows 87% women borrowers themselves have control over their loans and handle their loan money in their businesses. From the above statistics it is obvious control over loan money by women borrowers has increased from 60% to 87% in Bangladesh within a decade (2000-2011).

Muhammad Yunus admitted to some defects of the Bank's lending practices in addition to the rigidity of the system. Therefore, he made several fundamental changes in its operations in 2000 and called this new stage Grameen BankPhase -2. Yunus stated that, "Poor people are not trouble makers for the institutions, rather, the design of the institutions and rules make trouble for them" (2002). Now the questions raised to the GB are: (1) do micro credit projects help to empower women or increase their vulnerability, or (2) does this credit lead to increased tension and violence for these same women?

In reference to Evans and Shields (2000) study, it is found the Third Sector does good works. They suggest third sector organizations should lobby a 'mediation' role in society that can help people to build citizenship. According to them the third sector organizations are a central part of civil society. Civil society relates to the sector of 'space between public life and private life'. However, micro-finance institutions and non-profit organizations are controlled by the state through service contracts. Recently, in Bangladesh, a few small Third Sectors/NGOs like *Proshika*, *Nijera Kori*, Nari Pakka and *Unanyan Nari Bikalq* began to refocus their activities towards supporting civil society; however, the government placed injunctions on some of their activities causing them to malfunction. In addition, Islamic fundamentalists are strongly against of many MFIs and NGOs.

The Islamic fundamentalists (*Ulemas*) have raised strong criticize NGO activities and thus created tension in Bangladesh. They talk against Grameen Bank's credit program and others too. For example, *Ulemas* claimed that GB conducts interest earning investment activities which are prohibited (*Haram*) in Islam. They protest that the government must act against this revived form of imperialism and do so before the country loses its sovereignty and the nation, its Islamic identity (Nuruzzaman, 1994, p. 9). The *Ulemas* also charged that great majorities of NGOs are allegedly engaged in missionary activities. Therefore, their activities are seen as a threat, creating division in families which are the basic unit of Bangladeshi society (Islam, 1998, p. 84).

Hence there is persistent tension between MFIs and NGOs, and religious groups in Bangladesh. BRAC complained that 1,400 of its 20,000 schools in Bangladesh are vandalized with a good number of them burned. The Grameen Bank also has complained about the 'fundamentalist's' negative attitude towards it (Holiday-Dhaka 1994). In the socio-economic field, despite the important roles played by NGOs, especially poverty eradication, some scholars argue that most MFIs are taking high interest from the poor. Therefore, according to them, MFIs are merchants, and tools of exploitation.

Grameen Bank is neither a volunteer organization, nor a charitable organization. It has an autonomous board of directors who make its own policy and a decision, but the staffs of it is paid. Its profits return to the organization and to its beneficiaries. Studies have demonstrated that several MFIs/NGO programs have had a significant impact on social and economic development in many marginalized households in the country. Due to this success, Bangladesh is home to some of the largest indigenous NGOs in the world. GB is the giant credit- giving MFI in Bangladesh. According to Shamsul Haque (2002) Grameen Bank has been one of the most globally influential agencies regarding micro credit in particular.

The Board of Directors of Grameen Bank is the highest policy making body, comprised of 13 members of whom nine are elected from among the borrowers. GB board members are selected every three years. Muhammad Yunus is also a board member and the Chief Executive of the Bank during the period 1981-2011. Various activities of the Bank are organized and implemented by four tiers of administrative set-up: branch offices, area offices, zonal offices and head office. All these layers are interconnected and follow a bottom up policy and decision making approach. The branch office is the lowest unit of operations of GB and it is located in the village. The branch organizes clienteles and disburses loans directly to borrowers. The area office supervises about 10 to 12 branches. The zonal office is located in the district headquarters. The head office is in Dhaka. The GB head office coordinates and monitors all field activities, and provides general guidance to field offices of GB. All the field offices of Grameen Bank are accountable for their works to the respective reporting supervising offices and to head office. However, it does not mean hierarchical reporting system of GB is the top down organizational operation system.

According to Kevin P. Kearns (1996) the accountability environment is a collection of forces – legal, political, socio-cultural and economic– that place pressure on organizations and people who work in them to engage in certain activities and refrain from engaging in others. They mandate certain organizational actions and prohibit others with a vast array of rules, procedures, reporting requirements, and sanctions by outside entities. However, accountability is the bridge of answerability, responsibility and responsiveness.

The Grameen Bank's plans, programs and strategies are not developed by the head office; rather field workers make customized decisions in the branch office that are appropriate and beneficial to the borrowers. Currently ninety three percent of the shares in the bank are owned by the borrowers and 7% remain shares with the government. However, at the begening (1981) borrowers' shares was 75% and government share was 25%. GB borrowers share buying system is all borrowers buy share certificates (each borrower can buy one share and each share value is Tk. 100) and thus become part owners of the bank. Staffs of Grameen Bank at all levels are accountable to borrowers because in each branch there is a branch representative elected from the borrowers. Grameen Bank action plans are prepared and implemented through mutual dialogue among field staff and borrowers. However, in practice Grameen Bank branch staffs actually prepared the action plan for the branch in order to fulfil the target and perform well.

The Chairman of the board of Grameen Bank is appointed from the government is usually a high government official. The Board of Directors meets every quarter of the year at which time they review bank activities, accounts and performance and approve the annual budget and plan of the bank. Here is the bottom-up democratic decision making process embedded in the board. Within the GB all activities are accountable to the board. Representatives from the branch, area, and zonal offices give their feedback to the board secretariat. The board reviews the field inputs in its meetings and makes decisions. The board members of GB borrowers are informed about the agenda of the board meeting before the meeting of the same day. However, the board meeting agenda and related papers are not sending earlier to the board members who are elected board members of GB board from borrowers. So it can be said that the GB board has a democratic proceses; however, executive board members of NGOs are not elected from respective NGO clients neither NGOs' clients can buy respective NGO shares.

Although each MFI and NGO has its own agenda, strategies and programs for social development, most follow almost similar strategies, plans and actions in Bangladesh. For example, NGOs first motivate the isolated poor people to form groups to discuss their problems. After a period of conscientization, creating awareness, the needs for giving small loans for self-help projects are discussed by micro financing organizations. To do their jobs, they usually follow some strategies for promoting the participation of beneficiaries. For example, first *Localized Participation* attempts to increase the local people's abilities to participate in the social change process. The Second *Political Empowerment* which aims to promote involvement in broader social movements and increased political participation of those who are excluded from the national decision making process. GB has been providing credit to poor people through groups which simultaneously work to enhance social development. However, it has proved that it is difficult to attain a trickle down effect in the society where economic growth is concerned. However, it has no program for political advocacy program for its borrowers to achieve citizenry skills development. Nevertheless, the bank has some special strategies like solve neighbourhood issues through center borrowers' collective efforts that help disadvantaged people to solve their own problem by themselves. However, it is necessary to initiate directly some programs and services like political mobilization in its credit delivery system. This program could expedite the borrowers' citizenry skills development among GB botrrowers.

Grameen Bank is different from other commercial banks. Its actions are almost in direct opposition to other private banks. For examples, private banks provide loans to wealthy people, but GB gives loans to poor people; private banks only provide loans to men, while GB provides maximum loans to poor women. Schedule banks deliver large loans, while Grameen Bank provides small loans to poor people in Bangladesh. Commercial banks require collateral, but GB loans are collateral free. General bank clients go to the office, but GB workers go to the borrowers' doorsteps. GB provides loans through group formation whereas the transactions of general banks require no group formation. GB respects the local culture, norms, values, and religions. It works within the community as an insider. All the above are the strategies employed by Grameen Bank which has made it so popular to rural poor women in Bangladesh.

Grameen Bank targets and mobilizes the poor and creates social and financial conditions that help provide economic security through self-employment or otherwise, through the use of credit. The group lending, peer pressure mechanism helps to monitor and enforce contracts and aids in the screening of good borrowers from bad ones. GB mobilizes savings to develop good savings behavior among the borrowers. However, these savings mobilization schemes provide protection of loans against default, and provide an internal source of finance through stored funds. So savings are one kind of liquidity collateral. Moreover, field staff may deduct savings for delinquent loan adjustments.

The GB success in high volume lending, loan repayment rate and high profit that is well-liked among development practitioners. Grameen Bank operates nationwide through 2,185 branches. The repayment rate has been highly satisfactory (99%) since 1979. The majority of patrons (97.9%) are female borrowers. The Bank serves a total of 8.6

million borrowers through 130, 000 rural landless associations in 70,370 villages in Bangladesh. The total loan disbursement has been $5.65 billion since its inception. Of them $5.00 billion has been repaid. Current borrower savings are $2.2 billion (Grameen Updates, 2006). It runs on its own internal funds and investment incomes and that makes it economically sustainable. However, Isserles (2002) challenges that the Bank's high repayment rates do not indicate high efficiency, but he fails to point out the increase in the quality of women's lives.

Building capacity is about improving the quality of life for all. According to Sherri Torjman, building community capacity is a holistic approach to solving problems and improving the quality of life. It is built upon the intrinsic links among economic, social and environmental well-being. It is "pro-people, pro-nature and pro-jobs" (Torjman, 1998: p.3). Many scholars defined community capacity building is the "process of developing and strengthening the skills, instincts, abilities, processes and resources that organizations and communities need to survive, adapt, and thrive in the fast-changing world." Micro-finance community capacity building aims to enhance the capacity of governments, business, non-governmental groups and communities to plan and manage the coast efficiently and effectively. It also aims to improve institutional arrangements for coastal management. This implies addressing capacity building on a long-term, strategic level of the community organizations.

GB is working for poor people and its programs and policies are developed by the representatives of borrowers. However, it has no integrated development programs like literacy, family planning, rural infrastructural development, development of voting behaviors, citizenry skills development and efforts to work against patriarchy, etc. It only works for poverty through credit delivery to poor people. Thus GB's credit activities cannot significantly affect sustainable development unless it creates and implements holistic development programs. As an insider, I can say Grameen Bank has many social and green development programs in addition to its micro credit services in

Bangladesh. Sherri Torjman mentions seven strategies for sustainable development. These strategies are (1) poverty reduction, (2) broadened concept of investment, (3) civic engagement, (4) problem-solving, (5) partnership, (6) leadership development and (7) celebration. Grameen Bank only has a poverty reduction strategy; unfortunately all other strategies are important for sustainable development and to build skills among the poor. These are also important for accountability and for transparency within the organization.

Kevin P. Kearns (2006) in his article *'From Adequate to Outstanding Performance'* mentions six propositions that can make an outstanding organization. Such outstanding organizations continuously adapt and refine their missions, vision and aspirations with change, time and situations and refine innovative and effective approaches to accomplishing their mission. Outstanding performance begins with outstanding leadership. In the case of the Grameen Bank, such propositions have praxis at the ground level. For example, GB has changed its different plans, strategies, and revised its various loan products according to the needs of its borrowers. When the GB was established in 1979, there was only one loan product, but now it has more than one loan products delivering in Bangladesh. For example, it provides housing loans, disaster loans, struggling loans, seasonal loans, micro-enterprise loans, and higher education student loans in addition to its basic loan. However, it has moved to profit making for its financial sustainability. This change, effected for organizational survival, Kearns (2006) calls it mission drift.

According to Jim Collins (2001) an organization could be excellent if it has a clear focus on goals, expectations, and accountabilities and does not achieve greatness overnight. In this perspective, Grameen Bank can be in the category of an excellent organization because it has a clear vision of eradicating poverty among poor particularly poor women in Bangladesh. The leadership of Muhammad Yunus has been the guiding force for Grameen's initiation and expansion. However, over time, Grameen Bank has institutionalized a decentralized management structure with a cadre of dedicated professionals that is operating without much of his involvement. GB field staffs are implementing the credit program. There are several departments in the head office including administration, accounts, operation, audit, and MIS. These departments support and coordinate field activities. According to Collins, effective leadership connects with mission growth because the mission growth is a process of adapting and refining the organization's mission, vision, and aspirations for expanded community impact.

A good mission statement answers several key questions about the organization:

- What are the opportunities or needs that the organization addresses?
- What are the functions of the organization? How are these needs being addressed?
- What level of service is provided? and
- What principles or beliefs guide the organization?

The best way to develop a mission statement is to brainstorm with those connected to the organization. Ask employees and customers what they see as their biggest strengths and weaknesses to work in the organization. A good place to start is by defining organization's core values and functions. The value of a mission statement comes from when all stakeholders (management, staff, suppliers, partners and customers) can internalize it and use it as some sort of internal business compass for their day-to-day decision making. It is also important to remember that a mission statement is not evergreen. As a company evolves over time, its mission and intent may also change. A mission statement will keep organization on track, but it shouldn't become stale of irrelevant, so revisit it every few years to fine-tune it if necessary.

In Grameen Bank, there is a strong leadership which drives the mission to growth. To develop gender equality through women's leadership development each year the center chief for GB community groups are changed, which is an opportunity to develop each borrower's leadership qualities. Muhammad Yunus (1997) says, "The same person cannot be elected twice until other members of the group have had their chance". It is a system through which the center develops poor women's leadership in rural Bangladesh and raises their self-confidence (Chandler, 1993). However, Aminur Rahman (1999) discovered that one or two influential members had real control over the decision-making process of the center. Center chiefs hold *de facto* power as they decide almost every issue of the center. Perpetuation of such power relations in the loan centers is contradictory to the Grameen Bank ideology.

Armstrong and Mollenhauer (2006) discuss the culture of accountability within organizations. In their words, "A culture of accountability describes the critical success factors and indicators that need to be present in a highly accountable organization. The success factors are strategic leadership, performance culture, and rigorous decision; abilities to generate reliable information, create an environment of innovation, access and manage risk, and the possession of clear values and ethics" (p. 1). Grameen Bank shows such success in its work in Bangladesh. For example, in 1988 and 1998 there were some major floods which destroyed farmers/borrowers standing crops, resources and houses. GB borrowers were seriously affected by these two floods. In the periods following the post-floods, the Grameen Bank provided extra loans to its borrowers to rehabilitate their businesses. This disaster loan helped borrowers to recover their businesses, renovate their houses and cultivate crops. However, this disaster loan came with a 20% interest similar to the basic loan. Many journalists criticized it and compared GB to the East India Company in their dealings with the poor.

GB staff members are committed to implementing its credit programs for the benefit of poverty eradication and the creation of self-employment opportunities. Grameen Bank engages its stakeholders and creates meaningful dialogue with the more critical parties such as the NGO Bureau of Affairs and the Ministry of Finance Bangladesh, and invite them to participate actively in helping to achieve its mission. The bank also collaborates with Grameen Trust to replicate its peer support lending technology to other agencies with the help of UN agencies, CIDA and USAID.

According to Sonia Opina, William Diaz and James O'Sullivan (2002) negotiated accountability must encompass involving the range of stakeholders from the initial inception of the program, through to its implementation, evaluation and finally to the dissemination of results. Good communication mechanisms are important tools in negotiating the accountability environment in order to learn about and respond to the needs of the community. In the negotiation processes, stakeholders need to be flexible in their win-win situation. However, GB is always looking for a win-win situation and that sometimes creates problems with its shareholders. For example, in 1983, GB wanted 100% of share capital to be owned by its borrowers, but instead, the government registered it with 60% owned by the government. After a long process of negotiation GB achieved 93% of shares for its borrowers, while the government retained 7% of capital shares. However, the current Government of Bangladesh (2015-2018) is trying to control the bank. The election for new board members from GB borrowers is withheld for last five years. The current GB Board is run by the board members from GB borrowers those were elected in 2010.

James M. Ferris (1993) emphasizes the autonomy of MFIs/NGOs to implement their own decisions. Unfortunately, the government often regulates the activities of nonprofits organizations, using them as instruments for carrying out public policies; in particular, the expansion of welfare state expenditures at the national level. In practice, there is really no absolute autonomy in the nonprofits sector, but rather all organizations are held accountable to the NGO Bureau. Although the government should monitor MFIs and NGOs funding and activities, it is not acceptable to regulate and place conditions on them that might hamper their abilities to manage their programs effectively.

There are many NGOs in Bangladesh involved in adult literacy, maternal and child health, primary health care, nutrition, education, agriculture, relief and rehabilitation programs. For instance, BRAC itself has established more than 5,000 primary schools and kindergartens where about half a million students are enrolled. Grameen Shikka is providing child education in the villages in Bangladesh. It is very interesting that government schools have 15% attendance, whereas, NGOs have about 90% attendance (Holloway, 1998). Grameen Bank has introduced learning signatures to poor those are interest to receive loans from grameen bank. Through this introduction of signature learning for receiving loans from GB, all borrowers of GB learn and practice signature as when needed. Consequently, the literacy rate has increased. The latest statistics shows that the adult literacy rate has increased over the last few years, especially female, from 16% to 38.1%. However, very few MFIs/NGOs are involved in vocational skills development for the poor. Grameen Bank and other MFIs are not involved in vocational skills development. However, Grameen Shikka has been including vocational training for unemployed rural youths in Savar since 2012. However, large NGOs do not develop their role in the area of environmental sanitation, which includes provision of fresh water and disposal of waste (Chowdhury 1989). GB and other MFIs can step in for environmentalism. However, GB is providing environmentally friendly micro loans to its borrowers in Bangladesh. However, Grameen Shakti has been serving renewable energy services in Bangladesh since 1997.

Recently the Grameen Bank has shifted to a profit motive instead of retaining its original objectives. This profit-making focus diverted the focus of employees to credit disbursement and repayments rates; simultaneously turning them away from social and citizenship development issues. This is despite the fact that GB had objectives of creating organizational solidarity and networks among the poor and bringing groups together in co-operative activities such as the joint effort solution of problems. This system has led to more opportunities for women to show leadership. However, Anne Maria and Sengupta (1996) challenge this and infer that GB focuses on dispersal of credit and repayment, but it is unable to create solidarity among women. Rahman (1999) remarks that Grameen Bank has a really good objective, but now there is a gap between its original goals and field realities. Moreover, default borrowers' numbers are increasing in Grameen Bank. An external team or an external audit team can find out the reasons for increasing defaulter borrowers in Grameen Bank.

Drake and Rhyne (2002) concluded that instead of helping to eradicate poverty MFIs are involved in doing high profit business. Although Muhammad Yunus of Grameen Bank cautiously makes an important point in that the development finance community must continue to innovate in the areas of targeting tools, products, service delivery and operations in order to reach the full range of low income families. However, a focus on financial sustainability encourages MFIs to place a greater emphasis on making profit than on the well-being of clients. This has a negative impact on borrowers' lives (Goetz & Sen Gupta, 1996); Morduch, 1999; Rahaman, 1999; and Woller, 2002). For example, GB made a profit of $6.03 million dollars in 2005 (Grameen Bank, 2005, p. 54). Although Grameen Bank claims to be a social benefit institution, it now operates on a profit motive like as a private bank.

In 2000, GB reformed some of its products and introduced a new system called the Grameen Generalized System (GSS). Before 2000, all Grameen operations were termed Grameen Classical System (Phase-1) and after 2000 the same operation was renamed, Phase-2. In GB Phase-2, GB is more flexible and friendly to borrowers in loan transactions. The new system's main features are prime loan products including basic loans, housing loansand the higher education loan. Repayments can be made according to borrowers' income and loan size as per repayment records. Grameen Bank had tested this new mechanism in the field before establishing it in all branches. However, this new initiative has challenged the bank to sustain work with the poor in the lowest realms of poverty. GB in its Zonal Managers Conference in 2015, the managing director has developed strategies to reduce delinquent borrowers of grameen bank. This means many delinquent borrowers still exist in grameen bank. GB is trying to rehabilitate delinquent borrowers those who like to rehabilitate their businesses. However, GB is write-off its overdue delinquent loans every year. The Chaiman of Grameen Bank asked GB officials didsburse new loans to new micro-borrowers. This strategy can assist incorporate latest poor people in the community as well as increase loan disbursement amount. These strategies could assist increase GB loan outstanding that can drive to more profit of Grameen Bank.

One must consider why citizenry is important and what role the GB plays in citizenship skills development for low income women in Bangladesh. If we consider empowerment as 'the process of challenging existing power relations, and of gaining greater control over the sources of power then it gives conflicting information. For example, the Kabeer's (1998) study, *The Small Enterprise Development Program (SEDP) of Bangladesh* draws the conclusion that micro-credit programs have a positive effect, but it is largely men who benefit, because micro-credit has done little to move toward a situation of gender equality.

However, in Canada NGOs are diversified and are vehicles for the engagement of citizens and environmentalism. For example, the Ontario Coalition for Advocacy against Poverty (OCAP), Canadian Council on Social Development (CCSD) and Canadian Ethno Cultural Association (CEC) are involved in advocacy programs, as well as in protesting, advocating and lobbying for human rights and women's rights. Campaign 2000 for the National Child Benefit (NCB) in Canada has influenced the government to change some policies on child poverty and childcare. Although the Campaign 2000 is unpleasant, risky and controversial, it is successful in increasing child benefits for Canadian children. Likewise, Grameen Bank and other MFIs and NGOs can make alliances among them and lobby for participatory democracy and equity in all public policies. Canadian lobbyist organizations are strong and popular in Canada in contrast to the weakness of Bangladeshi NGOs in lobbying for women's rights.

Ilan Kapoor (2002) mentions that the PRA campaigns for local knowledge and puts forth a methodology aimed at enabling local people to take power over their own lives. Ultimately these strategies can help form an understanding of the power and politics of the society. Participatory rural appraisal (PRA) is an approach used by non-governmental organizations (NGOs) and other agencies involved in international development. The aim of this approach is to incorporate the knowledge and opinions of rural people in the planning and management of development projects and programmes. The philosophical roots of participatory rural appraisal techniques can be traced to activist adult education methods such as those of Paulo Freire and the study clubs of the Antogonish Movement in Canada and Zapatist Movement in Mexico. In this view, an actively involved and empowered local population is essential to successful rural community development. Robert Chambers, a key exponent of PRA, argued that the approach owes much to "the Freirian theme" that poor and exploited people can and should be enabled to analyze their own reality.

Participatory rural appraisal (PRA) is based on equitable and respectful partnerships and collaboration between clients and institutions with due attention to local knowledge (Chamber, 1997); Crush, 1995); Escobar, 1995); and Friedmann, 1992). According to Amartya Sen (1999) PRA is a process of developing individual capabilities through education and skills in order to empower individuals to fight for a better life, democracy and economic liberalization. Grameen Bank and all other MFIs are working closely with marginalized people at the grassroots level. This level of organizational development is an integral part of Grameen's credit program. It follows the Participatory Approach in working with the poor building from a location-specific context. GB believes that if group solidarity is strong, the poor can together form a socially and politically powerful entity. However, in practice GB borrowers are far behind to challenge the power structure of the society.

Source: Wikipedia- Bangladesh women talks about
their village development using PRA method

Robert D. Putnam (2000) says that if participation in political deliberation declines – if fewer and fewer voices engage in democratic debate – then politics will become shriller and less balanced (p. 338). Disadvantaged people will be further exploited in the public sphere. Therefore, GB follows the democratic process by electing group leaders; however, it does not have programs in which borrowers can be involved in the legislative electoral process that can create a real democratic voice in the public sphere especially in politics in order to establish their rights in the society.

Therefore, Grameen Bank and other MFIs and NGOs' programs on civic engagement are very essential in Bangladesh to mobilize citizenry because strong and caring communalities start with the citizen as the base of their development. Civic engagement or civic participation, according to the American Psychological Association, is "individual and collective actions designed to identify and address issues of public concern". It can be defined as citizens working together to make a change or difference in the community. Civic engagement or broad participation in decision-making is a prerequisite for achieving sustainable development. Yunus realizes this and took the initiative to be involved in politics in 2007. However, he did not continue his commitment to be engaged in politics. Other NGO leaders did not respond to his new mission. Even Grameen Bank does not take up the challenge of activism for citizenry.

The GB and other MFI's have been working in close contact with the rural poor. It is estimated that NGOs employ 200,000 young men and women as fieldworkers in Bangladesh. The educated NGO workers have daily contact with the villagers, visiting them in their homes. In the 1980s the staff of Grameen bank spent more time in the centers discussing various social issues with group members. However, now the bank workers are involved with different types of loan investments like basic loans and housing loans and collect them from the borrowers (Bernasek, 1992; Chandler 1993); Goetz & Sen Gupta, 1996). These activities, according to Hashemi, "this going to the poor breaks down some of the threatening distance between the educated NGO workers and the poor, that is so much a part of rural social stratification (Hashemi 1997b: p. 4). According to Karim (2001), "These activities in reality, introduce a new power elite into the existing dynamic of rural social relations (p. 96).

In West Bengal, popular political mobilization has successfully led to pro-poor economic reforms. The rural poor people were able to use local government as an alternative institutional channel for promoting their interests (Sengupta & Gazdar, 1998). Union council is a local government institution that has been involved in local political power, but is less powerful in helping the local people. Yunus recently tried to draw the government's attention to focus on this local institution Union Council; however, GB is not directly involved in lobbying for citizenry.

According to the Grameen Bank Annual Report of 2005, 58% of the families of Grameen borrowers have moved above the poverty line. The remaining families are moving towards the poverty line. However, if we compare Grameen borrowers' electoral success with their economic elevation, we can draw an assumption that political achievement is not as strong as its economic improvement. For example, in 1997, out of a total of 4298 unions of Bangladesh, 7 GB members and 39 members of the family were elected to the position of Chairman. In addition, 1,073 family members were elected as members of the union council (Grameen Dialouge 2001, p.16). However, this data is not as strong as its poverty reduction success statistics.

Recently, BRAC initiated a TUP program that re-engages social mobilization and advocacy programs. PROSHICA had been campaigning for poor engaging in rural power structure and increase their voice in Bangladesh. However, they are on a small scale. Massive expansion of such programs can help to create a voice for the poor. GB can initiate such an advocacy program that can help the poor gain access to political institutions; and thus challenge and reform public policy.

Since 1989, Grameen Trust (GT) has played a role in promoting the Grameen Bank type micro credit programs in Bangladesh and in different countries. It initiated a number of international dialogue programs where many overseas people came from different countries to participate and to learn and share their experiences with Grameen loan programs. By June 2006, GT partners had collectively reached more than 3.14 million poor families with micro credit in 37 countries through 143 projects in Asia, the Pacific, Europe, Africa and the Americas (Grameen Dialogue, 2006).

However, a number of problems arose during the initial replication and implementation phases. Some replication projects are not successful. For example, The Good Faith Fund in Arkansas initiated a Grameen type loan project in 1990. Although this project is popular in Arkansas, it has merged with the local credit union since

1998. However, Grameen type credit programs in India, Pakistan, Philippines, Myanmar, China, Nepal, and Bhutan continue to be successful. Grameen America, a MFI, has started in America in 2008 is popular in different cities of USA and it is expanding across America that mentioned earlier in this paper.

8.0. Conclusion

From the above discussion, it appears that the Grameen Bank and other MFIs and NGOs are playing a very important role in socio-economic development in Bangladesh and elsewhere although many of them have credit programs. Although there are some criticisms about the controversial roles of MFIs, the widespread existence of GB and other MFIs involved in social development programs cannot be ignored. They are well able to improve many people's living standards and eradicate poverty. The unfortunate truth; however, is that very few of them are involved in democracy and advocacy programs for citizenry skills development of the poor. Therefore, it is very important that GB and other MFIs include an alternative model of democratic development in their programs for strengthening awareness among the disadvantaged people. At the same time, government should not isolate MFIs from their development programs but rather, work in cohorts with such organizations. MFIs should also understand the local environment and culture. Furthermore, although the Grameen Bank is committed to its credit delivery program in Bangladesh it could initiate a pilot project for lobbying for women's equality rights. This initiative can be achieved through involving people in civic engagement programs.

Acronyms

Association of Social Advancement (ASA), Bangladesh Rural Advancement Committee (BRAC), Grameen Bank (GB), non-governmental organizations (NGOs), microfinance institutions (MFIs), Millennium Development Goals (MDGs), participatory rural appraisal (PRA), Proshika Manobik Unnayan Kendra (PROSHIKA).

Bibliography

Armstrong, R., and Mollenhauer, I. (2006). *A culture of accountability*. Toronto: Ontario Trillium Foundation

Bannerji, H. (1993). *Popular Images of South Asian Women. Returning the gaze: Essays on racism, feminism, and politics*. Toronto: Sister Vision Press

Barry, B. (1995). *Social Movements. In The Element of Social Theory* (pp.151-171). Princeton, N.J: Princeton University Press

BRAC Research and Education Department (2004). The elites, their perspectives of poverty, and the Gram Shahayek Committee: Some early explorations: CFPR/TUP *Research Preview*, Vol. 1(7)

Cathrine H. Lovell (1992). *Breaking the Cycle of Poverty*, Connecticut: Kumanan Press Inc.

Chambers, Robert (1994). The origin and practice of participatory rural appraisal. *World Development*, Vol. 22(7), pp. 953–969

Chowdhury, A., N. (1989). *Let Grassroots Speak: People's Participation, Self-help Groups, and NGOs in Bangladesh* (pp. 18-19). Dhaka: University Press Limited

Chowdhury, O., F. (2005). *The diversity of volunteerism: Bangladesh perspective retrieved from* http://www.un.org/dpi/ngosection/chowdhur.htm dated August 23, 2018

De Tocqueville, A. (2000). The Influence of Democracy on the Sentiment of Americas,' in *Democracy in America*,. P. Mayer, ed., New York, Perennial Classics

Drake, C. and Rhyne, E. (Eds.) (2002). *The commercialization of microfinance: Balancing business and development*. Blomfield, C.T: Kumarian Press

Dressen, A., J. (2000). *What do we know about the volunteer sectors? An overview*. Research Paper, Statistics Canada

Evans, B., M. and Shields, J. (2000). *Neoliberal restructuring and the Third Sector: Reshaping governance, civil society and local relations*. Department of Politics and School of Public Administration, Toronto: Ryerson Polytechnic University

Fuglesang, A. and Chandler, D. 1989. *Participation as process: What we learn from Bangladesh,* Dhaka: Grameen Trust

Goetz, A. M. and Gupta, R. (1996). Who Talks the Credit? Gender, Power, and Control over Loan Use in Rural Credit Programs in Bangladesh. *World Development,* Vol. 24(1), pp. 45-63

Grameen Bank (2006). *Grameen Bank at a glance,* Dhaka: Grameen Bank

Grameen Dialogue (2005). Impact of Grameen Bank microcredit, *Grameen Dialogue 60,* Dhaka: Grameen Trust

Grameen Dialouge (2006). *Group lending microcredit,* Dhaka: Grameen Trust

Grameen Trust (2006). *Monthly Report (June 2006).* Dhaka: Grameen Trust.

Haque, M., S. (2002). The changing balance of power between the government and NGO in Bangladesh. *International Political Science Review,* Vol. 23, pp. 413-415

Hollister, D. (1982). *The Knowledge and Skill Bases of Social development in Daniel S. Sanders (ed.), The Development Perspective in Social Work,* Honolulu: University of Hawai

Hossain, F. (1994). *Mullahs escalate NGO-bashing,* Holiday (Dhaka), April 1, 1994

http://www.un.org/dpi/ngosection/chowdhur.htm

IDB (2008). *Statistics and Quantitative Analysis Unit,* Internet Report

Isserles, R., G. 2003. Microcredit The Rhetoric of Empowerment, the Reality of "Development As Usual", *Women's Studies Quarterly,* Vol. 3 & 4, pp. 47-53

James M. F. (1993). The Double-Edged Sword of Social Service Contracting: Public Accountability vs. Nonprofit Autonomy. *Nonprofit Management and Leadership,* Vol. 3(4), pp. 336-376

Karim, L. (2001) Politics of the poor? NGOs and grass-roots political mobilization in Bangladesh. *American Anthropological Association,* Vol. 24(1), pp. 92-107

Kevin P. K. (1996). *Preserving the public trust: managing for accountability.* New York: Jossey-Bass publishers, pp. 29-44

Kevin P. K. (2006). *From adequate to outstanding performance.* The Forbes Funds.

Khan, A. K. (1981). *Christian Missions in Bangladesh: A survey.* London: Islamic Foundation

Khandker, S and Latif, M. (1996). The role of Family Planning and Targeted Credit Programs in Demographic Change in Bangladesh in *World Bank discussion paper no. 337.* Washington: The World Bank

Khanker, S. (1998). *Fighting Poverty with Micro credit- Experience in Bangladesh.* New York: Oxford University Press Inc.

Kholiquzzaman, Q. A. (1988). *Development communication and grassroots participation: Bangladesh Case.* Dhaka: Bangladesh Institute of Development Studies

Kobayashi, A. (2000). Advocacy from the Margins: The Role of Minority Ethno cultural association*s in Affecting Public Policy in Canada in the Nonprofit Sector in Canada: Roles and relationships, (Ed).* Banting, Keith G.). pp. 229-261. MacGil-Queen's University Press

Latifee. H. T. (2002). *Grameen Trust Experience (1991-2002).* Dhaka: Grameen Trust Publication

Mahamud, S. (2004). Micro-credit and Women's Empowerment in Bangladesh in *Attacking Poverty with Micro-credit (Eds.)* Salehuddin, A. and Hakim, M. A. (2004). Dhaka: Dhaka University Press

Michael, H. and Keith, G. B. (2000). The Nonprofit Sector in Canada: An introduction, 'in *the Nonprofit Sector in Canada: Roles and relationships.* Toronto: McGill-Queens University Press

Mizan, A. N. (1994). *In Quest of Empowerment: The Grameen Bank Impact on Women's Power and Status.* Dhaka: United Press Ltd.

Muttra Foundation (2004). Talking about Charities 2004, Muttra Foundation. Canada

Nuruzzaman S. (1994). *NGOs-The web of new colonialism: Aid merchant buying up Sonar Bangla,* Impact International (London), July 1994, p.8

Rahman, A. (1999). Micro-credit Initiatives for equitable and Sustainable Development: Who pays? *World Development*, Vol. 27(1), pp. 67-82. Elsevier Science Ltd.

Richard Holloway (1998). *Supporting citizens' initiatives: Bangladesh's NGOs and society.* London: International Technology Publications

Robert, P. (2000). *Democracy,' in bowling alone: The collapse and revival of American community.* New York: Simon & Schuster

Rouf, K. A. (2011). Citizenship Learning, Participatory Democracy and Micro-Financing: The Case of Grameen Bank's Peer-Lending System in Bangladesh. *Journal of Global Citizenship & Equity Education.* Vol. 1(1), pp 124-147. http://journals.sfu.ca/jgcee/

Rouf, K. A. (2011). Grameen Bank women borrowers familial and community relationships development in patriarchal Bangladesh. *International Journal of Research Studies in Psychology.* Vol.1 (1), pp. 17-26. ISSN 2243-7681.

Rouf, K. A. (2011). Grameen Bank women borrowers' private space and public space development in patriarchal Bangladesh. *T-Space, (PhD thesis) University of Toronto.* Identifier: http://hdl.handle. net/1807/31920

Ruth, A. and Linda, M. (2006). *A culture of accountability.* Ontario Trillium Foundation. Toronto

Shamsul, H. (2002). The changing balance of power between the Government and NGO in Bangladesh. *International Political Science Review*, Vol. 23, pp. 411-435

Sherri Torjman. (1998). Strategies for carrying society. *Caledon Institute of Social Policy Presentation.* Vol. 23(3). pp. 1-20

Sonia, O., Diaz, W., Sullivan, L. (2002). Negotiating accountability: Managerial lessons from identity-based non-profit organizations. *Nonprofit and Volunteer Sector Quarterly*, Vol. 31(1), 5-31. Retrieved from http://nvs.sagepub.com/cgireprint dated October 31, 2015

Syed, S., I. (1998). Impacts of Technology and NGOs on Social Development: The case of Bangladesh. *Journal of South Asian and Middle Eastern Studies*, Vol. 21 (2), pp. 51-63

The Grameen Bank Ordinance (1983). *The Grameen Bank Ordinance,* Dhaka: Grameen Bank

The Independent Dhaka (1999). *Internet Edition*, December 21, 1999

The Morning Sun Dhaka, (1993). *War on want: An NGOs Nijera Kori, supported by Christian Aid*, Dhaka, dated April 27, 1993

The New Nation Dhaka (1999). *Internet edition*, September 11, 1996

The UN Research Institute for Development (1963). The Commission for social development (New York: 1963). See also ILO, Perspectives: World Summit for Social development: Impetus to Concerted Action." *International Labor Reviews*, (1995). Vol. 134 (2), pp. 243-258

Thornton, P., J. Devine, P. Houtzager and Wright, D. (2000). *Partners in development. A review of Big NGOs in Bangladesh*. Report commissioned by DFID, Bangladesh

World Bank (1994*). World Bank Annual Report 1994*. Dhaka: Association of Development Agencies in Bangladesh

Wuthnow, R. (1991). The Voluntary sector: Legacy of the Past, Hope for the Future? in Between States and Markets: the volunteer Sector in *Comparative Perspective*, Robert Wuthnow, (ed.), Princeton, Princeton University Press. pp. 3-28.

Yunus, M. (2003). *What is Microcredit?* Dhaka: Grameen Bank.

Yunus, M. (2005). *Grameen struggling program*. Washington: State of the Micro credit Summit Campaign (2005), Washington D.C.

Yunus, M. (2006). *Grameen Bank at a glance*. Dhaka: Grameen Bank

Micro Financing Implementation and Expansion Strategies of Grameen Bank in Bangladesh

Abstract

Grameen Bank (GB) is a successful micro lending organization in Bangladesh that is initiated by Muhammad Yunus as a pilot project in Jobra village in 1976. It provides small loans to rural poor women, without collateral, following group lendingpeer support methodologies. It disburses $16.7 billion to 8.67 million borrowers through 2247 branches across Bangladesh. The loan repayment rate is 97%. It is a self-sufficient financial institution. GB's unique program implementation steps make it successful in achieving its goals of creating self-employment and creates choice among rural poor women; thereby, increasing their income, empowering them, and promoting environmentalism in rural Bangladesh. Obvious loan disbursement policy, simplified record keeping arrangement, monitoring and evaluation system, accounting procedures, auditing, decentralization policy, two way flow of information and communication (bottom-up approach) etc. are the outstanding process that empowered GB borrowers. Moreover, location specific solution by field staffs strategy, prompt respond to field problems, active community participation, and staff rewards for outstanding jobs altogether create competition and inspiration among employees to offer a high quality of services to its borrowers.

Guidance to field staffs by the executives, coordination with other stakeholders, bottom-up decision making, and the "learning by doing" approach are the core elements of the program of grameen Bank. Regular audits and inspections with monitoring information systems (MIS) are fabulous elements of GB's credit execution. GB runs its costs from its own investment income. Grameen Bank does not hire foreign consultants for its program design, development and implementation.

The sixteen decisions of the Grameen Bank that clients follow encourage them to develop their resource capital, human capital, social capital and other sustainable development in the borrowers' life. GB has succeeded in achieving its goals/objectives because it works in the community as an insider not as an outsider. Above all, Muhammad Yunus' dynamic leadership mobilizes staff to work hard for the betterment of the lives of clients. Now Grameen micro credit is recognized as a tool to eradicate poverty and to empower women. Its lending methodology has been replicating in 98 countries all over the world since 1993.

Key words: Empowerment, business capital, human capital, NGOs, self-employment, social capital, and sustainable development.

1.0. Introduction

There were several rural development and poverty eradication projects initiated by various government and non-governmental agencies in Bangladesh at different times. For example, the Bangladesh Rural Development Board (BRDB), Integrated Rural Development Program (IRDP), Food for Work Program, CARE Bangladesh, Rangpur and Dinajpur Rural Services (RDRS), Village Aid, and Bangladesh Rural Rehabilitation Program (BRRP) etc. However, few projects focused exclusively on poor women in development and the feminization of poverty. Many of them were temporary relief programs and handout projects. In contrast, the Grameen Bank (GB) micro financing program continued for more than three decades and is successful in sustainably addressing poverty and empowering rural women in Bangladesh. Now it is recognized as a model of development work in the world. This essay focuses on the implementation steps, features, policies and programs the Grameen Bank engages, which has made it a successful national financial institution in Bangladesh and has resulted in its replication across the world. Its micro lending technology is replicating across the world because of its uniqueness.

Bangladesh has 165 million people within a 147,570 square kilometer area (Bangladesh profile 2014). Half of the population is female. The majority of Bangladesh's people live in rural areas. The density of the population is 763 people per square kilometer. 67% of women live under the poverty line, which is significantly higher than the national average of 51% (Human Rights Report, 2000). Therefore, a majority of rural poor women are suffering from absolute poverty and miseries. The reasons for these sufferings may be found in the limited access to voice and choice of state resources. Hence, policies, programs and projects which focus on income generation and rural poverty are urgently needed to fulfill their basic needs.

Four decades ago banking facilities were not favorable to the landless poor in Bangladesh. Collateral for loans were a requirement and this proved to be a strong barrier against the rural poor accessing institutional credit. Therefore, a specialized bank was needed where alternative credit facilities without collateral could be delivered. This need was filled by the Grameen Bank which was established in 1976 by Muhammad Yunus. It delivers credit to the rural poor without collateral, giving priority to rural poor women.

Muhammad Yunus started credit operation on a pilot basis in a village named Jobra in 1976. This initiative was a flashlight to the poor women of Jobra village with little credit. This pilot credit project was desired by other villages and there was a great demand from many rural women to get loans for starting businesses (Yunus, 1994).

GB objectives involve extending banking facilities to the poor for their self-employment, to free them from exploitation by money lenders, and to empower women through providing them with collateral-free loans for doing businesses. GB introduced group-managed, peer support loan repayment system among borrowers in which they would repay loans in weekly installments at 2% of the principal amount, plus interest, within one year. After 2002, GB has changed loan repayment period for six months, but other strategies remain same. This credit program also included savings products which would help to develop better saving strategies among its borrowers. The whole mechanism of GB goes to the borrowers' doorsteps. They do not need to come to the bank office to repay their loans. The whole structure and operation of GB makes borrowing and repayment convenient and easy for its clients. There are no rigid structural policies and monitoring devices by outside consultants. The field staffs of the GB are responsible for developing its loan operation policies, programs and operation strategies, and accounting and monitoring devices. Yunus, its founder, coordinates all staff activities, ideas and recommendations and is the apex leader of GB loan operation in Bangladesh.

Many scholars and researchers studied Grameen Bank micro credit operation. This GB micro credit system has had a great impact on extreme poverty (Khondaker 2003). It can play a vital role in attaining Millennium Development Goals (MDGs). In the words of Kofi Anan, UN Secretary General, says "microfinance has proved its value, in many countries, as a weapon against poverty and hunger. Now it is recognized as a development model for income generation self-employment and empowers disadvantaged women" (Grameen Dialouge-60, 2005).

2.0. Implementation strategies of Grameen Bank

At the beginning Grameen Bank started as a pilot project, which had no formal organizational structure and procedures for delivering loans to poor people. The Grameen Bank project developed its implementation strategies, working methodology, and credit delivery mechanisms in the course of time. All credit delivery technologies were developed during its operation. GB has developed "learning by doing" method during its establishment. However, GB policies, implementation strategies, credit delivery and recovery mechanisms and other parameters are in a continual process of development and change to fulfill borrowers' needs and demands through situational analysis and through a bottom-up approach. It is obvious that rigidity in policies and guidelines have no place in GB.

3.0. Grameen Bank client development and client improving services

Micro financing institutions are working for supporting micro entrepreneurs to promote micro entrepreneurs micro enterprises. Grameen bank deals with GB borrowers like as GB customers through its different attractive products with quality service. GB developed strategies for reaching the clients more efficiently which enabled GB and its clients to make an adequate level of income. GB defines its clients as partner of the GB loan operations. It thinks client's success is the success of GB. GB looks for the origin of the demand of the poor people in the community and identifies related services for them. At the beginning, GB field staffs survey the area and survey the demographic segments of the poor people in the community, discern local physical infrastructures and social infrastructures in the community and analyses people's loans demands would be to GB. The next step is to find where the acute poverty sufferers target clients thrive and develop ways of relationships that could help poor people to be easy and comfortable to do banking with GB. Then field staffs started to provide unique simplified non-formal training in person within loan seekers neighbourhoods to familiarize poor people about the GB products and services for sxeven days. Information previously gathered help field staffs in formulating the appropriate products (size of loans, types of loans, modes of repayments) and service strategies.

4.0. Benefits of adapting the in-person client services of GB

- Encourages the GB micro entrepreneurs to think of creative ways to serve its clients
- Identifies and generates more loan receivers (clients) those can do business well by receiving loans from GB
- Allows the poor micro-entrepreneurs to grow steadily in profiting business, repay the loans and to empower them both economically and socially

- Enables the entrepreneurs to expand their businesses with new products and services
- GB in-person communication system helps GB clients to have direct relations and communications with GB. No need advertisement for GB to inform and expand GB in Bangladesh. GB has no advertisements on radio, TV, print media and in other social media
- GB in-person services to its borrowers give GB an advantage over the competition with its uniqueness
- The cliental relationships with GB has increased sustainable loan services to poor people in Bangladesh
- GB micro entrepreneurs relations with GB improved continuously
- GB entrepreneurs' microenterprises put in the best competitive position because of entrepreneur-client relationship
- Micro entrepreneurs easily obtain a competitive advantage over big enterprises by improving GB client's service and clients networking within the community.

5.0. Monitoring and Information System (MIS) of Grameen Bank

GB is more concern with calculating its vision and maintaining its organizational culture. Its' management has some motivational devices to ensure targeted performances. GB monitors its loan services to borrowers intensively. GB has an efficient MIS cell at its different stages of admin layers. It has developed its loan monitoring system that provides quick feedback to the fields by the GB executives. Grameen Bank uses its management information system (MIS) to generate information for decision making and to disseminate information back to lower level staff so that they can systematize their own performance. This MIS system has grown from field experience and that allows managers and field staffs to track its accomplishments.

6.0. Best practice parameters of Grameen Bank

GB has developed some parameters that are keys to the success of its objectives. These parameters are properly included in the operational structure at all levels and can be readjusted to the various needs of the poor in order to eradicate poverty. The GB target group is exclusively rural poor women. Its loan operations follow group lending methodology. It places special attention to and adapts community participation approaches to empower women. Loan appraisals and planning are conducted in the weekly centre meetings through mutual discussions and observance; not by complicated paper work or complicated financial and marketing analysis. Groups are composed of five poor women of similar socio-economic backgrounds, from the same village. Six groups make one center in a neighborhood/village. Borrowers themselves select their group members, but GB staff screen and verify members' portfolio backgrounds to ensure that they are indeed the poorest of the poor. This group formation system helps to maintain a homogeneous setting, networking and solidarity, in which clients can interact freely with each other. Nonetheless, strict credit discipline and close supervision is in place to guide each borrower towards proper control of loans.

7.0. Unique practices of Grameen Bank

To maintain equal opportunity and to address issues of participatory management, democracy and empowerment to all members of Grameen Bank, the positions of Centre Chief, Group Chairman, and Group Secretary change every year. Through this process, all members of the center get a chance to be Center Chief, Group Chairman, and Group Secretary by rotation every year. This practice helps to enhance leadership qualities and decision making skills in all members. In addition, this practice of rotating leaders adds to a decentralized power structure and holds each member accountable to the other within the center. These tools are essential to the efficient operation of the credit program including avoiding inequalities and maintaining corruption free loan transactions. These unique practices of the Grameen Bank start from making annual action plans at the field level. Branch managers set up some performance indicators like loan disbursements, loan repayment, group savings, and attendance in the centre meetings of borrowers (Annex-3) and borrowers' wealth creation by loan utilization etc. These parameters track the viability of the branch performances. The branch maintains all loans transections and other such related documents. Its performance is ensured by GB internal audit department and by external audit team every year. This internal auditing process enhances the leakage free credit delivery system.

The entire GB credit operation operates through a system of close supervision. There is an in-service training program in GB for its staff training. This practical training helps staff to be committed and to work for the poor as a cohesive team. There are no intermediaries between clients and the bank at the grass roots level. GB charges 20% interest on its general loans and 5% interest on its housing loans and student loans. There is no subsidy at any stage of the GB credit operation.

The simple, straight-forward program designed for loan proposals through mutual discussions among center members ensures diversified loan disbursements to its clients. All transactions are conducted within centre meetings and are intensively monitored. It ensures mutual accountability through a peer support mechanism. No information is kept secret, so there is no scope for corruption, misappropriation or irregularities. These strategies further contribute to the successful operations of the Grameen Bank.

8.0. Replication of Grameen Bank Model

The Grameen Bank credit program is widely accepted as a tool for poverty reduction. It attracts the attention of all development experts, researchers, universities, executives, policy makers and donors as a micro credit success story in Bangladesh for addressing poverty. Different countries have used Grameen Bank group-based credit experiences to replicate similar practices in their own cultural contexts. The Grameen micro credit model has been replicated worldwide since 1993. Now 98 countries follow GB group lending model, but they adjust their lending programs to their local culture, values and norms (Grameen Trust 2002, p.51).

The Global Micro Credit Summits of 1997, 2002, 2006 and 2011 helped to draw the attention of policy makers and practitioners' worldwide. Different international organizations like UNDP, UNHCR, UNICEF, ILO, CIDA, SIDA, USAID and several countries included the micro financing program in their policies to address poverty. All projects that were modeled on the GB reported loan repayment rates of more than 95%. These micro finance institution (MFI) initiators are trying to cover their cost of operation from their interest income. For example, Activist for Social Alternatives (ASA), Tamil Nadu, India, SHARE, Andrapradesh, India, CARD in the Philippines and NIRDHAN in Nepal, have their own banks to serve the poor (Grameen Trust Report 2006). The Grameen Bank Replication Program (GBRP) has set up a website that also helps people get information about its programs. The GB web site address is www.grameen.com/grameen/gtrust.

9.0. Facilitating factors for implementation of GB practice

The operational tools of GB which include projection meetings to plan for the program, direct contact with clients, mini meetings, rigorous training on group formation, weekly meetings, and group screenings ensure that all clients have equal opportunities to participate in decision making. These tools add to the successful implementation of the GB programs throughout Bangladesh.

GB is not a centralized decision-making organization. Management functions and decision-making powers are continuously being delegated to the branch offices to improve their managerial skills as well as to get grass roots information to hierarchal upper levels in area office, zonal office and head offices. This feedback loop involving head offices, zonal offices and branch offices enhances organizational management; decision making processes and improves program activities. Prompt responses to field problems by supervising officers are characteristic of Grameen Bank administration.

GB mobilizes its staff to be enthusiastic to do their assigned GB jobs by awarding them *star staff* and *five star branches*. Those who achieve star criteria receive appreciation letters from Managing Director, Muhammed. Yunus, monetary compensation, promotions, and opportunities to travel and conduct assignments abroad. A Grameen Bank Staff proudly displays his star on formal occasions. These awards encourage competition and help inspire field staff to be more active in their work for the poor.

Grameen Bank does not hire foreign consultants for its program design, development, and implementation. GB has taken experience directly from the field and looks at its needs. The GB staff review problems and needs, themselves. The solutions are based on local situations. The proposed solution is first tested in 2-3 branches for about 6 months on a pilot basis. Lessons are learned from the pilot experience and then the lessions learned expeiences are extended to other areas served by the bank. However, all solutions do not produce positive results.

GB has faced many problems during its operation. These have come in the form of bureaucratic influence from the government, income disruption to borrowers as a result of natural disasters like flood, cyclones and river devastation. Overlapping with other credit institutions, opposition by religious leaders and local money lenders, and political crises are also hampers to loan operations. These problems have impacted upon borrowers' income as well as loan repayment. Delinquent loans portfolios increased. These problems are solved by the GB field staffs by their continuous polite patient and respectful behaviors to borrowers, but strive to maintain credit discipline. GB staff may sometimes become disappointed, but are never disheartened about negative results. Both the head and zonal offices monitor field activities and lend constant support to their staff.

GB had served borrowers an approximate 2.54 million rural poor in 25 years in August, 2002; however, it has increased its client's services to about 6.7 million in September 2006 (GB report September 2006). This has been a huge increase within four years. This rapid expansion poses added challenges to GB to maintain quality service to its borrowers. GB offers loans to poor people for small businesses; however, it does not provide any training/orientation on small business management, marketing, loans management and book keepings that are very essential for businesses.

Although there have been many success stories of women who have been emancipated through Grameen micro-credit, Robin Isserles (2003) cautions that many women (16%) are still dominated by their husbands and do not actually enjoy the benefits from their financial gains or loan investments. In many cases, their husbands take the credit, and use the money for personal purposes (p., 43). GB gives loans to poor women for the improvement of their household economics as well as to generate social and human capitalamong them. However, GB has not put special implementation strategies to free women from patriarchal order. Rather, it believes that if women become earners, they can automatically empower themselves, promoting their own welfare as well as that of their family.

Moreover, although GB is successful in addressing poverty, 58% of its borrowers cross the poverty line (Grameen Bank 2006). Many borrowers are still living below the poverty line. Its investment interest rate is 20% to its borrowers, which is similar to other commercial banks in Bangladesh. GB covers its costs from its investment income. However, it is too much for poor people. The Government of Bangladesh could extend its subsidies to GB credit operation to reduce its costs and to reduce the burden of interest of borrowers.

22226266

10.0. Conclusions

Through working for the Grameen Bank since 1980, the author Kazi Rouf has observed that poor women are credit worthy and would have more self-confidence if they could earn money. Poor women could be more organized if they connect with institutions which support a bottom-up approach that respects poor people and their values. The projects are more successful in Bangladesh if high level socio-economic implementation technology or development ideas are not imported from outside. GB has succeeded because it works in the community as an insider not as an outsider (Rouf, 2011). Top down policy and operation contradicts with local values, norms, and culture. Hence, there is a cross relation among program design, program objectives, friendly program implementation strategies, local culture and community participation.

However, leadership is very important to mobilize people into activity, to achieve project objectives and to implement the program successfully. In addition, the project activities should exclusively focus on disadvantaged people issues; and strategies should be attentive to environmental sustainability. Poor people have less features and access to different public places, information, and resources; therefore, one stop information services to clients can help protect them from complex bureaucratic hazards. Moreover, guidance, coordination with other stakeholders, bottom-up decision making approach, and "learning by doing" approach are the core elements of the microfinancing program. Regular audits and inspection with monitoring information systems (MIS) altogether are very essential for micro financing institutions.

Feminization of poverty is increasing in Canada especially among single mothers. There are some NGOs involved in micro financing in Canada, but they are working in a limited scale. Therefore, it is necessary to initiate a micro financing project in Toronto using one stop services in one place and use some implementation techniques of GB credit operation in the project that can be adaptable to Canadian small entrepreneurs.

11.0. Bibliography

Asia Foundation Bangladesh Profile (2014). *Bangladesh Profile.* Retrieved on January 2015 from http://www.southasiafoundation.org/saf/bangladesh/banglastas.asp

Bangladesh Human Development Report (2000). *Fighting human poverty: An overview of the study.* Dhaka. Bangladesh Institute of Development Studies (BIDS), retrieved from http://www.sdnbd.org/sdi/issues/sustainable_development/bd

Brinkerhoff, D. W. (1996). Coordination issues: Policy implementation networks: An illustration from Madagascar's environmental action plan, *World Development*, Vol. 24(9), pp. 1497-1510

Coleman, G. (1999). Project planning: Logical framework approach to the monitoring and evaluation of agricultural and rural development projects, *Project Appraisal*, Vol. 2 (4), pp. 251-259

Found, W. C. (1999). *Techniques of project planning and implementation: Ten steps to success,* Toronto: Institute for Leadership Development

Grameen Bank (2002). *Grameen Bank Annual Report 2002,* Chittagong: Packages Corporation Limited

Grameen Bank (2006). *Grameen Bank Annual Report 2006,* Chittagong: Packages Corporation Limited

Grameen Bank (October 2002). *Revisiting the Wall Street Journal, the Financial Times and Grameen Bank.* Chittagong: Packages Corporation Limited

Grameen Trust (2006). *Grameen Trust Annual Report 2002,* Dhaka: Grameen Trust

Hadden, S.G. (1980). Controlled decentralization and policy implementation: The case of rural electrification in Rajasthan, in (Eds.) the *Politics and policy implementation in the Third World,* Susan G. Hadden: Princeton University Press, pp. 170-196

Khandker, S & Latif, M. (1996). The role of family planning and targeted credit programs in demographic change in Bangladesh in the *World Bank Discussion Paper* no. 337. Washington: The World Bank

Latifee. H. T. (2002). *Grameen Trust experience (1991-2002)*. Dhaka: Grameen Trust Publication

McLaughlin M. W. (1987). Learning from experience: Lessons from policy implementation, *Educational Evaluation and Policy Analysis*, Vol.9 (2)

Rogers, R.E. (1996). Preface, TQM in America- A review, and deming's 14 Points for TQM implementation', in *Implementing of Total Quality Management: A comprehensive training program,* New York: International Business Press

Rouf, A. (2018). *Organizing, designing, building and forming of groups and centers of Grameen Bank and its services implementation strategies in Bangladesh,* Toronto: Center for Learning Social Economy and Workplace, T-Space, University of Toronto.

Rouf, K. A. (2015). Micro financing implementation and expansion strategies of Grameen Bank in Bangladesh. *Global Journal of Management and Business Research (C),* Vol. 15 (10), pp. 7-14

Rouf, K. A. (2018). Views and reviews of the microcredit thoughts and MFIs services in the world. *International Journal of Research Studies in Management,* Vol. 7(2), pp. 1-20.

Rouf, A. K. (2011). The advantages of micro-credit lending programs and the human capabilities Approachfor women's poverty reduction and increased human rights in Bangladesh, *Prime Journals of Business Administration and Management (BAM).* Vol. 1(11), pp. 382-391

Warwick, D. (1980). *Bitter pills, Cambridge*: Cambridge University Press.

Yunus, M. (1994). *Grameen Bank as I See It.* Dhaka: Grameen Bank

Yunus, M. (2002). *Grameen Bank11-Designed to open new possibilities.* Dhaka: Grameen Bank

Yunus, M. (2004). *Grameen Bank at a Glance.* Dhaka: Grameen Bank

Yunus, M. (2006). *Grameen Bank at a Glance. Dhaka*: Grameen Bank

Eradication of Poverty through Community Blue Economic Development Utilizing Khas (Government Jurisdiction) Ponds: Lessons Learned from Grameen Motsho (Fisheries) O Pashusampad (Livestock) Foundation (GMPF) in Bangladesh

Abstract

Grameen Motsho O Pashusampad (Fisheries and Livestock) Foundation (GMPF)-is a sister organization of Grameen Bank (GB) involves in livestock and fish culture, mobilizing poor people engage in livestock and fish production, agriculture, horticulture, homestead gardening, social forestation and bio-gas plants and other community green income generating economic activities to bring improvement in the quality of life of the poor, in particular of poor women in Bangladesh. GMPF is managing leased of 1035 Khas (public) ponds having 2557.3 acres of water bodies and 20 fish seed farms leased from the Government of Bangladesh (GoB) for 25 years. The objectives of this study is to examine the policies, strategies and approaches of GMPF community economic development (CED) and to link CED concept with GMPF activities if it benefits to local poor people in Bangladesh. The study research questions are (1) is Grameen Motsho O PashuSampoad Foundation (GMPF) a CED program in Bangladesh? (2) If so, how it works, what approaches and strategies it follows, what are challenges it faces in implementing its programs in Bangladesh. The author writes this paper from his pre-and post-GMPF working experience. The paper contains author's live experience, review literature, secondary data and interpretative method of analysis.

GMPF has seven projects- Joygagor farm (JF), Dinajpur farm (DF), Jamuna Borrow-Pits Farm (JMBA), Empowerment of Coastal Fishing Community for Livelihood Security Project (ECFC), Community Livestock and Diary Development Project (CLDDP), Livestock Development Fund (LDF), Livestock Insurance Fund (LIF), Feed Supply and Fodder Cultivation Program (FSFCP) and Community Dairy Enterprises (CDEs).

A total of 14451.22 metric ton (MT) of fish was produced by Joygagor Farm since inception 1986 up to 2006. Fifty percent of the fish went to the share of poor beneficiaries. The Dinajpur Farm production of fish during the period 1988-1989 was only 18.60 MT per ha, which increased to 260 MT in 2006. Jamuna Borrow-pits Farm (JMBA) is a unique example of integrated farming through fish-crop-livestock and social forestation model. It has 1005 women village group members (VGMs)-the only one of its type in Bangladesh. The empowerment of coastal fishing community for livelihood security project (ECFC) developmental objectives are to promote livelihood security of the poor coastal fishing communities. Community livestock and dairy development project (CLDDP) has organized 3275 village group members (VGMs)-2750 male members and 525 female members in 655 villages in Bangladesh. Total TK 183, 09, 305 ($2.2 million) deposited to livestock development fund (LDF) and total Tk 31, 05,554 insurance premiums deposited to livestock insurance fund (LIF) by VGMs. Out of 5445 cow heifer 177 died, GMPF compensation paid against 148 dead cow heifers. GMPF has set up 6 community livestock centers (CLC), 5 livestock sub-centers and 85 trevice points had been equipped with all veterinary facilities including mini laboratory, which are managed by Community Livestock Officers (CLO), Livestock Field Assistants (LAs) and Veterinary Compounder s(VCs) located at the livestock service centers (LSCs). The veterinary clinical laboratory and vaccination services are given free of cost to project clients. GMPF has feed supply and *fodder cultivation program too. Under this program, it cultivated 1396 decimal Napier plots, 125 decimal guinea plots, 6.03 decimal ipil-ipil plots and 445 decimal maize plots. GMPF has initiated two community dairy enterprises (CDs) with milk cooling two tanks of 2000 liter each were established at Nimgachi and Dinajpur. GMPF has been executing shrimp farms at Chokoria and Satghira since 1985. GMPF had 8 fish seed multiplication farms with total area of 11.16 hectors across Bangladesh. Modern fish culture and livestock production technologies has introduced in the project. GMPF has conducted many workshops on fisheries and livestock management, community forestation and micro-credit management for local people that has impacted increasing local fish and livestock productions and community forestations in Bangladesh. Many local blue and green jobs are created by GMPF projects by expanding/ creating green small-businesses like fish cultivation, fish selling business, agricultural and artisan jobs there. GMPF runs all these projects/programs by 435 staff in Bangladesh.*

GMPF initiatives embrace the distinctive characteristics with a strong social mission. It earns revenues from the market and covers its costs from the revenues, which is hard for it to sustain financially. Moreover, the shock news is the Government of Bangladesh did not extend ponds lease agreement period to GMPF. Hence GMPF returned all ponds and fish seed farms to GoB in 2010. As result community members' access to these ponds management has declined. Hence these community members face challenges to continue their community blue and green economic development using Khas ponds in future.

Key words: Blue economy; community economic development (CED); Fish culture and Livestock Services; green economy; and social business.

Thesis: Grameen Motsho (Fisheries) O Pashusampad (Livestock) Foundation (GMPF) of Bangladesh is a very successful example of using Khas (government jurisdiction) ponds to create community blue economic development and foster local living blue economies and empower the marginalized people. The GMPF has managed to both increase local blue and green economic activities and build community social blue and green businesses through its highly successful and world renowned public ponds management.

1.0. Introduction

This paper is an overview of Grameen Motsho (Fisheries) O Pashusampad (Livestock) Foundation (GMPF), which is an example of the community resource asset-based ponds community blue economic development (CED) project in Bangladesh. The paper examines applications of theories of CED as a strategy for improving the quality of life of marginalized people through GMPF activities in rural Bangladesh.

The Grameen Motsho (Fisheries) O Pashusampad (Livestock) Foundation (GMPF) is a blue and green social business community economic development project serving marginalised people in Bangladesh from 1986-2006. The geographical areas of this project is in Bangladesh are covering 14 districts, 32 Thanas/sub- districts. The districts are Tangail, Sirajgong, Pabna, Bogra, Gaibandha, Rangpur, Kurigram, Nilphamari, Dinajpur, Thakurgaon, Panchaghar, Satkhira, Chittagong and Cox's bazaar, Satkhera and Jamalpur. GMPF involves in livestock and fish production, mobilizing poor people, engage in livestock and fish production, community forestation and other community green economic activities by managing leased 1035 Khas (public jurisdiction public) ponds having 2557.3 acres of water bodies, 20 fish seed farms lease of for 25 years (GMPF annual report 2006) from Government of Bangladesh (GoB) in 1986 (GMPF annual report 2006). It introduced two tiers accounting system that prevents project leaking and corruptions. It runs the project with 'no loss' principle. GMPF generates revenues from selling fishes, fingerlings and supply livestock vaccines. The profit generated from the project reinvested for ponds renovations, roads construction, and repair and project development.

GMPF is a social and blue business institution generating revenues and serving poor people by utilizing these leased Khas ponds in Bangladesh. The GMPF connects local poor people to these ponds; involve them in livestock and fisheries activities. These livestock and fisheries activities open local blue and green economic opportunity for marginalized communities there. The essay defines *Blue Economy* is ponds, lacks, canals marine-based economic development that leads to improved human well-being and social equity, while significantly reducing environmental risks and ecological scarcities. It includes: ponds, rivers, lacks, bays and oceans utilizing economy. Here *Green Economy* is defined as an economy that comes from natural resources, utilizing natural resources, but aims at reducing environmental risks and ecological scarcities, and that aims for sustainable development without degrading the environment. This green economy has direct valuation of natural capitaland ecological services. GMPF encourages local poor people to form fish culture and livestock associations in their areas in order to develop their capacity building to manage these Khas ponds for fish cultivation and to develop their partnership capacity and confidence among the beneficiaries. This asset-based community blue and green economic development project generates the power of local fish and livestock production associations to drive the community blue and green economic development process and leverage entitlements to local poor people (Mathieu & Cunningham, 2004) for their own benefit.

2.0. Objectives of the Study

The objectives of this study is to examine the motives, policies, strategies and approaches of GMPF community blue and green economic development (CED) and to link these concepts with GMPF if it benefits to local poor people in Bangladesh.

3.0. Research Questions

- Is Grameen Motsho (Fisheries) O Pashusampad (Livestock) Foundation (GMPF) a blue and green CED program in Bangladesh?
- If so, how it works, what approaches and strategies GMPF follows.
- What are its strengths and challenges it faces in implementing its CED mission?

4.0. Methodology

The author writes this paper from his pre-and post-GMPF operation job experience in Bangladesh. The author collected GMPF annual reports and other GMPF reports from GMPF office at Dhaka. The paper contains literature review and secondary data collected from GMPF. He directly talks with GMPF executives, field officers, and local elites of the project to know about GMPF activities, policies, strategies and approaches in Bangladesh. The author looks at GMPF 'Memorandum of Articles' and 'Memorandum of Associations' and GMPF lease agreement with the Department of Fisheries and Livestock, Government of Bangladesh. The paper follows interpretative method; however, it does not critically analyse GMPF activities, outcomes, strengths and weaknesses. Therefore, this paper is not an analytical paper rather it is an informative paper that provides readers with a synopsis of community managed Khas ponds contributed to local poverty reduction, blue economy fish culture and green economy livestock production, green technology transfer among marginalised people in Bangladesh.

5.0. Statement of the problem

The concept 'community economic development' is popular in micro and macro economics to eradicate poverty. However, there is a rare such practical example can be found in Bangladesh. Many community agencies could not find resources and capital to invest in business or farming or ways earning income to cover their costs; however, government jurisdiction ponds, lakes, canals, forests, and public unused lands exists within the community. However, these public resources are illegally captured by money lenders, political leaders and rural powerful elites. This illegal occupancy of Khas lands is increasing at exorbitant rate in Bangladesh.

Grameen Mosotho Foundation leases and utilizes government jurisdiction ponds, lakes, and lands since 1986. It extends community fisheries and livestock production in the community by utilizing these public ponds in Bangladesh, which is an example of community economic service facilities to the poor for their self-employment, to free them from deprivation of using these public resources and exploitation from rural elites and money lenders. Moreover, GMPF contributes to blue economy in Bangladesh. This initiative assists to empower marginalized community people in Bangladesh through providing and engaging them using these public resources and by involving them with fisheries and livestock production as a social blue and green business for their earning.

Many community development agencies are trying to scaling up their programs nationally, but they have not yet developed a strong system capable of serving massive numbers of poor in a sustainable fashion in Bangladesh. Author finds Bangladeshi many community development agencies are unable to scale up their programs because of scarcity of resources and unsuitable strategies and policies that are barriers to popular and expand in Bangladesh. Many NGOs could find these public resources in the community and use them for the benefit of marginalised people. Community organizations (COs) could get ideas from GMPF that could assist them initiating and implementing community economic development programs by utilizing public resource and get benefit from community public resources. The GMPF programs, implementation strategies, policies and monitoring devices narrated in this paper could help NGOs and community organizations (COs) get ideas from it.

6.0. Literature Review

Community economic development (CED) means a process through which citizens take charge of planning and managing economic development projects in their community areas with the aim of creating employment for them, improving their quality of life and developing greater community autonomy (Shragge, 1997, p. 103). It is an attempt to democratize the economic life of the neighbourhood's particularly marginalized people. Quarter et al. (2009) believe that CEDs are working for communities that are facing problems; unemployment, poverty, job loss, environmental degradation and loss of community control, need to be addressed in a holistic and participatory way (p. 95). CED initiatives embrace the distinctive characteristics of a strong social mission, but earn revenues from the market and require ongoing external supports, often from government (Brown & Iverson 2004; Dees, 1998; Quarter, Mook & Armstrong, 2009; Yunus, 2007). It refers to communities of common interest. CED programs can be considered as commercial non-profits. For example, CED Canada emphasizes distinct values: it has emerged as an alternative to conventional approaches to economic development. In Canada, there is an apex CED organization called Canadian Economic Development Network (CCEDNet) (Quarter, Mook, & Armstrong, 2009, p. 80). According to CEDNet, CED defined as action by people locally to create economic opportunities and enhance social conditions in their communities on a sustainable and inclusive basis, particularly with those who are most disadvantaged. Putnam (2000) refers to these dynamics as social capital development, social engagement, trust, and informal cooperation, as social capital can create multipliers, as strong communities pull together and initiate new projects. Therefore, CED projects have an important role in reducing the hardships associated with social inequalities. CED projects are mainly targeting below average standard of living people or involve groups who experience extraordinary challenges. Many community scholars think CED is a tool used to get economic equality. It is a program to address economic insecurity of the marginalised members of the community.

Government supported CED projects, either direct full funding or partial funding to CED projects, or lease/donate government properties like ponds, lands, bazaars, roads, public busses, industries to community organizations, can generate revenues from them, covers project costs and contribute to local living blue and green economics. The author believes that community blue and green economic development projects are social businesses that are not completely dependent on external continuous support rather it generates revenues from its products and services to cover project costs. Moreover, inclusion of marginalised people in project services could generate employment among disadvantaged people; get blue, green economic and social benefit from CED services. According to Quarter et al. (2009) CED involves organizations-nonprofits and cooperatives that are within social economy. These organizations earn a portion of their revenues from the market, sometimes in competition with other private sector firms, but they rely on support from government, and at times from corporations and individuals, both financial and volunteer labour. One of the intentions of CED project is reducing external funding/ public funding and ultimately reaching financial sustainability in order to be self-sufficient of its own after certain time. However, it is difficult for CED to survive as profit making business in the free market economy.

As CED project synchronize economic and social missions together in its social business model, CED project required ongoing external support for a while, but here the problem is external funding support decrease even funding support stopped before CED projects reach their financial self-sufficiencies. Canada and USA government agencies and foundations are important supporters of CED projects in North America although now government support is decreasing. Quarter et al. (2009) suggest that small business development funding could include CED initiatives in social businesses. Other alternatives could be private and CED project resource partnership sharing; public funding, foundations and community organizations collaboration project in the poverty prone area to generate employment among local disadvantaged people. In Canada, government initiated and supported many aboriginal businesses and projects that are running in Northern regions through the Department of Indian and Northern Affairs Canada, and Aboriginal Businesses Canada (ABC). Moreover, Community Futures Development Corporation has 268 CED projects across Canada. In Bangladesh, government supported CED projects are few although there are huge opportunities exist across Bangladesh. However, current government provides preference lease Khas lands to landless people in Bangladesh.

These are community development corporations (CDCs) and public sector non-profits agencies that have social economic contribution in Canada. They are the social economy organizations that have market orientation that combine a social mission and vision. They serve small and medium businesses within the communities. For example, Quint Development Corporation serves five neighbourhoods of Saskatoon through renting 45,000 square feet Community Enterprise Centre that combine retail and commercial office spaces. It also built housing cooperatives for ninety families including child care centre, family recreation and community gardens (Quarter et al., 2009). These are outreach programs and services within their jurisdiction, which could be difficult in centralised public institutions.

Author's experience finds that projects like the technical and vocational training assistance program, agricultural projects, urbane food security services, community gardens, community kitchens, community transport pool services and community printing press could help community unemployed people to work in these projects and learn technical and vocational skills to make them employable in the job market. Grameen Shikka has a vocational training center at Savar where it provides vocational training to poor youths with scholarships in Bangladesh. GMPF provides fish cultivation training to low income community people in Nimgashi Fish Culture Project.

Therefore, CED is a system of human activity directed to meeting human wants that is determined by deliberate allocations of scarce resources, including human time (Boothroyd & Davis, 1993, p. 230). Here people gain confidence when their opinions and experience are valued; their confidence strengthens their participation in community planningand decision making process (Shragge, 1997, p. 46). Therefore, CED agencies should be organized to promote cooperation rather than competition although they operate in the free market economy. Through this process, community people are concerned with each other's well-being and gain satisfaction from cooperating. GMPF is an example of community economic and social/emotional project where people feel connected with each other although the purpose of this project is to increase community livestock and fish production and increase income, solidarity, distribute justice and enhance quality life among GMPF beneficiaries. Through GMPF-CED activities and services, community marginalised members become empowered to participate in the community resource optimum uses, engage in community planning and decision making process for the well being of their own in the project areas. According to Mathieu and Cunningham (2004) this asset-based community development project could foster inclusive participation, fostering community leadership, foster relocation of power to communities and increase civic engagement in the community. It provides the source of constructive energy in the local communities. However, ideal community equality achievement is still hard to achieve in neoliberal market economy particularly in Bangladesh.

Under community economic development, it is seen as synonymous with promoting growth in jobs, income, or business activity. Here community is seen simply as the locality in which businesses get together to promote their interests through economic expansion (Alexander, 2000; Quarter et al., 2009). Many local green jobs are created by CED projects by expanding/ creating green small-businesses like agricultural and artisan jobs. It increases local control and brings local living green economics' stability in the community. Moreover, CED encourages local control and power ownership of resources; it creates organizations that are representative of and accountable to the local community, enables communities to address issues of poverty and inequality, environmental degradation and drives to basic social change (Shragge, 1997). Because CED principle is to utilize local resources, promote establishment of new green firms by local entrepreneurs and increase the productivity of the firms. Although CED approach is a single minded economic growth-commercialization approach and unable to structural change, CED projects increase the flow of money into local community. It has trickledown effect that helps the entire economy, which is very important to increase income among poor people and to address the issue of poverty. However, CED projects needs diversify external investment resources and use community resources, but it could reduce dependence on outside decision-makers by increasing local control over resource management. Moreover, community project initiators need to emphasis on planning for all relevant private, public and community agencies in setting targets, surveying opportunities and developing a wide range of strategies, which are sometimes absent in CED projects.

Although social enterprises, blue enterprises, community green economic development programs/servicers, public sector non-profits, non-profit mutual associations, civil society organizations, cooperatives, credit unions, micro-credit agencies and social financings all are social businesses and they are components of social economy, but they might have different in terms of approaches, structures, designs, strategies and policies. All these organizations have both social and economic missions, but all of them have different principles and operate strategies in the market economy. However, they have common provision for generating revenue from their operations in addition to social well being services to disadvantaged people. They are all different from charitable grants and relief organizations. Charitable organizations have traditions of social handout giving assisting those in need. Social enterprises are completely different from for-profit business organizations because for-profit business organizations main objective is profit maximizing; they don't have social and environmental commitment to society. In GMPF blue green social businesses organization community members are not handout receivers rather they are community beneficiaries who are part of community fisheries and livestock production economic actors and social actors in Bangladesh.

Boothroyd and Davis (1993) think that community development corporation institutions favour those most in need in the community. This approach includes production and distribution based on non-market principles of common ownership, mutual aid, and improving productive life at the expense of the efficiency. It creates alternatives to capitalism, rebuild and reconnect people with water, air, soil, agriculture and changes the quality of life for a number of people;

however, it requires a major shift in power which is usually not easy for local communities. Moreover, this entrepreneurial approach generally reinforces individualist and capitalist values, bringing poor people into competitive market economy(Shragge, 1997) that confirms by Jim Lotz (1987) community economic development research in USA.

7.0. Author's involvement with GBJMF before and after inception of Grameen Bank Joysagore Motsho Farm

On December 09, 1984, Muhammad Yunus, Managing Director, Grameen Bank (GB) Bangladesh requested the author to visit Government managed Nimgashi Fish Culture Project (NFCP), Sirajgong on his way return to Dhaka from Rangpur Grameen Bank branches tour. The author visited several Khas ponds of Nimgashi Fisheries Project (NFP) located in Raigong and Tarash Upzilla and collected preliminary information about NFP. The NFP has huge infrastructures in Nimgashi and Tarash sub-districts. Many cluster Khas ponds situated in Nimgashi area. Among these Khas ponds, Joyshagore Digi (pond) is the biggest one in the area with 22.35 ha of water surface. Mahango tribal people, 20% (approximately) of total population, live in this area; however, public has no access to these Khas ponds for fish cultivation although many poor people live on these ponds' embankments. Many rural powerful elites illegally occupied many Khas ponds and take benefit from them. Although many government officers work in this project, few of them stay in the project area. There is an excellent fish fingerlings production center in Nimgashi; however, it is in underproduction. The author's (Rouf) preliminary observation reported to Muhammad Yunus and to GB executives.

After one year (November 07, 1985) Yunus again sent the author to NFCP to survey it. At this time the author surveyed NFCP with GB another officer to explore the project resources and to asses if Grameen Bank and poor people could benefit from the project by managing it. The author writes a feasibility report on NFCP and identifies problems, potentialities, possibilities, and challenges for GB if GB is managing these Khas ponds and other resources of NFCP.

On March 20th 1986 the author returned to Dhaka after delivering 5000 Thai Camble baby ducks to GB branches in Tangail and Dhaka district, managing director of GB request him to join GB Nimgachi Area Office as an Area Manager in order to start Grameen Bank micro-credit services in Nimgashi and its surrounding area. The author worked in Nimgachi for two years as an area manager. During this time he opened twenty Grameen Bank branches there spreaded Sirajgong, Pabna and Bagura district. In addition to his GB responsibilities, he was involved with GBJMP operations in Raigonja, Tarash, Handial and Vangura sub-districts. He intensively traveled in each village of these sub-districts, visited all ponds of the projects, talked with local MP, rural elites, politicians, and general people and government officials. He friendly explained them the missions and visions of GB and GBJMF in these sub-districts. Although at the beginning many rural elites were protested against GJMP, later they were impressed of GB activities and appreciated GB and GBJMP activities in their area.

8.0. Grameen Bank operation starts in Grameen Bank Joygagor Motsho Project (GJMP) in Khas ponds in Sirajgong, Pabna and Dinajpur districts in 1986

The Ministry of Fisheries and Livestock (MoFL), Government. of Bangladesh (GoB) first transferred 782 ancients and derelict ponds with 675 ha water areas for 25 years to Grameen Bank in March 07, 1986 with the aim of improvement/better fisheries production and management, stop leaking/ corruptions by the government officials and to stop illegal occupancy of Khas (public jurisdiction) ponds by the local elites. Latter the government also decided to lease many other fish and shrimp farms and Fish Seed Multiplication Farms, spread over across Bangladesh. The Ministry of Fisheries managed Dinajpur Fisheries Project and Fish Seed Multiplication farms were handed over to Grameen Bank at the end of 1986. There were agreements between Government of Bangladesh and Grameen Bank for handing over physical possession of all assets and ponds on long term lease for community based management by organizing the landless poor people living on and rescue ponds those are occupied by locally influential people and around the embankments of the ponds. After receiving them, GB renamed this project to Grameen Bank Joysagore Motsho Project (GBJMP) in 1987. In 1994, GBJMP became a separate organization and named it Grameen Motsho Foundation (GMF). It again renamed Grameen Motsho O Pasusampad Foundation (GMPF) in 1999 (Grameen Motsho O Pashusampad Foundation Annual Report 2006).

The author was assigned to attend all 'GBJMP Advisory Committee' meetings in addition to his job in Grameen Bank Training, Research and Special Program portfolio at Dhaka. Although at the beginning the local elites protested against of GBJMP management, GBJMP is able to overcome this problem and smoothly run the project for the benefit of local disadvantaged people in the project area.

The primary objective of GMPF is to produce and to provide protein rich food and thus improve human dietary standard. GMPF other objectives are

(1) to undertake production, transportation, processing and marketing of products of fisheries, livestock, agriculture, horticulture, homestead gardening, social a forestation and bio-gas plants and other income generating activities to bring improvement in the quality of life of the poor, in particular of poor women; to finance, assist, take or give on lease, or otherwise support the management of fisheries, livestock, horticulture and forestry-based enterprises which are owned by the poor, in particular by poor women.

(2) to promote the increased participation of women in fisheries, livestock, horticulture and forestry production, storage, marketing, processing and other such related business; and

(3) to promote the increased participation of women in integrated fish-crop-livestock, horticulture, bio-gas, milk cooling, feed making and forestry production, storage, processing, marketing, and other related business.

The goals of GMPF are: diversifying rural production, increasing employment potentials, to provide alternative employment to rural people especially women, produce more fish, livestock and horticultural products for local consumption and to improve the nutritional standards in rural areas through additional supplies of animal proteins and vitamins, raising the net income of the rural communities, alleviation of poverty and increasing opportunities for earning foreign exchange and ensuring sustainable livelihood of the marginalized people in Bangladesh.

GMPF had many programs that are operated through (1) Fisheries Management and Aquaculture, (2) Livestock Dairy Development and Social Forestry, (3) Social Mobilization Technical Assistance Consultancy and NGO Execution Bangladesh, (4) Training Human Development and Research and Development (R & D), and (5) Planning, Monitoring and Evaluation. The GMPF has its fish culture training institute at Joysagar named Joysagar Training Institute. GMPF had five farm managers at Joysagar Mostsu Farm, Dinajpur Farm, and Jamiuna Borrow-pit Farm, Chokoria shrimp Farm and Satkhira shrimp Farm. GMPF had officers for empowerment of Coastal Fishing Community Project, Community Livestock Officers, Veterinary Surgeon, program organisers and community organisers for mobilizing community people for fisheries and aquaculture and livestock development. The GMPF had also provided micro-credit to fisheries farmers and livestock farmers through its credit field assistants.

9.0. Functions/activities of Grameen Motsho O Pashu Sampsad Foundation (GMPF)

The functions /activities of GMPF are as follows:

A. Community Fisheries Development: Fish farming, Shrimp farming, integrated aquaculture, fish mono-culture, fish poly-culture, fish-cum-shrimp culture, paddy-cum-fish culture, duck weed culture, fish hatcheries and nurseries, shrimp hatchery, brood management, marketing of fish, hatchlings & fry, Ice making and net-making.

B. Community Livestock and Diary Development: Cow farming, milk chilling, processing and marketing, beef fattening, goat farming, poultry farming, duck farming, pig farming, use of cow dung as slurry and fertilizer, development of bio-gas plants, community diary enterprises and community feed mills.

C. Community Farming and Social Afforestation: Social forestry, home-stead gardening, landscape gardening, horticulture farming, crops & fodder farming, and plant nurseries.

D. Training and Manpower Development: Programs include training of GMPF officers & staff, training of government and NGOs staff, training of group members, international training on social mobilization, groups and community development through integrated fish-crop-livestock and dairy development activities.

E. Social Mobilization Program: This program includes motivate and orient local people; formation of groups and centers, facilitation and communication skill development, gender awareness, legal awareness, awareness building for health, nutrition, safe water & sanitation, education and rights, training of poor men and women on facilitation and communication skill development, training on social mobilization and gender issues, group and community development, training on fisheries, livestock, social afforestation, horticulture and homestead gardening etc. (Memorandum of Articles and Memorandum of Association (GMPF), 2003; Memorandum of Articles and Memorandum of Association (GMF), 1994).

10.0. Joysagor Aquaculture Farm

The Nimgachi Fish Culture Project named as Joysagor Fish Farm (JFF) by Grameen Bank after the name Joysagor. Joysagor Fish Farm area is scattered over 200 square kilometres of remote rural areas of 5 Thanas of Sirajgong, Pabna and Bogra districts where ancient ponds of Paul and Sen Dynasties were left derelict and unused for hundreds of years. This has rendered these ponds as grazing grounds of cattle and goats. For rehabilitation and aquaculture, GB transferred these resources to Grameen Motsho (Fisheries) Foundation (GMLF) soon after its creation in 1994 as its sister organization of Grameen Bank. GMLF organised the local people living on embankments of the ponds and its close vicinity, formed them into groups of five beneficiaries and centers of 6-8 groups who were trained in aquaculture, rural development and social development activities and were given all inputs including fertilizers, manure, feeds, nets, boasts, etc. The possessions of the derelict ponds were given over from the vested interest groups to the down-trodden and resource less poor. It was an uphill task. GMPF has excavated/re-excavated 432 ponds with 417.50 ha water area and brought under scientific fish culture (GMPF, 2006). Table-1 shows year wise performance of Joysagar Fish Farm.

11.0. JFF year-wise fish production, share and income of beneficiaries

A total of 14451.22 MT of fish were produced by JFF since inception up to 2006. Fifty percent of the fish went to the share of poor beneficiaries. An amount of Tk. 179.21 million was received by the beneficiaries in 16 years as their share. Number of beneficiaries rose from 2249 in 1990-91 to 5876 in 2006. Per capita additional income through fish culture rose from TK. 1700 in 1990-1991 to Tk. 7223 in the year 2006. Per ha fish production rose from 700 kg in 1988-89 to 2734.30 kg in 2006-a rise of over 3905 in last 20 years or 19.53% per annum increase on an average. Out of 5876 of VGMs 2756 were involved in fish culture in 2006 (Grameen Mostsho O Pashusampad Foundation Annual Report 2006).

Table-1: Year Wise performance of Jaysagor Farm (JFF)

Year	# of ponds under cultivation	Water area (ha)	Prod. of fish (MT)	Prod. Of fish/ ha (kg)	Prod. Of hatchlings (kg)	Total income Tk. In Lacs	Share of benefi- ciaries @50% (Tk. in Lacs)	# benefi- ciaries	Av income/ head –Tk.
1986-87	185	225.20	157.0	700.0	193.2	12.9	-	-	-
1987-88	306	335.37	160.0	477.1	122.9	40.1	-	-	-
1988-89	356	399.06	173.0	433.5	142.9	48.1	-	-	-
1989-90	347	389.37	237.0	608.7	190.9	58.9	-	-	-
1990-91	388	404.48	456.0	1127.7	240.8	66.0	38.2	2249	1700
1991-92	392	382.98	503.0	1313.4	279.9	60.6	46.0	2301	2000
1992-93	392	382.98	810.0	2115.0	425.6	197.9	86.2	2165	3980
1993-94	396	386.16	920.0	2382.4	656.0	190.6	78.4	2198	3566
1995	396	386.16	968.0	2506.7	624.3	241.4	103.4	2247	4600
1996	397	386.83	986.0	2548.9	633.0	221.7	94.2	2247	4200
1997	406	393.52	867.0	2203.2	551.6	222.3	97.1	2322	4200
1998	421	401.55	621.6	1548.1	560.9	198.8	85.6	2293	3733
1999	423	411.00	842.7	2050.7	504.6	269.0	121.3	2548	4760
2000	427	415.52	869.2	2091.8	552.3	292.7	125.4	2628	4770
2001	427	418.27	907.7	2193.1	569.1	313.7	137.7	2724	5057
2002	427	415.52	987.1	2304.8	645.9	330.3	148.6	2776	5351
2003	430	415.74	950.1	2285.4	612.3	328.4	142.3	3128	5218
2004	430	415.78	881.8	2120.9	709.9	326.6	133.2	3855	4832
2005	432	417.5	1012.4	2420.1	739	381.9	155.5	4674	5582
2006	432	417.5	1141.6	2734.3	818	496.7	199.1	5876	7223
Total	-	-	14451.2	-	9773.1	4298.7	1792.1	-	-

Source: Grameen Mostsho O Pashusampad Foundation Annual Report 2006.

12.0. Dinajpur Farm (DF)

Dinajpur Farm (DF) was taken over from the DoF of GoB during 1987-1988 with 65 ponds having 155.46 ha of water areas scattered over the remotest rural areas of the greater Dinajpur district presently the new three districts of Dinajpur, Thakurgaon and Panchaghar (Grameen Annual Report, 1987). Most of these ponds were excavated by the local kings/ Zamindars about 500-800 years ago. Bangladesh's largest man-made pond 'Ramsagor Dhighi' with a water area of 30 ha is located about 10 km North of Dinajpur town. Out of these 65 ponds 51 ponds were brought under fish culture by organizing landless poor people of the area. Out of 1159 village group members (VGMs) 674 were involved in fish culture in 2006.

Table 2. Year-wise performance of DF

Year	# of ponds under cultivation	Water area (ha)	Production of fish (MT)	Production of fish/ha	Total Income (Tk. in Lacs)	Share of beneficiaries @40 (Tk. In Lacs)	# of ben-eficiaries	Income per head (Tk.)
1988-89	35	88.34	18.60	210.55	4.79	-	-	-
1989-90	50	133.18	19.62	147.32	6.53	-	-	-
1990-01	53	136.52	49.34	361.41	11.84	-	-	-
1991-92	53	140.81	96.34	684.18	15.10	6.04	451	1340.00
1992-93	50	133.48	121.00	906.50	17.42	6.98	439	1590.00
1993-94	50	134.82	1778.00	1320.28	33.39	134.37	496	2695.00
1995	54	154.00	209.00	1441.38	46.30	17.18	482	3564.00
1996	56	150.58	204.00	1354.76	36.82	13.41	492	2726.00
1997	56	150.58	128.73	854.90	29.02	11.23	480	2340.00
1998	56	149.65	137.44	918.48	37.34	14.79	619	2389.00
1999	56	149.65	147.00	982.30	40.29	15.98	615	2598.00
2000	54	151.79	161.20	1062.00	47.59	17.70	636	2783.00
2001	52	144.8	187.18	1292.7	54.07	20.66	666	3102
2002	52	153.8	201.00	1304.65	55.95	22.18	722	3072
2003	51	146.40	208.17	1421.93	56.04	22.29	776	3488
2004	51	146.40	215.34	1470.90	60.21	23.95	873	3772
2005	52	150.00	237.10	1580.67	68.30	27.11	942	4236
2006	46	106.67	260.00	2437.42	92.60	33.10	1159	4911

Source: Grameen Mostsho O Pashusampad Foundation Annual Report 2006.

The DF production of fish during the period 1988-1989 was only 18.60 MT per ha, which increased to 260 MT in 2006. The income out of fish sales increased from tk. 4.79 lacs to k 92.60 lacs during 1988-2006. 400% of the sale proceeds were given to the group members of DF. Beneficiaries' per capita additional income was raised from Tk. 1340 in 1992 to Tk. 4911 in 2006. Per ha fish production rose from 210.55 kg in 1988-99 to 2437 kg in 2006 - a rise of 1157% in last 18 years or 64% per annum on an average (Grameen Mostsho O Pashusampad Foundation Annual Report, 2006).

13.0. Jamuna Borrow-Pits Farm (JMBA)

The Jamuna Borrow Pits were created as result of construction of East and West Approach roads of Jamuna Bridge in Tangail and Sirajgong. Due to acquisition of land on both sides of the road, many people were rendered homeless and landless. The people are called Project Affected Person s (PAPs). Jamuna Multipurpose Bridge Authority (JMBA) has its moral and legal responsibility to 42 km of slopes of the approach roads for construction of ponds for fish culture and developing the farms for agriculture and horticulture and the slopes for plantation. Jamuna Multipurpose Bridge Authority (JMBA) invite to GMPF to manage the ponds for fish culture and developing the farms for agriculture and horticulture and the slopes for plantation project in 1997. JMBA accepted the offer from the government for fish culture in the ponds and plantation besides the road and took over possession in 1997 by virtue of agreement for 25 years lease singed between Jumuna Multipurpose Bridge Authority (JMBA) and GMPF on 12-03-1997. Under this project the major component was excavation of 90 ha of new water areas (ponds) for creating physical resources for the poor people living adjacent to the 42 km long East and West approach Roads of the Jamuna Multipurpose Bridge (JMB) in Tagnail and Sirajgonj districts. During 1998-2004 only 65 ponds having a water area of 67 ha were excavated under JBPF. This project is a unique example of Integrated Farming through Fish-Crop-Livestock and Social Afforestation having 1005 women VGMs-the only one of its type in Bangladesh.

Table 3. Group formation, Centers, VGMs, Ponds and Water Areas

Activities	Total	Comments
No of Centers	45	
No of Groups	274	
No of Members	1259	100% women
No of Ponds	65	
Water Area (ha)	69.60	
Fish Production (MT)	52.84	

Source: Grameen Mostsho O Pashusampad Foundation Annual Report 2006.

14.0. Chokoria Shrimp Farm

GPF has also been executing shrimp farm named Chokoria Shrimp Farm at Chokoria sub-district in Cox's Bazaar district. This farm was handed over by Department of Fisheries (DoF) to GMPF in 1986 for 25 years on lease. It has area of 300 acres of water area and producing shrimps since inception. In 1992-1993 semi-intensive shrimp culture was started in 42 ponds. From 1996 the farm did not culture any intensive semi-intensive shrimp, but traditional extensive shrimp culture was re-introduced to get rid of the diseases problem. The farm had one dairy farm with 49 cows/cattle and it has over 1911 coconut trees. It produced 19.26 MT shrimps and 6.47 MT fish in 1996 (Grameen Mostsho O Pashusampad Foundation Annual Report 2006).

15.0. GMPF Micro-credit Implementation Project

Grameen Motsho O Pashu Sampad Foundation (GMPF) has been executing the Ponds Command Area Development Project and Micro-credit Implementation Project funded by Asian Development Bank (ADB). This project was operated in three sub-districts (Sathia, Bera, and Sujanagar) of Pabna district. GMPF had been organizing the ponds, borrow-pits, and irrigation canals of Pabna Irrigation and Rural

Development project. The project owners' preferably landless poor, marginal farmers, fishermen, hatchery/nursery operators, net makers, and sellers and other aquaculture related persons. GMPF had organised 499 groups of 5005 beneficiaries, and gave them training in fish culture, gender issues, social development issues, legal awareness etc. It covers 134 villages, and 519 hectors of water areas. The project gave micro-credit to the beneficiaries not in the form of 'cash' but in the form of 'input'. During the project period the project disbursed Tk. 17.05 million as input credit to the beneficiaries and the recovery rate is 86.30%.

16.0. Table 4. No. of groups, no. of beneficiaries, fish cultivation areas, loan disbursement, savings collections from the GMPF Micro-credit Implementation Project

Description	# of group	# of beneficiaries	Area under cultivation	# of villages covered	Savings collections million in (TK.)	Loan disbursement in million in (TK.)	Loan recovery in million (TK.)
Actual	341	3553	367	126	7.93	17.05	118.94
Target	341	3410	341	126	-	17.05	14.50
%	100%	104.2%	107.6%	100%	-	100%	81.37%

Source: Grameen Mostsho O Pashusampad Foundation Annual Report 2006.

17.0. Empowerment of Coastal Fishing Community for Livelihood Security Project (ECFC)

Grameen Motsho O Pashu Sampad Foundation (GMPF) was executed the social mobilization program 'the Empowerment of Coastal Fishing Communities and Livelihood Security Project' (ECFC) in Cox's Bazaar, Ramu, Teknaf, Ukiya, Moheskhali and Kutubdia sub-districts under Cox's Bazar district covering 65 fishing villages, and 149 village organizations. This project was basically a social mobilization and community empowerment project following a multidimensional approach. The project engages a numbers of service providers from the private sector to assist the project in achieving its objectives within the framework of project concept, strategy, and institutional arrangements. The developmental objectives of the project were to promote livelihood security of the poor coastal fishing communities. The ECFC immediate objectives were to: (1) assist the communities to empower themselves to collectively address their problems and needs; (2) introduce various economic and community approaches which are operated and managed by the community organizations; and (3) facilities sustainable conservation and management of coastal marine and estuarine fisheries resources and habitats through strengthening of community based management of the resources. ECFC target people are marginalized women, children and men are from the coastal fishing communities and the people who are most prone to recurrent natural disasters.

The project concept is based on the Sustainable Livelihood Approach-includes the vulnerability context, peoples coping and adaptive strategies, the livelihood assets, and the livelihood outcomes. Poor fishing communities have access to information, assets and resources as well as knowledge and technologies, employments and alternative income options in the area. ECFC emphasises on marine fishing technologies and strength capacity building for disaster managementamong coastal people.

18.0. Community Livestock and Diary Development Project (CLDDP)

The objectives of the CLDDP project are to contribute to national efforts for poverty alleviation by providing a model for sustainable rural development opportunities for women. The project is located in GMPF's three-existing farm areas namely (1) Joysagar Farm, (2) Dinajpur Farm, and (3) Jamuna Borrow-Pits Farm (JBPF) in 18 sub-districts of 7 districts in Northern West of Bangladesh. CLDPP works in 375 villages of 18 sub-districts of seven districts in Bangladesh. It has 360 centers, 1150 groups and 7750 beneficiaries where 4600 were male (59.35%) and 3150 females (40.65%) under 22 GMPF unit offices (Grameen Mostsho O Pashusampad Foundation Annual Report 2006). The following table shows GMPF meat, milk, dung and eggs production of GMPF under CLDDP.

Table 5. Production of Milk, Meat, Cow Dung and Eggs

Produces	Total (as of 2006)
Total Milk Production (Litre	6723871
Milk received by CDE (Litre)	3560999
Eat (Fattening Cattle) (MT)	1478.99
Cow dung: produced (MT) (Estimated	62434
Egg (nos.)	1329591

Source: Grameen Mostsho O Pashusampad Foundation Annual Report 2006.

19.0. Livestock Development Fund (LDF)

Savings account has been opened at each of the GMPF village centers to make up a local Livestock Development Fundby the village group managements (VGMs). Each VGM contributes TK. 5 at every fortnightly meeting as a compulsory savings into the LDF. This is considered to be a personal savings of each VGM and proper records were maintained at the centre to determine the amounts saved by each VGM so that he/ she may be able to withdraw the full amount with interest at the time the VGM leaves the center. Every time a VGM receives a loan for a livestock package through the center, a sum equal to 2.5% of the value of the livestock (milch cow and pregnant heifer) procured is deducted from the total loan amount and deposited into the LDF at the centre. When the group repays the loan capital and interest at the fortnightly meeting of the centre, 25% of the interest is deposited into the DF account. Each VGM is expected to contribute to the LDF at the rate of thirty paisa (TK. 0.30) for every litre of milk sold, irrespective of whether it is sold direct to the market or through the Community Dairy Enterprise (Grameen Mostsho O Pashu Sampad Foundation Annual Report 2006).

Bank interest for the fund accrued in the savings account gets added every quarter into the LDF. Any fine imposed by the centre on the GM is also deposited into the LDF.

19.0. Livestock Insurance Fund (LIF)

2.5% of the purchased value of cows/heifers realised as premium have been deposited to the insurance account. Out of 5445 cow heifer 177 died and compensation paid against 148 dead cow heifers. The details of livestock insurance fund position are shown in Table below.

Table 6. Insurance Fund: Premium and Compensation

Description	Total
No. Of insured cows heifers	4250
Total premium realized (Tk.)	27,21,809
No. Of insured cows heifers died	177
No. of Insurance claimed settled	148
Amount of insurance claimed settled	3,79,170
Total LIF	31,05,554

Source: Grameen Mostsho O Pashusampad Foundation Annual Report 2006.

20.0. Livestock Support Services

The Livestock Support Services project provided adequate facilities for treatment, vaccination, artificial insemination, fodder cultivation and pregnancy test for cow heifers. Moreover facilities like treatment, vaccination and other facilities for goats, poultry, ducks etc. provided with necessary equipment, instruments, trevice, LFA kit box and other ancillary appliances. In addition, linkage has been established with Department of Livestock Services (DLS) to provide more necessary inputs and veterinary services.

20.1. Community Livestock Centers and Livestock Sub-centers

In order to provide needed veterinary services for the livestock distributed to the VGMs, the project has set up 06 Community Livestock Centers (CLC) at Nimghachi, Tarash, Sujan, Elenga, Ramrai and Dinajpur. Moreover, five livestock sub-centers setup at Nandigram, Nalka, Deul, Vitargarh, Belowa and Ramarai units. 85 trevice points had been equipped with all veterinary facilities including mini laboratory. They had been managed by a Community Livestock Officer (CLO), Livestock Field Assistant (LA) and Veterinary Compounder (VC) located at the SC. The CLO, LFA VCs services are given free of cost. If the livestock is owned by a non-VGM the cost of medicine, vaccine, artificial insemination and emergency call fees are realized and deposited into a Livestock Services Fund maintained at the respective farm. Required number of community members also given training on AI techniques by DLS for a period of 3-months. These trained personnel earned money by privately insemination. The following table shows scenario of the treatments, vaccinations of cattle, poultry and ducks and artificial insemination and pregnancy test of cow heifers.

Table 7. Livestock, Poultry, Breeding and Treatment

Description	Total (as of 2006)
No. of various types of Vaccination	114631
Artificial Insemination and Pregnancy Test	
No. Of Artificial Insemination done by the project	7429
No. Of Pregnancy Diagnosis done by DLS	1665
No. De-worming done by the project	17103
No. of Infertility treatment done by the project	1216
Total no. of cases treated at	
Trevice Points	13559
CLC LSC	13258
VGMs house on emergency call	960
VGMs houses services provided	28157

Source: Grameen Mostsho O Pashusampad Foundation Annual Report 2006.

20.2. Feed supply and fodder cultivation

The project motivated the VGMs on the advantages of feed and fodder for dairy cows setting up demonstration plots in Units. Distribution of milch cow was subject to a condition that every VGM should plant at least a small plot of improved grass such as Napier, Guinea grass, maize or ipil-ipil whatever land available in the backyard of the beneficiaries or on pond embankments. Grass cutting and ipil-ipil seedlings were distributed to the VGMs. VGMs cultivated 1396 decimal Napier plots, 125 decimal guinea plots, 6.03 decimal ipil-ipil plots and 445 decimal maize plots and others 700 decimal. The project has also set up feed mills for supplying quality cattle feed to the VGMs. Since inception 3 feed mills produced and distributed 5184 metric tons of feed (Grameen Mostsho O Pashusampad Foundation Annual Report 2006).

20.3. Community Feed Mill (CFM)

Although there is a provision for two feed mills at Nimgachi and Dinajpur, the project established three feed mills one more at JBPF for facilitating steady supply of quality feed to the VGMs. All the feed mills are functioning well with highly satisfactory management and producing quality cattle feed by procuring raw materials from the local market and supply them to feed mills. Feed samples of collected ingredients are sent to nutrition laboratory of DLS in every six- months. The results compare well with national analytical figure. Moreover, feedback information from VGMs about feed is also promising. The price of feed is fixed by the committee and their selling price varies depending on their price of ingredients. A profit margin of TK. 0.50-1.00 is kept in the Feed Mills account to build up working capital. The feed mills are jointly owned and managed by the community and GMPF with 70:30 share of profit. Feed mills employ managers and staffs from the community only.

21.0. Community Dairy Enterprise (CDE)

Two Community Dairy Enterprises (CDEs) with milk cooling tanks of 2000 litre each were established at Nimgachi and Dinajpur. Under changed situation and market demand more facilities had been developed in 3 farm areas for preservation and marketing of milk. Beyond 2 cooling tanks of 2000 litre capacity each set up at Joysagar and Dinajpur 8 more cooling tanks of 2000 litre capacity-4 and 1000 litre capacity-4 have been set up at Nalka, Nandigram, Tarash, Belwa and Ramrai. Total cooling capacity of milk was 16,000 litres per day (Nimgachi 4000, Tarash-3000, Nandigram-2000, Nalkas-2000, Belowa-1000, Dinajpur-1000 and Ramrai-3000 litre) (Grameen Mostsho O Pashusampad Foundation Annual Report 2006).

22.0. Implications of the study

The experience of GMPF is one of the examples of CED blue and green program in Bangladesh. In theory CED approach has many advantages in producing local jobs creation, increase income among community members, empower people, and address the issue of povertyby using local resources for local community members. It is an approach where private-public-community agencies make partnerships among them and serve to local communities for their wellbeing. GMPF has community Khas ponds project. This community project cultivates fish by employing local poor people. Moreover, GMPF project encourages community members to become involved in fish culture; livestock productions and community forestations in its project area. They are an asset-based community economic development projects that have an innovative strategy for community-driven development for rural communities in Bangladesh. Therefore, community economic development workers, researchers, policy makers, academicians and executives could learn from GMPF different services, products, tools and its implementation strategies from this paper. This paper can assist them to plan and to initiate CED projects in their own communities lesions learned from GMPF.

Limitation of the study

This paper is a description of GMPF activities, implementation strategies, policies and monitoring devices. The author does not critically analyse the GMPF programs and activities. The paper does not contain national and international fisheries and livestock production statistics. The paper has no graphs and diagrams rather it directly records the GMPF resources, fisheries and livestock production statistics and tables collected secondary data from GMPF.

23.0. Conclusion

GMPF employed local people to work in the GMPF fish culture firm and GMPF livestock farm. GMPF mobilise local villagers to make fish culture associations and let them jointly (association members and GMPF field staff) work with the project in order to increase livestock and fish production in the area. GMPF livestock association members benefited from the GMPF services. It has setup milk collection chilling points at different locations near to villages where people sell their milk. The Grameen Yogurt plant uses the collected milk for producing Grameen Yogurt. Many local people employed in this Yogurt plant for producing and selling yogurt.

Modern fish culture and livestock production technologies were introduced to the GMPF project. GMPF conducted many workshops on livestock management, fish culture management, community forestation and micro-credit for local people that have impacted increasing local fish and livestock production and community forestation. Many NGOs' field workers, government officials and international agencies visited the project and learn GMPF activities and management strategies. For example, Bangladesh Fisheries Development Corporation, DFID, UK, JICA, Indian Livestock Association, Nepal Fisheries Department, Kenya Livestock Department etc. visited GMPF and they have learned about GMPF ponds management from GMPF.

The author finds GMPF beneficiaries gain access to modern livestock and fish production through this project that resulted in an increase to their income, created excitement, confidence, access to better food, housing and social activities, acquire new skills and information and developed coping strategies through GMPF. The GMPF technology transfer process helps local poor to develop their leadership skills, exposed to technologies on modern fish culture, and livestock production and community forestation. GMPF these activities, programs and services have created many employments in project area and help the community to be self-help at the local level.

In the GMPF area, Grameen Bank field staff works hard to serve local poor people in providing micro loans, open cost free center schools for the poor children in addition to other benevolent activities of Grameen Bank in Bangladesh. Moreover, GBJMP has developed a people centered decentralised local community partnership ponds management model for low cost fish culture and livestock production in the project area that become an examples for the local communities and other agencies in Bangladesh. The author and his GB staff of this area extend their full cooperation to GBJMF in order to run the ponds smoothly under GBJMP management. All people were impressed of Grameen Bank and Grameen Bank Joysaghur Mostho Project (GBJMP) (later called GMPF) activities. The author narrated his GB and GBJMP working experiences in his monthly official report received from the project during his tenure at Nimgashi. It was a great experience for him.

The Khas ponds lease agreement between Grameen Bank and GoB was for 25 years (1986-2010). The Government of Bangladesh did not extend the lease period; hence GMPF returned all these Khas ponds to GoB in 2010. Khas ponds return to Government by GMPF has declined community members' access to ponds management and fish cultivation. As a result GMPF association members and beneficiaries are deprived from the pond management participations although they are conscious about their rights to access to Khas ponds fish culture. Hence the sustainability of this GMPF community economic development project faces red tape challenges to develop and flourish. Moreover, there is a question would the government bureaucrats red tape be able to carry people centered GMPF fisheries and livestock associations services to communities because government officials do not have experience working with the local communities in Bangladesh.

References

Alexander, J. (2000). Adaptive strategies of nonprofit human services organizations in an era of devolution and new public management. *Nonprofit management and Leadership,* Vol. 10(3), pp. 287-303

Boothroyd, P. and Davis, H.G. (1993). Community economic development. *Journal of Planning Education and Research*, Vol. 12, pp. 230-240

Brown, W. A., & Iverson, J.O. (2004). Exploring strategy and broad structure in nonprofit organizations. *Nonprofit and Volunteering Sector Quarterly,* Vol. 33(3), pp. 377-400

Dees, J. G. (1998). Enterprising non-profits. *Harvard Business Review* (Jan.-Feb.), pp. 55-67

Grameeen Bank Annual Report (1987). *Grameen Bank Jaoysagor Project 1986 in Grameen Bank Annual Report (1986).* Dhaka: Grameen Bank

Grameen Mostsho O Pashusampad Foundation Annual Report (2006). *Grameen Mostsho O Pashusampad Foundation Annual Report (Grameen Fisheries and Livestock Foundation) 2006.* Dhaka: Grameen Bank.

Lotz, J. (1987). Community development: A short history. *Journal of Community Development* May- June, pp. 40-46

Mathieu, A. and Cunningham, G. (2004). *From clients to citizens: Asset-based community development as a strategy for community driven development.* Antigonish: Coady International Institute

Memorandum of Articles and Memorandum of Association (GMF). (1994). *Grameen Motsho Foundation Memorandum of Articles and Memorandum of Association.* Dhaka: Grameen Bank

Memorandum of Articles and Memorandum of Association (GMPF) (2003). *Grameen Motsho O Pashu Sampad Foundation Memorandum of Articles and Memorandum of Association.* Dhaka: Grameen Bank

Putnam, R. (2000). *Bowling alone: The collapse and revival of American community.* New Work: Simon and Schuster

Quarter, J., Mook L., and Armstrong, A. (2009). *Social economy: A Canadian perspective.* Toronto: University of Toronto Press

Rouf, K. A. (2014). Community Green Economic Development by leasing and utilizing Government Jurisdiction Ponds by Grameen Fisheries and Livestock Foundation in Bangladesh. *International Journal of Research Studies in Management.* Vol. 3(2), pp. 1-16

Shragge, E. (1997). *Community Economic Development: In search of empowerment.* Montreal: Black Rose Books

Yunus. M. (2007). *Creating a world without poverty: Social businesses and the future of capitalism.* New York: Public Affairs.

Marketing of Community Banking Services to the 'Bottom of the Pyramid' in Bangladesh

An Examination of the Successes of the Grameen Bank using Prahalad and Hart's article 'The Fortune at the Bottom of the Pyramid'

Abstract

This paper describes how Grameen Bank (GB) has built a local support base with its stakeholders; it highlights GB's research and development (R&D) contribution to poor people; and show GB's human resource management; and how GB the financial structure become financially sustainable services dealing with the poorest of poor in Bangladesh. In addition, this paper discusses GB's social capital for sustainable business management. The paper uses literature review and incorporated his (author's) three decades personal working experience working with Grameen Bank Bangladesh.

The practices of profit making traditional businesses of multinational corporations (MNCs) have directly affected people's lives, increase their poverty and injustice to them, destroying their ability to teach their younger generation about the value of sustainable business and preserve their structure. However, there are four billion poor people in developing countries who are at the base of the market pyramid. The perception of the bottom of the pyramid is not only that of a viable market but that it also includes 70% of the total economy and they are inclusive to MNCs business market. However, there is no doubt that the Grameen Bank has successfully marketed to the poorest of the world's poor and led a revolution in seeing these people as true economic and social actors in Bangladesh.

The bank has successfully banked the unbankable. Lessons can be learned from where the Grameen Bank has been, and as the poor become stronger economic actors in the world's economy, other corporations can follow suit assisting with the goal of bringing more and more people out of extreme poverty. The study could be directly benificial to new youth enytrepreneurs in Bangladesh and elesewhare. Moreover, this study could broaden and improve Grameen Bank micro-financing model and its implications in Bangladesh and elsewhere. The author concluded with the words Grameen Bank is a successful role model of "The Fortune at the Bottom of the Pyramid" where many MNCs have failed.

Key Words: Bottom of Pyramid; corporate social responsibility (CSR); Grameen Bank; Grameen DANONE; Grameen Shakti; Grameen Struggling Members Program; strategic human resource management (SHRM); micro-finance marketing; Multinational Corporations (MNCs); social capital; and sustainable development; zero wastage.

1.0. Introduction

The Grameen Bank was formally established in 1983 as a specialised bank, but general people think it is an NGO designed to assist small businesses in Bangladesh. Serving the poorest of the poor, the Bank provided microfinance loans to individuals by forming groups in their neighbourhoods, through the innovative use of lending circles, to help lift them out of poverty. It introduced many new programs to the poor like small business loans, agriculture loans, housing loans, and loans to beggars, student loans, housing loans, pension funds, and loans to purchase mobile phones to assist the poor in conducting business. As this new innovation in banking has grown, it has been copied throughout the world and the Grameen Bank have become increasingly similar in structure and style to commercial banks; to the point that the Grameen Bank is now a registered corporation in Bangladesh and operates more like a business than an NGO. This paper examines the Grameen Bank through the observations laid out by Prahalad and Hamel in their article '*The Fortune at the Bottom of the*

Pyramid'. There is no doubt that the Grameen Bank has successfully marketed to the poorest of the world's poor and led a revolution in seeing these people as true economic actors. The bank has successfully banked the unbankable.

2.0. Problems with the profit maximizing enterprises

The market is an institution not equipped to address social problems. It is contributing to the expansion of social problems, environmental hazards, inequality, health hazards, unemployment, ghettos and such like. In capitalism the market turns corporations into the Profit Making Enterprises (PMEs), ignoring the common interest of the people and the planet. A business or other organization whose primary goal is making money (a profit), as opposed to a non profit organization which focuses a goal such as helping the community and is concerned with money only as much as necessary to keep the organization operating.

The Business Directory defined profit business as a business or other organization whose primary goal is making money (a profit), as opposed to a non- profit organization which focuses a goal such as helping the community and is concerned with money only as much as necessary to keep the organization operating. Most companies considered to be businesses are for profit organizations; this includes anything from retail stores to restaurants to insurance companies to real estate companies. PMEs only mission is profitable; having the objective of making profit or financial gain through free markets. However, the neo-liberal free market has no capacity to solve social problems; rather, its responsibility is handed over to the state. However, the state has no capacity to deal with all social problems.

Market is a regular gathering of people for the purchase and sale of provisions, livestock, and other commodities. It benefits people to buy and sale products in a convenient place of local people. However, modern market has developed in different ways. The modern free market makes business people for making money by doing different types of business in society. It is not necessary for a business owner to be physically present in selling and buying the products, they (MNCs) are absentees; they are employees or representatives deal with buying and selling the products and receiving money. However, MNCs, and all other PME's emphasis on economic development results in communities losing control over resources, environmental degradation, and concentrating wealth in too few hands.

The practices of profit making traditional businesses (MNCs) have directly affected people's lives; they do not care people's well being rather they preserve their business structure. Big business owners carry out unethical activities in Bangladesh. For example, they buy and store food grains at a cheap price during harvesting time to create an artificial crisis, and then sell them at higher prices in the lean season. As a result, in the 1970s many people died of starvation, famine and poverty. In these severe poverty situations, the Grameen Bank credit program initiates and promotes alternative small business facilities in the villages in an effort to address these acute problems. However, in the 1990s and onward many Multinational Corporations (MNCs) began doing business in Bangladesh and are destroying small business development harmony and initiatives.

A multinational corporation (MNC) has facilitied and created other assets in at least one country other than its home country. Such companies have offices and/or factories in different countries and usually have a centralized head office where they coordinate global management. Very large multinationals have budgets that exceed those of many small countries.

2.1. What is a Multinational Corporation (MNC)

A multinational corporation (MNC) has facilities and other assets in at least one country other than its home country. Such companies have offices and/or factories in different countries and usually have a centralized head office where they coordinate global management. Very large multinationals have budgets that exceed budgets of those of many small countries.

Multinational corporations are sometimes referred to as transnational corporations. Nearly all major multinationals are American, Japanese or Western European, such as Nike, Coca-Cola, Wal-Mart, AOL, Toshiba, Honda and BMW. Advocates of multinationals say they create high-paying jobs and technologically advanced goods in countries that otherwise would not have access to such opportunities or goods. On the other hand, critics say multinationals have undue political influence over governments, exploit developing nations and create job losses in their own home countries.

2.2. Largest multinationals

The 10 largest multinational corporations in the world, as of 2015 revenue, are WalMart ($485.65 billion), Sinopec ($433.31 billion), Royal Dutch Shell ($385.63 billion), PetroChina ($367.85 billion), Exxon Mobil ($364.76 billion), BP ($334.61 billion), Toyota Motors ($248.95 billion), Volkswagen ($244.81 billion), Glencore ($209.22 billion) and Total ($194.16 billion).

WalMart has operations in 28 countries, including over 11,500 retail stores that employ over 2.3 million people internationally. There are a number of advantages to establishing international operations. Having a presence in a foreign country such as India allows a corporation to meet Indian demand for its product without the transaction costs associated with long-distance shipping. Corporations tend to establish operations in markets where their capital is most efficient or wages are lowest. By producing the same quality of goods at lower costs, multinationals could reduce prices and increase the purchasing power of consumers worldwide. However, multinational corporations take the opportunity of free trade marketing and business globalization.

3.0. Globalization

Globalization is the process by which businesses or other organizations develop international influence or start operating on an international scale. It is the increasing interaction of people through the growth of the international flow of money, ideas and culture. It is a dominant hegemonic elements of neo-liberal capitalism. Globalization is primarily an economic process of integration which has social and cultural aspects as well. It involves goods and services, and the economic resources of capital, technology and data. A trade-off of globalization, or the price of lower prices, is that domestic jobs are susceptible to moving overseas. Data from the Bureau of Labor Statistics (BLS) shows that between 2001 and 2010, the United States lost roughly 33% of its manufacturing jobs (5.8 million jobs). This data underscores how important it is for an economy to have a mobile or flexible labor force, so that fluctuations in economic temperament aren't the cause of long-term unemployment. In this respect, education and the cultivation of new skills that correspond to emerging technologies are integral to maintaining a flexible, adaptable workforce. A few of the fastest-growing industries in the United States are peer-to-peer lending platforms, medical marijuana stores, telehealth services and motion capture software development; together, these industries are replacing many of the American jobs that were displaced by overseas manufacturing.

Globalization refers to the tendency of international trade, investments, information technology and outsourced manufacturing to weave the economies of diverse countries together. In business and finance, it primarily refers to the economic integration of global markets, but the term is also used to describe socio-cultural integration among countries. Altogether, globalization has had the effect of markedly increasing both international trade and cultural exchange.

Globalization has been credited with helping shift wealth to less-developed countries. However, globalization is also often blamed for the loss of employment in developed nations, as corporations ship manufacturing facilities and jobs overseas in order to save costs; critics say it weakens national sovereignty as well.

The goal of trans-globalization is to provide organizations with a competitive advantage through lower operating costs and the gain of greater numbers of products, services and consumers. One of the key ways this is done is through diversification of resources, opening up additional markets and accessing new raw materials. And indeed, it has brought the entire world together, with multinational corporations manufacturing, buying and selling goods across the globe. For example, a car company based in Japan might have auto parts manufactured in several different developing countries, then ship the parts to another country for assembly, and then sell the finished car to nations everywhere.

Multinational corporations can provide developing countries with many benefits. However, these institutions may also bring with them relaxed codes of ethical conduct that serve to exploit the neediness of developing nations, rather than to provide the critical support necessary for countrywide economic and social development.

When a multinational invests in a host country, the scale of the investment (given the size of the firms) is likely to be significant. Indeed governments will often offer incentives to firms in the form of grants, subsidies and tax breaks to attract investment into their countries. This foreign direct investment (FDI) will have advantages and disadvantages for the host country.

3.1. Benefits of a multinational investing

The possible benefits of a multinational investing in a country may include:

- **Improving the balance of payments** - inward investment will usually help a country's balance of payments situation. The investment itself will be a direct flow of capital into the country and the investment is also likely to result in import substitution and export promotion. Export promotion comes due to the multinational using their production facility as a basis for exporting, while import substitution means that products previously imported may now be bought domestically. However, this process of multinational trading policy affects the local small manufacturers because local business products face competition with the multinational low quality products.

- **Providing employment** - Employment Development Initiatives (EDI) will usually result in employment benefits for the host country as most employees will be locally recruited. These benefits may be relatively greater given that governments will usually try to attract firms to areas where there is relatively high unemployment or a good labour supply. However, it is not the reality. Usually unemployment rate is higher in the remotest less development transpotation areas. Multinational corporations set up their plants near main cities. Therefore, remotest areas people do not get the employment opportunities from MNCs.

- **Source of tax revenue** - profits of multinationals will be subject to local taxes in most cases, which will provide a valuable source of revenue for the domestic government. However, in reality, MNCs have bad practices of lobbying government, bribing and hiding their real income and they do not pay proper amount of tax to the government.

- **Technology transfer** - multinationals bring with them technology and production methods that are probably new to the host country and a lot can therefore be learnt from these techniques. Workers will be trained to use the new technology and production techniques and domestic firms see the benefits of the new technology. This process is known as technology transfer. However, techlogies are expensive so small farms can not afford high tech in their manufacturing business.

- **Increasing choice** - if the multinational manufactures for domestic markets as well as for export, then the local population will gain form a wider choice of goods and services and at a price possibly lower than imported substitutes.

- **National reputation** - the presence of one multinational may improve the reputation of the host country and other large corporations may follow suite and locate as well.

3.2. Disadvantages of multinational corporations

The possible disadvantages of a multinational investing in a country may include:

- **Environmental impact**- multinationals want to produce in ways that are as efficient and as cheap as possible and this may not always be the best environmental practice. They often lobby governments hard to try to ensure that they can benefit from regulations being as lax as possible and given their economic importance to the host country, this lobbying often be quite effective.
- **Uncertainty** - multinational firms are increasingly 'footloose'. This means that they can move and change at very short notice and often close their plants. This creates uncertainty for the host country.
- **Increased competition** - the impact the local industries can be severe, because the presence of newly arrived multinationals increases the competition in the economy and because multinationals should be able to produce at a lower cost.
- **Influence and political pressure** - multinational investment can be very important to a country and this will often give them a disproportionate influence over government and other organisations in the host country. Given their economic importance, governments often agree to changes that may not be beneficial for the long-term welfare of their people.
- **Transfer pricing**-multinationals always aim to reduce their tax liability to a minimum. One way of doing this is through transfer pricing. The aim of this is to reduce their tax liability

in countries with high tax rates and increase them in the countries with low tax rates. They can do this by transferring components and part-finished goods between their operations in different countries at differing prices. Where the tax liability is high, they transfer the goods at a relatively high price to make the costs appear higher. This is then recouped in the lower tax country by transferring the goods at a relatively lower price. This will reduce their overall tax bill.

- **Low-skilled employment**-the jobs created in the local environment may be low-skilled with the multinational employing expatriate workers for the more senior and skilled roles.
- **Health and safety**-multinationals have been accused of cutting corners on health and safety in countries where regulation and laws are not as rigorous.
- **Export of profits** - large multinational are likely to repatriate profits back to their 'home country', leaving little financial benefits for the host country. For example, Grameen Phone remittance and its huge profits to Norway from Bangladesh.
- **Cultural and social impact**-large numbers of foreign businesses can dilute local customs and traditional cultures. For example, the sociologist George Ritzer coined the term McDonaldization to describe the process by which more and more sectors of American society as well as of the rest of the world take on the characteristics of a fast-food restaurant, such as increasing standardisation and the movement away from traditional business approaches.

However, it is now time to move away from the narrow interpretation of business development through the globalization of capitalism and broaden the concept of recognition to Social Business Enterprises (SBEs). It is these enterprises that are social value-based resources that serve the mass people.

In "*The Fortune at the Bottom of the Pyramid*" K. Prahalad and Stuart L. Hart (2002) say that there are four billion poor people in developing countries who are at the base of the market pyramid. The perception of the bottom of the pyramid is not only that of a viable market, but that it also includes 60% of the total economy. Therefore, the MNC can be a leader in products that do not repeat environmental mistakes. Today they tend to make products and services that are not resource intensive but polluting the nature. Prahalad calls this market the *Tier 4 MNC Market*. It provides multinational corporations with opportunities to infiltrate these countries. Their investment at the bottom of the pyramid can lift billions of people out of poverty, prevent social decay, and can reduce the gap between the rich and the poor. Prahalad and Hamel (p. 368) make a strong case that MNCs should focus on the 'bottom of the pyramid' and not dismiss the world's poor as an unprofitable market. The Grameen Bank is a shining example of Prahalad and Hamel's ideas. The bank has successfully marketed banking products to the poorest of the world's poor in Bangladesh. They have done this through innovative and unique techniques.

According to Prahalad and Hamel, an MNC must make the following changes in order to succeed in marketing to the poor, or Tier 4: (1) Build a local base support with stakeholders, (2) Conduct R&D on the poor, (3) Form new alliances, (4) Increase employment intensity and (5) Reinvent cost structures. However, Prahalad and Hamel did not mention corporate social responsibility, which is essential for sustainable business development. Therefore, it needs to add CSR to its list to ensure a sustainable business model because only the most solid and sustainable businesses will survive into the coming centuries. Grameen Bank is an example of a company that can apply the Tier 4 concept in Bangladesh. It is the first in the world to have applied a micro lending model in the banking world. In 1979 Professor Muhammad Yunus began a lending service to the poor in Bangladesh that has now inspired thousands of micro lenders, serving 100 million clients worldwide in developing countries and wealthy nations, including the United States (Microcredit Summit 2006).

Below this paper first describes how GB has built a local support base with its stakeholders; highlights GB's R&D contribution to poor people; illustrates Grameen Bank's alliances with its different stakeholders and the benefits from these alliances; shows GB's human resource management; and fifthly present the financial structure for GB's institutional sustainability. In addition, this paper discusses GB's social capitalfor sustainable business management.

4.0. Build a local base support with stakeholders

In order to be accepted by the local communities, businesses must build support within these communities. This can be a difficult and time consuming process, and in fact may even be dangerous at times. However, the Grameen bank has successfully built coalitions with local board of director leaders' electted from its micro borrowers, NGOs, governments and other businesses to create that base of support. In this regard, Ansoff, Freeman and McVera (2001) pointed out that identifying these stakeholders is critically important in the core competence of businesses and mentions that the stakeholder approach places and emphasis on the active management, which has several benefits such as providing a single strategic framework flexible enough to deal with the environment and adopt new strategic paradigms (p. 194). Therefore, the stakeholder strategic approach helps to develop a relationship with those who have a stake in the firm. The stakeholder approach is an approach of organizational management and business ethics that addresses morals and values in managing an organization. It was originally detailed by Ian Mitroff in his book "Stakeholders of the Organizational Mind," published in 1983 in San Francisco. However, stakeholder theory provides the interests of the various stakeholders can be, at best, compromised or balanced against each other.

The relationship between Grameen Bank and Grameen Shakti (Solar energy) is a good example of intensive networking and bonding between Grameen sisters organizations that has facilitated the building of a local base in the villages of Bangladesh. Grameen Shakti is a green enterprise that demonstrates the success of a densely networked approach involving mutually reinforcing investments in human, social, ecological and financial capital by a number of organizations. This company sells solar home electricity systems to families that do not have access to electricity otherwise, which includes more than 75% of the country's population. GB is providing small loans to solar recipients to help pay for their systems. Grameen Solar has installed 75,000 individual solar energy systems that have provided more than 200,000 lower income individuals with access to reliable electricity Grameen Shakti, 2006). Thus, Grameen Shakti is the stakeholder of GB who serves the poor solar electricity lights and environmentalism by working to eradicate poverty from their lives. Infrastructure development corporation limited (IDCOL) is Grameen Shakti's one of the business partner. However, Grameen Shakti have limited alliance outside Grameen sister organizations.

Government power has been eroded by globalization and transitional corporations in Bangladesh. NGOs and civil society stepped in to stop this expansion and to protest against it. However, a smarter approach to globalization can address the social and environmental concerns of fringe stakeholders, fringe stakeholders are stakeholders who could not directly impact the firm; however, they can join together and voice their concerns using the Internet or other medium. However, the firm needs to consider a strategic management process. Stakeholders' network can help to deal with threats from MNCs. The strategy of engaging fringe stockholders is required first to alter their consciousness towards the powerless and isolated. Hart and Sharma (2003) call it *Radical Transitiveness (RT)* (2005: p. 10). Hart and Sharma (2003), suggest a new entrepreneurial capability know as *Radical Transitiveness (RT)*. They defined RT as 'a dynamic capability which seeks systematically identify, explore, and integrate the views of the stakeholders on the fringe-the poor, weak, isolated non-legitimise and even non-human for the purpose of managing disruptive change and building imagination about future competitive business model.

GB engages its fringe stakeholders and uses their experience in its credit operation for the benefit of the poor. For example, it focuses on diversely spreading its activities to distant and marginal stakeholders (micro borrowers of GB). Hart and Sharma (2003) termed it *fanning out*, meaning spreading the business to poor people to identify opportunities for new businesses, rather than the protection of existing big businesses. This trust-based interactive strategy enabled the Grameen Bank and its stakeholders to confront many conflicts and contradictions. This process facilitated the mutual learning of diverse information making it possible for the *fanning in*of opportunities that did not previously exist in big businesses in Bangladesh (p. 16).

According to Green and Clarke (2003) there are three levels in which stakeholders can participate and contribute to achieve their companies' objectives: (1) information participation-pass information to one another, (2) consultative participation- ask about views and perspectives on issues, and (3) participation in the decision. Although Grameen Shakti and Grameen Bank are managed as separate entities, Grameen Shakti and Grameen other umbrella organizations have a close relationship with the Grameen Bank that allows them all to benefit from the bank's financing and the exchange of views and information.

Grameen Bank high officials are the board members of these umbrella organizations. For example, Grameen Shakti actively collaborates with Dhaka based Grameen Phone Ltd. By purchasing a cell phone and solar home energy system package and selling phone services to the villagers, these entrepreneurs create attractive revenue from these micro enterprises resulting in the improvement of borrowers' standard of living. All these organizations help to build a local base of support and benefit the local people. Hence, Roper and Cheney (2005) termed these organizations are social business enterprises (SBE) who take responsibility for the needs of the poor. Social entrepreneurship has been run as a non-profit sector for a long time; however, recently some hybrid social enterprises found in the non-profit sector with an entrepreneurial offshoot that generates revenues to fulfill the organization's social objectives.

Grameen Bank is a social business enterprise; it promotes credit as a human right. Its mission is to help poor families help themselves to overcome poverty. Its loans are collateral free and are based on trust. This loan is for creating self-employment for income generating activities and housing for the poor. It provides service at the door step of the poor based on the principle that the poor should not have to go to the bank; instead, the bank should go to the borrowers in order to provide loans to them. Five loan applicants form a group from the local community and conduct loan transactions with the bank.

Grameen bank branches are located in the local areas within the borrowers' community, close to their location. It brings problem-solving close to borrowers by locating field offices close to their homes. This policy reduces transaction costs for borrowers. It has bottom-up approach to decision making process and it uses a simple accounting system and less administrative and bureaucratic structure.

All loans of GB are to be paid back in installments (weekly). Grameen Centers are the places where loans are approved in front of the people and other loan activities carried out. These centers provide a forum for borrowers to pool information regarding credit decisions. Therefore, GB centers perform various development activities that are promoted by the credit program for the poor.

Grameen Bank created a methodology that meets the financial needs of the poor and created access to credit on reasonable terms that enable the poor to build on their existing skill to earn better an income in each cycle of loans. Therefore, GB's method is the reverse of the conventional banking methodology. Conventional banking is based on the principle that the provide loan to rich people is safe because rich people can provide collateral their assets against the loan. As a result, more than half the population of the world is deprived of the financial services of the conventional banks. Conventional banking is based on collateral, whereas the Grameen system is collateral free. Conventional banking is owned by the rich, generally men, while Grameen Bank is owned by poor women. Conventional banking motive is maximizing profit.

Grameen monitoring information system (MIS) pays a lot of attention to monitoring the education of the children, housing, personal hygiene, access to clean drinking water, and their coping capacity for meeting disasters and emergency situations. Ninety-six percent of Grameen Bank borrowers are women. It works to raise the status of poor women in their families by giving them ownership of assets in Bangladesh. Therefore, Grameen Bank is a socioeconomic public wellbeing development bank for the disadvantaged people particularly for poor women in Bangladesh.

5.0. Research and development unit of Grameen Bank

Grameen Bank portfolios have developed through its Research and Development (R & D) process that built within the organization that generates and tests different technology and then expands them to its clients. Through R&D GB, has initiated socially, economically and environmentally suitable products for the poor, which are beneficial to them. For example, micro-enterprise loans, loans to beggars, housing to the poor, higher education loan, deposit collection, etc are the products of R&D of Grameen Bank. GB initiated the technology loan in the mid 1980's where borrowers practice some form of technology for their livelihood, such as bee keeping, hand looming, batik printing, treadle pumping, oil extruding and candle making. Now the technology loans have shifted to micro-enterprise loans. GB provides larger loans, called micro-enterprise loans, for the fast moving members for power-tillers, irrigation pumps, transport vehicles, and river-crafts, as transportation and fishing are popular items for micro-enterprise loans among Grameen Bank borrowers. GB passed its development stage in the 70's and early 80s when it tested many of its products. The Bank attained the sustainability stage in the 90s at which point it achieved a degree of financial viability. From the late 90s, GB started its expansion stage while it underwent a structural transformation in order to scale up its operations to extend all over Bangladesh. Today, it lends out a half billion dollars of depositors' money, each year, without collateral in the amount of about $13 billion to 8.6 million borrowers; and maintains a 99 per cent repayment record (Grameen Updates 2016).

According to Prahalad and Stuart doing business with 4 billion people, requires radical innovation in technological and business models. The poorest people are large in number; therefore, this raises a new managerial challenge for the wealthiest companies in attempting to settle the poor and helping them to improve their lives and produce products that are culturally sensitive, environmentally sustainable and economically profitable. This Tier 4 MNC market has some core assumptions that are an influence in LDC: (1) the poor are the target consumers because they are not in a profitable market, (2) the poor cannot afford products that are sold in DC and (3) the bottom of the pyramid is not a long term viable business. The motive of the private sector is to leave Tier 4 (the poor) to the government and non-profit sectors because managers are not excited by business challenges that are humanitarian. Therefore, it is hard to find managers who agree to work with the bottom of the pyramid. However, GB is an exception in this regard.

For example, in 2003, GB took up a separate special program, called *Grameen Struggling Members Program*, to reach out to the beggars. About 100,000 beggars have already joined the program and received these loans. They returned the loans smoothly and all loans are interest free; they are covered under life insurance without paying any cost. Moreover, GB has introduced housing loans for the poor since 1984. It became a very attractive program for the borrowers. This program was awarded the Aga Khan International Award for its simple, long lasting housing methods in 1989. The housing loan of GB maximum size is USD$250 to be repaid over a period of 5 years in weekly installments. 638,008 houses have been constructed with the housing loans. A total of US$121 million has been disbursed in house loans thus far. It provides scholarships, every year, to the high performing children of Grameen borrowers, with priority given to women, to encourage them to stay ahead in their classes. The scholarships amounting to US$420,000 have been awarded to 32,380 children (Grameen statistics. 2006). GB also has loans paid off in what is called the Death Welfare. Under this program, the families of the deceased are not required to pay off their debt burden any more, which is instead paid off by their life insurance, being shareholders of the bank. As of September 2006, the total loan insurance savings account stood at US$51.63 million.

6.0. Form new alliances

According to David Wheeler (2005), and Sharma and Rudd (2003) sustainable businesses involve relatively dense networks of local business communities, NGOs and other actors who are involved in creating value in economic, social, human and ecologically and secure financial sustainability. This Sustainable Local Development Network (SLDN) is important for sustainable business development because it provides opportunities for business communities, individuals, government agencies and NGOs to create shared assets that have many benefits; such as reliable returns on investments, local living economic development and trade expansion to enhance the quality of life and ecological enhancement. The local community development partnerships are usually composed of public, private (banks), NGOs, philanthropic organizations could increase the accountability of the MNCs and its stakeholders.

David Wheeler says, "The sustainable business investments can contribute to human capital, social capital, financial capital, and ecological capital. Ecological capital means it is a natural capital that is one approach to ecosystem valuation which revolves around the idea, in contrast to traditional economics, that non-human life produces essential resources. It is an extension of the economic notion of capital (resources which enable the production of more resources) to goods and services provided by the natural environment. For example, a well-maintained forest or river may provide an indefinitely sustainable flow of new trees or fish, whereas over-use of those resources may lead to a permanent decline in timber availability or fish stocks. Natural capital also provides people with essential services, like water catchment, erosion control and crop pollination by insects, which in turn ensure the long-term viability of other natural resources. Since the continuous supply of services from the available natural capital assets is dependent upon a healthy, functioning environment, the structure and diversity of habitats and ecosystems are important components of natural capital. All these capitals need to be present, in some form or other, in the organization, in order to restore resources and for networks to grow and to become self-reliant." (p. 36).

Grameen Bank has shared asset networks with its umbrella organizations. For instance, Grameen Bank has created many other social business enterprise (SBE) companies like Grameen Renewable Energy, Grameen Health, Grameen Phone, Grameen Telecom, Grameen Agriculture, Grameen Fisheries and Livestock, and Grameen IT Park etc. They are independent from Grameen Bank; however, their mission is also to serve the needs of the poor, but through the supply of solar panels, health services, phone services, crop production, and various IT services. Grameen Bank extends its managerial, advisory and funding support to these organizations. For example, it gave an endowment of $3.16 million of its revolving loan fund to Grameen Health (Grameen Statistics: 2002, p. 5). Grameen Bank becomes the guarantor to Grameen Solar, and Grameen Fisheries while their need for borrowing funds from outside. GB provided financial guarantees to Grameen Solar of half a million dollars to receive loans from the government and other financial organizations. GB borrowers buy solar panels from Grameen Shakti. These GB stakeholders shared their services that helped to channel more services to the rural poor. GB also networks with international organizations like UNDP, CIDA, and NORAD for the replication of Grameen-type lending technologies in different countries

Recently, Grameen America micro lending program in the United States has replicated the Grameen type group lending method in poor urban neighborhoods. The Project Enterprise New York is receiving loan funds and technical support from Grameen Foundation USA to provide credit to minority entrepreneurs. Recently it formed an alliance with the Clinton Global Foundation and now it receives funding from it.

According to Cik Prahalad and G. Hamel (1990) the core competence is the collective learning in the organization. It is about delivering organizational value, coordinating diverse productive skills and integrating multiple technologies. Competence is the glue that binds existing businesses. They are the engine for new business development. An example is Grameen Bank sister organizations like Grameen Telecom, which puts cell phones in the hands of Grameen Bank female borrowers even in the remotest villages of Bangladesh. GB has provided loans to 258,884 borrowers to buy phones and offer telecommunication services to half of the villagers of Bangladesh where this service never existed before. Telephone-ladies run a very profitable business with these phones. Telephone ladies play an important role in the telecommunication sector of the country (Grameen Bank, 2002).

Another Grameen company called Grameen Shamogree is linking up the traditional handloom weavers of Bangladesh with the garments sector. All these GB stakeholders create potential access to a wide variety of markets to poor that helps them to participate in diverse businesses and contribute to customers' benefits with end products. According to Sharma and Rudd (2003) public policy is not sufficient for achieving sustainability; rather corporate sustainability could be achieved through multi-stakeholders. GB's various stakeholders like borrowers, board members, employees, NGO Bureau, Bangladesh Central Bank, Ministry of Finance, investors, GB's umbrella organizations, suppliers, and media contribute to GB's portfolio development. It seeks stakeholders' inputs in its business operations through these stakeholders' networks, customers feedback and from international dialogues. GB is always free to share and deliver information to all parties that seek it.

MNCs can build social capital by creating an environment where different stakeholders can contribute and be acknowledged by a farming vision. This shared vision can create social capital for communities and enterprises that are built on trust, reciprocity, care and mutuality (Sandra Waddock, 2001). According to Palus & Drath (2001) dialogue is the best way to create the sharing of ideas in a group for action. Dialogue allows people to let go of their own ideas, share those of others, and participate in a decision that challenges their own ideas. Grameen Bank has organized many international dialogue seminars where thousands of national and overseas researchers, implementers, academicians, micro credit practitioners, donors, and community leaders participated. They reviewed the GB credit operation and exchanged their ideas in the meetings and seminars. Grameen Bank received their ideas that applied to borrowers if it is applicable. These dialogue workshops have contributed to improving Grameen Bank's different products and services and have facilitated the replication of Grameen technology to different countries.

7.0. Increase employment intensity

As mentioned earlier Grameen Bank's 22, 000 staff meets 8.6 million borrowers at their door-step in 72,096 villages all over Bangladesh, every week, and deliver bank services to these borrowers. (Ninety Six percent of its customers are women, who, as the traditional breadwinners and entrepreneurs in rural Bangladesh, are better credit risks than men). All these borrowers become self-employed by utilizing Grameen Bank loans.

Sustainable business strategy emphasizes an employees' leadership and empowerment and quality services to customers. Sustainable business, or green business, is an enterprise that has minimal negative impact on the global or local environment, community, society, or economy-a business that strives to meet the triple bottom line. Often, sustainable businesses have progressive environmental and human rights policies. In general, business is described as green if it matches the following four criteria:

1. It incorporates principles of sustainability into each of its business decisions.

2. It supplies environmentally friendly products or services that replace demand for non-green products and/or services.
3. It is greener than traditional competition.
4. It has made an enduring commitment to environmental principles in its business operations.

GB is dedicated to the delivery of quality credit delivery services to its borrowers. Its credit business practices and processes are designed to achieve results that can give both qualitative and quantitative results to its stakeholders and shareholders. These qualitative and quantitative results are the outputs of employees' services. According to Colbert (2004) Strategic Human Resource Management (SHRM) is important for the sustainability of an organization because SHRM deals with employees' skills, behaviors and interactions in an organization. These attributes and practices are instrumental in developing human resource capability. Staff training is essential to motivate performance and increase their skills. GB staff training integrates into ongoing operations to ensure that staff members receive training in a structured and systematic way. Recently Grameen Bank has collaborated with Grameen communication in supporting Grameen branch computerization. Now the bank is trying to develop its online business model to reduce the costs of manpower.

Grameen DANONE is a socially responsible investment (SRI) which produces thousands of rural employment through its different food production plants and distribution outlets. Its mission is to reduce poverty by a unique proximity business model that brings daily healthy nutrition to the poor. It is sharing the benefits with its community fringe stakeholders. It allows lower income consumers of Bangladesh to have access to a range of tasty and nutritious foods and beverages on a daily basis, in order to improve their nutritional status. In addition, it has involved local suppliers (farmers) for helping them to improve their skills in livestock raising practices, and involved local people in the manufacture of its milk food products contributing to the creation of new jobs in the rural area. The profit generated by Grameen DANONE is reinvested in the development of its business in a manner to be mutually agreed upon by Grameeen Bank and Grameen DANONE. Like DANONE, different MNCs, donors and foundations can start creating social business equity (SBE) funds in recipient countries to support SBE initiatives. These SBEs can become very powerful players in the national economy if we can recognize them and empower them.

8.0. Reinvent cost structures

Contrary to popular assumptions, Tier 4 can be very profitable if MNCs change their business models. Tier 4 is not a high margin; rather profit is driven by volume and capital efficiency. The main values here are that margins should be low, but unit sales high. Electricity, water, refrigeration and many other essential services are all opportunities for running social and green businessesin developing countries. Tier 4 communities are physically and economically isolated. Therefore, better distribution systems, education and communication links are essential to develop the bottom of the pyramid and allow creative local companies can lead effective rural distribution for them.

MFIs of Bangladesh became specialized lending institutions whose primary objectives are to improve the quality and efficiency of their lending operations and expand them significantly to the disadvantaged people. Maria Otero mentions that there are some institutional and financial characteristics like the number of clients reached, sources of funding, achieving self-sufficiency and staff development strategies (Oterio & Rhyne 1994: p. 94). However, to succeed micro-lending organizations there must improve and use sound lending principles to guide their financial operations and cut costs. GB provides some financial intermediation such as receiving savings from the borrowers, paying interest on savings, and receiving interest from credit investments. However, in most countries, regulations prevent non-profit organizations from capturing savings from the public, but it is an essential ingredient of financial intermediation for MFIs.

Governments of different countries should give legal protection for financial savings deposits made by borrowers in the MFIs. These institutions need to gradually scale-up their loan functions in order to reach thousands of small-scale entrepreneurs. They must develop their products with the market perspective and focus on financial services that respond to the preferences of their clients. According to Otero, effective financial management is essential for continued growth and any move into financial intermediation of the MFIs (Oterio & Rhyne 1994: p. 100). The decentalised GB's central accounts have outlets to its area offices by which it delivers funds to its branches. This process helps the smooth management and flow of funds throughout the Bank.

MFIs need to maintain their social development objectives in addition to financial viability. In this regard GB uses profits to create long-term financial sustainability and expansion; however, the challenge for GB is to maintain the integrity of this duality of purpose and not allow one part to overtake the other. It has savings, emergency funds, and life insurance provision to its borrowers. However, GB does not provide vocational training or vocational training loans to its clients, which are important for trade businesses. GB measures its financial condition by profitability, excess of income over expenses and return of equity, portfolio quality that measures default loans risk, liquidity, and capital adequacy. In 2005, GB made $680,000 in profit. Doing business this way means a lot of work for the bank, but it is inconvenient for the borrowers. However, the popularity of its services has generated more local competitors, but its portfolios are expanding day-by- day to poor. At the same time it maintains its financial sustainability.

The Tier 4 model also works for environmentally friendly businesses like solar energy in different countries. For example, Prahalad and Stuart mentions that the Solar Electric Light Fund (SELF) has creatively adapted technology and applied micro credit funding to bring electrical service to people in remote villages in Africa and Asia who otherwise use hazardous kerosene, wood, or dung. SELF has funded this project in China, Sri Lanka, Nepal, Brazil, Uganda, Tanzania and South

Africa. The success of the small scale rural renewable resources project draws other companies like Honeywell Inc. and makes micro turbines. Therefore, there are huge opportunities for MNCs to work with Tier 4 people and to profit from their businesses. However, as Tier 4 communities are often physically and economically isolated; therefore, better distribution systems and communication links are essential to develop the bottom of the pyramid.

According to Kevin P. Kearns (2003) all the above features together can make outstanding performance of a firm. For example, the GB credit delivery program carries out an outstanding performance by continuously adapting and refining its mission and vision and developing revenue strategies that are appropriate to its financial sustainability. GB continually refines innovative and effective approaches to accomplishing its mission and makes decisions about competition and collaboration on a case-by-case basis. For example, GB totally changes its classical micro-lending services in 2000. The Grameen Bank new lending system is called Grameen Type-2. In Grameen type-2 lending system, abolish group fund elements, introduce six months repayment system, the grammen pension scheme (GPS) etc. According to Jim Collins (2001) GB characteristics distinguished it from other MFIs because it has unique social, economic and environmentally friendly objectives. It has clear goals, and it is accountable to its different stakeholders.

9.0. Social value capital development

Phahalad and Hamel do not mention social value capital development in their Bottom Pyramid Tier-4 approach. However, SBEs are very important for value creation and socially-driven ventures. They are designed and operated as a business enterprise to pass on all the benefits to the customers rather than translating them into profits for the investors. According to Clarke and Clegg (1998) a value creating business culture means that companies think more about quality and commitment to continuous value creation for people within communities. The elements of the value culture are alternatives for value creation, continuous learning, disciplined decision making, and open information flow (p. 239). For example, recently GB has created a joint venture SBE with Grameen DANONE Foods where the capital ratio is 50:50 between Grameen Bank and DANONE Company. It is innovative in solving intricate social and economic problems in Bangladesh and improving malnutrition and the living conditions of the poor. In addition, this Grameen-DANONE link creates sustainable value from its intangible assets – human capital, database information system, customer relationship brand innovation capabilities and culture. According to Kaplan and Norton (2004) intangible assets are (1) human capital: skills, talent, know-how; (2) information capital: availability of information system and networks, (3) organizational capital: ability of organizations to mobilize and sustain the process to change and execute strategy. All are strategies that promote intangible assets in the internal processes of an organization that create unique values in the organization.

- Following are points Jeremy Bloom, a business man in US, believes to be the cornerstones of a solid business culture:
- Transparency: Here the goal is for all employees to feel they know the thinking, responsibilities, and strategy at various levels of the company and can share ideas and feedback no matter who they are. Everyone in the company can participate and ask questions.
- Time to disconnect: Employees can't come in early and leave late every single day without getting sick or personal emergency at some level. It's important to understand that sometimes life will get in the way of business and everyone should be allowed to take care of pressing personal matters.
- Empowerment and a sense of freedom: Business owner can empower employees by not only micromanaging, erring on the side of giving people general guidelines rather than explicit, detailed directions. Informed employees are more involved and empowered in a company. And the more freedom people have to take on tasks, manage them, find solutions, and execute

them, the more they feel connected to and woven into the company's culture.

- Physical space: It's important to consider the comfort level of the employees before employer decides how to lay out space or what type of office space to lease.
- Talking to customers and employees: Company's another maturation process is employer guaranteed to go through weeks or even months where he feels lost. Through regular visit, it's also important to touch base with the employees. Another way to try to solve these problems is by talking to customers.
- Organizational design: Organizational design is the processes, structure, and hierarchy can put into place that allows employer to put his organizational culture into practice. This can include your communication, company policies, team building, performance indicators, and performance evaluations, division of responsibilities, and even how schedule, and run meetings.

If business designed well, everyone in the business can do his or her job more effectively. Business culture will significantly be enhanced if the organizational design puts into place clarifies authority, responsibility, and accountability. Grameen Bank practices above all Jerimy Blooms notions of employees' social value development. For example, it is fair and transperant to its all employees; it motivates, encourages and follows the notion of time connection and employees empowerment. It has convenient and hygenic office spaces for its employees at each levels of its administration. GB has excellent customer services for its borrowers, and for its well simple, appropriate micro lending policy. Grameen bank prefers cordial relationship among hierchy employees and soft team building spirit. Moreover, Grameen Bank has negoatiable performance indicators, fair job performance evaluation and promotion system for its employees. These are social value capital development elements of Grameen Bank that practices by GB in its credit deliverying design and operations in Bangladesh.

GB is not only a credit delivery organization, but also promotes leadership, and citizenry skills development process among the poor in Bangladesh. For example, Grameen credit delivery system makes the borrowers familiar with the election process. They routinely elect group chairmen, secretaries, and center chiefs every year. They elect board members for running Grameen Bank every three years. This experience has prepared them to run for public offices. They are contesting and getting elected in the local governments. For example, in the 2003 local government election 7,422 Grameen members contested in the reserved seats for women, out of which 3,059 members were elected. During the 1997 local government election 1,753 members got elected to these reserved seats (Grameen Bank, 2003).

Although Grameen Bank believes in financial sustainability, because it cannot expand its outreach without funds; moreover, it gives high priority to building social capital. This social capital is promoted through the formation of groups in the centers and maintain networking among clients aiming to develop leadership quality among the poor through annual election of group and centre leaders. GB has *sixteen decisions* that help borrowers to make a social agenda. The Grameen Bank system encourages the borrowers to adopt some goals in the social, educational and health areas. These are known as *sixteen decisions*. (No dowry, education for children, use sanitary latrine, planting tress round the year, eating vegetables to combat night-blindness among children and arranging clean drinking water etc.) Conventional banks do not see this as their business; however, GB places special emphasis on the formation of human capital development among its borrowers and concern for protecting the environment. It monitors children's education, provides scholarships and student loans for higher education. For the formation of human capital, it makes efforts to provide technology like mobile phones, wind pumps, and mechanical food processing to poor people.

Corporate social responsibility is one of the vital components for social businessequity (SBEs) funds that Prahalad and Hamel ignored. However, CSR makes the company environmentally responsible (Cramer, 2005: p. 256). According to Cramer, the CSR approach has a social vision, a mission and code of conduct that is embedded in the process of quality management system. To extend CSR to MNCs requires commitment from the senior management, and sufficient internal support from the business. If employees and middle managers are accountable for their performance on CSR, they will be more willing to take the issue seriously and commit to action.

The concept of Corporate Social Responsibility was first mentioned 1953 in the publication 'Social Responsibilities of the Businessman' by William J. Bowen. The concept is started popular in 1990s in the business world. Corporate social responsibility is a concept whereby companies decide voluntarily to contribute to a better society and a cleaner environment. Corporate social responsibility is represented by the contributions undertaken by companies to society through its business activities and its social investment or donate to public wellbeing programs.

Over the last years an increasing number of companies worldwide started promoting their Corporate Social Responsibility strategies because the customers, the public and the investors expect them to act sustainably as well as responsibly. In most cases CSR is a result of a variety of social, environmental and economic pressures.

The term 'Corporate Social Responsibility' is imprecise and its application differs. CSR refers not only to the compliance of human rights standards, labour and social security arrangements, but also to the fight against climate change, sustainable management of natural resources, consumer protection, philanthropy and volunteering.

Therefore, Wheeler et al. (2003) asserts that CSR and sustainable development are interrelated in the creation of business value. According to them, sustainable businesses have three interwoven concepts: (1) corporate social responsibility (CSR), (2) sustainable development and (3) stakeholders approach to strategic management. The CSR and sustainable development with the stakeholders approach can be developed by focusing value creation in the business is an integrating ground for Tier-4 sustainable business development. MNCs take advantage of economic globalization, but they bypass their social responsibility. CSR value-based networks can generate both economic and social benefits to the bottom pyramid.

10.0. Sustainable development and sustainable business development

According to the World Commission on Environment and Development, (WCED, 1987) sustainable development means that "we meet the needs of the present generation without compromising the ability of future generations to meet their own needs" (p.8). However, WCED talks about preservation of a particular social order rather than preservation of nature. Hopwood et al. (2005) define sustainable development as the combination of environmental issues with socio-economic issues. It challenges humanity now and in the future. It concentrates on sustainable livelihoods and well-being rather than well-having. Although GB works under the existing social structure, it believes that problems are rooted in fundamental features of society and interrelated with environment. It sees human interactions with the environment and views problems within the economic and power structure of society as it concerns human and environmental well-being. However, although GB is not challenging the existing political values, but GB serves sustainable development as its program is designed for human centered development and deals with socioeconomic and environmental issues.

Community participation approach is one of the major elements of sustainable business development that is not mentioned by Prahalad and Hamel; but participatory rural appraisal (PRA) is very important to social business development. GB follows this community participatory approach in its program implementation because it is based on equitable and respectful partnerships and collaboration between clients and institutions with due attention to local knowledge (Chamber (1997, Crush 1995, Escobar 1995, Friedmann 1992). According to Amartya Sen (1999) this is a process of developing individual capabilities through gaining education and skills in order to empower individuals to fight for a better life, goals of good governance, democracy and economic liberalization. Grameen Bank and all other MFIs are working closely with grass roots marginalized people and following a community participation approach.

In Canada, Alterna Savings follows community participatory strategy by providing loans for environmental businesses like Naturfriend Services Inc., is involved in organic fertilizing, weed control, grab grass control, cutting, trimming lawn grasses and seasonal cleanup services. All these activities are fulfilling the bottom pyramid Tier 4 model that makes mutual partnership among MFIs and clients. Conversely, MNCs are far away from fulfilling the greening of the world and providing sustainable development for people. Rather they are concentrated on making money and maintaining their brand. Therefore, it needs to develop a local living ecologically balanced economy (LLC) so that it does not need to import products from outside but rather cares for and promotes local resources and reduces the rate of pollution in the environment. Ecological economics/eco-economics refers to both a transdisciplinary and interdisciplinary concept addressing the interdependence and coevolution of human economics and natural ecosystems both intertemporally and spatially. Ecological economists point out that, beyond modest levels, increased per-capita consumption and suggest an interdisciplinary approach combining social and natural sciences as a means to address local poverty, and social and environmental injustice.

GB works closely with local people, respects local values and beliefs. It provides loans for agriculture, and other green businesses. It promotes gender equality. However, modern management failed to challenge capitalism and to address the issues of environmental degradation, equity, equality, and futurity. Therefore, the earth's ability to sustain life is threatened by human activity and MNCs because industries look only at exploitable resources of eco-system such as oceans, forests and plains. The government and companies are not serious about it because the values of environment services do not appear in the balance sheet, but the economy is in the nature. We cannot live without it. Lavinson asserts that *natural capitalism* includes increased natural productivity, and biologically-inspired production models. It is a solution-based business model reinvesting natural capital. According to Lavinson (1999), the productivity of natural resources can be increased by fresh designs of industrial systems and can replace old systems of technology. Biological models reduce wastage and can provide a vast business opportunity. This biological business model has sustainable value.

Sustainable value is a way of managing and measuring sustainability performance. The concept was developed by researchers who are working today for Euromed Management School (Marseille/France) and the IZT - Institute for Futures Studies and Technology Assessment (Berlin/Germany). Sustainable value differs from existing approaches by the fact that it is value-based while all other existing approaches to sustainability assessment (such as environmental impact assessments) are burden-based, i.e. they are assessing environmental and social resource use based on the burden that is created. Using the sustainable value approach, economic, environmental and social resources are assessed and aggregated based on their relative value contribution and can be expressed in a monetary unit like Euros, dollars or pounds.

According to Faerkas and Backer (1996) sustainable values have four drivers (1) reduce maternal consumption and pollution, (2) operate in greater transparency, (3) reduce human footprints by technological improvements, and (4) meet the needs of the bottom people through pollution prevention. SMEs are in a better position because they are small, and can change and adapt promptly. They are less polluting and can recycle wastages (Zero wastage). However, MNCs are not attentive to zero cvarbon and they are not attentive to their wastage products recycling them although they are aware of it. Small purchases amount to major wastage. Many executives pay little attention to saving resources. Natural capitalism can address the issue of the wasteful economy by reintegrating ecological with economic goals (Lavison, 1999: p. 158). GB provides loans for recycling businesses and makes packets from leaves, which helps to reduce pollution in borrowers' neighbourhood.

From the above discussion, it is clear that there are many distinctions between MNCs and small businesses, ecological businesses. The main distinction between MNCs, small businesses and ecological businesses is that MNCs focus globally and nationally. They build, expand and protect their own brand names. For example, Coca Cola, IBM, and Dell computer is attentive to maintaining their own brand names. They are involved more in advertising and marketing their products to different countries from a distance; however, these companies do not have strategy for taking back or disposing consumers thrown unused mechaniries that are garbage in the community

Thus there is a big gap between MNCs and customers. Contrarily, small businesses are close to customers' doors, they know each other. Small business owners live within the customers' community, and respect their values and traditions. SMEs receive customers' feedback quickly and respond to them promptly. Brian Milini (2000) emphasizes that SMEs can create a vibrant community local living economics where local skills, local resources, local wastes recycling, and local renewable resources can be geared towards community currency. SMEs can customize solutions promptly. GB promotes small business, works very close to its borrowers and becomes partners with them. GB takes care of its borrowers.

MNC has a top down management approach, but SMEs are bottom up. Big businesses want to sell everything and defeat the SMEs until they die. They do not want to *cannibalize* (kill) their existing businesses. MNCs create more packaging wastages. They ignore corporate social responsibility and avoid socially responsible investment. Alterna Savings Toronto, Access Riverdale and Ottawa Community Loan Fund provide loans to social enterprises. These micro lending organizations are emphasising on individuals' characters, commitment and ability to serve local people. These Canadian MFIs are promoting Tier-4 business strategy and support SMEs.

The Bottom Pyramid Tier 4 business strategy is a shift from high-margin business to high-volume business model. MNCs current business price reflects high-margin strategy. A high-price leads to an impediment for mass adoption. Therefore, the bottom pyramid Tier-4 supports sustainable businesses and pursues a low-margin high-volume sale approach. The Tier-4 lower price strategy enables the mass adoption of consumptions by low income consumers. The reasonable price reduces the burden to the mass of the people at the bottom of the pyramid. To achieve sustainable businesses purpose and mission, MNCs should focus on values like integrity for the highest ethical standards and products and processes of highest quality. GB respects people and recognizes that people are the cornerstone of its success, and treat them with dignity. Grameen Bank believes in teamwork and customer satisfaction instead of simply high profit. It puts community values in the first place. It is innovative and is dynamic in meeting the needs of the poor. Creating buying power, shaping aspiration, improving access and tailoring local solutions are Tier 4 elements of bottom pyramid. Innovation is a key leverage (Prahalad & Hart, 2003; p. 376). Prahalad suggests that MNCs can be involved in Tier 4 business through resource building of commercial structures for the bottom pyramid, leverage MNC transfer of knowledge from one market to another market, and bridging. MNCs must provide an organizational infrastructure to address the bottom pyramid.

GB has proved itself a successful role model in micro financing and has become a leader in promoting micro enterprises and social business enterprise. It generates reliable information about its performance and creates an environment of innovation for the bottom poor people. It has a clear line of authority and responsibility to its stakeholders. It has clear and comprehensive values and standards of ethics: in the written value statement that clearly describes what the organization stands for. Board and staff members regularly refer to these values. It has engaged all its stakeholders in providing opinion, and in the decision-making processes. Moreover, it is transparent to providing accurate information to its stakeholders. Therefore, it is a successful role model of "*The Fortune at the Bottom of the Pyramid*" where many MNCs have failed. In fact, the Grameen Bank has begun to export its success model outside of Bangladesh and into other businesses within Bangladesh. Having fulfilled the plan laid out in "*The Fortune at the Bottom of the Pyramid*", the Grameen Bank has managed to market monetary services to the poorest of the world's poor. This is a remarkable achievement one which has succeeded in helping the world's poor to escape poverty although there are many limitations can be found in Grameen Bank portfolios particularly citizenry skill development services to its clients in Bangladesh.

11.0. References

Clarke, T. and Clegg, S. (1998). Strategy in Changing Paradigms, *Journal of Management Study*, Vol. 35(2), pp. 163-194

Colbert, B. (2004). The complex resource-based view: implications for theory and practice in strategic human resource management, *Academy of Management Review*, Vol. 29(3). pp. 341-358

Cramer, J. (2005). Company Learning about Corporate Social Responsibility, *Business Strategy and the Environment*. Vol. 14, pp. 255-266

Daly, H. E. (2003). *Ecological economics: The Concept of scale and its relation to allocation, Distribution, and Uneconomic Growth*. Alberta: CANSEE, Jasper.

Delimas, M. and Toffel, M. (2004). Stakeholders and environmental management practices; an institutional framework, *Business Strategy and the Environment*, Vol. 13, pp. 209-222

Farkas, C. and Backer, P. (1996). The quick and the dead: the strategic approach in maximum leadership in chapter *The world's leading CEO's share their five strategies for success*, pp. 27-60, Collingdale: Diane Publishing Company

Freeman, R. and McVea, J. (2001). A stakeholder Approach to Strategic Management. In Hitt, M. et al., eds., *The Blackwell handbook of strategic management*, pp. 189-207

Green A. and Clarke, L. (2003). A typology of stakeholder participation for company environmental decision-making, *Business Strategy and the Environment*, Vol. 12. pp. 292-299

Hart, S. and Milsten, M. (2003). Creating sustainable value, *Academy of Management Executive*, Vol. 17(2), pp. 56-69

Hart, S. and Sharma, S. (2004). Engaging fringe stakeholders for competitive imagination. *The Academy of Management Perspective*. Vol. 18 (1). pp. 7-18

Henry, S. (2006). *How MFIs and their clients can have a positive impact on the environment. Good practices in business development services: how do we enhance entrepreneurial skills in MFIs clients?* Paper personated in the Micro Credit Summit Halifax held in November 2006. Toronto: Alterna Savings

Hopwood, B. and Hopwood, B., Mellor, M. and O'Brien, G. (2005). Sustainable Development: Mapping different Approaches, *Sustainable Development*, Vol. 13, pp. 38-52

Hulme, D., and Mosley, P. (1996). *Finance against poverty*, 2 Volumes, London: Rutledge

Jain, P. (2000). *Managing fast expansion of micro-credit programs*. Dhaka: Association for Social Advancement (ASA).

Jain, P. S., (1996). Managing credit for the rural poor: Lessons from the Grameen Bank. *World Development*, Vol. 24 (1), pp. 79-89

Kaplan, R. and Norton, D. (2004). *Strategy Maps: Converting Intangible Assets into Tangible Outcomes*. Harvard Business School Press, pp. 3-15

Kearins, K. and Springett, D. (2003). Educating for sustainability: Development critical skills. *Journal of Management Education*, Vol. 27 (2), pp. 188-204

Kevin Kearns (2006). *From Adequate to outstanding performance*. The Forbes Funds, pp.1-18.

Lovins A. and et al. (1999). A road map for natural capitalism, *Harvard Business Review*, pp. 143-158

Milani, B. (2000). *Designing the Green Economy: the post-industrial alternative to corporate globalization*. Lanham MD: Rowman and Littlefield

Milani, B. (2001). *From Opposition to Alternatives: New Productive Forces and the Post materialist Redefinition of Wealth.* Paper presented at the Environmental Studies Asso. of Canada (ESAC). Laval Quebec

Oterio, M. and Rhyne, E. (1994). *The new world of microenterprise finance: Building healthy financial institutions for the poor.* Connecticut: Kumarian Press

Otero, M. and Rhyne, E. (1994). *The new world of micro enterprise finance,* Connecticut: Kumarian Press, Inc.

Palus, C. & Drath, W. (2001). Putting something in the middle: An approach to dialogue. *Reflections: The SOL Journal of Knowledge, Learning and Change,* Vol. 3(2), pp. 1-22

Prahalad, K. and Hamel, G. (1990). The core competence of the corporation. *Harvard Business Review,* pp. 2-15

Prahalad, K and Hart, S. (2002). The fortune at the Bottom of the Pyramid. *Strategy +Business,* Vol. 26, pp. 1-22

Roper, J. and Cheney, G. (2005). Leadership leaning and human resource management: The meaning of social entrepreneurship today. Corporate Governance, *the International Journal of Business in Society.* Vol. 5(3), pp. 95-104

Rouf, K. A. (2016). Eradication of Poverty through Community Economic Development using Micro Financing: Lessons Learned from Grameen Bank Bangladesh. *International Journal of Research Studies in Management,* Vol. 5(2), pp. 1-10

Rouf, K. A. (2016). Grameen Bank services to Women in Development (WID), Gender and Development (GAD), Women in Business (WIB), Women and Development (WAD) and Women in Environment (WED) approach in Bangladesh. *International Journal of Research Studies in Management,* Vol. 5(2), pp. 11-20

Rouf, K. A. (2018). Concepts, theories, and approaches to management practices for sustainable businesses, *International Journal of Research Studies in Management, Vo*l. 7(1), pp. 13-36.

Sharma, S. and Ruud, A. (2003). On the path to sustainability: Integrating social dimensions into the research and practice of environmental management, *Business Strategy and the Environment* Vol. 12, pp. 205-214

Waddock, S. (2001). How companies can build social capital internally? Reflections: *The SOL Journal on Knowledge, Learning and Change,* Vol. 3(1), pp. 18-24

Wheeler, D., Colbert, B. and Freemanet, R. E. (2003). Focusing on value: Reconciling corporate social responsibility, Sustainability and a Stakeholder Approach in a Networked World, *Journal of General Management,* Vol. 28(3). pp. 1-28.

Wheeler, D., McKague, K., Thomson, J., Davies, R., Medalye, J. and Prada, M. (2005). Creating sustainable local enterprise networks, *MIT Sloan Management Review,* Vol. 47(7), pp. 32-41

Yunus, M. (1978). *Bidhimala: By-laws of the Grameen Bank Project.* Dhaka: Oslow Printers.

Yunus, M. (2006). *Grameen Bank at a glance.* Chittagong: Packages Corporation Limited:

Yunus, M. (2006). *Social Business entrepreneurs are the solution.* Chittagong: Packages Corporation Limited.

Religious Patriarchal Values obstruct Bangladeshi Rural Women's Human Rights

Abstract

Patriarchy and religious customary laws, private and public realm, gender division of labour, and colonization contribute to women's subordinate position in Bangladesh. Women are stereotyped as passive, docile, silent, illiterate, and keeps them invisible, voiceless, choice-less, faceless and as objects of men in the society. This paper argues gendered division of labor; patriarchy and religious customary laws and values have denied Bangladeshi women access to equal rights. Customary laws dominate rural women, who are governed by the rural religious male elites. This promotes a dichotomy of private and public realm, which in turn is barrier to women's participation in economic activity outside home. Changing customary law, modifying traditional Muslim and Hindu laws, and women having equal access to property rights and income-generating strategies are needed to improve women's access to the legal system to address the violation of human rights and to improve Muslim family laws in Bangladesh. Gender balance adult women education and women's empowerment advocacy can enable women to oppose the authoritative patriarchal power structures and customary religious laws through collective networking and action. With these aims, Grameen Bank Sixteen Decision campaigns and group-based credit program creates opportunities for poor women in Bangladesh to find them free from male dependence.

Keywords: Bangladesh, gender balance, gender division of labor, Grameen Bank, Muslim customary laws, private sphere, patriarchal values, poverty, public sphere, and women's human rights.

1.0. Introduction

Bangladesh is a highly patriarchal Muslim dominated society where men make household decisions. This gender-based discrimination in Bangladesh has eroded women's fundamental rights to life, health, education, security, bodily integrity, food, work, and shelter. Women are stereotyped as passive, docile, silent, illiterate, unclean, fertile and smelling of curry. This stereotype keeps women 'in their place, invisible and as objects of the ruling social organization (Bannerji, 1993: 149). Therefore, rural women are imaged negatively, becoming the invisible and faceless in the society. Women are limited in their choices in practically all spheres of life and occupy the lowest level in the society. Bangladeshi rural women experience discrimination, exploitation and a robbed of their human rights. This paper argues that Bangladeshi rural women are denied access to inherent property rights and other financial resources because of British colonization, gendered division of labor, patriarchy and religious customary values.

Currently, Bangladesh has 164 million people within a 147, 570 square kilometer range (Bangladesh profile 2016). Half of the population is female. The density of the population is 763 people per square kilometer and an individual's per capita income is $1070. Only 30% of the total population has access to basic health services, and 76% of all households are deficient in calorie intake (CIDA 2001: Gender Profile Bangladesh). Without access to health care, poor women face malnutrition and death. 67% of women live under the poverty line, which is significantly higher than the national average of 51% (BIDS Human Rights Report, 2005).

2.0. Women status in Bangladesh

Family types in Bangladesh are predominately extended families, although this is changing. Women's subordinate status is almost an established fact in Bangladesh (Begum, 1988). Women are dependent upon men throughout their life cycle (Quddus et al., 1985, 30). Since men hold the status of family head and control the resources, they enjoy the most power in the family. Women are often socially and economically isolated. Under patriarchy women internalize the sexist values that dictate their actions. Accordingly they defer to the authority of their husbands and teach their daughters to assume a traditional role dependant on a subordinate status to men. Women, themselves, engage in actions that seem to actively contribute to the continuation of their subordinate status, because it is presented to them as biologically given (Ahmed, 1990:365). Women teach their daughters traditional roles. Women's subordinate position is not inevitable fact of biology; rather it is a product of socialization process starting at birth.

In Bangladesh, women are socialized to identify not as persons, but as mothers. The book, "Village Women as I Saw Them" written by Tahereen Nesha Abdullah (1974) sparked a new era of feminist writings in Bangladesh. Abdullah mentions that during the last two decades a considerable amount of literature had been produced depicting the subordinate condition of women from different perspectives. Interestingly, there has hardly been any attempt on part of the government or NGOs to examine how far the victims (Women) think and feel about their exploitation and subordination in patriarchal society.

Kinship arrangements in Bangladesh are rigidly patrilineal. Under this system, sons are given preferential treatment. Sons are seen as essential to carry on the family lineage. The main productive assets are passed through the male line and daughters become the property of their husbands and live at their houses. Since only boys remain in the lineage, only the names of sons and grandsons are listed in the traditional family geneogram. It is through the father that a child acquires a social identity and is incorporated into the social order. Women are recorded only in the capacity of the wives of the men who gave rise to succeeding generations of men. This also means that sons provide labor and economic support to their parents as they grow older. Feminists' scholarship widely accepts the belief that male preference is a function of cultural values born under patriarchy. Therefore, girls and women are exploited and subordinated by men through the control of the resources of society. For example, parents see the education of sons as more important than daughters. This reality is reflected in the fact that the adult female literacy rate (43%) is much lower than the national average (86%) (Bangladesh Human Rights Report, 2000). Education of sons is seen as profitable because parents will later depend on their sons in their old age.

Nine out of ten persons are Muslims in Bangladesh (BBS, 1994,p. 103). Muslim traditional cultures and laws dominate people lives. These laws and cultures place men in control of women's labor, choice of marriage, access to resources, and legal rights (Ahamed, 1990 , p. 365). Men enjoy privilege over women in almost every sphere in the family (Jahan, 1975, p. 270). Both Islam and Hinduism have discriminatory inheritance laws against women (Ahamed, 1979, p. 293). *Islamic Sharia law* encourages male dominated patriarchy. Although Bangladesh declared itself a secular state, Islamic religious leaders and values still hold a lot of influence in politics that affect women's rights. However, the solution is not to simply reject Muslim rather knowledge of the actual Al-Quranic verse and women being involved in consciousness raising at the grass- roots level is important to reconcile their equal rights in Islam.

Under patriarchy, women in Bangladesh do not have equal rights to inherit property. For example, in orthodox Hindu religion daughters have no property rights to their father property. In Islam, a widow can only own 12.5% of her husband's property under *Sharia Law*. However, in practice widows cannot even own this property due to village politics of *Fatawa and customary laws*. Therefore, most widows give up their claims to property because fear of violence, anger, and torture by men. Widows also are often unaware of what they are rightfully entitled to.

2.1. Women position under customary law in Bangladesh

Customary laws dominate rural women, who are governed by the rural religious male elites. Although some reform has been made in property rights in Bangladesh, women in practice still do not have property in their names. If women do not have ownership of property, they do not have access to bank loans, or other community finances. One such example is that a mortgage is required to receive loans. When women do not have access to loans, it becomes impossible to own their own business or seek self-employment. Islamic values, Mullahs and other customary values prevent women from working outside the home. This promotes a dichotomy of private and public realm, which in turn is barrier to women's participation in economic activity outside home. Therefore, women are not economically independent in the family, which, means they suffer from poverty and malnutrition. This means they must struggle to fulfill their basic needs like: food, clothing, shelters, education, and health.

3.0. Feminists view of women property law

In Bangladesh, many feminists talk about women's equality regarding access to work and education, but little attention is paid to rural women's deprivation of wealth and access to financial resources by the state. For example, in 1993, feminist Farina Rahman challenged the *"Muslim Family Property Laws Ordinance 1961."* She raised the question of male bias in village council. However, her proposal did not pass in the male dominated parliament. Praxis (theory and practice) oriented programs and their implementation are important to allow women to access property and financial independence. Changing customary law, modifying traditional Muslim and Hindu laws, and women having equal access to property rights would help them to be economically, socially and politically empowered in the society. Such empowerment would facilitate women leaving abusive, violent and male dominated environments. This would also aid in overcoming poverty.

Patriarchy is systemic and very powerful in Bangladesh. For example, one Member of Parliament (MP) warned a feminist in 1994 to "never try to touch the Hindu Law in the name of women's welfare; otherwise blood will be flooding the floor of parliament". (State of Human

Rights 1994, p. 91). Nonetheless, Bangladesh National Women Lawyers Association and Coordination Council for Human Rights in Bangladesh (CCHRB) and Bangladesh Human Rights Council challenge the male dominated customary lawon property rights. However, *Shura* (high level religious leaders) and Islamic organization united together to maintain *Islamic Family Law*.

The media is totally silent in these affairs. One journalist says, "Women's property rights are a tough and complicated issue that is closely related to religion and male chauvinism. It has no end itself." (State of Human Rights 1994, p. 93). Hence patriarchy and women's inequality in property rights is a societal problem in Bangladesh where women are victimized, deprived and discriminated against. National and International human rights commissions and feminists are strongly challenging these male dominated property right laws to open the door for equal rights for women.

There are many laws and customs that limit women's equal rights to property. Although Muslim marriage laws protect women partially through the custom of *Mahar* (*Mahar* is money, property, jewelry or clothing that is to be given to the bride upon divorce), most women especially those from the lower socioeconomic classes may not have written these conditions in the marriage registration, *Kabin Nama*. Surprisingly the practice of *Mahar* now has been replaced by dowry in Bangladesh that exploits, victimized and discriminates women's equal rights to wealth. Dowry is a demand for wealth by the groom's family for the bride. Dowry related violence is common in Bangladesh. For a dowry, women can be tortured, killed, or burned if their husbands' dowry requests are not fulfilled. As soon as a daughter is born, the family knows it will be burdened with dowry demands. This causes girls and women to be treated differently in Bangladesh. Unpaid dowries are causes for divorce, separation, torture, and sometimes even death. Women have not recourse for seeking justice from these beatings, assaults and unfair treatment because rural women have no voice to complain about negative effects of injustice in this male dominated religious society.

Additionally, Muslim laws often contradict legal laws and therefore, impede the application of justice for women. If a woman chooses to leave her husband against her family will, she will more than likely wind up homeless? Woman is not only face financial insecurity if they divorce their husbands, her reputation is also ruined in the community. People blame her that she was incapable of keeping her husband and abundant in the society. Society expects women to act in a certain way and when they "disobey" these so called "rules" or "norms", they are seen as an outsider of the community or they are deviant.

4.0. Dichotomy of public and private realm of women in Bangladesh

The dichotomy of public and private realm in Islam underpins gender subordination, and dependence. Pardah dominates women. Women are dependent upon men due to the rigidity of the Purdah system, which restricts them from participation in economic activities outside the household (Kabeer, 1988, p.108). If women are unable to find jobs, they cannot provide for themselves and their families. These further reinforce male dominance over females (Mizan, 1994, p. 33).

Both men and women support the present sex specific division of labor in the family. Men work outside, earn money and provide financial support to the family, while women are responsible for domestic obligations. Men are the breadwinners and women are the homemakers. Interestingly enough some women argue that women have taken their present position in society as natural and desirable. They define their position in society as fair and non-discriminatory because they see it as tradition: men work outside and women work inside for their family (Begum, 1988, p. 7). Women have taken these socially prescribed roles for granted and don't know alternatives to these. The domestic work is stereotyped as "women's work" and therefore, is not as valued.

They are involved in unpaid family subsistence agricultural work. Both male and female have internalized the existing societal values of men's instrumental and women's roles in the family. Undisputedly it goes at the advantage of men since the labor is organized in a manner that confines women at home with unpaid domestic chores. But women hold up half the sky. Although Asian women have only 1% of the wealth in the world, they do 66% of the work that is needed for human survival (Wong, 2002, p. 47).

Men of all classes benefit from women's unpaid labor in the home and therefore, they enjoy a higher status in society (Mead et al. 1979, p. 417). Women's paid labor is restricted due to social norms and religious values often leaving them in stereotypically feminized jobs such as rice processing, cooking, child bearing and rearing and quilt making etc. When women do work they are given a lower wage. Thus women have fewer earnings and so they presently suffer more in modern agricultural economy. To challenge this traditional male dominated custom, rural women must be recognized equally for their economic contributions and their work must be rewarded accordingly.

Below the paper first is discussing British colonial negative impact on Bangladeshi women, second the paper is talking consequences of gender division of labor on women, thirdly women oppression under patriarchal society. Lastly the paper discusses how religious customary laws deprived women from various human rights like property rights.

5.0. British colonial negative impact on Bangladeshi women

Before the British colonized India, it was a *self-sufficient village community* with a *land-based agriculture* that fostered an egalitarian status for women in the family. However, this self-sufficient agricultural village collective culture and economy was destroyed by the imposition of the British capitalist colonialism in Indo-Pak-Bangle subcontinent from 1750. These colonizers introduced the male dominant nuclear family norm and private lands ownership system that promotes individuality, and hierarchal organizing. They created a new male class called *Zamindars*, who were revenue collectors during the Moghal Empire (Karim 1976, p.102). The Permanent Land Settlement Act by British in India in 1773 robbed women land ownership. Moreover, the British created the new *petty bourgeoisies*as the ruling class in India. From then, the state experiences hegemonic crisis and political instability. Therefore, colonialism produced misery in the society and created unequal inheritance laws for women in Bangladesh (Alam, 1995, p. 5).

6.0. Consequences of gender division of labor on women

As Boserup's (1970) says, changes in the production of agriculture effects women and the land, their roles, and the decline of women's equality from pre-colonial to colonial times. Bangladeshi women contribute the majority of agricultural production as well as within the informal sectors of the economy. This new land tenure system forced farmers into cash crop production and commercialized agriculture. In the new system women were left out from land ownership, and the new system of agriculture cash crop production and commerce. In addition, current trade economy does not allow for women to be included so many of them become street beggars after losing all that they own through the informal mortgaging of all their assets. Consequently, these women are left with no rights and no power in the society.

The Constitution of Bangladesh appears to strongly approve gender equality and positive action that guarantees women's full participation in the social, economic and political life. For example, Article 10 of the Constitution notes, "Steps shall be taken to ensure participation of women in all spheres of national life" (BMSP, 1997). However, there is still a big gap between the law and its actual implementation. That is why the bottom 50% disadvantaged poor people, largely women, are struggling to fulfill their basic human needs.

The author believes that an income-generating program for women could create the potential to enhance women's power and status at home over men. This would boost rural women's role in family as well as independent decision-making, and encourage the development of self-confidence to empower not be silent in male violence. In addition, it would help them to overcome their poverty, so they would have the finances necessary to leave violent situations. This is important for achieving the goals associated with women's human rights.

7.0. Women oppression under patriarchal society and initiative to reduce it

Strategies are needed to improve women's access to the legal system to address the violation of human rights and to improve Muslim family laws in Bangladesh. Women's empowerment can also enable women to oppose the authoritative patriarchal power structures and customary religious laws through collective networking and action.

With these aims, Grameen Bank credit creates opportunities for poor women in Bangladesh to find from male dependence. This project provides distressed women with education, life skills training, credit, and other support services for income generating purposes. Grameen Bank borrowers still are not free from male dominance in their loan transactions. The husbands control the loans. A study by Isserles suggests that 57% of women saw a rise in verbal aggression after they received loans from their husbands (Isserles, 2003, p. 49). However, Rouf survey study (2011) indicates 87% women borrowers of GB control their loan money; however, it is wise all women borrowers could control over their loan money. This shows how patriarchy has deep roots interconnected among class, gender, religion, and education.

To reverse this order and to free women from men dominance and to enhance women propriety ownership recently Grameen Housing Loan Program introduced a policy that house loans could only disburse to those female borrowers who have house land in their own name. Borrowers' husbands registered land in their name in order to get housing loans. As result 3.6 million Bangladeshi rural women are able to have land in their own name.

In recent years, there have been efforts initiated by the government and NGOs to improve the status of women by providing free education up to class V111, and launching several development programs for women. However, all these programs don't seem to have produced desirable results as women still hold traditional views regarding division of labor in the family (White, 1992, p. 15). Therefore, strong gender development policies along with encouragement of human capabilities can give a positive impact on both gender equality and economic growth (Nussbaum, 1988).

Mohila Samilty (women cooperative), Bangladesh Rural Advancement Committee (BRAC), Bangladesh Rural Development Board (BRDB), Nijera Kori, Gono Unnayan Prochesta, and Proshika in Bangladesh runs various programs to help women to achieve self-reliance; however, their initiatives are confronting the customary religious Muslim and Hindu laws and traditional rural values. These NGOs have less power to lobby for the necessary changes in the legal system (Quadir, 2003, p. 437). A national woman NGO in Bangladesh like *Fulian* in China should be set up and supported by state law enforcement agencies to work for women's human rights.

8.0. Conclusion

Patriarchy and religious customary laws, private and public realm, gender division of labour, and colonization contribute to women's subordinate position in Bangladesh. Naila Kabeer says, "the denial of women's autonomy is everywhere in Bangladesh" (Kabeer, 1983, p. 8). In order to establish gender equality in property rights, and female empowerment and reduce female poverty, Bangladesh needs to close the gender gap in employment and wages, Muslim Family Laws and Customary laws. Hence like Grameen Housing Loan Program feminists and other civil society organizations can initiate gender equality action program in collaboration with state law enforcing agencies with good governance to fight for what is needed for women to have equal rights in Bangladesh.

9.0. References

Abdullah A. T. and Zeidenstein, S. A. (1982). *Village women of Bangladesh Prospects for Change,* Oxford: Pergamon Press

Abed, F. (1998). *Towards Gender Equity: BRAC Center Policy.* Dhaka: BRAC Printers

Ahamed, M. (2002). *Key to achieving sustainability: Simple and standard microfinance services of ASA,* Dhaka: Prominent Printers

Ain O, Salish K (2005). *Human Rights in Bangladesh-2004.* Dhaka: Shahitya Prokash

Ain O Salish Kendro (2004). *Human Rights in Bangladesh-2003,* Dhaka: Shahitya Prokash

Alam, S. M. S. (1995). *The state, class formation, and development in Bangladesh,* New York: University Press of America, Inc.

Ali, A. F. I (1993). *Samajtatta.* Dhaka: Centre for Bangladesh Studies

Bangladesh Bureau of Statistics (2007a). *Key Findings of HIES 2005,* Dhaka: Bangladesh Bureau of Statistics

Bangladesh Bureau of Statistics (2016). *Demography of Bangladesh, Retrieved from* http://www.bbs.gov.bd/dataindex/poverty.pdf. dated November 26, 2016

Bangladesh Bureau of Statistics, (2010). *Distribution of household by size of household and residence -2005.* Retrieved from http://www.bbs.gov.bd/RptHIES_2_2.aspx

Bangladesh Country Profile (2010). *Bangladesh country profile,* BBC News, Retrieved from http://news.bbc.co.uk/2/hi/europe/country_profiles/1160598.stm

Bannerji, H. (1993). *Popular images of South Asian women. Returning the gaze: Essays on racism, feminism, and politics.* Toronto, On: Sister Vision Press

Belal, A. R. (2008). *Corporate social responsibility reporting in developing countries-A case of Bangladesh*. England: Ashgate Publishing Ltd.

Beneria, L. (2003). *Gender, development and globalization: Economics as if people mattered*, New York: Routledge

Biddimala Grameen Bank. (1978). *Bidhimala*. Dhaka: Oslo Printers Ltd.

Boserup, E. (1970). *Women's role in economic development*, London: Earthscan

Cain M, Syeda R. K., and Shamsun N (1979). Class, patriarchy and women's work in Bangladesh, *Population and Development Review*, Vol. 5(3), pp. 405-438

Dua E, and Robertson A (1999). *Scratching the Surface: Canadian anti-racist feminist thought*, Toronto: Women Press

Grameen Bank Annual Report (2009). *Grameen Bank Annual Report-2009*. Chittagong: Packages Corporations Ltd.

Hashmi, T. J. (2000). *Women and Islam in Bangladesh, Beyond Subjection and Tyranny*, London: MacMillan Press Ltd.

Hossain, H. E. (2001). *Human Rights in Bangladesh 2000*, Dhaka, Ain O Salish Kendro (ASK).

Isserles, R. G. (2003). Microcredit the rhetoric of empowerment, the reality of development as usual, *Women's Studies Quarterly*, Vol. 31(3/4), pp. 38-57

Jahan R (1995). *The Elusive agenda: Mainstreaming women in development*, Dhaka: The University Press Ltd.

Kabeer, N. (1999). Resources, agency, achievements: Reflections on the measurement of women's empowerment, *Development and Change*, Vol. 30(3), pp. 435-464

Kabeer, N. (2003). *Gender mainstreaming in poverty eradication and the millennium development goals*. Ottawa: International Development Research Center (CIDA)

Kar, P. V. (1993). *Samajtatta*. Calcutta: West Bengal State Book Board

Karim, A. Nazmul K (1976). *Changing society of India, Pakistan and Bangladesh*, Dhaka: Nawroze Ketabistan

Lorde, Audre (1984). *Sister Outside*, New York: Crossing Press

Mahmud S (2004). Microcredit and women's empowerment in Bangladesh, in Ahmed, S. and Hakim (Eds.). *Attacking poverty with microcredit*. Dhaka: The University Press Limited.

Mies M (2005). *Search for a New Vision*. Dhaka: Narigrantha Prabartana

Miles A (2006). Local activisms, global Feminisms and the struggle against globalization. In Andrea Medovarski and Brenda Cranney (Eds.), *Canadian Women's Studies: An Introductory Reader*, (pp.58-64) Toronto: Inanna

Mizan, A. (1994*). In quest of empowerment: The Grameen Bank impact on women's power and status*. Dhaka: University Press Limited

Mohanty C (2003). *Feminism without borders: Decolonizing theory, practicing solidarity*. Durham, North Carolina: Duke University Press

News Network (2005). *How people suffer in Bangladesh*. Dhaka: Probe Printers Ltd.

Nussabaum, M. (1988). Women's capabilities and social justice, in Molyneux, M. and Razavi, S. (Eds.), *Gender, Justice, Development and Rights*, (pp. 45-74): New York: Oxford University Press

Pereira, F. (2001). *Women's rights to equality and non-discrimination in Human Rights in Bangladesh*. Dhaka. Ain Salish Kendra. Publications

Quadir F (2003). How "civil" is Civil Society? Authoritarian state partisan Civil Society and the struggle for democratic development in Bangladesh, *Canadian Journal of Development Studies*, Vol. 24(3), pp. 425-438

Rouf, K. A. (2013). Religious patriarchal values obstruct Bangladeshi rural women's human rights. *Journal Research in Peace, Gender and Development (RJPGD)* Vol. 3(5), pp. 75-79

Rouf, K. A. (2015). Against all odds: Socio-economic and political factors related to female labor force participation and decision making power in Bangladesh. *International Journal of Research Studies in Management*, Vol.5 (1), pp. 53-63

Rouf, K. A. (2011). *Green microcredit for environmental development- a Master Degree Thesis*. Toronto: York University

Sania, S. A. and Sally, B. (2004). One able daughter is worth 10 illiterate sons': Reframing the patriarchal family, *Journal of Marriage and Family*, December, 66:1332-1341, Toronto: Women's Press

White, S. (1999). NGOs, civil society, and the state in Bangladesh: The politics of representing the poor, *Development and Change*, Vol. 30(2), pp. 307-326

Wong, W. A. (2002). *The Poor W omen- A Critical Analysis of Asian Theology and Contemporary Chinese Fiction by Women*: New York: Peter Lang.

Promoting Participatory Rural Appraisal (PRA) through Micro Financing Institutions (MFIs) in Bangladesh

Abstract

Participatory rural appraisal (PRA) is a development approach must come from within the community people, build trust, confidence and cooperation among community people and legitimize popular praxis through community participation. Chamber's original idea is learn from local people of the Southern countries. It negates outsiders' prescription for rural community development. However, World Bank uses this PRA concept for their project appraisal in order to implement their projects as a process of community people's participation at the grass roots to help the rural people. This paper explores how micro financing institutions (MFIs) are working in Bangladesh as participatory organizations that are interested in promoting a bottom- up approach for solving poverty and promoting community development. It is found that Grameen Bank implementation has a bottom-up strategy and a process that encourages, enhances and promotes rural poor people participations in the Grameen group-based micro-credit program in Bangladesh since 1976. Rural poor people's participation has driven the success of the Grameen micro-credit program in Bangladesh.

Key words: Bangladesh Rural Development Program (BRDB); Grameen Dialouge; microcredit institutions; PKSF; participatory rural appraisal (PRA); sustainable development; and World Bank.

1.0. Introduction

Participatory Rural Appraisal (PRA) is preoccupied with local ideas, identifies the structural problems, and allows the individual to overcome these structural barriers. However, this PRA benefits have eroded by some outsiders' intervention. Therefore, the proponents of PRA think PRA must come from within the community and legitimize popular praxis. However, it neglects how power operates and is constituted because the current participatory praxis fails to deal with politics and power rather it increasing social disparities in the society. Although Chamber's original idea is learn from local people of the South than trust research that is grounded in the North. World Bank uses this PRA and tries to implement this process at the grass roots to help the people. This paper examines how micro financing NGOs claim themselves as participatory organizations that are interested in promoting a bottom up approach for solving povertyand promoting community development.

2.0. Features of the PRA

Through PRA, it builds and promotes trust, confidence and cooperation between and among the community people and staff; it organizes and mobilizes people, increases people's awareness of issues affecting their lives and build people's capacity to manage their own affairs. This approach builds trust and confidence between and among people's organizations. People can be prime movers of their own development with the right opportunity and motivation. It is a continuos process of sharing of knowledge, consciousness-raising of the people and a strong desire from the people for sustainable development.

Haberma's PRA legitimizing procedures could formalize and discipline it; however, Chamber is panic about its coercive practice at the community level. Therefore practitioners should see power from positive perspectives. For example, Foucault argues that power can help people understand their own problem and solve these problems in a very systematic manner. Hence Fahim Quadir says, "NGOs can organize people as a countervailing force where they can construct a new form of politics through NGOs mobilizations" (class lecture April 04, 2007). To explore such possibility, the author has studied Simeen Mahamud's Article "Micro-credit and Women's Empowerment in Bangladesh" and read some NGOs of Bangladesh activities to relate this inference.

3.0. Micro credit and women empowerment

Simeen Mahamood (2004) in her article micro credit and women's empowerment in Bangladesh examine whether MFIs Bangladesh contribute to women wellbeing and tries to find relationship between micro credit program participation and the process of empowerment. Her findings states that women have good access to credit through NGOs. There is a strong co-relation between women participating in microfinance programs and use of birth control, indicating greater welfare for women. However, the norms and practices in the country put them at a definite subordinate position to men, which means they have a lack of choice and little power in decisions making process that shape their welfare. These findings confirmed by Robin Isserlses findings (2003). This is because of patriarchal male dominant values over women exist in Bangladesh for long time.

Grameen Bank gives loans to poor women through peer support lending methodology for the improvement of their household economics as well as to generate social and human capital among them. However, this patriarchal male dominating value over women cannot change overnight. Grameen Bank believes that if women become earners, they can then empower themselves and promote their own well-being; as well as that of their families. With this aim, GB creates a ray of hope for empowering rural poor women in Bangladesh.

In the Micro Credit Summit 2002 New York, Muhammad Yunus, winner of the Novel Peace Prize 2006 states, "Micro credit can play a vital role in attaining Millennium Development Goals (MDGs)". It gives high priority for building social capital; it gives special emphasis on formation of human capital". Kofi Anan, UN Secretary General says that microfinance has proved its value, in many countries, as a weapon against poverty and hunger. Because micro financing in Bangladesh has created tremendous positive impact on poor women's life and created millions of self-employment opportunities for them. A revolution has happened in female entrepreneurships there. Now it is recognized as a development model because it is a vital means of income generation, self-employment, and social inclusion and empowers disadvantaged women (Grameen Dialouge-60, 2005).

However, GB and other microcredit institutions (MCIs) are focusing mainly to economic participation (business basics) which is not enough to create freedom of speech to this disadvantaged people. They (MCIs) ignore political basics that have broader social empowerment components like group participation in social action, networking with government organizations (GOs) and non-government organizations (NGOs), participation in local Salish (arbitration trials), or Union Parishid (local councils), understanding of social issues, and group action against social repression. If one's political right is violated, the right to speak suppressed the human right. The current PRA masked mass people voices and choices by domination of a few rich people because of their economic and political strength. That is why Muhammad Yunus says (1994), "If we had established as the first human right the right to credit there is no reason why anybody in the world would remain poor and excluded" (p,20). Therefore, GB and other MCIs emphasis more on economic development in the first place with a hope that borrower's income generation may lead to other socio-political development.

4.0. Micro credit institutions and PRA

The ground of political process could be prepared as an ultimate output of empowerment of micro-borrowers. However, economic participation and community political participation are two sides of the same coin, but the existing micro credit institutions (MCIs) participatory development strategy instead of looking at people as a whole-participatory development approach, MCIs look at individual economic initiatives. PRA talks about community development as a single element, but there are moments of empowerment that can be explored through community initiatives. Many other issues are related to community development like class, gender, race, and environmental degradation. Therefore, the whole notion of participatory development (PD) obscures local power indifferences.

Simen Mahamud offers a framework of women's empowerment that shows how positive changes can women's lives improves their fallback position and bargaining power within patriarchal structure. She mentions that different dominions of empowerment includes material gain, cognitive perceptual (improve self-esteem and self- confidence) and relational. According to Mahmud, these disadvantaged women dimensions can be triggered by schooling them, create equal labor force participation in the market, and receive credit. However, her dimensions are missing political component voice for opening their public space; rather her women welfare empowerment study only looks at women's pattern of time use in the home, use birth control, health care and immunization. The study does not look at political basics.

5.0. Women borrowers of Grameen Bank participation in the Union Councils in Bangladesh

Few NGOs also work for citizen consciousness raising with their specific program in Bangladesh. For example, GB membership is allowing borrowers to expand their networks among them and lobbying for enhancing members to get essential services from various government agencies at the local levels. GB borrowers' participation in the formal local councils is increasing although it has no core program for mobilizing citizenship rights. However, in 1997 (as erlier mentioned) out of a total of 4298 unions of Bangladesh, 7 GB members and 39 members of the family were elected to the post of Chairman of Union

Prashad. In the membership election in the union councils, out of 51,396 seats, 261 male and 1,343 female GB borrowers were elected by contest and 34 members were elected uncontested. In addition, 1,073 family members were elected as members of the Union Council (Grameen Dialouge 2001, p.16).

Moreover, as earlier announced 58% of Grameen borrowers' families of Grameen borrowers have crossed the poverty line. The remaining families are moving towards the poverty line stated (Grameen Bank Annual Report, 2005). However if we compare this statistics with borrowers political achievement, we can draw an assumption that although the social and political empowerment process has started among credit recipients; however, political achievement has left behind economic achievement. Fahim identified the reason is micro financing institutions see and work with single elements of the segment of the problem.

6.0. Conclusion

The existing NGOs activities do not have core program to address the issue of power and politics, patriarchy, market and international order distortions that are barriers to move forward achieving democratic objectives because citizenship notion is not in priority to MCIs. For Example, Bangladesh Rural Development Program (BRDB) tries to address the issue of poverty. However, its services benefit only few peoples in the community. No equal benefits go to all segment of the society. Therefore, it needs to look at the power dynamics of the whole community and analyses of its elements that are essentials for opening up new spaces for political action by all people to achieve equal choice and voice opportunities in the community. However, MCIs are working under government conditions and regulations in Bangladesh. Therefore, they have self- regulation mechanism control (on-site and off-site) within the fold of an agreed 'Code of Conducts' for the growth of MCIs in Bangladesh (PKSF Annual Report, 1998-1999, p. 27).

Simeen Mahamood study concluded that micro credit expands women's access to valuable resources like self-employment and mobility into certain public spaces like visit health care offices; however, women wage employment is not increased. Therefore, protest against women's subordination, discrimination and exploitation in the labor market needs to be mobilized. Therefore, institutional lobbying for continual citizen rights can open up space for disadvantaged citizens. These initiatives should incorporate the poor into mainstream modernity capitalism and explore alternatives in addition to economic agenda. Fahim says, "If participation can do these three things, it can be seen as a new form of social, political and cultural parameters to enhance opportunities for all people having equal voice, and choice in the community development (Class lecture, April 03, 2007).

7.0. References

Chambers, R. (2008). *PRA, PLA and Pluralism: Practice and Theory in Practices,* pp. 297-318

Grameen Bank (2005). *Grameen Bank Annual Report 2005.* Grameen Bank, Dhaka

Grameen Dialogue (2001). *Grameen replication,* Dhaka: Grameen Bank

Habermas, J. (1987). *The Theory of Communicative Action,* Volume- I, Translated by Thomas McCarthy, Boston: Beacon Press

Mahamud, S. (2004). Micro-credit and women's empowerment in Bangladesh in *Attacking poverty with micro-credit,* (Eds). Salehuddin Ahamed and M. A. Hakim. Dhaka: Dhaka University Press.

Palli Karma Sahayak Foundation, (PKSF) (1999). *Palli Karma Sahayak Foundation Annual Report 1998-1999.* Dhaka: Sangshita Mudran & Prokasani

Singh, K. (2001). Handing over the stick: the global spread of participatory approaches to development, in M. Edwards and J. Gaventa (eds.), *Global Citizen Action.* Boulder, CO: Lynne Rienner, pp. 175-87

White, S. and Pettit, J. (2004). Participatory methods and the measurement of well-being, *Participatory Learning and Action*, Vol. 50, pp. 88-96

World Bank (2000). *Attacking Poverty: World Development Report 2000/2001*, London: Oxford University Press for the World Bank

Yunus, M. (1994). *Credit is a Human Right*. Dhaka: Mahtab Offset Printers.

Possibility of Citizenry Mobilization to Micro-borrowers through Micro Credits Institutions (MCIs) in Bangladesh

Abstract

Rural elites and politicians monopoly power exercises, exploitation and corruptions increasingly vulnerable to poor people. It exacerbates the erosion of democratic institutions and the public spherein Bangladesh. Although microcredit institutions are credit delivering organizations have been working closely with local people for engaging them micro businesses for increasing their income; they (micro credit institutions) have limited citizenry skills development education and political mobilization program for their clients. However, these programs are necessary for micro borrowers' individual and collective empowerment, develop citizenship rights and increasing human right voices. As MCIs are following participatory rural development approach that favors the process of poor people empowerment, hence MCIs could rethink incorporate political activism agenda in their programs to empower micro-borrowers and make state accountable to the public (good governance). Without political mobilization, they are unable to get equal status, rights, choice, and voice in the society and free them from rural elites political, social and economical exploitations and injustice.

Key words: Ashraf; Atraf; Bangladesh Human Rights Council; citizenry empowerment; centre chief; citizenry skills development; civil society; collective empowerment; customary law; gender discrimination; good governance; Gram Panchayet; Hindu Laws; Krishak Samilty; Mullah; participatory rural development approach;

political mobilization; right-based approach; Salish Muslis; Tabaga Andalon; and traditional Muslim laws.

1.0. Introduction

There is a growing realization that increases income is not enough to empower poor people unless their citizenship rights ensures because poverty alleviation efforts eroded by lack of good governance and discriminatory public policies in neo-liberal free market. That creates rich and poor disparity and inequality. Fahim Quadir says," Current Bangladeshi MCIs/NGOs' are the provider of goods to poor consumers rather facilitators of actual women empowerment. However, different studies show that the non-government organizations (NGOs) in Bangladesh indicated a vibrant civil society that helped Bangladesh economic and social development and is a model for participatory development. They have been working closely with local people; however, micro credit institutions have limited involvement to promote good governance and effective policy implementation although they have limited smooth relationship with the government agencies. NGO activity can help animate civil society, consolidate the political rights of citizens and can promote women human rights. This paper argues although current NGOs and MCIs focus mainly economic and social development, they can built in pro-political mobilization for the citizenry empowerment along credit delivery services.

2.0. Role of farmer movements and NGOs contribution to citizenry mobilization

In the 1970s, The Tabaga Andalon, Krishak Samilty and other new organizations were politically active to mobilize farmers for farmers' rights. However, many of them shifted their initiatives to relief works, rural infrastructure reconstructions and rural development work. Now maximum NGOs shifted their programs to credit, health, and education service delivery. Rural elites and politicians monopoly power exercises, exploitation and corruptions increasingly vulnerable people. It exacerbates the erosion of democratic institutions and the public spherein Bangladesh; however, they could social mobilizing central tools for empowering rural disadvantaged people. As NGOs are following participatory development approach that favors the process of empowerment, hence it is urgent needs NGOs rethink incorporate political activism agenda in their programs to make state accountable to the public.

According to Devine (2003), there are 22,000 NGOs are working in Bangladesh where 35% Bangladeshis are receiving credit, education, heath, sanitation and other services from these NGOs and MCIs. Taj Hashemi (1995) says, "Bangladeshi NGOs focused primarily on social mobilization programs aimed at organizing the poor into independent groups to resist exploitation." However, they shifted to the market driven service delivery paradigm like disburse credit. Mute their political mobilization over time that hampers empower people politically. This credit delivery approach helps NGOs to run their programs from investment income.

Moreover, political mobilization is highly costly for the poor, since it involves an investment of time and resources that the NGOs can hardly afford from their credit investment. On the other hand, according to Escobar and Ferguson the financial dependence of NGOs on donors creates technical apolitical projects that follow donors' objectives. Ferguso also agrees that NGOs constitutionally unfit to engage in explicit political activism necessary to bring genuine social change (Ferguson, 1994, p. 226). Therefore, MCIs main focus is on financial sustainability in economic benefits than qualitative development. They excluded vested interest to structural inequalities. Therefore, NGO eroded democratic institutions and practices to achieve the goal of a state responsive to its citizens' needs.

However, interest payments and fees for micro credit services (NGOs and MFIs interest rate more than 20%) into the programs undermined NGOs ability to act as legitimate representatives of the poor and weakened it's to engage in social mobilization. GB also charges interest for its credit delivery services. Although GB runs its costs from its income, GB activities result welfare and empowerment to the poor; however, there is increasingly criticizing GB for being financial self-sufficiency. NGOs depoliticizing undermines the achievement of the genuine empowerment of the poor that high lights in Simmen Mahamud's study 2004 in Bangladesh.

Amatya Sen (2002) high lights the importance of collective action and political mobilization is needed to stop government agencies leakage and get the highest benefits from credit program. For example, Reinikka and Stevenson (2003) have found that the introduction of a newspaper awareness campaign dramatically increased the responsiveness of state education spending and reduced the government spending from 80% to 29% in 2001.

ADAB, Nijera Kori, Proshika and Gono Shahaisgo Shantha (GSS) had engaged in social mobilization programmes while receiving donor support, but recently they have faced depolarizing pressures from government and other civil society. Government conditionality, centralized control, harassments, political authority undermined the efficacy and viability of NGOs as institutions of voice. Their funding constraints make them no longer exist in activist empowerment program. NGOs engaging in social mobilization programs find themselves under greater government scrutiny (Hashemi, 1995, p.105). Therefore, NGOs development activities now are technical issue of service delivery rather than as a political issue involving the empowerment of the poor (Hickey & Mohan 2004). However, in West Bengal Gram Panchayet, a popular political mobilization institution under government blessing successfully has led to pro-poor economic and political reform. This local government institution acts as an alternative channel for promoting public interests at the village level (Sengupta & Gazdar, 1998).

However, local government Union Parishad of Bangladesh increasing corruption in the provision of social services at the local level and see it as irrelevant to citizenry (Khan and Asaduzzaman, 1996). Poor people distrust this institution and viewed a place of corruption although they vote for their representatives.

Although recently BRAC-TUP program engage in social mobilization in a limited scale could revive public sphere. However, it requires restoration of active political citizenship program built in the existing NGOs and MCIs mainstream program so that poor people can organize advocate for reform public policy along their economic development programs.

3.0. Participatory approach for citizenry mobilization

Participatory approach is people-centered development strategy is the spirit behind the community. It believes that people have inmate capacity, but opportunities and social mobilization to achieve their rights can transform them to citizenship rights. Here it emphasizes the active participation of people in designing, planning and managing community development issues, people's basic rights issues. For example, participatory approach in micro enterprise development enables beneficiaries to eventually own, control and sustainable manage their businesses once the support institutions withdraws.

3.1. MFIs/NGOs and participatory approach

The community participation workers encourage and awaken people to realize that they themselves have abilities, energies, and resources to take initiative to better their lives. It develops people's decision making confidence and to be self-reliant and access to use local resources. However, Shragge, E. (1997) says "progressive, community empowerment approach linking not only linking social and economic objectives rather encouraging local control, ownership of resources and address the issue of inequality, self-reliant communities develop beyond traditional government controls i.e. basic social change" (Shragge, 1997, p. 13). However, Bangladeshi's NGOs like BRAC, Grameen

Bank, Proshika, ASA, and Gono Gahasgha Shantha (GSS) are world renowned for community participation development by providing services like credit, health, education services in rural areas. They are the project-based service oriented institutions targeting interventions to specific local groups, and initiating social change. However, individual and collective empowerment is necessary that also create self-esteem and consciousness-raising towards citizenry. Their entrepreneurial approach generally reinforces individualistic and capitalist values bring women into the competitive market economy. Self-employed women are vulnerable because they do not have access to employment insurance, pensions, or union membership etc. (Shragge, 1997, p. 39).

However, the NGOs participatory approach in Bangladesh mainly focuses on providing micro credit, health services, education and relief works. They are not providing political education basics to people. Their activities are mainly to service delivery to local people, mainly focus economic, health and educational achievement, but by pass social mobilization citizenry and good governance issues. MCIs institutions are not advocating for reform judicial system, public administration reform, anti-corruption, strengthening local government accountability, and public expenditure management. Extension workers can motivate, support, and train people to be partner of local political institutions; however, their services tailored to economic and social issues. They are away from political agenda because government tries to control and monitor NGOs activities through NGO bureau. So they are elusive to political discourses and services although NGOs provide much higher service quality (World Bank,1999, p. 43). The relationship between the government and NGOs has not always been smooth (World Bank, 1996c).

Barbara Cruikshank (1994) comments that empowerment connote a spectrum of political activity ranging from acts of individual resistance to mass political mobilization that challenges the basic power relations in our society. For women, it should start from their powerlessness in systemic oppression and deal with root cause of poverty (Cruikshank,

1994, p. 30). The reason is poor people are experiencing deprivation and inability to participate in the wellfare right approach. Therefore, the civic engagement is important in building civil society that embraces a wide range of social and economic roles including service delivery, cooperative social, and economic activity advocacy, protection of the public interest and public education. MCIs and NGOs could be the vehicle for active citizenship or strong democracies where they can foster not only inclusive to economic, education, environmental participation, but they also can inclusive to political basics education.

4.0. Grameen Bank group leadership development process is a participatory approach

GB clients join a group of five men or women who are the same socio-economic background who need a seven days intensive training on how poor people exploited in the society, how GB can help them to overcome from poverty and GB activities with them. Each group elects a chair and a secretary. The positions are rotated on an annual basis among members to give everyone the chance to be a group leader. Up to eight groups constitute as centre, headed by a centre chief and an associated centre chief who is elected by the group chairs. The centre chief ensures attendance and discipline at the meetings.

This whole process helps poor people develop their leadership quality; develop networking skills among clients, with other local institutions. Through the loan, borrowers participate in the economic development process and earn income for their families, open the door for self-employment, and they are more capable of changing their lives for the better, contribute to capital formation and wealth creation. The borrowers of Grameen Bank also participate in the social development process: attentive to children education, family health, and rejecting dowry; however, women are not completely free from patriarchal exploitation of dowry, they do not challenge the existing exploitative power and politics in the society. Without, it they are unable to get equal status, rights choice and voice in the society.

KAZI ABDUR ROUF

Centre members of Grameen Bank discuss their activities and conduct all the banking transactions in the weekly centre meeting of Grameen Bank. The weekly meetings are conducted in a disciplined manner and end with recitation of the 16 decisions, codes of conduct that the members are supposed to follow in their daily basis. Development issues like personal hygiene, health, nutrition, children and education, moral ethics, are also discussed during the centre meeting. Other GB success factors are its exclusive focuses on disadvantaged people, close supervision and connection with clients by the field staff. Moreover, Grameen Bank is able to create collective accountability through peer support of micro-borrowers, transparency in loan operation, decision making decentralized to the field staff. It provides education, visibility and mobility of the staff in the working area. GB social development program embedded in the 16 decisions. However, here it needs very cautious to discuss case based local power and political exploitation and critics of state policies which are necessary for creating and advocacy for citizenship rights. However, GB does not challenge opposition by some religious fundamental leaders, local elites and politicians.

For example, patriarchy takes away women's right from equal inherent family wealth thus women have nothing to live on. Hence they suffer from poverty. Male dominated religious customary laws and values effects women's exploitation deprived them from access to property and their economic upliftment. Here the question is how patriarchy got power. The answer is patriarchy got power through religion (Hindu and Islamic values), colonialism, capitalism, and customary law. Below the paper is only narrating religious factors that exploit women.

5.0. Are religious and customary property laws deprived women in Bangladesh?

Majority Indian Women have been pushed to economically poor through Hindu caste system and Muslim Ashraf (royal) and Atraf (bottom) segregation. In Islam according to Sharia Law widowed wife can only own 12.5% property of her husband. But in practice

358

widowed cannot own propriety rather facing lots of hassles and Fatawa (religious decision) problems. Therefore, maximum widowed give up to claim the property rights. Customary laws are dominating in the rural areas that dominated and governed by the rural elites. Although some reform made in property rights in Bangladesh, but in practice women do not have property in their name. Women lack of ownership to property makes them not access to bank loans or from any other state financial services because mortgage is required. Islamic values and other customary values prevent women to work outside of their home because of Mullahs'(religious leader) fatawa on purdha. So they can not involve in any economic activity outside home. Rather they suffer from to earn income. Therefore, women are economically dependent to men and are struggling for to fulfill their basic needs and citizen rights.

Man take advantages to inherent and increase wealth and religious customary laws support men in Bangladesh. So women are deprived from inherent property. They do not have any meaningful participation in property decision making. "Salish Muslis" in the village decide village matters by the religious leaders where all of them are male and oppressed women in the name of religion. Ubeniq, a feminist organization in Bangladesh, talks about women's equality access to women property rights issue, but little success. For example, in 1993 feminist Farida Rahaman challenged the Muslim Family Property Laws' Ordinance 1961 and raised the question of male biased arbitrary village council. However, her proposal did not pass in the male dominated parliament.

Therefore, Fahim Quadir urges for Praxis action oriented program like change customary law, change traditional Muslim laws, Hindu Laws and implementation them are important to create women access to inherent property, but patriarchy is systemic that even embedded in the state system.

Bangladesh National Women Lawyers Association and Coordination Council for Human Rights in Bangladesh (CCHRB) and Bangladesh Human Rights Council challenged the male dominated customary lawon property rights, but Shura (high level religious leaders) and Islamic organization united together and protest for to maintain Islamic family law. Patriarchal male dominating values and women inequality in property rights is a societal problem in Bangladesh where women are victimized, deprived and discriminated from property rights. In such situation, GB is trying empower women in their property rights. For example, GB provides housing loans to its clients if the housing land deed is in women's name. However, here the concern is GB does not mobilize its borrowers even it has not included programs for gender inequality property right issues in Bangladesh. Therefore, GB needs to design strategy for educating clients on patriarchy, citizen rights, local, and macro political awareness discourses to its clients and also participate in citizen rights advocacy activities, which can help women micro-borrowers to challenge customary laws. ADAB, Prosheka, and Nejara Korri, Bangladesh National Women Lawyers Association and Coordination Council for Human Rights in Bangladesh (CCHRB) and Bangladesh Human Rights Counciletc. agencies are trying to step in such citizenry activities; however, government conditionality, repressive laws restrain them massively involve in advocacy program (Karim, 2002).

6.0. Lessons learned from Grameen Bank PRA activities

The participatory approach is time consuming and resource intensive. Empowering the poor requires patience to continue despite all odds. However, the rural people can be reliable partners in development if given the chance and an enabling environment. In MCIs, include credit plus programs like citizenry advocacy are critical to enhance participation towards organizational viability and sustainability. However, GB has a consciousness program that GB clients have to follow. For example, among GB sixteen decisionslike the 12th, 14th, 15th and 16th decisions are related to micro-borrowers' of Grameen Bank participation in community activities. For example, 12th decision is campaign for 'they shall not inflict any injustice on anyone, neither shall they allow anyone to do so'; moreover, 14th decision is about borrowers of GB shall always be ready to help each other. 'If anyone is in difficulty, they shall all help the sufferers and the victims of sufferers, if they come to know of any breach of discipline in any GB centre'. The 15th decision message is they shall go there and help restore discipline, and they shall introduce discipline in all centers.

Moreover, the 16th decision of GB talks about borrowers of GB shall take part in all social activities; participate in all citizen rights awareness creation campaigns and civic activities. All these stated decisions of *GB Sixteen Decisions* promote the *right-based approach*. These civic activities are for women borrowers of Grameen Bank. However, GB itself is not directly involves in challenging/ advocating, protesting against patriarchy, violence and for government good governance on behalf of its clients. Nevertheless, MCIs and many NGOs are successful pooling of resources and provide leverage for the people to access support like credit and technology. Clients of MCIs make networking among them through group-based micro-credit program, but NGOs do not discuss different discriminatory state macro-policies and religious gender discrimination. Author thinks MCIs and NGOs are very cautious about dealing with religious gender discrimination issue because this a sensitive issue in Bangladesh.

Increased participation in elections at the local and national levels, greater ability to make collective decisions and solve problems, participation in informal community problem solving, increased awareness of women's rights, child welfare rights, and participate in local leadership activities are crucial for micro-borrowers families. Mobilization and utilization of local resources, and sharing social problems, and good governances of the local government are essential for them. These rights could be enhanced in Bangladesh if micro borrowers aware of their different rights with the support of state enforcing agencies, and MCIs and NGOs.

Women are suffering from the burden of gender discrimination like gender biased (inequality of using family income) family resource distribution and others. With the help of Grameen Bank's credit and social programs, women in Bangladesh have gradually become more self-reliant, more confident and much aware of prevailing social issues. It is now generally accepted that micro-credit programs providing small loans to allow poor families to start and expand individual businesses are very effective in reducing poverty. Their benefits are not just economic, but also contribute to social development in Bangladesh. For women, it means greater self-confidence and increased hope in the future. Micro-credit programs also strengthen community relationships. Therefore, providing small loans to poor women has now become a door of endless possibilities in their empowerment and development in Bangladesh.

7.0. Conclusion

Under neo-liberal free market ruling paradigm and as external body, neither Word Bank PRSP strategy nor any other ideas derived from the ruling paradigm can promote citizenry participatory cohesive development and promote human rights equality. However, NGOs cannot stay forever in a community to support its socio-political and environmental initiatives because of time consumption and costs. At a certain point, the people themselves have to carry on, to continue and sustain the actives started. The people have to be enabled and empowered to take charge. However, it is only possible if NGOs and MCIs could mobilize their clients and initiate discuss agenda like the citizenship equality, state accountability to public, transparency to public fund allocation and their proper expenditures, good governance of public policies for disadvantaged people and gender equality etc. These social development agenda could be achieved if community people are actively participate in social development discussions and socio-economic projects in Bangladesh because the participatory approach offers a gradual and progressive transfer of management responsibility and authority from the support institutions to the entrepreneurs to avoid overwhelming the people with rigidity of managing their businesses.

Although right based-citizenry mobilization process may be slow, costly and tedious, it provides atmosphere conducive for learning and enabling the people to release their full potentials to manage themselves and their enterprises in Bangladesh and elsewhere.

8.0. References

Chambers, R. (1994). The origins and practice of participatory rural appraisal, *World Development*, Vol. 2(7), pp. 953-69

Chambers, R. (1997). *Whose reality counts? Putting the first last*, London: Intermediate Technology Publications

Cruikshank, B. (1994). The will to empower: Technologies of citizenship and the war on poverty. *Socialist Review*, pp. 29-55

Grameen Annual Report (2005). *Grameen Bank at a glance*, Dhaka: Grameen Bank

Grameen Dialogue (2001). *Grameen Trust micro-credit replications*, Dhaka: Grameen Bank.

Grameen Dialogue (2006). *Grameen Bank borrowers local election performance.* Newsletter #63, April 2006. Dhaka, Bangladesh: Grameen Trust.

Grameren Bank (2009). *Impact* of *Grameen Bank on local society*, Retrieved from http://www.rdc.com.au/grameen/impact/htm dated June 23, 2009

Hickey, S. and Mohan, G. (eds.) (2004). *Participation: From Tyranny to Transformation? Exploring New Approaches to Participation in Development.* London and New York: Zed Books

Holmes, T. (2001). *A Participatory Approach in Practice: Understanding fieldworkers' use of PRA in Action Aid The Gambia* (Working Paper No. 123). Sussex: IDS.

Kabeer, N. (1983). *Minus Lives – Women in Bangladesh.* Dhaka: University Press

Khan, S. and Asaduzzaman, M. (1996). Politics of people's participation: Focus on government development project, *Social Action* Vol. 46, pp. 325-9

Lee, B. (1999*). Pragmatics of community organization*, Mississauga: Common Act Press

Mahamud, S. (2004). Micro-credit and women's empowerment in Bangladesh in *Attacking poverty with micro-credit*, (Eds.), Salehuddin Ahamed and M. A. Hakim. Dhaka: Dhaka University Press

Mayoux, L. (2003b). *Participatory action learning system: an empowering approach to monitoring, evaluation and impact assessment, Manual.* Draft, June [www.enterprise-impact.org.uk]

Mayoux, L. and Anandi (2005). Participatory action learning in practice: Experience of Anandi, India, *Journal of International Development*, March, 2005, Vol. 2(11), p. 4

Pathways to Participation (c. 2001). *Critical Reflections on PRA.* Sussex: IDS.

Results Canada (2006). *Results Canada Action Sheet*, September 2006, Ottawa

Robb, C. (2002). *Can the poor influence policy? Participatory poverty assessments in the developing world*, 2nd edition. Washington, DC: World Bank

Rouf, K. A. (2017). While poverty is a global problem resulting from global issues, its definition and solution can only be found locally, *International Journal of Research Studies in Management*, Vol.6(2), pp. 39-52

Sen, A. (1999). *Development from freedom*. New York: Anchor House.

Shragge, E. (1997). *Community economic development-in search of empowerment.* Montreal: Black Rose Books

Wong, W. A. (2002). *The poor women-a critical analysis of Asian theology and contemporary Chinese fiction by women.* New York: Peter Lang.

Concepts, Theories, and Approaches to Management Practices for Sustainable Businesses

Abstract

This paper is the literature review of different concepts, ideas, approaches, research findings and management practices of different businesses and companies. The paper takes a triple bottom line approach, defining sustainability in business as a balanced progress towards green, social and economic performance, social justice and environmental quality. Intensively read all these articles and many carefully followed by creating a brief review of each of them. These articles contain critical analysis of different sustainability tools and techniques used by different business managers to create environmental values in marketing, product development, community relations and other functions of the business. In-depth knowledge and a clear understanding of these articles are crucial to green sustainable business practice research. This research paper draws sustainable business practitioners' attention towards sustainable business investment practices in their future management roles.

Key terms: Business management practice; corporate social responsibility (CSR); eco-efficiency; environmental pollution; eco-design; environmental management system (EMS); environmental restoration; fringe stakeholders; life cycle assessment (LCA); globalization; multinational corporations (MNCs); green marketing; profit making enterprises (PMEs); sustainable businesses; socially responsible investing; sustainability balanced scorecard (SBC); and sustainability reporting.

1.0. Introduction

Management practices for sustainable businessesis very essential because the practices of profit making traditional businesses (MNCs) have directly affected people's lives, destroying their ability to teach their younger generation about the value of sustainable business and preserve their structure. There are four billion poor people in the world who are at the base of the market pyramid are suffering from poverty, injustice and environmental degradation. Feminization of poverty is increasing at an alarming rate all over the world. The free market economy is an institution not fully equipped to address social problems. It is contributing to the expansion of social problems, environmental hazards, inequality, health hazards, unemployment, ghettos and so on. In capitalism, the market turns corporations into the Profit Making Enterprises (PMEs), ignoring the common interest of the people and the planet. However, PME's emphasis on economic development results in communities losing control over resources, environmental degradation, and concentrating wealth in too few hands. Moreover, the market has no capacity to solve social problems; rather, its responsibility is handed over to the state.

2.0. Rationality of the paper

Big business owners like traditional profit making enterprises carry out unethical activities in the planet. Moreover, the multinational corporations (MNC) tend to make products and services that are resource intensive and polluting the environment. Prahalad calls this market the *Tier 4 MNC Market*. Tier 4 are: (1) Build a local base support with stakeholders, (2) Conduct R&D on the poor, (3) Form new alliances, (4) Increase employment intensity and reinvent cost structures. Tier 4 MNC Market provides multinational corporations with opportunities to infiltrate these countries. However, "*The Fortune at the Bottom of the Pyramid*" K. Prahalad and Stuart L. Hart say that MNCs can be a leader in products that can practice sustainable businesses and do not repeat environmental mistakes. Therefore, this paper emphasises for people-centered sustainable business practicesthat can have triple bottom-line benefit to people (society), planet and public wellbeing economy.

The Brundtland Commission's brief definition of sustainable development is the "ability to make development sustainable to ensure that it meets the needs of the present without compromising the ability of future generations to meet their own needs." The Brundtland Commission's this sustainable development is surely the standard definition when judged by its widespread use and frequency of citation. The use of this definition has led many to see sustainable development as having a major focus on intergenerational equity. Although the brief definition does not explicitly mention the environment or development, the subsequent paragraphs, while rarely quoted, are clear. On development, the Brundtland Commission's report states that human needs are basic and essential; that economic growth, but it also requires equity to share resources with the poor is required to sustain them; and that equity is encouraged by effective citizen participation. On the environment, the text is also clear: the concept of sustainable development does imply limits-not absolute limits, but limitations imposed by the present state of technology and social organization on environmental resources and by the ability of the biosphere to absorb the effects of human activities.

Management practices for sustainable development are an interdisciplinary praxis where several stakeholders' management techniques involve business decision-making with reference to the environment, social issues and economics. Also, this paper looks at the private sector challenges in implementing different approaches and assumptions. The challenges arise from green marketing; Life-cycle Assessment; environmental management systems; environmental and social audits; stakeholders' dialogue and inclusion; sustainability reporting and communications. The material of the paper identified some organizational issues: the use of environmental and social information and techniques and the development of reflective practitioners who can effectively implement value-creation sustainability development. It shone light on including organizational active participation in organizational management practices' career. Moreover, the paper's exploration of the notion of sustainable business practices and their different options can make readers knowledgeable about the value of environmental and social stakeholders' contribution to environmental and social marketing, product redesign and new venture opportunities for sustainable business management development.

3.0. Literature review and theories of sustainable business practice

The literature review of this paper has forty five articles and four books. These literatures have several main themes like organizational connectivity to markets, organizational commitments to environmental management systems and environmental reporting in creating environmental value for the firm and its stakeholders; organizational capabilities in environmental sustainability; and organizational culture toward sustainable business practice. In this paper, business sustainability means it is managing the triple bottom line-environmental, social and economic blended business management practices. It is a process by which business companies manage their financial, social and environmental risks, obligations and opportunities. These three impacts are sometimes environmentalist referred to as profits, people and planet.

According to Center for Sustainable Business Practices, a business practice that is economically viable, socially responsible and environmentally friendly is usually regarded as being sustainable business. However, corporations that include socially responsible and environmentally sound policies as core elements in their growth strategy very often create sustainable economic values.

There are many ways sustainability can be defined. While there is no universal definition of sustainability, there is broad consensus that sustainability can be viewed as a holistic system, inclusive of nature and man-made, but it needs to be regenerative and balanced in order to last a very long period of time for the benefit of people, wildlife, environment, society and well-being economic performance. Therefore, in the paper, sustainability is viewed as a form of triple-bottom-line reporting system whereby a business enterprise communicates to their stakeholders for its economic (profit) performance; environmental (planet) performance, and social (people) performance

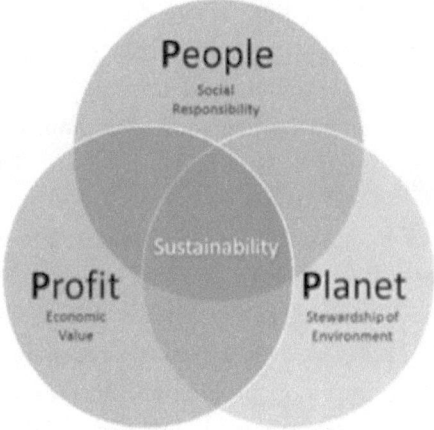

Source: Center for Sustainable Practices

Moreover, the goal in managing sustainable business practices is to create policies, methods and strategies that preserve the long-term viability of People, Plant and Profit. In addition, sustainability business requires an integrated system that connects businesses to people, society and the environment through business operations. This triple bottom line business management practices are very essential because pollution in one part of the world affects others thousands of miles away. Socially responsible corporate business strategies impact communities, peoples and environment not only today, but also leaves lasting impressions for our future generations.

With this framework of sustainable business practices, below the paper discusses each article and books main concepts and my views related to sustainable business management practices.

Ansoff, Freeman and McVera (2001) in their article pointed out that identifying the social and green business stakeholders is critically important in the core competence of public wellbeing businesses. Moreover, Ray Anderson (2000) in his *Climbing Mount Sustainability* article, he mentions that it is not only needed to reach sustainability in business, but also to create restorative measures. Here, the first priority is sustainability, then restoration. However, the widely accepted sustainability definition is to meet the needs of our generation and future generations without depriving future generations of meeting their needs.

From this point of view, Anderson's the restorative process creates more balance and does well for the earth. It is not only based on a company's zero-based waste management, but also do not do that is not right (Anderson, 2000, p. 9). So it is a cyclical process inside the factory that maintains the zero-loop production. Moreover, it is recycling renewable energy rather than fossil fuel-derived energy. Therefore, Anderson suggests reorganizing the whole transportation system, which is a terrific complex environmental issue. Therefore, the focus is needed to sensitize people to their role in the environment because MNCs are resource-extractive, linear, fossil fuel-driven, abusive and wasteful to the earth. Hence, the redesigning of commerce and business practice is important to revitalize environmental services to people because manufacturing industries are liable for landfill waste.

Thomas Dyllick and Kai Hockerts (2002) in their article *Beyond the Business Case for Corporate Sustainability* suggest that profit motive business progress towards global sustainability is suspiciously absent. International treaties have stalled protection of biodiversity and climate change. However, the governments of different countries can initiate their own national sustainability programs. Today, many business managers accept corporate sustainability and follow eco-efficiency guiding principles, but this is insufficient. Therefore, Dylick and Hockerts suggest for three elements of corporate sustainability: (1) integrate triple bottom line business strategies that include economic, ecological and social aspects of community, (2) make long-term profit strategies instead quick profit and (3) create economic capital along with natural capital and social capital.

Economically sustainable companies guarantee cash flow at all times in order to ensure a company's liquidity, but within ecological sustainability, companies use natural resources to keep a company afloat. However, these natural resources are consumed at a rate below the natural reproduction or below development substitutes. Moreover, the natural resources do not cause emissions that accumulate in the environment beyond the capacity of the natural system, neither do they absorb and engage in activities that degrade eco-system services. Therefore, Dyllick and Kai Hockerts speak about socially sustainable companies who add value to communities by increasing human capital of individual partners as well as societal capital of the communities. However, sadly, the *Business Case Model* for sustainable development is not enough, rather corporations need a natural case for corporate sustainability and firms need to make the Societal Case for sustainability (p.135).

John R. Ehrenfeld (2005) in his article *The Roots of Sustainability* talks about eco-efficiency. According to him eco-efficiency means delivering more value for the environmental burden. Here, the problem is none of them benevolence that is spread allows for the adoption of sustainability. Therefore, it temporarily slows down and drifts towards sustainability. Contrarily, management fails to see the problem is in deep-seated systems, which requires radical thinking and action upon the sustainability trajectory. However, now, businesses are focused on reducing the 'unsustainablity' of the flawed economic system, the addiction to commoditization and material consumption. According to Ehrenfeld sustainability means a condition where all forms of life flourish forever (p. 24). Unsustainablity stems from the deepest cultural structures that shape everyday activities through capitalism. Therefore, sustainability cannot change until these structures change. Despite this, profit motive businesses focus on production and economic efficiency. However, the monopoly business profit motive internalizes the social cost and damages the long-term interest of sustainability. However, here, Ehrenfeld's idea of reducing of unsustability is not the same as creating sustainability. Cultural values should always triumph over technology to determine business behavior. So culture and technology are the foundation for building sustainability.

The article entitled *Sustainable Development: Mapping Different Approaches* written by Bill Hoopwood, Mary Mellor and Goeff O'Brien (2005) talks about environmental, social and economical justice issues and sustainability approaches that can promote business sustainability. They espouse that in the last couple of years, the environment has been viewed as being external to humanity by business people. Hence they link environmental sustainable development with environmental and socio-economic issues and claim that mainstream economic policy is dominating international property human beings and expanded global trade. However, past economic growth models fail to eradicate poverty globally and locally. Rather this economic growth creates a downward spiral in poverty, social injustice, environmental injustice and environmental degradation. Therefore, poverty, social justice and environmental justice are a crucial component of sustainable development and for sustainable business practice.

Moreover, in the article, Bill Hoopwood, Mary Mellor and Goeff O'Brien (2005) use two terms: weak sustainability and strong sustainability. Weak sustainability sees natural and human capitalas interchangeable with technology filling human produced gaps in the natural world (p. 40). Strong sustainability criticizes weak sustainability, pointing out that human-made capital cannot replace a multitude of processes that are vital to human existence, such as the ozone layer and photosynthesis. According to them, there are five sustainable development principles based on equality: intergenerational equity, intergenerational social justice, trans-frontier responsibility (geographical equity), procedural equity(treating people fairly) and inter-species equality (importance of bio-diversity). Hence these authors urge for political, economic and human environmental relationships that are needed for business sustainability practices to achieve sustainability development.

Moreover, to achieve sustainability, these authors (Bill Hoopwood, Mary Mellor and Goeff O'Brien, 2005) analyze the status quo approach; the reform approach and the transformatory approach; and eco-feminists' and eco-sociologists' attitudes towards sustainable development. Although a reform in the beliefs of the people who maintain the status quo is necessary for change, it must be acknowledged that they work within the economic and power structure of the society, because they believe in an adjustment policy without any fundamental change. Conversely, reform approach is critical to government and businesses, but they do not consider the fundamental change needed to prevent the collapse of the ecological or social systems. They do not see the root of the problem. Transformationist approach believes a human relationship with the environment is necessary to avoid environmental crisis and the future collapse of sustainability. They (Bill Hoopwood, Mary Mellor and Goeff O'Brien, 2005) emphasize social and political actions for indigenous groups, the poor women and the working class. However, these transformationists are not directly concerned about sustainable development (p. 45). So this tranformatory approach has a strong commitment to social equity (access to livelihood, good health, and resources).

Economics and politics are related to environmental development. Eco-feminists see environmental degradation with the subordination of women. The eco-sociologists, Marx and Engle, have a strong attitude toward the environment. They say, "By no means rule over human nature...(W)e with flesh, blood and brain belongs to nature and exists in its midst." (p. 46). Therefore, from the above discussion it can be concluded that sustainable development is not possible through a single factor change rather it is multifaceted.

The article *I Don't Have Time to Think" versus the Art of Reflective Practice* composed by Joseph A. Raelin (2002) uses the term reflective practices, which means the practice of periodically stepping back to provide careful analysis of what has recently transpired between people. It privileges the process of inquiry, leading to an understanding of experiences that has been overlooked in practice. Raelin says, "Reflective practice tends to be deeper level than trial-and-error experience." (p. 66). Because there are several reasons reflective social business practice needs to be brought about because for example, Government power has been eroded by globalization and transitional corporations in Bangladesh even many other developing countries.

There are many NGOs and civil society stepped in to stop this expansion and to protest against it. However, a smarter approach to globalization can address the social and environmental concerns of fringe stakeholders; but the business company needs to consider a strategic management process. Stakeholders' network can help to deal with threats from multinational corporations MNCs). Joseph A. Raelin mentions, for example, people who are unaware of their behaviors and its consequences may have a 'cognitive error' in their perceptions. Therefore, reflective culture supported by public, private and social business could make it possible for people to constantly challenge the profit oriented environmental destroying businesses without fear of retaliation.

Hence Raelin suggests some strategies that might be useful in reflective practice. (1). A person can demonstrate the value of inquiry, (2) the building of a network among community people and (3) the improvement of the process. According to him, there are three types of reflexivity: reflective skill of speaking that articulates a collective voice from within the group; skill of disclosing means unveiling feelings at a given moment and testing. Therefore, reflective business practice is a new way of thinking and behaving for sustainable development(p. 73).

4.0. Debates on sustainable green business practices

Michael L. Barmet (2004) in his article *Are Globalization and Sustainability Compatible* documents and reviews two books named, (1) *Walking the Talk and a Better World Is Possible* and (2) *Alternatives to People's Eco-globalization*. The former book sees globalization as the market place and the best path toward sustainable human progress. The book has two parts: The first part says there are ten building blocks for sustainable development. Business, government and citizens can cooperate in creating a market that maximizes opportunity for all (p. 523). Eco-efficiency produces more goods (value added) with less resources, waste and pollution. Here the overarching question is whether a profit can be made for corporate sustainability because the first building block is the free market. However, policy and regulatory architecture of business practice need to be overhauled and streamlined in the free market because most policies and regulations are awkward hybrid tools that do not serve sustainability.

Therefore, Michael L. Barmet suggests for four business practice aspects like: dematerialization, closed-loop production, service extension and functional extension can decompose eco-efficiency. However, here Michael L. Barmet's sustainability approach missing point is the social justice issue. Moreover, he thinks corporate social responsibility (CSR) is the commitment of businesses to contribute sustainable economic development and to improve their quality of life. However, CSR is running within the model neo-liberal market economy capitalism and this concept is not challenging the exploitative unjustified capitalism.

The other book named *Alternatives to People's Eco-globalization* written by Joseph A. Raelin (2002) highlights an alternative to economic globalization, which is against the forces of global corporate rule. Joseph A. Raelin (2002) says that the policies of the last half-century have lead to a concentration of economic and political power that is unaccountable to government, people and the planet and that it undermines democracy, equity, and environmental sustainability (p.

527). Therefore, all decisions should be made at the lowest level of governing authority because localization is important to guarantee democratic equity and human rights. Contrarily, globalization guarantees absentee rules by giant corporations that are designed in their own interests without concern for local daily lives because corporate principles are to make profit by continuously growing and expanding. These two both books call to decrease economic ecological disparity because open market policy benefits solely a wealthy minority which creates inequality in society.

People want an alternative to economic globalization, which is against the forces of global corporate rule and this phenomenon has reflected in different studies. For example, in 1999 the *Environics Internationals* conducted a survey in 23 countries around the world on corporate social responsibility. All the respondents of the survey thought that every country should focus more on social and environmental goals than economic goals. Two out of three citizens of this survey wanted companies to go beyond their roles of making profit, paying taxes, employing people by contributing to broader societal goals. Half of the people in the survey were paying attention to the social behavior of companies. One in five consumers reported either a reward or punishment for companies based on their past social performance. They said that major companies should demonstrate their commitment to society's values and to environmental and economic goals through actions. They also thought that they should protect society from the negative impacts of companies' operations. Corporate social responsibility (CSR) is a business's concern for the welfare of society. This concern is displayed by managers who take into consideration the long-term interests of the company and the company's relationship with the society which it operates. However, CSR concept is not out of the capitalist exploitation circle. CSR concept accepts MNCs activities in the capitalist market.

CSR is a phenomenon that thinks profit oriented corporations can share their shares to the wellbeing of society. Corporate social responsibility

(CSR) is growing fast in response to global expectations that require a comprehensive corporate response. Many problems have been created by corporations such as pollution and poverty-level wages. It is the ethical responsibility of business to correct these wrongs. Another point is that businesses have many of the resources needed for solving society's problems and they should use them to do so. Many corporations, banks have started to put funds for CSR and invest this money for public wellbeing. For example, in Bangladesh many banks distribute winter clothes, support sport events, supply relief materials to the disaster victims etc. Therefore, CSR can be a great way for a company to build positive public relations and attract top talent in the industry. Although today, many people argue that corporate social responsibility is important, few people debate about the degree and forms of social responsibility in which businesses should engage

Beyond Greening: Strategies for A Sustainable World written by Hart, S. (1997) mentions that the environmental revolution has been percolating for three decades has changed companies' businesses modalities, but in the 1960's and 1970's corporations denied their impact on the environment. As a result, a series of highly visible ecological problemshave arisen in different countries. Today, many companies accepted responsibility to not do harm to the environment. The challenge; however, is to develop a sustainable global economy that supports the planet indefinitely. This article sees sustainability is not only a matter of pollution control, but also to allow future generations the ability to meet their needs. However, the root problems are population growth and rapid economic growth. There are three factors that may control environmental pollution, strict environmental regulations, greening the industry, and relocating the responsibility of polluting activities to the emerging market. Short-term survival pressures lead growing rural populations into practices that cause long-term damage of forest, soil, and water.

The natural economy supports the market and the survival economics. However, the greatest threat for sustainable development today is the depletion of the world's renewable resources, although technological innovation has created substitutes, many used non-renewable resources. S. Hart makes formula functions of environmental burden (EB). The total environmental burden created by human activity is a function of four factors: pollution (P), consumption (C), affluence (A), and technology (T). They are multiplicative of the environmental burden. The EB equation is = PxCxAxT. However, the primary pollution actors are corporations. Therefore, environmental-friendly manufacturing industrial plants and products, and anti-pollution campaigns should start from corporations.

Mathew J. Kiernam and James S. Martin (1998) talks about Eco-Industrial Revolution and its benefits to environment in their article *Wake-up for Fiduciaries (Relationship between trustee and beneficiaries): Eco-efficiency Drives Shareholders Values.* Currently there is a worldwide economic and industrial restructuring has begun. It is acknowledged by leading financial analysts that there is a strong positive and growing correlation between industrial companies' eco-efficiency and the competitiveness and financial performance (p. 17). However, fund managers and plan sponsors in North America continue to conduct businesses as usual. However, in environment, there are some investment funds in Europe that uncovering the hidden value created by superior eco-efficiency. These European funds are not flaky rather ideologically-driven 'Green Funds' (p. 18). The author hopes that the far-sighted company leaders and investors will position themselves accordingly. However, green funds are very few, so green projects and their products cannot massively serve to cover people's need all over the world.

In the article *Eco-efficiency Warriors* written by Mathew Kiernan and James Martin (1998) mentions that it is not widely recognized by financial analysts and investors that there is a strong, positive and growing correlation between industrial companies' eco-efficiency and their competitiveness and financial performances measured in terms of total stock market returns. However, superior eco-efficiency can help generate competitive advantage that has five well-recognized value drivers: Cost containment (keep negative effect under control), sales and market share growth, franchise and brand value, stakeholders' satisfaction and innovation capacity. However, Carl Frankel (1998) concept of green consumers is different from Michael l. Barnet and Robert M. Salomon (2003) CSR thoughts.

Carl Frankel (1998) in his article *Whitecaps, Green Consumers and the Infrastructure-Building Blues* emphasis on products life cycle costs and related it to the benefit of green consumers. He says that companies can offer environmentally friendly products at consumers' affordable prices two ways: Increase supply and stimulate demand. He suggests government agencies should purchase green products for two reasons: to stimulate demand and to inspire state/local government and private sector to follow the suit because the green products have longer benefits over their life cycle costs to consumers. Frankel defines life cycle costs is the amortized annual costs of a product including capital costs, installation costs, operating costs, maintain costs and disposable costs over the life time of the products (p. 137). He says that if the costs are more than non-green products, it can cover its extra costs by with lower disposable costs.

This life cycle costing has the potential to help level the procurement playing field green products. However, green consumerism hasn't boomed although it hasn't been bust. Since 1990, Green consumerism movement has followed a bell curve showing mild rising followed by decline. Statistics shows that 40% Americans are indifferent to environment (p. 141). However, green consumerism is important because it bridges the gap between environmental issues and ideology (p. 141). In America every school has environmental education program that provides environmental education to the present youth generation. So the kids are receiving more environmental education than their parents. Frankel's study indicates that although the size of the official green consumer segment has declined; however, green values are steadily penetrating mainstream culture (p. 143).

5.0. Socially responsible investing

According to S. Hart sustainability can be achieved by reducing environmental burden. This can be done by decreasing the human population, lowering the consumption, and change the technology that does not harmful to environment. The article narrates three stages of achieving sustainability: pollution prevention, product stewardship-focus not only pollution minimizing, but also focus full cycle of a product. Therefore, the design for environmental efficiency (DFE) is an important tool that can create products that are easier to recover, reuse or recycle (p. 72). The most commonly used socially responsible investing (SRI), or social investment definition is also known as sustainable, socially conscious, "green" or ethical investing, is any investment strategy which seeks to consider both financial return and social good to bring about a social change. However, the public policy innovations and changes individual consumption patterns needed to move forward sustainability, but corporation can help shape public policy and change consumer's behavior plus good business strategies can build sustainable world. Moreover, many corporations receive SRI public funds, but they do not use them properly.

The article *Throwing a Curve at Socially Responsible Investing Research* written by Michael l. Barnet and Robert M. Salomon (2003) talk about corporate social responsibility (CSR) has been abandoned as companies engage in activities that can give highest financial return. Because corporate social responsibility (CSR) by most common definition means it is a business approach that contributes to sustainable development by delivering economic, social and environmental benefits for all stakeholders. However, the firm is judged by its financial reward, but its morality is concerned secondary. However, this certainly does not mean that firm should not behave morally and can govern a variety of social issues. CSR can improve relationships with key stakeholders and increase firm's ability to attract resources in the community. Although standard measures of public firm's financial performance are available; however, their social performances are not available. Authors assert that investment in CSR has maximum pay-off. However, this concept is not only supports the capitalism neoliberal environmental degradation, but also encourages MNCs profit maximization.

The article *Sustainability: Consumer perceptions and Marketing Strategies* written by Seonaidh McDonald and Caroline J. Oates (2006) talks about environmental marketing. Here the authors predict that there is a sudden powerful movement anticipated in green consumer behavior in 1980's and in 1990's. However, recent emphasis on environmental concerns is environmental marketing. The green movement has been viewed as an opportunity to identify and segment new markets. However, the problem is in identifying the *'Recycler'*. Because it observes that many people concerned about environment, but this does not indicate their purchasing or disposal to landfills actions unless they effected by individually. Authors' mention that there are two factors that effects individual environmental purchase behavior: the degree of price compromise, and the degree of confidence to address genuine issue and represent environmental benefits. Therefore, green purchasing falls into two folds: (a) Acts of purchase represents the process of consumption, (b) environmental, ecological or green relate to unsustainability. However, environmental marketing needs to relate social and ethical issues with it to get full picture of interrelated concern.

Seonaidh McDonald and Caroline J. Oates interviews several people and presented these information in a metrics form. The metrics has five activities of categories. The environmental stable activities fall into the high difference/low efforts category. It finds in the matrix that some activities are more consistent to the top, bottom, right or left of the matrix then in individual cells. The matrices that show equal distribution of activities across all four matrices are considered them as balanced respondent. However, it finds more optimist then pessimists in this matrices category. However, in practice this strong endorsement does not reflect into environmental actions in any free market capitalist society.

6.0. Green marketing

In the article *Green Marketing, Public Policy and Managerial Strategies* written by Aeem Prakash (2002) uses the term green marketing that refers to the strategies to promote product by employing environmental claims either by their attributes or by the systems, polices, process of the firms through manufacture or sell them (p. 285). According to Prakash firms can be green by themselves in three ways: value addition process, management systems and through products. The third greening strategy is products related to product services. This service could take place in several ways like repair-extend the life-cycle of the product by repairing them, recondition-extend product life-cycle by overhauling them, remanufacture-new products based on the old one. He emphasises for reuse and design a product in such a way that can be used multiple times, recycle-reprocessed the products and convert them into raw materials to be used in other products.

Finally this process can reduce-less use of raw materials and generate less disposable waste. Although in United States 87% adults are concerned about the condition of the natural environment; however, the problem is such concerned and attitudes to environmental product do not translate into actual behavior. Therefore, mass consumer markets for green products in most categories have yet to develop because most consumers are not ready to pay increased direct costs of green products or organic products. Hence many mass merchants continue to focus on the conventional product price, quality and product features. However, if firms can offer green products at no additional costs, but have same quality, dilemmas will not occur.

7.0. Approaches to sustainable business practices

The article *Industry Codes as Agents of Change: Responsible Care Adoption by US Chemical Companies* written by Jennifer Howard, Jennifer Nash and John Ehrenfeld (1999) asserts that industry generates codes of environmental health and safety practices for the benefits of people and to improved corporate environment management. These codes developed collectively by all members of the industry to improve their members/other stakeholders' environmental performance. However, the adoption of voluntary code of environmental practices does not guarantee that companies follow uniform practices and compiles desired norms. Recently it is found that public demands for environmentally sustainable manufacturing driven companies to adapt environmental practices specially health and safety management. Therefore, industrial management codes establish new norms of behavior among the manufacturing companies. Peer pressure is the key enforcement mechanism for ensuring companies comply with the industry generated codes. These practices benefit the companies to legitimacy.

Although the US manufacturing Association (CMA) set up the responsible care program in 1988 to re-establish public confidence in the chemical industry with the hope that mimic success among peers will take place. However, it is not in practice. The authors predicted that companies will adapt a variety of practices in response to the responsible care code if companies are not at stake. Howard, Nash and Irenfeld conducted a survey on responsible care practices among the chemical companies and find four patterns exist in this sector. (1) drifters companies do not follow responsible care, (2) promoter companies adjusts to existing environmental health and social (EH & S) programs, (3) adaptor practice and belief responsible care is a valuable care tool for improving their EH & S functions and (4) company leaders belief it is whole new way of thinking that EH & S practices should be strong prior to responsible care. At the end of the article the authors concluded that although some skeptic exists about environmental codes; however, the above categories are uniform response that elicit from companies in the area of image manipulation.

Michael J. Lenox and Jennifer Nash study four American Trade Associations and write a paper entitled Industry Self-regulation and Adverse Selection; A Comparison Across our Trade Association Programs that published in 2003. The survey studied a number of trade associations have promoted industry regulation through the voluntary association of firms to control their collective behaviors to avoid costly regulation and liabilities. This industry self-regulation tools serves as a mechanism to facilitate the collective improvement of environmental performance within the industry. The success of self-regulatory program is contingent on individual members abide by program requirements. This mode of self-regulatory programs attracted other firms but the problem is there is no mechanism for screening member firms. However, these self-regulatory programs face a number of challenges like unchecked adverse selection undermine self-regulatory programs.

Therefore, Michael J. Lenox & Jennifer Nash (2003) proposed the viable way to avoid adverse selection is simply expels non-compliant firms from the program. This means that self-regulatory programs must make structures to monitor individual firms to compliance with self-regulatory program objectives, and establish procedures for removal firms from the program. Therefore, state may create incentives for firms to adapt strict governance structures by rewarding firms that participate in effective self-regulatory programs.

Bruce Paton (2000) in his article *Voluntary Environmental Initiatives and Sustainable Industry* mentions in the article that voluntary environmental initiatives in private or public efforts try to improve corporate environmental performance beyond existing legal requirements. In America, its global climate change policy almost entirely based on voluntary programs. Allenby (1997) for example, points out that extensive voluntary action imply a fundamental and inappropriate shift in the theory of the firm from profit seeking to social welfare maximizing behavior. However, Strut Hart (1995), on the other hand, argues that the goal of business sustainability is entirely consistent with the profit motive. He suggests that a 'sustainable' corporation may achieve significant competitive advantage by exerting leadership by meeting environmental and social needs (p. 330).

According to Bruce Paton there are four types of Voluntary Approach: (1) Unilateral initiatives are actions that improve environmental performance within a single firm, (2) private codes include initiatives by industry associations, and non-government organizations, (3) voluntary challenges are government sponsored challenges that encourage firms to improve environmental performance and (4) negotiated agreements involve contracts reached between government and industry. Bruce Paton thinks his all these approaches should be attached to: (1) environmental effectiveness, (2) economic efficiency and (3) equity. Moreover, he suggests for a third parties involvement for effective transparency and openness to voluntary participation. The third party involvement can give some benefits like environmental effectiveness, intergenerational equity, intra-generational equity and transparency. According to him environmental effectiveness refers to the ability of a voluntary approach to achieve its intended results: typically emissions reductions and energy savings. The intergenerational equity refers to the fairness in allocation of resources between current and future generations.

Bruce Paton says, "the principal efficiency gains from voluntary approaches may come from the ability to address barriers to change within the firm" (p. 335). Therefore, Voluntary initiatives can increase efficiency relative to a compliance baseline, by overcoming the detrimental economic effects of inefficient behaviors. However, the voluntary approaches are not adequate by themselves. In the absence of explicitly articulated coercive or market-based measures, voluntary initiatives may be less ambitious and less economically efficient than the more conventional policy alternatives. However, this voluntary approaches may be ineffective and economically inefficient if they are poorly designed or in conflict with existing public policies.

The *Private Costs and Benefits of Environmental Self-Regulation: Which Farm Have most to Gain* is written by Natalie Stoeckl (2004) that paper refers to Robert COASE theory (1960). *Coase theorem* is theorised by Ronald Coase which is a legal and economic theory that affirms that where there are complete competitive markets with no transactions costs, an efficient set of inputs and outputs to and from production-optimal distribution is selected, regardless of how property rights are divided. This COASE theory argued that victims of pollution damage have an incentive to take corrective action. This theory says if private individual seek recourse through the courts, then no need governmental intervention for pollution control (p. 135). The traditional pollution control strategies largely relied on command and control policies such as emission standards and market based approach and is excessively costly. Therefore, Stioeckl concludes that these two approaches have not fully solved the problems of pollution regulation (p. 136). Hence the self-regulatory pollution controls strategy growing interest to many firms. However, this approach has several advantages like it is less costly to tax payers then government imposed regulations. Moreover, self-regulation participation has identified as being a fundamental barriers to success the self-regulatory mechanism because a profit maximizing firm choose pollution control that equates with its private costs benefit.

Moreover, Natalie Stoeckl contrarily thinks command and control regulations are accused of being inefficient of stifling innovation have enforcement difficulties and they are focusing on end-of-pipe solutions (p. 139). However, self-regulation often fails to fulfill its original assurance to control pollution. However, traditional environmental abatement programs are costly yet this not to be the case. Stoeckl says that consumers are carrying about the environment are necessary, but not sufficient. Hence consumers demand side effects of environmental programs if (a) firms are able to differentiate their production environmental grounds. In the articles *Private Costs and Benefits of Environmental Self-Regulation: which Farm Have most to Gain* of Natalie Stoeckel (2004) identified seven characteristics of firms likely to benefits from environmental self-regulation programs: They are (1) large firms, (2) dirty firms, (3) firms that are capable of differentiating products on environmental point, (4) environmentally sensitive operating firms, (5) firms selling products to affluent consumers, (6) firms operating in highly competitive market and (7) firms that are members of industry associations (pp. 151-152). However, Natalie Stoeckel classifications of firms are always not attached with industry associations particularly in developing countries.

The key theme of the article *Different Strokes: regulatory Styles and Environmental Strategy in the North American Oil and Gas Industry* written by Sanjoy Sharma (2001) is stringent command and control to environmental regulations defer the entry of firms into an industry on the incumbents. Such regulation may not stimulate innovations by organizations looking to influence environmental regulations (pp. 344-345). Therefore, there is an argument that this command and control regulate technology rather than environmental solutions. Sanjoy Sharma makes two advices for the effectiveness of stringent command and control legislation. The first one is firm response to sticks and second is stringent regulations enhances corporate competitiveness by fostering innovation. However, the Canadian managers considered regulations more important to address environmental abatement issues, which is opposite from US managers and from many other country MNCs that regulations are not important to environmental strategy (p. 347). Sharma concluded in the article by saying that environmental regulations need some minimum standard regulations to drive the environmental strategy although enforcement makes minimum compliance. Therefore, public policy makers need to find creative ways to stimulate proactive environmental actions by the oil and gas companies who are unwilling to go beyond compliance (p. 362).

David Annadale, Angus Morrison-Sanders and George Bouma (2004) in their paper *The Impact of Voluntary Environmental Protection Instruments on Company Environmental Performance* says that traditionally the predominant approach to addressing the environmental problems emanating from the private sector through direct command and control regulations. This instrument for environmental protection has been increasing criticizing now. As a result of this voluntarism, education and information and economic instruments emerged. Japan has implemented the voluntary pollution control agreements over 30 years have benefited local government and companies (p. 3).

However, there is no investigation made on volunteering environmental outcomes, but many environmentalists focus on to improve the process of development of *environmental management system* (EMS) and *corporate environmental reporting* (CER).

CER is being implemented by larger companies with their traditional financial reports. However, standards for CER are less defined than EMS. Authors claim that EMS has a greater positive influence on environmental performance than CER (p. 6). Contrarily, EMS needs to be more focus on its systematic approach and provide better documentations and to drive for change. Moreover, the CER thought is similar to CSR concept that supports capitalistic neoliberal free market economy.

The article *Environmental Management System, Communicative Action and Organizational Learning* written by Fredrick Burnston Von Malmborg (2002) thinks many private organizations have voluntarily established in administrative environmental management system. EMS is traditionally worked as a technical tool for analytical management action. Contemporary EMS has fast and vast ecological, technological, economic, social and cultural and political change. It is a learning process, where it changes organizational behavior on the basis of experience. The author uses the term unlearn for organizational cultural change. To promote cultural change, the organization must unlearn. According to Malmborg unlearn is promoted when (1) the organizational culture encourages openness to experience, (2) encourage to risk taking, and (3) willing to accept mistakes and learn from them. There is a reward system encourage risk taking. However, there is a common critique about EMS that it emphasis to much the creation of formal procedures.

8.0. Measuring the sustainable business practices and sustainable business management models

Another suggestion coporate business performance can be improved by integrating social, economical and environmental dimensions made by Frank Figge, Tobis Hahn, Stefan Schallegger, and Marsus Wagner (2002) in their paper *The Sustainability Balanced Scorecard-Linking Sustainability Management to Business Strategy*. This article mentions that although market prices are important in the market system business; however, economic scarcities exist in this system. Environmental and social management is often not linked to the economic success of the firm. Therefore, economic contribution of environmental and social management remains unclear (p. 270). However, it is desirable that corporate performance improves three dimensions of sustainability –economic, environmental and social-together. Integration of all these three pillars of sustainability in the businesses management has three advantages: sustainable business management is not engendered by economic crisis and unsure corporate sustainability management. The other benefit is environmental restoration.

The environmental and social aspect makes integration in the existing business standard. The authors suggest for a specific environmental and social scorecard for ranking companies sustainable management. Moreover, Figge et al. (2002) thinks there needs three steps in preparing *Sustainability Balanced Scorecard Card* (SBSC). (1) A strategic business unit (2) identify the environmental and social aspects of the business unit and (3) determine the relevance of the business strategic unit. However, SBSC measures cannot be used universally because different business practices are varying by different business companies at different places (countries) and in different times. Moreover, business practices need to tailor to local situation. Therefore, SBSC cannot be used universally all time.

Vesela Velva and Michael Ellenbecker (2000) propose a measurement system for measuring business sustainability in their article *A Proposal for Measuring Business Sustainability*. They suggest for a sustainable production framework to measure sustainable business development. Such kind of sustainable production framework does not exist to measure sustainable production system (p. 102). The sustainable production indicators can serve as a roadmap for sustainable business companies in their every day practice. According to Vesela Velva and Michael Ellenbecker all sustainable production is the creation of goods and services that are non-polluting, conserving energy and natural resources and socially rewarding for all working people (p. 103). Therefore, sustainability business has three dimensions: environmental, social and economic.

Vesela Velva and Michael Ellenbecker measurement tool is called *Indicators for sustainable production* (IPS). This IPS tool develops mainly for production facilities with the aim to address key productions like energy and material use, natural environments, economic viability, community development and social justice. However, these need desirable qualities for developing sustainable production indicators like (1) Appropriate to the tasks, (2) allow comparison between companies; (3) indicators need to be verifiable. ISP should be a manageable number an easy to apply and evaluate. Fortunately ISO 14031 links environmental condition indicators with operational indicators and creates a common framework for companies to use and integrate all information related to production; however, ISO considers environmental sustainability with no reference to social or economical sustainability of companies.

Vesela Velva and Michael Ellenbecker (2000) draw the example of *global reporting initiative* (GRI), World Business Council for Sustainable Development, (WBCSD) and Center for Waste Reduction Technology (CWRT) framework to support the ISP arguments. The global reporting initiative (GRI) provides a common framework for companies to report their achievements towards sustainability that promotes awareness and business accounting. It covers all missing aspects of sustainable production and addresses key issues of global concern. However, GRI framework has several service indicators like it does not have a clear operative definition of sustainability. However, it guidelines have large number of indicators (about 100) with no guidance how to select from hem. It is developed by multinational corporations.

The World Business Council for Sustainable Development (WBCSD) and it has small manageable number of indicators. Centre for Waste Reduction Technology (CWRT) developed a sustainable metrics. It includes environmental effect indicators like acidification, eco-toxicity, and human toxicity. However, it does not address all aspects of sustainable production like social issue, workers and products are missing in the lists of categories. From the above discussion it is clear that only single approach ISP, or CWRT or GRI or WBCSD is not sufficient to promote sustainable production change. Therefore, it is necessary to standardize the ISP methodology and specify them.

W. Gary Wilson, and Dennis R. Sasseville (1999) talk about the environmental business management System. Here authors emphasis on cooperative relationship among the environmental regulating agencies and business companies so that it can be cost effective to both of them and fulfill environmentalism. They say that environmental liability is the biggest cash drain on a business. Therefore, it needs to encourage creative thinking for cost-effective approaches to deal with environmental issues (p. 64). Wilson and Saseville defined environmental management system (EMS) is a process to assist management to deal with the significant environmental aspects of the business. This EMS approach creates an overall management approach to identify and control environmental impact.

However, this definition of EMS is limited than Business Dictionary because Business Dictionary definition of environmental management system covers organizational structure, planning activities, responsibilities, practices, procedures, processes, resources, and standards (such as ISO 14000 or BS 7750) employed in formulating an organization's environmental policy and achieving its objectives on both short- and long-term basis. W. Gary Wilson and Dennis R. Sasseville say that EMS measurement should cover all these points.

Therefore, the implementation of EMS decision needs to come from top management and carry it by them to different levels of the business staffs. The EMS needs to set goals that management wants to achieve its goal through EMS. It needs to develop an EMS framework, assigning responsibilities, communicate essential EMS information, documenting EMS elements and develop the necessary operational procedures to make the EMS function. Awareness training, EMS procedures training, and specific job training for employees could facilitate EMS promotion in the companies.

The article *Engaging Fringe Stakeholders for Competitive Imagination* written by Hart, S. and Sharma, S. (2004) mentions that government power has eroded by globalization and growth of traditional corporations in different countries have increased. NGOs and civil society stepped into the break their expansion. Internet connected coalition of NGOs and individual and smart mob-make impossible government, corporations to do monopoly decision to public. To avoid extreme danger of mob, it needs to proactively seek voices from the fringe that previously ignored. Therefore, the firm needs to consider strategic management process. Corporate strategies control critical resources influences. Authors Hart and Sharma use the term *Radical transactiveness (RT)*, which focuses on gaining access to stakeholders to manage disruptive change and create competitive imagination among them.

The RT strategy is put the last first for include those are powerless, non-legitimate and isolated. His concepts of RT strategy implementation can be found in Grameen Bank borrowers' inclusion in its Board. GB shareholder system included its borrowers in the board decision making process as stakeholders of the bank. GB focuses on "fanning out" (the term uses by Hart and Sharma) if activities to distant and marginal stakeholders to identify opportunities for new business rather than to protect existing businesses. The GB trust-based interaction strategy enabled the bank and its micro-borrow stakeholders to confront the conflicts and contradiction. In the 'fanning in' system, there are scope for mutual learning and integration of diverse information that make possibility of fanning in for opportunities that did not exist previously in Bangladesh banking system. Therefore, GB banking system in Bangladesh is considered as *Radical transactiveness (RT)* in Bangladesh banking sector.

Adams A. Carol and Geoffrey R. Frost have researched web-based corporate sustainability reporting that they incorporated in their article *Accessibility and the Functionality of the Corporate Web site: Implication for Sustainability Reporting.* According to them reporting is a function of the need for organizations to respond to external pressure or scrutiny of their performance. However, reporting has increased an environmental disaster, but there has been a growing awareness by companies of their shared social responsibilities, and growing demands for their accountability with respect to social and environmental impacts. However, web based reporting has here several limitations.

For example, many companies' free standing report has no link to general corporate communications; secondly environmental performance data are not linked to corporate environmental reports; and thirdly companies are not interactive and customized their environmental reporting. As a result, many corporate web sites are difficult to negotiate for less experienced users. However, companies have two advantages reporting for sustainability issues are: accessibility and functionality. Companies see the Website as an extension of the traditional reporting process where sustainability reports are uploaded as a PDF. However, the traditional reporting system overlooks the web as a dynamic environment, where users are familiar with live data or continuous updates.

Moreover, not all corporate sustainability reports (CSRs) are created equal. Some reports are glossy marketing brochures that lack substantive data. Others are so data focused that reading them requires a strong cup of coffee to resist boredom-induced sleep. The best reports provide a balance of accessible, engaging text and comprehensive, material data presented in a well-designed format. It is both art and science. There are five elements that are vital to producing a quality report: Transparency, authenticity stakeholder engagement, intuitive structure and meaningful. The green enterprise (GE) sustainable growth report is particularly successful at creating a structure that leads readers through the company's sustainability story. The content is divided into three easy-to-understand sections: People, Planet, and Economy. Then each of those sections has three layers of information from the high-level, at-a-glance "Highlights," to the narrative details in "Progress," to the detailed data in "Metrics." This enables readers to easily find the information that interests them. The structure is always visible in the navigation, providing readers the signposts that allow them to feel comfortable exploring the report with the confidence of knowing where they are and how to get back to where they started.

In the article *Trends in Sustainability Reporting by the fortune global 250* Ans Kolk (2003) provides sustainability reporting statistics of the global big 250 companies. Here he mentions that most multinational companies signed out from corporate governance and social responsibility. Therefore, government has started corporate accountability through reporting legislation or voluntary disclosures. After then corporate reporting (1998) on non-financial reporting has increased from 35% to 45%, but sustainability reporting have not changed much with chemical, pharmaceuticals followed by computers and electronics, automotive, utilities, and oil and gas all scoring above average. Exceptions find in food and beverages industries. Finally, successful reports will do all of the above in a way that is truly meaningful to each audience. At *Emotive Brand*, we believe that people (i.e. stakeholders) are increasingly skeptical and sophisticated, and that they will support companies that offer them meaning. Sustainability reports present an opportunity for organizations to communicate authentically about issues that matter to people. So, it is important to tie each of the previous elements together in a way that speaks clearly and directly to stakeholder interests, while providing an opportunity for continued dialogue.

However, the sustainability reporting did not increase in US and in many other countries. However, many Japanese companies follow the recommendations on environmental accounting guidelines. Ans

Kolk even himself predicted that sustainability reporting is like more window dressing (p. 289). However, he concludes in the article that the environmental reports professional capture and a managerial turn than helps increase accountability with an audit process that lacks transparency (p. 290).

The term *"greenwashing"* was added to the Oxford English *dictionary* in 1999, where it is *defined* as "disinformation disseminated by an organization so as to present an environmentally responsible public image." In reality, the company may actually be doing very little that is environmentally-friendly. According to Catherine A. Ramus and Ivan Montiel Green washing means disinformation by an organization to present an environmentally responsible public image. Authors Catherine A. Ramus and Ivan Montiel in their article *When Are Corporate Environmental Policies a Form of Green washing?* says environmental policy statements are not required by law rather they are voluntary commitment to public. However, corporate environmental policy (CEP) statements are important in business practices. Environmental literatures talks about environmental regulations, the degree of stakeholder pressure, economic advantages and mimic pressures from the environmental institutions to reduce use of fossil fuels, to create environmentally sustainable business. The article disagrees with self-regulatory notion of MNCs for achieving green policy commitment and implementation. They say that firms will implement corporate green policies if they get potential economic benefit from implementing corporate greening policies.

Catherine A. Ramus and Ivan Montiel (2005) argue that firms will commit to environmental policies because of coercive, normative and mimic pressures plus if there is economic incentives (p. 383). Regulative environmental aspects are coercive in nature, using roles and laws to bring organizations into compliance. Normative aspects are morally governed with organizational performer with social obligations. The authors Catherine A. Ramus and Ivan Montiel assert that manufacturing companies, oil and gas industries will implement the environmental policies than service industries if environmental policies enhance manufacturing, gas and oil industries businesses. However, environmental policies are not enough for enhancing and implementing environmentalism in fossil fuel business practices. However, enforcing governing the policy is very important to execute the environmental policies.

According to WECD (1987) the definition of sustainability is the development that meets the needs of the present without comprising the ability of future generations to meet their own needs. Helen Tregidga and Markus J. Milne (2006) think business has the key role to achieve such sustainability. They mention in their article *From Sustainable Management to Sustainable Development: A longitudinal Analysis of a Leading New Zealand Environmental Reporter* that it can be achieved through corporate environmental reporting because they can play a part of forming social ideology (p. 224). According to them there are four ideological assumptions constitute corporate environmental management: (1) the environment can be managed, (2) corporate managers should be left to manage the environment, (3) environmental management is a win-win opportunity for the companies, and (4) science and technology are the means to manage the environment. Helen Tregidga and Markus J. Milne emphasis environmental management is a source of value that can serve economic interest of the firms, but it needs to be managed carefully.

David Wheeler and John Elkington (1998) assert in their paper *The End of the Corporate Environmental Report? Or the Advent of Cybernetic Sustainability Reporting and Communication* that effective communication with stakeholders is a powerful way of building trust and thereby contributing to business performance. In Europe, duty to the environment, public relations, and legal compliance are the most driving force for environmental reporting, but in North America it is less important. However, in Japan consumer and shareholders pressure, environmental duty and public relations scored higher than legal compliance in environmental reporting

(Wheeler & Elkington, 1998, p. 2). The cybernetic reporting and communication of environmental, social and economic information are the triple bottom line, which adds real value for stakeholders and assist companies to navigate their market successfully. I, Kazi Rouf, think without good governance and strong government enforcement and support, the corporations might not really follow and publish their corporate environmental reports. Government needs to pressure corporations for regularly monitor the corporate environmental reports.

9.0. Eco-efficiency in business practice

The notion of eco-efficiency delivers more value to the customers at lower environmental costs. This is measured by the Brundtland Report that creatively helped to reduce the rate of unsustainability. This term was coined by the World Business Council for Sustainable Development (WBCSD) in its 1992 publication "Changing Course," and at the 1992 Earth Summit, eco-efficiency was endorsed as a new business concept and means for companies to implement *Agenda 21* in the private sector. However, according to Erenfeld creating sustainability is not the same as reducing unsustainablity. John R. Ehrenfeld in his paper *Searching for Sustainability: No Quick Fix* asserts that unsustainability is exacerbated the situation by generating more wealth and more consumption.

Erenfield define sustainability as the possibility that human and other forms of life will flourish on the Earth forever. He says; however, flourishing sustainability depends on three critical domains: (1) the natural domain, (2) the human domain and (3) the ethical domain (pp. 3-4). To achieve this true sustainability Ehenfield suggests corporations should follow two parallel paths and follow six steps for achieving true sustainability. The paths are: (1) change the paradigms that guide business and environmental thinking in traditional way, (2) use appropriate technology that can satisfy both human and natural needs. The six steps of Erenfield for future sustainability are: (1). don't settle for simply reducing unsustainability, (2), Change thinking enterprises are independent, autonomous entity in the complex living network, (3) Implement sustainability that harmony to the natural, human and ethical domain, (4) Follow the principles of industrial ecology built on Natural Capitalism, The Natural Step, Cradle to Cradle, etc., (5) Design most efficient way technology use, and (6) Implement the environmental design (p. 12).

However, eco-efficiency by definition says it is a management philosophy that aims at minimizing ecological damage while maximizing *efficiency* of the firm's production processes, such as through the lesser use of energy, material, and water, more recycling, and elimination of hazardous emissions or by-products. However, eco-efficiency has been proposed as one of the main tools to promote a transformation from unsustainable development to one of sustainable development. It is based on the concept of creating more goods and services while using fewer resources and creating less waste and pollution. However, this notion of environmental eco-efficiency is not covered by Ehenfield suggestions.

William McDonough and Michael Brauntgart (1998) in their paper *The Next Industrial Revolution* talk about eco-efficiency and relate it to the recycling of packaging waste management (those composed of biological nutrients) and respect for environmental diversity with economic benefit and social justice. Their definition of eco-efficiency is close to Earth Summit eco-efficiency thinking. According to the authors, eco-efficiency means doing more with less (p. 82). They predicted that eco-efficiency has been functioning within industries with the notion of reducing, reusing, and recycling. Their definition of eco-efficiency; however, does not go far enough. Rather their thought works within the same system that caused the problem in the first place. They prefer the term *down-cycling* instead of recycling. They say, "Recycling is more expensive for communities because traditional recycling tries to force materials into more lifetimes that they were designed for" (p. 86). If this process is to save money and materials, products must be designed from the very beginning to be recycled or up-cycled, because human industries create things that are inclinators or need landfills; even waste materials are poison.

Therefore, McDonough and Brauntgart suggest for cradle-to-grave instead cradle-to-cradle life cycle products (p. 88). Their second principle of the Next Industrial Revolution is respect diversity. According to McDonough and Brauntgart, the sustainability movement in the industrial revolution should have three categories of concerns: equality refers to social justice; economy refers to market viability (consumers afford to buy their needs) and ecology. The products should have biological nutrients at their end of life cycle.

In the article *Industrial Ecology, Life Cycles, Supply Chains*, Stefan Seuring argues for environmental supply chain management and life-cycle assessment for industrial ecology management. He says that industrial ecology covers both a geographical and a product-based approach where human activities and natural ecosystems are connected (p. 309). A product's life cycle assessment (LCA) places emphasis on the product design. The author suggests for integrated chain management, which stresses the involvement of different stakeholders for a positive impact on all parties. The environmental supply chain management approach is where a fully integrated supply chain contains all the elements of the traditional chain that includes a closed-loop product cycle and packaging recycling, re-using, and remanufacturing.

Mathew Simon, Steve Poole, Andrew Sweatman, Steve Evans, Tracy Bhamra and Tim McAllone (2000) in their article *Environmental Priorities in Strategic Product Development* speaks to the "The Design for Environmental Decision Support" (DEEDS) project and the tools for Design for Environment (DFX), which have different approaches. For example, DEEDS involves assuming a product and recycling it in order to meet *eco-label standards* such as energy consumption. Now, supporters of DFX believe in new successful designs and that the marketing of green products requires organizational change. This article asserts that successful eco-design requires activity at two levels:

the strategic level: to set the issue and at the operational level: for product development. The authors suggest a framework that contains four stages: Analysis, Reporting, Prioritization and Improvement for successful eco-design. People perceptions on ecology are very important and this can be achieved through educating and campaigning of the potentiality of the proposed eco-design. Analysis of data of eco-design could be one of the components of the DEEDS, but without people's perception and awareness eco-design DEEDS would be successful.

According to Richard Welford (1998), eco-design life cycle assessments are able to identify areas of environmental damage, give direction to the redesign of products and improve the distribution methods to reduce environmental damage. Lastly, they can improve businesses and their environmental performance. It is about the cradle-to-grave approach. It is an analysis that covers every stage and impact of a product from extraction to decomposition back to natural elements. It requires active cooperation and collaboration of suppliers to facilitate positive environmental impact. There should be an integral management tool in life cycle assessments to minimize the negative impact of environmental products. Welford mentions in his paper *Life Cycle Assessment* four stages that involve LCA: (1) identification of the areas of environmental impact; (2) quantification of energy and material inputs, emissions and waste output; (3) identification of impact mechanisms; and (4) the establishment of options and strategies for improving product life cycles.

LCA has four stages in its methodology: (1) gathering inventory data for emissions, (2) discharge and waste, (3) impact analysis, impact assessment and (4) the receipt of feedback for improving the environmental profile. There are, however, some problems that exist in LCA. The prioblems are (1) LCA is dependent on the scope to be applied to the situation; (2) it is difficult to compare its data, because different data has different perspectives; (3) issues of disposal and decomposition (some products have been used up economically and sometimes it is environmentally more efficient to throw them away rather than to recycle them); and (4) since property rights do not exist for the environment, exact quantification of environmental damage is subjective (Welford, 1998, p. 146).

John Kotter (2001) explores what business leaders really do for environmental restoration. John Kotter in his paper *What Leaders Really Do* identifies that leadership and management are two distinctive and complementary systems of action. Each has its own function and characteristic activities (p. 3). However, the real challenge is to combine strong leadership and strong management and use each to balance the other, because without good management, complex enterprises tend to become chaotic.

Good management brings a degree of order and consistency to key dimensions like the quality and profitability of products. By contrast, leadership is about coping with change. Usually management develops the capacity to achieve its plan by organizing and staffing that creates an organizational structure. Management ensures plan accomplishment by controlling and problem solving; however, according to the author, leadership activity is about aligning people (p. 4). The central feature of modern organization is interdependence. Businesses that are well lead tend to recognize and reward people who successfully develop leaders.

Senge, Peter M., Art Kleiner, Charlotte Roberts, Richard B. Ross, and Bryan J. Smith (2004) in their papers *Awakening Faith in an Alternative Future: A Consideration of Presence: Human Purpose and the Field of the Future* and *A Conversation on Leadership* identify four major sources of confusion in the area of leadership studies: (1) equating leadership with personality; (2) equality leadership with authority; (3) the tendency to equate leadership with knowledge, and (4) leadership as being value-neutral. Senge et al (2004) say that the term, leadership, it is value-laden. It is suppose to be good and positive. (p. 61). According to them, 'leadership' is to gather and create a community where people can learn from each other. However, his leadership definition is not complete. Because ledear is about an action of leading a group of people or an organization and it is the state or position of being a leader who has the qualities like able to motivate, encourage, guide, organize, direct, administrate and manage people and institution with good governance and command. Moreover, he can influence people with his personal capacity, power and ascendancy quality.

The article *'Engaging the Future'* written by Smith, B. (2006) talks about strategies of engagement for key decision-makers in their businesses. A clear engagement strategy can improve the quality and the capacity of the team's thinking power for the future. Smith states three steps for an effective engagement strategy: (1) seeing past the 'Big Bets' that stimulates an initial conversation about the future strategy among the decision-makers; (2) identifying driving forces that could engage businesses for future potential impact, while monitoring the strategies needed to be adjusted sooner; and (3) creating scenarios that portray a set of imaginative, but plausible stories to describe the world of tomorrow (p. 49).

Waddell, S. (2002) in his article *Six Societal Learning Concepts for a New Era of Engagement* mentions about the societal learning process and its different subtext for the new era of engagement. According to Steven J Waddell, societal learning is associated with individual, groups and organizational learning. It articulates new paradigms that alter the perspectives, goals and behaviors of societal systems larger than particular organizations. It develops new relationships, strategies and organizational structures to address issues such as sustainability, poverty, and cultural clashes.

Steven J Waddell (2002) notes that societal learning involves triple-loop learning, which has six core societal learning concepts for the new era of engagement: (1) Action framework: building societal systems that knit together societal systems and create cross-functional activities in business; (2) appreciating different power sources' (3) dynamic co-production operation through mutual gain among the socially responsible and corporate citizens; (4) collaboration through the spirit of relationship: emphasizing shared power among stakeholders. In collaboration, the general decision-making process is rooted in the concept of consensus; (5) lubricating forces through dialogue and learning. Here, dialogue requires four capacities: voicing, listening, respecting and suspending and last; (6) hard work for an emerging desirable future. Waddell suggests three types of distinct sets of organization for encouraging development and societal earning: business, governmental and civil society (p. 25).

The paper entitled *Including the Stakeholders: The Business Case'* written by Wheeler, D. and Sillanpaa, M. (1998) talks about the effective management of business issues. They identified effective management of business some issues, such as product quality, learning (knowledge transfer) and environmental protection may be achieved in one of two ways. They may be done top-down, based on the development of detailed process prescriptions and individual job specifications; and accomplished within a 'command and control' framework. Alternatively, they may be managed in a spirit of continuous improvement. Wheeler and Silanpaa say, "knowledge-creating organization has both problem solving and enhances the systems towards potential creative forces" (p. 202). Knowledge-creating organization has two basic principles of stakeholder inclusion: (1) Alignment of values, which has two active commitments: (shared perspectives and an active dialogue from collective values) and (2) dialogue-based empowered relationships that can deal with organizational chaos.

D. Wheeler, D. and M. Sillanpaa emphasize the practice of stakeholder inclusion in the business. The key stakeholders of the company are the customers, employees, local communities, suppliers, other business partners and investors. The social stakeholders represent the civil society; however, the non-social stakeholders do not involve human relationships. The social stakeholders and non-social stakeholders should work together for the betterment of the natural environment, non-human species, and future generations. The organizational stakeholders' inclusions of clear policies help provide a framework for quality relationship with the company's stakeholders. Every organization requires a clear long-term vision in order to secure stakeholder commitment. The article places importance on a shared publication statement and dialogue with stakeholders. In order to have a cycle of effective inclusion of stakeholders, it is important that there is effective communication among the stakeholders. Wheeler and Sillanpaa advise that stakeholders' inclusion can be made on the grounds of ethics, public policy, and risk management (p. 209).

9.0. Strategies for implementing the sustainable business corporation

The article *'Implementing the Sustainable Corporation'* written by Dunphy, D. (2000) deals with strategies for implementing sustainable corporation. The sustainability movement addresses the social, economic and political environment of corporations that facilitate sustainable corporation practices. Dunphy identifies six phases in corporate progression towards full sustainability integration and a corporate philosophy of sustainability that abandons the exploitation and degradation of both human and natural resources. Tendency to quick fix to problems, however, created troubles in the rapid transformation of markets, economic deregulation and the globalization of businesses.

Constant change of producing new products increased waste and pollution; however, change prepares the ground for potentially rapid transformation to new sustainable practices. Dunphy says that for transformative change to occur it requires rapid, radical redefinition of the core business; new business strategies and market redefinition; and workplace restructuring and reformulating of a corporations' core culture (p. 265). However, this phenomenon is a paradigm-shifting exercise, requiring courage and visionary leadership. Moreover, the article suggests two important approaches for transformational change: *charismatic transformation* and *turnaround transformation* (p. 91).

In *charismatic transformation*, the change is led by a charismatic leader who inspires and enthuse others to make dramatic changes in the operation of the organization. This model creates high energy for change and maintains the momentum of change in different circumstances. The *turnaround approach* is the alternative path and is a high-risk strategy mounted by committed business elite. Following, are some suggestions made by Dunphy to implement a sustainable corporation: the elimination of societal, organizational or individual rewards for unsustainable practices; the elimination or reduction of unsustainable practices; cost-saving by eliminating wasted products; increased competitive advantage through product or process of innovation; and corporate contribution to overall community welfare. However, the elimination of societal and organizational change is not easy, rather huge radical challenge involve that usually profit oriented business people do not want. Moreover, corporate contribution to community welfare is an imagination. Corporations are private sector businesses who are focus on maximization of profit.

E. Schein first differentiates the types of change that occur in human systems and then provides a model that makes it possible to understand the nature of stability. According to Schein, there are three types of change that occur in all human organizations: (1) natural evolutionary changes (2) planned and managed changes and (3) unplanned revolutionary changes. Again, the author in his article *Models and Tools for Stability and Change in Human Systems* conceptualized three stages in the change process: a stage of unfreezing, a stage of change, and a stage of refreezing. Schein says, "No change will occur unless the system in unfrozen, and no change will last unless the system is refrozen" (Schein, 2002; p. 36). Two change mechanisms need to be considered for human system change: (1) Scanning the environment until a new formulation is found, (2) finding a role model and learning a new viewpoint through psychological identification.

Moreover, Senge, Peter M., Art Kleiner, Charlotte Roberts, Richard B. Ross, and Bryan J. Smith (2004) termed global corporation as a new species on earth who has titanic forces of globalization and information revolution. The industrial-age institutions continue to expand blindly, unaware of their part in a larger system that make people lose their social identity. Here, Senge et al. identifies that the basic problem with global institutions is that they have yet to realize that they are 'living'. In the article, *Awakening Faith in an Alternative Future*, Senge, P. et al. (2004); therefore, suggests an alternative future that can actually open people up (p. 10). Their idea is good; however, they do not specify what would be the alternative future and what are the policies, strategies need to be taken for creating the alternative future.

This article *Searching for a Simpler Way to Lead Organizations* written by M. Wheatley (1994) focuses on the process of discovering and inventing the new organizational forms that will inhabit the twenty-first century. One organizational model cannot change or develop elsewhere. There are not any recipes, nor formulae, nor checklists, nor advice that describes the reality elsewhere. Therefore, it is necessary to reorganize organizations as systems, constructing them as 'learning organizations and crediting them with some type of self-renewing capacity' in different socio-economic and environmental context (p. 13).

J. Ehrenfeld predicts in his article *'Colorless Green Ideas Sleep Furiously: Is the Emergence of "Sustainable" Practices Meaningful?'* that sustainable strategies in the green field will win in the future; however, few new practices are being touted as green. He says, "Sustainability is a radical concept, unavailable within the existing set of institutional and societal action-producing structures within the current dominant social paradigm" (Ehrenfeld, 2000, p. 35).

An alternative way of thinking about sustainability is important, because it is a future vision that constructs human living, forces governments and other institutions to act responsibly in taking care of the future and shares equitable ecological resources to satisfy human needs and human aspirations." According to the author, ideal, sustainable firms should have: (1) a set of sustainability tools to guide actions; (2) operate the same set of policies and standards in every location; (3) maintain high levels of employment and flatten wage discrepancy between management and workers, (4) market services that confirm sustainability principles and understand societal values; (5) focus on services that take account of life cycle impacts over the entire value chain; (6) educate its customers and strategic partners along the entire life-cycle value chain implementation; and (7) publicly report on all of its activities that impinge on sustainability.

The article also talks about eco-efficiency and product stewardship. Eco-efficiency focuses on the inefficiency of material and energy consumption that is prevalent in current practices. It has five core themes: (1) emphasis on service; (2) focus on needs and quality of life; (3) consider the entire product life cycle; (4) recognize eco-capacity; and (5) review the process. Ehrenfeld says, "...product stewardship is a shift in responsibility from merely delivering a product that meets its legal provisions to one that accepts responsibility across the entire product life cycle" (p. 41).

Peter Senge (2003) in his another article *Creating Desired Futures in a Global Economy,* he talks about human local identity vs. alien identity. Previously, people identified with their families, tribes, and local social structures. Today; however, it is the reverse. Human identity looks alien. Previously, people spoke about depleted topsoil, local fishery etc. People paid a price. Today it is called 'sustainability'. Senge differentiates 'creating' from 'problem solving'. In 'creating', people care about their existence, but in 'problem solving' they ignore it. He suggests that organizations must resolve day-to-day problems and generate new results. This day-to-day problem solving process generates new results process that is needed to connect between two missing points: redressing the imbalances in global society in income distribution and that of living systems. Also, it is necessary acknowledging that the need to connect permeates natural and social aspect of the society.

10.0. Implications of the paper

The above mentioned articles, books and my views and debates on business and sustainability management issues and views in different organizational contexts. By reading all of these articles intensely by the author, these literature provided him and possibly readers with critical thinking skills around sustainable management practices and sustainable business development for organizational sustainability. These literatcreative writings offered me as well as readers an overview of public attitudes towards socially and environmentally focused business organizations, social accounting, social auditing for corporate governance, and business social capital. Kazi Rouf personally learned different approaches of stakeholders' management and engagement the application of in different changing situations, and the value of stakeholders' integration in management practices in order to maximize social and environmental benefits.

Moreover, by reading this thematic paper, readers and investors can learn socially responsible ethical investments, global market places and their marketing influence on customers, and green marketing. In addition, this paper also talks (abrupt taken from the above mentioned articles) about different voluntary initiatives for sustainable business management, environmental management systems (EMS) and linked sustainable management to business strategy. In addition, readers can receive ideas about eco-efficiency through eco-innovations, eco-compass-product life cycle analysis: theory and applications of life-cycle inventories of products and service impact assessments, supply chain management, and socially and environmentally responsible purchasing.

Furthermore, the paper can be exposed to readers the role of leadership in stakeholders' inclusion of building social capital and natural capital for competitive advantages in the business world. Some articles speak about organizational change and sustainability dynamics for the development of sustainable organizational culture, leadership development and human resource management to achieve a vision of sustainability. All of the articles abstract and their review can draw sustainable business practitioners' attention towards sustainable business investment practices in their future management roles. Readers and sustainable business practitioners can apply the paper's ideas, concepts and approaches of sustainable business management to their various business practices.

10.0. Conclusion

In conclusion, the paper thinks it can be achieved sustainable business practice goals through engaging in dialogue with related business stakeholders to determine best practices and opportunities for knowledge sharing. Secondly, collaboration and working with business different stakeholders, particularly business owners and businesses employees, academia, green business scholars and public social enterprises to develop innovative business procedure and practices. And thirdly, make connections among them in order to discovering others with similar interest in advancing sustainable business practices and creating a community business of practice. Fourthly, it is necessary educate corporate executives/managers and small/medium business owners with practical social and green business strategies that foster ecological and economic sustainability. Fifthly, it is needed to support the social and green businesses for mushrooming these social businesses. Readers can be knowledgeabled about green business strategies and business owners can be benefited of all these sustiainable business practices notions by reading this paper.

As Brundtland Sustainable Development Report argued that the environment does not exist as a sphere separate from human actions, ambitions, and needs; and attempts to defend it in isolation from human concerns that have given the word "environment" a connotation of naivety in some political circles. Moreover, the word "development" has also been narrowed by some scholars into a very limited focus, along the lines of "what poor nations should do to become richer," and thus again is automatically dismissed by many in the international arena as being a concern of specialists, of those involved in questions of "development assistance." But the "environment" is where we live; and "development" is what we all need to do in attempting to improve our lot within that abode. These two concepts 'development' and 'environment' are inseparable. Therefore, our attention, themes and analysis should around the Brundtland Sustainable Development Report commissioned by OECD and later by the United Nations Conference on Environment and Development (UNCED).

Therefore, it is necessary work with existing businesses and organizations to develop the tools for success in an emerging sustainable economy. In order to achieve triple bottom line social, economic and environmental business practices, business people need a platform where they can create forums and develop speaker series so that it can serve as a forum where business community and other potential business groups can collaborate to remove barriers to achieving ecological and economic sustainability while learning and sharing ideas about sustainable enterprises.

11.0. Bibliography

Adams, C. and Frost, G. (2006). Accessibility and functionality of the corporate Website: Implications for sustainability reporting. *Business Strategy and the Environment*, Vol. 15. pp. 275-287

Anderson, R. (2000). Climbing mount sustainability. *Reflections,* Volume1 (4), pp. 1-20

Annadale, D., Morrison-Sanders, A., and Bouma, G. (2004). The impact of voluntary environmental protection instruments on company environmental performance. *Business Strategy and the Environment*, Vol. 13, pp. 1-12

Barmet, M. (2004). Are globalization and sustainability compatible. *Organization and Environment*, Vol. 17(4), pp. 523-532

Barnet, M. and Salomon, R. (2003). Throwing a curve at socially responsible investing research. *Organization and Environment*, Vol.16(3), pp. 381-389

Bradbury, H. (2000). On the plural attentions necessary for catalyzing and implementing sustainable development. *Reflections*, Vol. 1(4), pp. 13-21

Burnston, F. and Von Malmborg (2002). Environmental Management System, Communicative Action and Organizational Learning. *Business Strategy and the Environment*, Vol. 11. pp. 312-323

Dunphy, D. (2014). *Implementing the sustainable corporation: The corporate challenge of the 21st Century*. Australia: Alen & Unwin Book Publishing. pp. 251-273

Dyllick, T. and Hockerts, K. (2002). *Beyond the cusiness case for Corporate sustainability*. Switzerland: John Wily & Sons, Ltd.

Ehrenfeld, J. (2000). Colorless green ideas sleep furiously: Is the emergence of "Sustainable" practices meaningful? *Reflections*, Vol. 1(4), pp. 34-47

Ehrenfeld, J. (2004). *Searching for sustainability: No quick fix*. Retrieved from WWW.reflections.solonline.org dated October 10, 2017

Ehrenfeld, J. (2005). The roots of sustainability. *MIT Sloan Management Review*, Vol. 46(2), pp. 23-27

Environics Internationals (1999). *The Millennium poll on corporate social responsibility Environics*, Toronto: International Ltd.

Figge, F., Hahn, T., Schallegger, S. and Wagner, M. (2002). The sustainability balanced scorecard- Linking sustainability management to business strategy. *Business Strategy and the Environment*, Vol. 11. pp. 269-284

Frankel, C. (1998). *Whitecaps, green consumers and the infrastructure-building blues*. New Society Publishers, pp. 135-147

Hart, S. (1997). Beyond greening: Strategies for sustainable world. *Harvard Business Review*, pp. 66-76

Hart, S. and Sharma, S. (2004). Engaging fringe stakeholders for competitive imagination. *Academy of Management Executive*, Vol. 18(1), pp. 7-18

Hoopwood, B. Mellor, M. and O'Brien, G. (2005). *Sustainable development: Mapping different approaches*. UK: University of Nothhumbria

Howard, J. Nash, J. and Ehrenfeld, J. (1999). Industry codes as agents of change: Responsible care adoption by US chemical companies. *Business Strategy and the Environment,* Vol. 8, pp. 281-295

Kiernan, M.J. and J.S. Martin (1999). Eco-efficiency warriors. Investments and Pensions, *Europe Magazine,* Vol. 46

Kiernan, M.J. and J.S. Martin 1998. Wake-up call for fiduciaries: Eco-efficiency drives shareholder value. *In Today's Corporate Investor,* pp. 17-18

Kolk, A. (2003). Trends in sustainability reporting by the fortune global 250. *Business Strategy and the Environment,* Vol. 12. pp. 279-291

Kotter, J. (2001). *What leaders really do?* Harvard Business School Publishing Corporation.

Lenox, M. and Nash, J. (2003). Industry self-regulation and adverse selection: A comparison across our trade association programs. *Business Strategy and the Environment,* Vol. 12, pp. 343-356.

McDonagh, W. and Braungart, M. (1998*). The next industrial revolution.* The Atlantic Monthly

McDonald, S. and Oates, C. (2006). *Sustainability: Consumer perceptions and marketing strategies.* Willy Inter-science. Retrieved from WWW.interscience.wiley.com dated October 12, 2017

Paton, B. (2000). Voluntary environmental initiatives and sustainable industry, *Business Strategy and the Environment,* Vol. 9. pp. 328-338.

Peter M. Senge, C. Otto Scharmer, Joseph Jaworski, and Betty Sue Flowers (2004). Awakening faith in an alternative future, *Reflections,* Vol. 5(7), pp. 1-11

Prahalad, K. and Hart, Stuart L. (2002). *The fortune at the bottom of the pyramid:* New York: Columbia Business School

Prakash, A. (2002). *Green marketing, public policy and managerial strategies.* Retrieved from WWW.interscience.willey.com dated October 12, 2017

Raelin, J. (2002). *I don't have time to think" versus the art of reflective practice.* Massachusetts: North Eastern University

Ramus, C. (2005). When are corporate environmental policies a form of greenwashing? *Business and Society*, Vol. 44(4), pp. 377-414

Rouf, K. A. (2018). Concepts, theories, and approaches to management practices for sustainable businesses, *International Journal of Research Studies in Management*, Vol. 7(1), pp. 13-36.

Rouf, K. A. (2018). Views and reviews of the microcredit thoughts and MFIs services in the world. *International Journal of Research Studies in Management*, Vol. 7(2), pp. 1-20.

Schein, Edgar H. (2002). Models and tools for sustainability and change in human systems. *Reflections*. Vol. 4(2), pp. 34-46

Senge, M. Peter, Scharmer, C. AU, Jaworski, Joseph, Sue Flowers, and Betty, P. Y. (2004). Awakening faith in an alternative future: A consideration of presence: Human purpose and the field of the future, *Reflections: The SoL Journal*, Vol. 5, pp. 1-11

Senge, Peter M., Art Kleiner, Charlotte Roberts, Richard B. Ross, and Bryan J. Smith (2003). A conversation on leadership, *Reflections*, Vol. 2(1), pp. 121-136

Senge. P. (2003). Creating desired futures in a global economy, *Reflections* Vol. 5(1), pp. 1-12, Retrieved from www.reflections. solonline.org dated October 12, 2017.

Seuring, S. (2004). Industrial ecology, life cycles, supply chains: Differences and interrelations. *Business Strategy and the Environment*, Vol. 13, pp. 306-319

Sharma, S. (2001). Different strokes: Regulatory styles and environmental strategy in the North American oil and gas industry. *Business Strategy and the Environment*, Vol. 10, pp. 344-364

Simon, M. Poole, S. Evans, S. and McAloone, T. (2000). Environmental priorities in strategic product development. *Business Strategy and the Environment*, Vol. 19. pp. 367-377

Smith, B. (2006). *Engaging the future*. Retrieved from www.reflections. solonline.org dated October 12, 2017

Stoeckl, N. (2004). The private costs and benefits of environmental self-regulation: Which farms have most to gain? *Business Strategy and the Environment*, Vol. 13. pp. 135-155

Susse Georg and Füssel, Lanni (2000). Making sense of greening and organizational change. *Business Strategy and the Environment.* Vol. 9(3), pp. 175-185

Tregidga, H. and Miline, M. (2006). From sustainable management to sustainable development: a longitudinal analysis of a leading New Zealand environmental reporter. *Business Strategy and the Environment,* Vol. 15. pp. 219-241

Velva, V. and Ellenbecker, M. (2000). A proposal for be assuring business sustainability. *Greener Management International,* Vol. 31, pp. 101-120

Waddell, S. (2002). Six societal learning concepts for a new-era of engagement. The society for organizational learning and the Massachusetts Institute of Technology. *Reflections,* Vol. 3(4), pp. 18-26

Welford, R. (1998). Life Cycle Assessment: Environmental management 1, *Business Strategies and the Environment,* Vol. 1(7), pp. 1-12

Wheatley, M. (1994). *Searching for a simpler way to lead organizations.* California: Berrett-Koehler Publishers.

Wheeler, D. and Elkington, J. (2001). The end of the corporate environmental report? *Business Strategy and the Environment,* Vol. 10, pp. 1-14

Wheeler, D. and Sillanpad, M. (1998). Including the stakeholders: The business Case. *Long Range Planning,* Vol. 32(2), pp. 201-210

Wilson, W.G. and Sasseville, D. R. (1999). *Environmental management* system. John Wiley & Sons Ltd., pp. 63-77

Compare and Contrast NGOs/ MFIs Developed Social Safety Net Services (SSNs) in Bangladesh and State Managed SSNs Measures in Canada

Abstract

Social safety net (SSN) measures are usually managed by the state for the vulnerable people like seniors, physically and mentally disability diagnosed people, vulnerable widowed and people living with the economic crisis. Recently many NGOs of Bangladesh have developed social safety net services for the vulnerable poor people in Bangladesh. The paper is an attempt to find out (1) what are the SSNs measures are taken by NGOs/ MFIs in Bangladesh and how they work; (2) to discern what are the state managed Canadian SSNs services that have served to Canadian vulnerable people and or people living with economic crisis; and (3) compare and contrast SSNs strategies governed by NGOs/MFIs in Bangladesh and public agencies have managed in Canada. This study follows descriptive ethnographic and participatory observation methods working with Grameen Bank and BRAC Bangladesh as well as researcher working experience with Toronto Social Services and Ontario Disability Support Services in Canada. Study uses secondary data and reviews works of literature to provide evidence of the narrations.

The research finds Grameen Bank, BRAC and Nijera Kori Bangladesh have developed different SSNs services for vulnerable people in Bangladesh as an alternative of the state-managed SSNs services although Bangladesh Government has initiated many SSNs services through its public and external resources. However, government supported SSNs services are yet not massively reached to all vulnerable people in Bangladesh who have suffered from poverty. Contrarily, Canada SSNs programs are universally followed by the Social Acts of Canada. The Canadian SSN many services have reached massively to its vulnerable population to address their social and economic crisis and poverty. However, SSNs financial supports have not complied with the rise of prices in Canada at different time. By reading this paper, readers could learn different social security measures developed by NGOs and MFIs in Bangladesh and the state managed SSNs measures in Canada that are narrated in the paper.

Key words: BRAC-IGVGD program; Bayashka Vatha; Canada Universal Health Care; Employment Insurance; Food for Works, Food for Education; Food vouchers, Old Age Pension; Grameen Bank baggers loan services; Grameen Bank Emergency Fund; Grameen Healthcare Program; Grameen Pension Scheme; Grameen higher education loans; National Childcare Benefits; Ontario Disability Support Program; School Feeding Program; Social Housing; and VimoSEWA; Zakat.

1. Introduction

There has been a greater diversification of social protection coverage through a combination of government, and non-governmental provisions in different countries. For example, in Bangladesh private sector business organizations, private banks and private foundations donate funds to the Prime Minister Relief Funds. This money is using to provide relief to flood victims, drought rehabilitation, and other natural disasters. The Bangladesh Islamic Bank donates a million of dollars to the government agencies for public relief and rehabilitation programs. Grameen Bank, BRAC and other NGOs have developed social security measures for the destitute women and poor people for overcoming their poverty; many NGOs have health care services for the poor at lower costs that assist them to receive medical services for their family members. Although recently developing countries are destined towards a western welfare state model, the paper explores areas of organizations contributing to social safety net measures in Bangladesh; find out organizations contributing to social policy inputs including non-state private, NGOs/MFIs, international NGOs and public institutions; and narrates comprehensive set of concepts of different social protection systems. On the other hand, Canada has Universal Health Care Services to its all citizens. Canada also has social assistance 'income support program' which is given only to those who have exhausted all other avenues of support and can prove they are in need (Raphael, 2007).

The Welfare State Services of Canada is unique and world-famous. Moreover, Canada has private health insurance like Blue Cross is providing life insurance coverage to its clients. However, Canada non-state and non-market organizations are peripheral within a welfare mix contribution to public welfare. The Center for Policy Dialogue (CPD) Bangladesh calls it 'semi-public' safety net measures. This paper explores what are the public, private and NGOs social safety net measures exists in Bangladesh and in Canada. Moreover, the paper talks about social policy of Bangladesh that has wider concepts that are different from the conventional western social policy state funded. The purpose of writing this paper is also to inform the readers' about different initiatives of social protection measures taken by different public institutions, private foundations and NGOs/MFIs, and how bottom people particularly destitute women are benefiting from these institutional services in Bangladesh and Canada.

Both Bangladesh and Canada have acknowledged welfare investments are the investments in 'human capital' to uplift the bottom people's sustainable development in their livelihoods. There is a lively debate about state sponsored social safety net services and non-state social protection measures. For example, when the welfare management approach is brought into the Bangladesh context, a few more social safety net measures are introduced by the government's own funds, international funding support to government and NGOs/MFIs services to bottom people. Canadian social safety net services mostly from public institutions. Even though usually, state sponsor Canada welfare system recently acknowledge both state, labour market, family and NGOs contributions, community based organizations in the field of social safety measures, public financing support and governing still in is predominant.

2. Objectives of the study

(1) To find out what are the SSNs measures are taken by NGOs/ MFIs in Bangladesh and how they work;
(2) To discern what are the state managed SSNs services in Canada that have served to Canadian vulnerable people and or people living with economic crisis; and
(3) To compare and contrast SSNs strategies governed by NGOs/ MFIs in Bangladesh and publicly managed SSNs services in Canada;
(4) To explore what are the challenges they are facing in providing social safety nets services to their citizens; and
(5) The paper also discerns the history of social security measures taken by different countries in the world.

3. Methodologies

This study follows descriptive ethnographic and participatory observation methods working with Grameen Bank and BRAC Bangladesh as well as Toronto Social Services (TSS) and Ontario Disability Support Services (ODSP) in Canada. The study uses secondary data and review literature to provide evidence of the narrations.

4.0. Meaning of social safety nets

The Social security is basic human rights (Chappell, 2006; Hick, 2004; Pal, 1987; Raphael, 2007; Rice & Michael (2000); and Sobhan, 2004).

Social safety nets are programs that offer protection to poor people by providing income through cash transfer programs, subsidies on staple foods and other items, employment services to unemployed people by the employment support agencies for developing their social capital and human capital development (Chappell, 2006; Epstein, 1980; Eichler, 1987; Findlay, 1983; Hossain & Ali, 2012; Hussain & Mahbub, 1995; Mahmud, 2004; Raphael, 2007; Steinhauer, 1995; and Zhiqin, 2002). Social security is the protection that a society provides to individuals and households to ensure access to healthcare and to guarantee income security is an essential element of the safety net that keeps working people and their families from failing into poverty. Social safety nets are part and parcel of social development (Clarke, 1991; Feit & Feit, 1996; Laliberte, 1998; Mahmud, 2004; and Raphael, 2007). In 2001, the ILO Conference defined principles and approaches of basic social security. It is considered that there is no single right model of social security, and that priority should be given to policies and initiatives that can bring social security to those who are not covered by existing systems. Social security should promote and be based on the principle of gender equality. This program should be open to all who are eligible. The World Bank finds social safety net programs protect families from the impact of economic shocks, disasters, and other crises.

According to Business Dictionary, it is the social welfare services provided by a community of individuals at the state and local levels. These services are geared toward eliminating poverty in a specific area. Social safety net works in conjunction with a number of other poverty reduction programs with the primary goal of reducing/preventing poverty. Social safety nets and anti-poverty programs have overlapping target populations particularly in Bangladesh. The targets of social safety nets are those people adversely affected by natural or economic crises or sudden shocks, accidents who mostly are poor people. They are the same people who are the targets of anti-poverty programs (Science Direct). Social safety net is a social protection systems help the poor and vulnerable cope with crises and shocks, find jobs, invest in the health and education of their children, and protect the aging population.

Social safety net programs are crucial to ensure that all groups of the population have reasonable access to minimal income and basic social services in the event of diverse contingencies such as involuntary unemployment, old age or sudden natural and economic crisis. Fewer than 10 percent of people in the poorest countries have social security coverage. This has an enormous impact on their lives and on work itself (Hossain & Ali, 2012; Kabir, 2007).

According to the ADB's definition of social protection contains five components: 1) labor market policies and programs designed to facilitate labor adjustments and promote the efficient operation of labour markets, (ii) social insurance programs to cushion the risks associated unemployment, disability, sickness, maternity, work injury, and old age, (iii) social assistance and welfare service programs to provide a floor for those with no other means of adequate support, (iv) Micro and Area-based Schemes to cushion the risk to agricultural incomes from crop failure or temporary market disruptions, and address reduction of risk and vulnerability at the community level: and (v) Child Protection. Of the five components, the first three (labour markets, social insurance and social assistance) are normally included in any social protection strategy. Recently a growing number of developing countries are investing in social safety nets to improve the lives and livelihoods of billions of poor and vulnerable people. Safety net programs include cash and in-kind transfers targeted to poor and vulnerable households, with the goal of protecting families from the impact of economic shocks, natural disasters, and other crises. Yet in low-income countries around the world one in five of the world's poor still lack safety net coverage.

4.1. What is the role of safety net?

Safety net programs have two key functions in economic policy. Their traditional role is to redistribute income and resources to the needy in society, helping them overcome short-term poverty. More recently identified role for safety nets is to help households manage risk (Rahman & Hossain, 1995; Raphael, 2007; and Rice & Michael, 2000). Safety nets can increase options for the poor. Safety nets can bring potentially higher returns to poor households, such as growing high yielding varieties of crops and using modern farming methods particularly in Bangladesh. When hard times hit households, safety nets reduce the need to make hasty decisions that diminishes the chances of escaping poverty in the long run. At the national level, if sound safety nets are in place, the pension program can focus on improving the efficiency of providing benefits to contributing workers rather than finding ways to provide cash transfers to those who have not made adequate contributions. Recently Canada moving towards SSN institutional approach instead residual approach in Canada

4.2. Why safety nets needed?

The elderly and disabled are often more immediate threatening than those faced by others in society (Feit & Feit, 1996; Rahman & Hossain, 1995). These risks can be either household (i.e., illness, disability or death and unemployment), community based (i.e., floods, famine) or nationwide drought, global financial risk or shift in terms of trade) (Hossain & Ali, 2012). The adverse effects of these risks can be found in Bangladesh and will be far more damaging to the poor than those better-off in terms of income, physical and mental well-being, and long-term human development. For example, in Bangladesh, poor people, low income people may force them to sell their land, their livestock or their tools, send their children to work rather than to school, or eat less. These drastic measures may help families survive from day-to-day, but they will make it that much harder for these families to escape poverty in the future (Hussain & Ali, 2012; Kabeer, 1997; Mahmud, 2004; and Raphael, 2007).

Governments and international financial institutions play an important role in helping households manage daily risks and cope with losses when they occur. The notion that safety nets should be a permanent feature of social policy and not simply a temporary response to crisis is increasingly being embraced by the international development community. But, even when a country prospers, some households will face hard times. During economic downturns, such as the Asian financial crisis and crises in Latin America, problems are much more serious and immediate and the appeals for public action undeniable (Mishra, 1999).

5. Different models of social safety net program in the world

Many Asian countries rely on traditional safety nets provided by family or community. However, the traditional, informal social safety network has gradually diminished with increased industrialization and urbanization. However, according to most researchers, the comprehensive welfare system is the best form of social safety net where the state provides all kinds of social security to its citizens like Canada. It is remarked that it is the left-wing who argued for government provision of welfare. But, Bismarck's government in Germany in the 1880s is actually the first to initiate steps towards a welfare state. These views are reflected in the Kaiser's announcement that: "the cure of social ills must be sought not exclusively in the repression of Social Democratic excess, but simultaneously in the positive advancement of the welfare of the working masses" from Rimlinger-Welfare Policy Industrialization in Europe, America and Russia-Wiley, New York (Chappell, 2006; Hick, 2004). Ensuring workers' basic needs is one of the main motives behind the introduction of the welfare state. Further justification for it is outlined by the Beveridge Report in Britain, which formed the basis of Britain's post-war policy and influenced the development of welfare in other countries. It emphasized the need to preserve the population's morale and efficiency in wartime and to help offset of any social discontent after the war (Briggs, 2006; Chappell, 2006, and Raphael, 2007). After World War 11, spending on welfare rose under several non-left governments who all unambiguously stated their belief in it-McMillan in Britain Adenaur in West Germany, de Graulle in France, and Nixon and Kennedy in the US. The social and economic reasons for introducing the welfare state are thus apparent to governments of all colors. However, difficulties soon arose. The continuous rises in economic growth and prosperity which is expected after the war evaporated, particularly from the late 1960s onward reconstruction, has run its course with the return of world slumps (Briggs, 2006; Chappell, 2006; Ralphael, 2004).

The welfare state became more difficult to finance out of sustained economic growth at exactly the time the burdens of poverty and unemployment placed increasing demands on it. Idea of the 'welfare state' means the state accepts responsibility for the provision, where the state accepts responsibility for the provision of comprehensive and universal welfare for its citizens. However, in many welfare states, social protection is not delivered by the state at all, but by a combination of independent, voluntary and government services. Asa Briggs (2006) mentions British welfare state, identified three principal elements: a guarantee of minimum standards, including a minimum income; social protection in the event of insecurity; and the provision of services at the best level possible. This has identified the 'institutional' model of welfare: the key elements are social protection, and the provision of welfare services on the basis of right. In practice, social welfare in the United Kingdom is very different from this ideal.

The German social market social safety net measures initiated in the post-war German settlement, which is based on the idea of a 'social state', sometimes rendered as a 'special market economy'. Here the central idea is the general concern to ensure that public expenditure on welfare is directly compatible with the need for economic development and growth. Second, the German economy, and the welfare system, developed through a corporate structure. This principle is developed by Bismarck on the basis of existing mutual aid associations and remained the basis for social protection subsequently. Social insurance, which covers the costs of health, some social care and much of the income maintenance system, is managed by a system of independent funds. Third, there is a strong emphasis on the principle of subsidiarity. This principle is taken in Germany to mean both that services should be decentralized or independently managed and that the level of state intervention should be residual- that is, limited to circumstances which are not adequately covered in other ways (Briggs, 2006; Chappell, 2006). Higher earners are not covered by the main social insurance system, but are left to make their own arrangements.

The French social protection model is called 'solidarity and insertion' social protection. Social protection in French is based on the principle of Solidarity: The commitment is declared in the first article of the French Code of Social Security. This idea refers to cooperative mutual support. Some terms it 'mutualist' group (friendly societies) that emphasis that people insured within national schemes are called to contribute and benefit on an equal footing. The French system of welfare is a complex, patchwork quilt of services. However, recent French policy has controlled the expenditure of the social protection. Here the main areas of concern are not dependency or unemployment, but pensions because market-led services present considerable problems in cost control (Kabir, 2004).

Sweden social safety net model is called the institutional redistribution model. Canada is following this model with modification. It is seen as an ideal form of 'welfare state', offering institutional care in the sense that it offers universal minima to its citizens. It goes further than the British Model in its commitment to social equality. Social protection is not necessarily associated with equality; the French and the German systems offer differential protection according to one's position in the labor market. The Swedish system has many of the same characteristics: "selective by occupational experience". However, the importance of equality-sometimes identified with 'solidarity', in the sense of organized co-operation. The model of this is the 'solidaristic wage policy' advocated by the labour movement, which emphasized improving standards, limited differentials and redistribution (Briggs, 2006; Kabir, 2004).

The United States has also a safety net measures described as a Liberal welfare, in the sense that it represents individualism, laissez-faire, residual and a punitive view of poverty. These issues often seem to dominate US debates on welfare: Examples are the introduction of 'workfare', the exclusion of long-term benefit dependents, and the criticism of the under classes. The US does not; however, have a unified welfare system. For example, Minnesota and Hawaii have state-funded health systems (Kazemipur, 2001). By comparison with other developed countries, US central government has a limited role in social welfare provision; the main developments of federal provision are during the Roosevelt administration of the 1930s, which laid the foundations for the social security system, and the 'War on poverty' of the 1960s, which provided some important benefits (notably health care for people on low incomes) and engaged the federal government in a wide variety of projects and activities at local level. These are significant departures from the residual model-state schooling, social insurance or the Veterans' Administration, which provides health care for nearly 40 million people in US (Briggs, 2006; Kazemipur, 2001; and Ralphael, 2007).

The social policy of the European Union the emphasis of community social policy changed towards improving 'living and working conditions' in the community and to include workers who are not part of the labour force. The EUC approach to the development of policy is based on the incremental development of services, the progressive expansion of solidarity and the insertion of those who are excluded (Midshra, 1999; Kabir, 2004).

Social policy in developing countries is to reduce poverty because nearly half of the world's population lives on less than $2 a day. For Amartya Sen, poverty stems not just from a lack of resources, but from lack of entitlement: Famines happen, not because there is not enough food, but because poor people are not allowed to eat the food that is there. Economic development is essential for welfare; however, economic growth creates social inequality and division in the society.

He provokes for the economic development that promotes integration and interdependence and extends people's entitlements. It has clearly beneficial effects on social welfare. Access to basic amenities like water supplies and fuel, and the provision of services like health care and education increased, but these facilities equally do not provide benefit to bottom people. Rather, poor people become vulnerable through economic growth in the developing countries. It led to social polarization in the society everywhere in the world. For example, the structural adjustment policy favored by international organizations are moving to developing countries towards a formal market economy pushing developing countries into a situation where poor is unprotected. Even the economic development does not guarantee social protection. Some countries initiated social security schemes, but a few people receive effective protection for a short period. For example, Vayaska Vatta yet to massively served to seniors in Bangladesh.

Social safety can play an important role in alleviating poverty and promoting a long-term growth by providing households with the protection those markets and informal networks may not supply (Mahmud, 2004; and Yunus, 2008). A social safety may redistribute resources towards disadvantaged groups. Unfortunately, the growing awareness of the importance social safety nets in developing countries has not been translated into effective action because of the failure of traditional social welfare ministries to effectively reach and engage the poor (Kabir, 2004). This led to experimentation with new bottom-up service delivery options and poverty alleviation mechanisms that more actively involve the poor and their communities in program design, implementation and monitoring. Examples are reforms that decentralize the delivery of public services to local government, community management of forests and other natural resources, and group-based micro-credit programs.

The Demand-driven social funds that aim by design to elicit community involvement have become increasingly popular with governments and donors, and international organizations. For example, the World Bank now make community participation social safety net program as an explicit criterion for funding approval for a growing list of social safety net projects (Kabir, 2004; World Bank, 2018; and World Food Program, 1998).

Food stamps, vouchers and coupons are another mechanism used to deliver an income transfer for a target population. Because they are linked to food, they also tend to increase food consumption more than a cash transfer. Such instruments may restrict beneficiaries to buying only a few specific foods or allow them buy any food in the market. The vouchers or stamps may be demonstrated in cash value or in terms of quantities. The food stamp program can only be implemented in countries with a well-developed commercial retail sector, a solid banking system, and public faith in the government's ability to back the value of the stamp. Only few countries like Jamaica, Honduras, Sri Lanka, Mexico, Colombia and the US have tried to implement them (Kabir, 2004; Mishra, 1999).

Consumer food subsidies operate by lowering the price of certain food stuffs, ideally inferior foods (that is, foods consumed by the poor but not by better-off households). Some subsidy programs ration the quantity that may be purchased at the subsidized price to control costs, with additional quantities available on the open market at higher prices. This approach also reduces the incentive for a black market in the subsidized food to emerge. After independence (1973-1977) of Bangladesh, there was a huge food crisis in Bangladesh and the food price was skyrocketed. Many municipalities of Bangladesh had distributed rice, wheat, sugar, and soybean oils on weekly basis at fewer prices by issuing ration card to households of the municipal dwellers. The qualities of rice, wheat were very poor. The author had gone to collect ration food every Monday morning from Chokbazar, Chittagong dealer shop in 1973-1977. Author had waited for a long to collect this rationed food, but this had disturbed his studies in Grade 11-12. Many people had suffered from intestinal diseases eating these low quality foods.

Emergency feeding programs are implemented to protect lives and livelihoods when food entitlements decline following the disruption of production and market due to armed conflict, natural disasters, or other causes of acute for insecurity. Although emergency supplementary food should ideally be distributed at the community level to prevent distress migration, it is most often disbursed from a centralized distribution point to populations who have already disposed of their productive assets and migrated as a last resort (Hossain & Ali, 2012; Kabeer, 2002). When food provided in camps for refugees or internally displaced persons (IDPs), emergency feeding may replace rather than supplement the household diet (Hossain & Ali, 2012; Kabir, 2004). Many of the subsidized ration programs are created during World War 11 as a provisioning mechanism rather than as anti-poverty programs. In the US, both the Food Stamp Program and direct food distribution program are originated as outlets for surplus disposal during the Depression. Mother and Child Health (MCH) supplementary feeding is designed more than therapeutic intervention than as part of a safety net. Food for Work Programs evolved where governments lacked cash and food aid is available. For example, Maharashtra Employment Guarantee Scheme in India uses this program for lack of cash for the targeted people.

5.1. Social safety net by religions

In all Muslim countries, people give donations and reliefs to poor people that is a part of Iman, next to obligatory prayer. Islam has built-in many social safety net donations and measures like Zakat, Sadaqah, Fitrah and Korjee Hasana as part of religious obligation of the Muslims. Zakat, Fitra and Sadaqah are mandatory to rich people to donate to his neighboring poor. Zakat is an obligatory payment (tax) made annually under Islamic law on certain kinds of property and used for charitable and religious purposes that is next after prayer (salat) in importance. Zakat is one of the most important pillars of Islam. It is mandatory for every Muslim who is financially stable to pay zakat to the poor and needy. Fitra is a charity given to the poor at the end of the fasting in the Islamic holy month of Ramadan. Sadaqah, meaning 'charity', is the concept of voluntary giving in Islam sadaqah encompasses any act of charitable giving done out of compassion, love, friendship or generosity. In every Mosque and Madrasa put donation boxes where affordable people donate money as Zakat, Fitrah and Sadaqah for poor people. Moreover, likewise, every religion has voluntary donation program that endorses a part of religious reward and public well being. In Sikh religion, Langorkhana (religious food house) attached in every Sikh temple. Christian religion has Salvation Funds for feeding poor and providing relief to natural disaster victims. These are all social safety net measures that are serving to poor people in the community everywhere in the world.

6. Social safety net programs supported by international agencies

The World Bank (2018) strategy mentions sustainable and affordable safety net programs can protect families from shocks; assist to ensure that children grow up healthy, well-fed, and stay in school and learn; empower women and girls; and create jobs. Building sustainable and affordable safety nets in each developing country is a key component of the World Bank's Social Protection and Labor Strategy 2012-2022. This model of social safety net is helping countries move from fragmented and token programs to affordable social protection systems that enable individuals to manage risk and improve resilience by investing in human capital development and improving people's ability to access jobs.

For example, Uruguay's food program for the poor children and elderly, Indonesian target-based programs, Panama's school–feeding program, Albanian social assistance, Uzbekistan's Mahalla development and Argentina's Trabajar program are some activities that have been acclaimed all over the world who are contributing to vulnerable people's social protection although some are still token (Kabir, 2004). World Bank finds social safety nets have positive and significant impacts on education, health, and food security as well as promote households' ability to generate income that can lead to positive effects in local economies. For example, to respond to the extreme drought in the Southern Africa region, cash transfers have become the primary response to support the recovery of disaster-affected population in Lesotho, Madagascar, Malawi and Mozambique (World Bank, 2018).

Ethiopia's Productive Safety Net Program reaches about eight million poor people. Analysis shows that the direct effect of payments reduces poverty by 7%. In Madagascar, with support from the World Bank's Fund for the Poorest (IDA), cash transfers were provided to more than 80,000 poor households, while promoting nutrition, early childhood development, children school attendance and productive activities of families. In Peru, the Juntos cash transfer program helped address chronic malnutrition, reducing childhood stunting rate in half in just 8 years, from 28% in 2008 to 13% in 2016 (Hussain & Ali, 2012). Even in the Philippines, the country's conditional cash transfer program has reached 4.4 million families, covering 21% of the vulnerable population. The program has successfully kept poor children in school. And for children who are part of the program, it helped reduce stunting by 10% (Kabir, 2007).

Asian countries hit by the 1997 economic crisis. These countries have social insurance schemes such as health care, vocational injury compensation, and pension. Over time, each of those countries has developed social insurance schemes of varying levels of coverage and generosity. However, it is difficult to say that social insurance in Indonesia, Malaysia, Thailand and Philippines plays a role as a safety net due to the low ratio of insurance premium contributors to total labour force or to total population. Among these countries, Malaysia has social insurance schemes that are the most advanced, but it does not mean that these insurance schemes function as a safety net for all Malayans (Isabel, 2001 and Kabir, 2004).

Asian Development Bank (ADB) thinks well-designed labor market policies may serve the majority of the active population of a country.

For example, households in the formal sector may be reached by structured social insurance, crop insurance and social assistance, including child protection. However, those in the informal sector like family or households supports are more likely to be reached by less structured social assistance, child protection, micro-insurance, social funds and other community-based programs. The family, household and kinship support services are less expensive and easily available to family and household members as when they needed.

Traditional family-based care for the elderly has broken down in many developing countries without adequate formal mechanisms to take its place. For the elderly, inadequate transfers from either formal pension systems or from informal family and community transfers can severely reduce their ability to cope with illness or poor nutrition. In low-income countries, only one in nine workers contributes to a pension program (Kabir, 2007). This proportion has remained stagnant for decades, affecting their ability to receive adequate pension benefits. The World Bank has been involved in pension reform in more than 90 countries and provided financial support for reform to more than 70 countries. The World Bank has collaboration with various development partners in building strong pension systems in developing countries. Researchers find predictable Cash grants to poor households are one of the most effective poverty reduction strategies. Moreover, the World Bank Group is ensuring that individuals have access to quality education and training opportunities for skills development that can reduce unemployment, raise incomes, and improve standards of living.

The Lao People's Democratic Republic is one of the least developed countries in Asia, with half of its population of 5 million living below the poverty line and 85% of its workforce in the agricultural sector. International Labour Organization (ILO) helps the government design a national social security plan that is currently being implemented in the capital city, Vientiane. The scheme covers 70% of private sector workers in Vientiane and provides pensions (retirement benefits and death benefits) and short-term payouts for maternity, employment injury and sickness (Kabir, 2004). The scheme also includes health coverage based on contributions from employers and workers. However, the country has yet not expanded social security plan to agricultural and informal economy.

Interesting social safety nets exist in sub-Saharan countries and Muslim countries. For example, labor exchange is common in sub-Saharan Africa; and Zakat, Fitra, Sadaque- charitable given safety net tend to be focused on emergent situations caused by socio-economic crisis or natural disaster in Muslim countries.

7. 0. Social safety nets services in different countries

The Netherlands has complex relationship between providers and sponsors. A good example of the potential complexity in the relationship between providers and sponsors is the Dutch disability Act (WAO) introduced in 1969. It intends is to provide a social benefit to persons who become disabled and lose their capacity to earn. In the original institutional design of the Act, persons were entitled to receive a benefit of maximum 80 percent of the last earned wage after being ill for more than 12 months and after being accepted as disabled by a controlling physician and the provider named "bedijfsvereniging". The benefits are defined as entitlements and are paid out of a general fund common to all providers (this means providers are financed by a flexible capitation grant and financed by nationwide uniform premiums paid by employers and workers. It is executed by Social Security Council Sociale Verzekerinsraa). Both the Bedrijifsvereningingen (provider) and Sociaale Verzekeringsraaad (governance) are controlled by the labor unions and the employer-federations (Chappell, 2006; Hussain & Ali, 2012; Ralphael, 2007). The program is popular and received one million of people got disabled benefits. However, the cost is very high and part of the disabled are not defined as disabled. The reformed Act finds the maximum benefit under the disability act was 10 percent higher than the maximum benefit under the unemployment act: so benefits are lowered.

In Maxico to address the "Tequila Crisis" which began in 1994, developed both the short run and long term safety net measures for access to the social services needed by the working poor (Miller, 2000). Usually the safety net as a whole provides coverage to three different groups: (1) the chronic poor-even in 'good times' (2) the transient poor-lives near the poverty line, (3) those with special circumstances- sub–groups of the population stem from disability, discrimination due to ethnicity, displacement due to conflict, social "pathologies" of drug and alcohol abuse, domestic violence or crime (Kabir, 2004). These groups may need special programs to help them attain a sufficient standard of well being. Brazil is using 'social pensions' to fight poverty. Brazil has been steadily improving its pension system, with the goal of reducing poverty among the country's elderly population. A key element of this initiative is tax-financed 'social pensions", targeted primarily to rural areas, to provide coverage to people who do not participate in the more traditional contributory plans that cover many of the country's salaried workers in both the private and public workers (Schwarzer, & Querino, 2002). These social pensions provide the equivalent of the minimum wage to elderly beneficiaries. Nearly 80% of Brazilians over age 60 live in families that receive pension benefits. Recently social benefit age has reduced from 65 to 60 years of age for men and to 55 for women.

Tunisia is striving for universal coverage in social security: Tunisia succeeded in raising social security coverage for healthcare, old age pensions, maternity and employment injury-from 60% to 84% of its workers and their families in just ten tears (Chaabane, 2002). Nearly all Tunisians who work in the public and private non-agricultural sectors are now covered. Recently, Tunisia includes casual and seasonal agricultural workers, construction workers in labour intensive public works programs, domestic workers and the unemployed in social security coverage program.

The author had been working in Namibia through UNDP from 1998-2001. Its different social safety net programs designed during this period. However, it has excellent health care facilities received from its pre-independence regime. Now it has established its social security system. The present system consists of tax-financed benefits, administered by the Ministry of Health and Social Services and paid universally to people over age 60, as well as invalids and disabled people who are younger. Additionally, the ILO has worked with Namibia's Social Security Commission to create a national social insurance scheme, financed by contributions from employers and workers and providing income security in the event of sickness, maternity and of a breadwinner. Within this system, a pension scheme is being planned to supplement the tax-financed universal pension. The universal pension contribution is \$25 a month per person is a major source of economic support to Namibia's impoverished communities. The Ministry of Social Development issues "Smart Cards" with the beneficiaries' photograph and a fingerprint that can be immediately verified by a machine. Pension is the only regular cash income in many rural households (Schleberger, 2002). The pension provides the source of financing for basic items like school fees and machines. Author visited a King's house (traditional leader) in the North of Namibia, and he found behind the king's house there are many big buckets full of grains. The king told these grains are reserved for the victims who are suffered from famine during drought. Farmers have given their 5% of their produced crops to the king's grain reserve program. This is an example of an informal food security system in Africa for the famine victims of the tenants of the king.

Uruguay has both public and Private Sector involvement in food program targeted to school aged children. Uruguay Food program is for poor children and for elderly. The programs call 'Programa Nacional de Complementacion Alimentaria (PNCA)', 'Programa Nacional de Complementacion Alimentaria- Materno infantil (PNCA-M' and Programa Nacional de Complementacion Alimentaria-Pansionistas (PNCA-P). These two programs have many common characteristics; the benefit and nutritional content are largely similar, and the food baskets are distributed in a PNCA center which delivers food for beneficiaries of both programs. Nevertheless, the incidence of these two programs is very different, with 84.6 percent of the PNCA-M reaching the poorest quintile of the population, but only 39 percent of the PNCA-P reaching that quintile. The main difference between the programs lies in the determination of eligibility. While the PNCA-M uses the health card to identify eligible individuals, the PNCA-P requires a certificate issued by the BPS (Banco de Prevision Sociale- Social Security Institution) system to determine an individual's entitlement to receive the benefit. The health care card (Carnet de Salud) indicates self-reported household income and occupational characteristics and is used as a targeting device in the PNCA-M program (Kabir, 2004).

This health card is issued by the Ministry of Health of Uruguay to individuals who cannot pay for their services in public healthcare facilities and upon completion of the monthly health check-up the mother and her children are then entitled to receive the food basket in the PNCA center. This increases not only the targeting performance of the feeding program, but also improves the health situation among the poor. Indonesia is targeting safety net program to local needs and condition. Indonesian safety net program has two types: one is "cheap rice" (OPK) program and the labour-intensive public works program "Padat Karya" program (Kabir, 2004). Both programs are based on people's local conditions and needs. In cheap rice program, targeted poor families identified by the National Planned Parenthood Coordination Agency using a standard set indicators. Poor would be considered if the family has (household) wealth equivalent to ten cows, but these criteria also debatable. The second criteria the labour-intensive public works faces similar problem of poor identification (Irawan, 2001). For example, it was found that in some areas it is a very popular program because it generates additional income for the poor family. However, in other areas it does not yield the expected results. This program undermined the tradition on voluntary collective work (Gottong royong), making people less willing to participate in cheap rice public works program safety net scheme. From the designed program experience, Indonesia again needs to be tailored this safety net program to local needs.

7.1. Social Security System in the Republic of Korea

The Republic of Korea has four major social insurance systems (a) Industrial Accident Compensation Insurance, Health Insurance (1964); (b) Medical Insurance (1977); (c) National Pension (1988); and (d) Employment Insurance (1995). In response to the massive unemployment that struck the domestic labour market before the system matured, the public works arrangements and loan programs are put in place to supplement the existing system. The current safety nets in Korea; therefore, are characterized into two layers: The primary layer of the social insurance scheme comprising the above four social insurance systems and the secondary layer of the protection mechanism consisting of passive labour market policies, public assistance (APEC, 2001; Bark & Hwang, 2006).

Social Insurance of Korea program has the employment insurance is introduced in July 1995 to cover firms with 30 or more employees, and it is extended to cover all full-timers, temporary workers and part-times as of October 1998. The national pension system has been supporting the livelihood of the unemployed by decreasing the minimum contribution period for benefit entitlement from the previous 20 years to 10 years in 1999 (APEC, 2001).

Health insurance is introduced in 1977 in Korea and expanded to cover the self-employed in rural areas in January 1988, and the urban self-employed in July 1988, thus, providing universal coverage. The annual benefit period is also extended continuously: 270 days/year (1997), 300 days/year (1998, 330 days/year (1999) and 365 days/year (2000). However, the burden of equity paying is decreasing the minimum contribution period for benefit entitlement from 20 years to 10 years in 1999. 2.5 percent of the total households are covered by these benefits (APEC, 2001). Moreover, Korea also developed the industrial injury insurance, implemented in 1964, is a system that pays benefits to those employees with sickness or injuries arising out of duty from its fund financed by employers' contributions. This is applied only to workers at firms with more than 500 employees during its initial phase, the current insurance system (as of July 2000) covers every worker in the country, including the self-employed (Bark & Hwang, 2006; and Kabir, 2004).

The Korean National Basic Livelihood Security system has introduced in 1999 that has helped those living under absolute poverty, irrespective of their ability and age (APEC, 2001). However, the livelihood protection system is too limited to surmount the large-scale economic crisis. Moreover, this public pension scheme has been widely criticized for inefficiency in dealing with mass unemployment since its inception. Korea has an employment insurance system (EIS). The EIS is financed by employer and employee contributions. Current contribution rate for the unemployment benefits program amounts to one per cent of the total payroll (0.5 per cent from employers and .5 per cent from employees). The contribution rate for the employment stabilization program stands at 0.3 per cent of the total payroll and that for the job's skill development program varies from 0.1 to 0.5 percent depending on the size of the firm (Bark & Hwang, 2006; Kabir, 2004). Employers are responsible for the contribution to the employment stabilization and job skills development program. However, workers who quit their jobs without justifiable reasons (voluntarily quit for jobs) are not eligible for benefits in Korea. However, although vocational training introduced through employment program, the quality of vocational training has not been improved in proportion to the expansion in quantity.

7.2. Panama School Feeding Program

The school lunch program of Panama is supported by the Social Emergency Fund (FES) is one of the two national school-feeding programs that constitute the largest social assistance transfer program in Panama. While the second program (MINEDUC snack program) is becoming explicitly universal, the FES lunch program is geographically targeted using poverty, malnutrition, and education indicators. The programs' objective is two folds: improving the nutritional status of pre-primary and primary school children and improving school performance

(Kabir, 2004). The FES lunch program was initiated in 1991, and is geographically targeted using nutritional, poverty and education indicators. The FES lunch program of community participation is high: teachers and school directors deal with the administration at the local level and mobilize community involvement where parents participate in preparing food and maintaining school gardens on rotation; the program meetings are held regularly in recipient communities. The food was first delivered to satellite schools in the district in Panama.

7.3. Albania's social assistance program

In 1995, Albania's social assistance program underwent a reform which made legislation more compatible with the kind of block grant program. The program is administered by the Ministry of Labour and Social Protection; allocate a certain amount of funds to each commune that then decides on the allocation among its inhabitants. The allocation process at the communal level takes the following form: Families apply to the local office of social assistance and they are then listed as eligible recipients according to their estimated household needs, which are mainly determined by the household's size, landholding, and family member's wages or receive a pension. From the calculated benefits are then subtracted unemployment insurance and pensions received and potential earnings from land owned. The final decision of a household's eligibility and the allocation of the benefit are then taken by the elected commune council. However, still many poor people are not covered by the social assistance program (Alderman, 2000).

7.4. Uzbekistan social assistance program

In 1994, a new social assistance system has been introduced in Uzbekistan which is mainly aimed at benefiting families with children, is a very interesting example of a highly decentralized system because the local administration is carried out by traditional community groups called "Mahallas". These local communities try to solve their social problems and conflicts in the community. At the beginning of each year, the

Ministry of Finance distributes the central funds through its regional and sub-regional officers to special accounts in savings banks held by each Mahalla. The chairman and the committee members elected by each of these community groups decide which families in the community are the neediest and to some extent, what amount of support they deserve (Coudouel & Macklewright, 1999). The Uzbek statistics (1997) find about 11 per cent of all households are recipients of the benefit. Although this system is very decentralized and flexible system, it has many problematic issues. For example, the amount of benefit paid to households is unrelated to observed measures of household well-being. The children's nutritional statuses are not having a strong influence on the award decision. There are no guidelines from the central authorities for allocating funds to regions. There is a need a closer examination of the process and a closer monitoring of the mahallas decision-making process by the central authorities (Ibid, 1999).

7.5. Argentina's Trabajar Program

The Argentina's Trabajar Program is an interesting example of a social program in which key decisions like the allocation of funds are decentralized. The program aims at reducing poverty by both generating employment opportunities and improving the social infrastructure of poor areas. The issues of intra-regional inequalities that are not taken into account, and of the weak performance of poorer provinces at targeting their poor, with local elite possibly capturing the gains from an expanded social program, can be explored (Kabir, 2004). Employment opportunities offered are low wage jobs on a variety of community projects, and by providing this kind of short-term employment at rather moderate wages it is intended to self-select unemployed workers from poor families. Additionally, the social infrastructure of poor areas is need to be improved by locating these community projects in poor areas. The projects and NGOs have to cover the non-wage costs and wage costs are paid for by the center. These projects are approved on the regional level using central government guidelines.

7.6. Self-employed Women Association (SEWA) India

The Maharashtra State Employment Guarantee Scheme in India is a good example of providing income-generating work to every family in the state who are even in need to work. Self-employed Women Organising for Economic Security India has governed by Self-employed Women Association (SEWA), which is a labour union that now represents more than 1000,000 informal economy workers in five states in India. Its members consist of primarily of home-based workers, vendors, manual labours, service providers and producers. Economic security and self-reliance have always been the central focus of SEWA strategy to organize women. SEWA designed and developed its own insurance plan, known as VimoSEWA. The plan provides a series of packages offering life, health and casualty insurance at premiums ranging from $1.77 to $8.33 per year (Hussain & Ali, 2012; Kabir, 2004). VimoSEWA functions as a cooperative where services are managed by a team of 120 grassroots women leaders who promote and explain the plans, process claims and develop new products and negotiate with government and private insurers. It is serving more than 100,000 people. VimoSEWA is one of the world's largest social security organizations for the informal economy. Recently it introduced health insurance for children and plans to introduce maternity insurance.

The International Labour Organization (ILO) has been working in Asian countries to design and to improve their social security systems. Some examples are narrating below:

7.7. Thailand and Indonesia social safety net programs

Thailand is one of the worst affected countries, with more than 6.7 million people falling into poverty. The country covers safety net measures only 9% of the total population. It introduces old age pensions and limited child allowances and this program opens to all public, private employees and self-employed, who covers 45% of the labour force (Zhiqin, 2002). A universal health care system is introduced giving nearly three-quarters' of the labor force access to medical care at a nominal fee. In Thailand, currently safety net programs are focusing on poverty alleviation, job creation, income distribution and risk reduction and so on. Job creation and income generation are impressive. Recent statistics of Thailand indicate that unemployment has fallen to 2.1% of the workforce. Thailand launches 30 baht medical care schemes and it expanded to 75 provinces and 13 districts of Bangkok (Ibid, 2002). The main objectives of the scheme are to develop the country's primary healthcare system, and to encourage people to visit any healthcare units nearest to their homes. There are three kinds of health insurance for Thai people: the social security system, the medical welfare scheme for state officials and 30-baht medical care scheme. The 30 baht gold-card schemes covered people aged over 60, children below 12, disabled people, monks and community leaders eligible for free medical services (Ibid, 2002).

Indonesia has more workers in its informal economy, experienced a major increase in joblessness and lacking unemployment insurance and social assistance, a substantial increase in poverty. The country's largest retirement savings plan allowed members to take small lump sum benefits to survive, leaving them with nothing for their retirement. The Government with ILO's assistance has established a National Task Force to develop plans extend basic social security coverage to informal economy workers, to improve health care coverage, to introduce pensions for private sector workers and to provide social assistance and unemployment benefits (Irawan, 2001).

8. Target groups of the SSNs services in Bangladesh and Canada

Social safety nets benefits as a share of the poor's income and consumption are lowest in low-income countries, at only 13 percent. For example, Sub-Saharan African countries spend an average of US$16 per citizen annually on safety net programs, whereas countries in the Latin America and the Caribbean region spend an average of US$158 per citizen annually. Globally, developing and transition countries spend an average of 1.5 percent of GDP on safety net programs (World Bank, 2018). World Bank finds evidence now shows how safety nets cash transfers not only help nations invest in human capital, but also serve as a source of income for the poor, improving their standard of living. Today, approximately 2.5 billion people are covered by safety net programs and around 650 million people or 56 percent of the poorest quintile.

Social safety net programs utilize many eligibility criteria to identify their specific target groups. Many eligibility criteria develop to identify their specific target groups. Generally social safety nets targeted people who are suffering from poverty. Many scholars think poverty is not an accidental; it is not a by-product; it is an inherent and crucial feature of a society whose economic structure is grounded in class and exploitation. There is a huge debate on MFIs and or state should fully concentrate properly for addressing the absolute poverty in Bangladesh. However, in practice, these are often vague and lack comprehensiveness of the term. Study information have been collected to develop a generic profile of safety net target group. The typical safety net target household is: those who has no land or land up to 10 decimals, Average income per person per day below Tk. 300 (US$4), a financial profile where debts exceed savings by an average of around Tk.2500 (US$36). There is a greater number of disadvantaged vulnerable women are living in poverty in Bangladesh. About a quarter of households have members participating in MFI (Kabir, 2004). However, if we look at Canadian context, social assistance levels are clearly set below LICO level associated with absolute poverty. However, most measures of low income developed and applied in Canada assess depth of relative poverty (Chappell, 2006; Hick, 2004; and Raphael, 2007).

AS mentioned earlier, Canada social safety nets measures targeted peoples are who are living below LICO levels (16% Canadians, 18% children, 14 older Canadians, unattached non-elderly 38% Canadians and female lone-parent families 51% and 31.2 % of the Aboriginal Canadians, 55.9%

unattached Aboriginal Canadians who are living in poverty (Statistics Canada, 2004). Dannis Raphael (2007) finds in his study 75% of his respondents living with low incomes who do not have enough money to participate in community activities. Half of the people who are living in poverty in Canada are employed, but they do not earn wages that lift them out of poverty. Therefore, poverty rates ebb and flow as the result of economic growth and recession; and because of globalization free trade market economy. Canada has both individual and household targeted social safety net measures and universal safety net measures. Although poverty is related to lots of health issues exist in Bangladesh, public health sector in Bangladesh unable to provide universal healthcare services to its poor people. Therefore, the Government of Bangladesh should be taken more seriously to improve the public healthcare sector in addition to other social measures in Bangladesh.

9.0. NGOs/MFIs managed Social Safety Nets services in Bangladesh

At present, there are more than 1,400 NGOs registered with the NGO Affairs Bureau Bangladesh. NGOs have has a particularly prominent role in anti-poverty programs with the scale of their activities increasing as donors have considered them to be more effective for poverty reduction objectives. A number of local Bangladeshi NGOs start their activities on eradication of poverty after Bangladesh independence. Their services are like patron-clients structured hierarchies in Bangladesh. In the 1980s, many of these NGOs scale-up their services on the delivery of micro credit. A number of them became deliverers of micro-finance services to their clients in Bangladesh. Many of them have significant impacts on poverty, reduction through the provision of credit, health services, non-formal education, public works schemes, agricultural extension, immunization and a number of other activities (Hossain & Ali, 2012; Mahmud, 2004). Grameen Bank, BRAC, ASA, Proshika, Nijera Kori are large national non-state organizations that are providing social services to poor people in Bangladesh. However, in the 1990s, these large organizations particularly Grameen Bank and BRAC have faced pressure to cover their own running costs by themselves. The paper is an example largely narrates these two organizations safety net strategies that are helpful to bottom people of Bangladesh.

10. Social safety net service in Bangladesh

The major social safety net (SSNs) programmes in Bangladesh can be divided under four broad categories: (i) employment generation programmes; (ii) programmes to cope with natural disasters and other shocks; (iii) incentives provided to parents for their children's education; and (iv) incentives provided to families to improve their health status. SSNs programs can also be grouped into two types depending on whether these involve cash transfers or food transfers. The review indicates that SSN programs in Bangladesh have led to increased school enrolment and attendance especially among girls in secondary schools and closing the gender gap; additional employment generation; provision of food during crisis; building infrastructure; and increased access to and utilisation of maternal health care services. Such programmes deserve high priority to ensure the rights and entitlements of the disadvantaged groups, including the urban poor and the poor living in rural areas (Hossain & Liaquit, 2012).

In Bangladesh, social safety nets initially focused only on protection goals, they are now increasingly combining promotional goals too. Over the years, Bangladesh has introduced a plethora of safety net programmes. However, such growth has often been ad hoc and lacking a systematic overview. Therefore, there is a need for a comprehensive and strategic framework within which to consolidate social safety nets has emerged as an increasing preoccupation within the wider policy community of Bangladesh.

11. Success stories of social safety net services in Bangladesh

11.1. Social Safety Net through Microcredit

The proliferation of NGO-led microfinance programs, many of which deliberately set out to target women from poorer households, is partly in response to the perceived failure of government efforts (Mahmud, 2004). The Grameen Bank is now internationally renowned for innovation of the idea of lending to poor women organized into groups and responsible for ensuring weekly repayment of loans (Khandker, 1998). Other organizations like BRAC, and Proshika, have combined lending to the poor with some attention to social mobilization while others still, like ASA, have modified the Grameen Bank approach to offer a more diversified range of financial services.

There are *absolute poor* who are suffering from poverty and these hardcore poor suffer from chronic food deficits. The MFIs are operating (particularly Gramen Bank) in the minimum economy in which production, consumption, trade, savings, borrowings and earning occurs in very small amounts (Khandker, 1998).

ASA started up a flexible 'open-access' savings service for its core group and set aside a quota for them in its entrepreneurship development program. Proshika gives loans to its very poor borrower's access to risk-reducing technologies from its Income Generation Program profiles so that borrowers feel less threatened by actual or potential income losses.

12. Grameen Bank community micro-insurance program in Bangladesh

The Grameen Bank community micro-insurance program is an affordable and quality healthcare service in Bangladesh initially supported by ILO for the Grameen Bank micro health insurance plan for its borrowers in Bangladesh. Each member of GB contributes

Tk.200 annually to this plan and the whole family get free healthcare services annually from the program. The program is governed by Grameen Kalyan (GK), a sister organization of GB. Grameen Kalyan continues to provide affordable health security to more than 100,000 people in Bangladesh by its different clinics and hospitals. It is constructing a big hospital with modern facilities in Dhaka where GB insured members can receive healthcare services with fewer costs from the Grameen health hospitals (Grameen Kalyan, 2017).

Grameen Bank changes its lending approach in 2001 when it found that its borrowers in Rangpur area are falling behind on their repayments. Rangpur is one of the most economically depressed areas in Bangladesh. There is little economic activity and during the lean season, food security is so great that declining body weights are recorded in the period between mid-September and mid-November. Instead, Grameen Bank embarked on a goat-leasing program, providing defaulting borrowers with goats, which they could raise and then pay back in the form of a kid from the first litter and another from the second litter. No cash repayments are required. Since goats are hardly animals, women have repaid their loans by the end of the first year. The program has proved to be successful and brought many of the poorest sections back into its micro credit program.

12.1. Grameen Bank Emergency Fund

The Grameen Bank Center Emergency Fund is one of the safety net services to the members of Grameen Bank in Bangladesh. This emergency fund generates from borrowers contribution. After payment of the total interest accrued on bank loan, an amount equal to half that amount is deposited in a special fund of the Center/Association which is called 'Emergency Fund'. This fund creates through compulsory contributions of all the members of the center deposited in the Emergency Fund. Money accumulates in the Emergency Fund of the center/association can spend for to repay the bank loan of any member who becomes unable to repay the loan due to any accident

(e. g. the death of a cow purchased with the loan money, damage of a rickshaw in accident etc.) and to pay of the desist borrowers' family to recover unpaid loan. This emergency fund can extend grants for repayment of the outstanding amount of loans in case a member of any group fails to repay his/he loan for any other reason where the total saving of the particular group is not sufficient repayment of the same. Moreover, this Grameen emergency fund utilises for other activities making arrangement for veterinary services, adoption of health care programmes for the members etc.). However, the expenses for such programmes shall not exceed 50% of the total savings in the Emergency Fund. Moreover, arrangement of insurances of different types for the members e.g. cattle insurance, crop insurance, life insurance etc. pay from the emergency fund. The money from the Emergency Fund can be spent in such programs only on the basis of decisions taken by the General Assembly of the Center/Association.

The Emergency Fund operates under the joint signatures of the Center Chief and Associated Center Chief and the field Manager. However, the center emergency fund dismantled in 2001, but currently the emergency fund operates from centrally. If any borrowers died, his/her unpaid loan waived. Even, GB provides Tk. 2000 to the desist family for the desist funeral service.

12.2. Grameen housing loans program

In Grameen Bank Phase-1 (Classical phase (1978-2000), Grameen Bank has initiated the housing loans for the members for constructing their houses. This loan is introduced on small scale in 1984, but it is expanded rapidly after the devastating flood of 1987. First housing loan was distributed by the researcher provided when he was an area manager in Vhuapur, Tangail. Grameen Bank thought that better housing for the poor should be categorised as an investment rather than as consumption, as the borrower can use a good house both as factory space and as protection from natural calamities detrimental to health. The housing loan provides to borrowers for a longer-period to be repaid by weekly installments over several years, with an annual interest rate of 8% per year. Initially, a sum of TK. 7000 is given to housing loan borrowers as the "Moderate Housing" loan. However, the amount of housing loan was raised to TK. 25,000 taka to account for the rising cost of building materials. The houses built with the loans to purchase four concrete pillars, a sanitary latrine, and corrugated iron roofing sheets. This type of houses provides protection against floods, cyclones, and rain. This loan was exclusively given to poor women borrowers. The land on which the house is built has to be in the woman's name.

Grameen Bank included this condition to make sure that the women would not be evicted from her home in case of dissolution of the marriage. Owning a piece of land through a housing loan from Grameen Bank may be the only way for a woman to have "a house of her own." GB also introduced "Basic Housing Loan" to rebuild homes of the borrowers that were damaged by the flood of 1987. The loan size was Tk.7000-Tk.12.000. The maximum period for repayment of a housing loan is five years (Dowla & Barua, 2006). However, the repayment rate of housing loan was not satisfactory. As the loan repayment rate was for more than one year, borrowers are relaxed to pay the loans regularly. However, they could complete repaying their housing loan in their life time. GB introduces to awards to those workers who provide more housing loans to borrowers and recovers the loans regularly. As of June 2018, GB provides housing loans to 721,306 borrowers of GB in Bangladesh.

12.3. Grameen Bank higher education student loans program

In 1997, the higher education student loans are introduced by Grameen Bank with easy terms and conditions for the children of GB borrowers. By receiving this loan, many children of GB borrowers completed their education and become doctors, lawyers, engineers, chemists, biologists, physicist, and social scientists in Bangladesh. Loan receiving graduated students are regularly repaying their loans. As of June 2018, GB disbursed higher education loans US$ 52. 25 million (female student loans US$ 13. 89 million and male student loans US$ 38. 36 million) to 53, 933 students (male students 40,970, and female students 12,963) in Bangladesh. Grameen Bank decides to provide this student loan to finance higher education to the children of GB members. Currently, all children of borrowers who are on a basic loan or flexible loan and have been members of the bank for at least a year are eligible to receive student higher education loans. Grameen Bank introduces scholarships for the children of GB borrowers in 2001. Scholarships are given with priority to girls every year, to encourage them to get better grades in schools. On an average 3,000 children, at various levels of school education, receive these scholarships every year (Dowla & Barua, 2006).

12.4. Grameen Bank phase- 2 social safety net services in Bangladesh

In 2000, GB reforms its some products and it has introduced new system called *Grameen Generalised System* where it designed a new operational manual based on its experience. Before 2000, all grameen operations are termed *Grameen Classical System* (Phase-1) and after 2000, Grameen operation named Phase -2. Phase-2 is more flexible and borrowers-friendly system to borrowers to transactions with the bank. The new system main features are prime loan product called *basic loan*, housing loan and the higher education student loan, repayment according to borrowers income, loan ceiling as per repayment record and deposits, weekly savings varies with loan size full repayment at any time allowed, fresh loan after every six months on top of the existing loan, interest pay with principal installments, *Grameen Pension Savings* (GPS), larger savings for larger loans, overdue loans are routinely written off, loan loss provision, loan insurance fund (loans paid off after death, struggling members (baggers loan with no interest). Here welfare products to borrowers like struggling members' loans without interest, generous loan loss fund etc. that help to hardcore poor to mushroom them/survive them in adverse situation. Baggers' loans gave priority to the poorest of poor where GB gives special attention to mentor their businesses. By the end of June 2006 Grameen Bank has provided baggers loan services to 75,672 beggars. Their successes are tremendous to cross the road from baggers' life to small entrepreneurs. Borrowers used their savings to withstand the flood and other crisis situation. Bank also used the cushion of large amounts of internal members' savings to deal with the two stages of the flood- the first in July and second in September 2004 (Dawla & Barua, 2006).

12.5. Grameen Pension Scheme (GPS)

In 2000-2002, GB develops the new loan products (mentioned earlier in the paper) and an attractive insurance policy (Grameen Pension Scheme) that motivates default borrowers of GB to revive the center disciplines and to receive new loans, *flexible loan and easy loan,* for reviving their business capital. Borrowers start to deposit their weekly savings, voluntary savings and premiums of their pensions (Grameen Pension Schemes (GPS)). The Group Fund and Emergency Fund are abolished in Grameen Bank Phase-11. Although Emergency Fund safety net stopped, each year families of deceased borrowers of GB receive an average total of TK. 8 to 10 million in life insurance benefits. Each desist family receives up to a maximum of TK. 2,000. A total of 54,469 borrowers died in Grameen Bank. Their families collectively received a total amount of Tk. 114.0 million (Dawla & Barua, 2006). Borrowers are not required to pay any premium for this life insurance. Borrowers come under this insurance coverage by being a shareholder of the bank (Yunus, 2008). As of June 2018, GB life insurance accumulated US$ 194. 039 million and total amount paid out from life insurance to borrowers of GB US$5.91 million in Bangladesh.

Field staffs reenergize them through new financial incentives and promotional incentives designed for them. Now GB repayment rate regains to 97%. The premium deposits of Grameen Pension Scheme (GPS) are 100% although all members of the center are not present on time in their weekly center meetings. Now GB is flexible to the attendance of the borrowers in the weekly meetings than before. If any reason all members need to sit together or need to resolve any problem, they organize special meetings at their own convenient places at nights.

13. Handicrafts create opportunity for distressed women in Bangladesh

Training on handicrafts by a local NGO, *Satrong Jubo Beker Mohilla Samilty'* has helped over 500 distressed women of Gopallgonj district who earns their livelihood with their own efforts and become self-reliant. Sarang Jubo Beker Mohilla Samilty, working in Gopallgonj sadar, Muksudpur, Kashiani, and Tungipara upazilas of the district, has been paying a prominent role in improving the lot of the socially oppressed and distressed women. This organization is imparting intensive training to these helpless women on the art of making handicrafts and other income generating activities. It has providing 30-day practical training to over 500 women on making jute, cotton and woolen handicraft goods, decorated floor mat, table mat, pillow cover vanity bag, cap, shital pati and 'Sheeka". This organization manufactured Grameen Shamogree's garments when the researcher was working in Grameen Shamogree in 1995-1997.

13.1. Integrated Food for Security Project in Bangladesh

Food security project in Bangladesh is helping the poor in Bangladesh. The Integrated Food for Security Project of the World Food Program has helped approximately 18,500 distressed people of 25 unions under five upzilas of Kurigram district in their struggle to come out of poverty trap. The Local Government Engineering Department in collaboration with Rangpur Dinajpur Rural Services (RDRS), an NGO, had chalked out a five-year program to alleviate poverty to the extreme poor of the district. Many have-nots have found work to manage at least two square meals a day and meet other daily household demands. The poor are earning their livelihood by putting in physical labour in the activities such as road construction, repair of flood shelters, raising the level of homesteads in the flood-prone areas.

Another scheme the self-help healthcare model changes Chakoria: Once thousands of people in Cox's Bazar's Chkoria upzila used to beg for relief materials. Now self-help model of primary health care started replacing that odious post, which is established by the self-help organization with community-arranged land, housing, furniture, etc., proving that people are willing to pay for better health services. The number of families buying into the scheme is rising and the annual fee has been reduced, but immunization has increased and people are lesser suffering from diarrhea. Health awareness improved dramatically among the clients. So, there have been real benefits, according to the local people as well as the physicians working under project.

The Education Department of Government of Bangladesh has distributed stipend TK. 2.36 crore among 62,223 girl students in six upazilas of Narshingdi with a view to encouraging female education. Under the girl students' sub-stipend project, the amount is distributed among the students of different secondary schools and madrassahs of the district as the first six-month stipend (January to June). Of the total amount, over Tk. 1.72 crore is given to the students for purchasing books, stationary and dresses, and over Tk. 64 lakh is given for tuition fees of the students of 178 schools and madrassahs (Kabir, 2004). The objective of the monetary assistance is to stop dropout of female students. The initiative of the government has increased the attendance of girl students at different schools in Narshindi district.

Some distressed women and children, most of them victims of trafficking and rape, are languishing at what is called 'Safe Home' in Rajshahi (United News of Bangladesh April 12, 2004, New Age). Eighteen victims at Rajshahi Safe Home have detached these women from their families who are leading wretched lives. These women and children have been staying at the Safe Home for last 14 years. Moreover, a good number of trafficked and other crimes related victims are shifted to the Safe Home from different jails, including Rajshahi Central Jail. Social and human rights organizations come up to extend their helping hands for their rehabilitation.

Radda Burn, an international community MCH clinic, is working in Mirpur Dhaka Bangladesh. It has MCH feeding programs in the clinic for the needy patients of it in order to prevent or alleviate malnutrition in certain physiologically vulnerable subgroups of population (infant or child anthropometric status as well as pregnant mothers' exhibit poor nutritional status or inadequate weight gain or have low birth-weight babies). It provides MCH services in addition to child feeding nutritional program in Dhaka. Here MCH malnourished women receive food services on site with a minimum fee cost. This program is run under the primary health care services in Bangladesh. The Institute of Food Science and Nutrition, Dhaka University has nutritional food services for the malnourished children and lactating mothers funded by UNICEF Bangladesh. Researcher received 'Applied Nutrition and Food Science Diploma' from this institute. His apprentice to feed vulnerable malnourished children and to serve MCH mothers was in this institute for six months. There are critics on this program; it is not a national program of Bangladesh. It provides a perverse incentive to households if they believe they will receive a transfer only if they have malnourished members. This program is only targets its clinic clients, all children under the age of two and all pregnant or lactating low income women, but this program could also include services for preventive functions.

Famine in Pabna and Kurigram locally call as *monga*, prevails in rural areas of Pabna and Kurigram district due to lack of jobs during the Bengali months of Ashwin and Kartik. The poor farmers and day-labors are the worst sufferers. Ashwin and Kartick called as monga period when hundreds of farmers and landless people of the district have no work to earn their livelihood. Grameen Fisheries Foundation provides fisheries loans to fish cultivators, but it freezes its loans of the borrowers during the monga months.

The Government of Bangladesh has recognized safety nets can play an important role in alleviating poverty and promoting long-term growth by providing households with the protection. A more recently identified role for safety nets is to help households manage risk. Safety nets can also increase options for the poor economy for the welfare of the poor. When people are struck by poverty or any other crises in Bangladesh, the state provides them with financial support although it is not covered to all crisis victims. However, whenever an accident or disaster-natural or manmade-occurs, poor and low-income group of people suffer most. Although the Constitution of Bangladesh recognizes the citizen's right to social security and support from the government during unemployment, sickness, disability, widowhood, old age and other circumstances beyond control, the government is yet to initiate remarkable and effective programs for the welfare of the distressed people, except some insignificant measures, including a pension scheme for the elderly people (Kabir, 2007).

Bangladesh has state supported many programs. For example, the government distributes vulnerable group feeding (VGF) and vulnerable group development (VGD) cards among the poor people, but the number is too insufficient to cover all the poor. Therefore, the process of card distribution has raised question. The government supported social safety nets services are narrating below:

13.2. Vulnerable Groups Development (VGD) Program

In Bangladesh, programs like Food for Work (FFW) and Vulnerable Groups Development (VGD) programs have been successful, even though there have been leakages and corruption associated with FFW in particular since 1980s. The VGD program played a very effective role during the post-food of 1998 in providing entitlements to the victims of the flood and averting severe hunger. Informal ways of safety nets have always been there in Bangladesh, but these programs should cover more and more people in Bangladesh. Researcher Kazi Rouf was involved with the Grameen Bank VGD wheat distribution program for Grameen Bank clients in post-flood period in 1998. However, although GB distributes wheat in-kinds, it credited wheat prices to clients. GB clients paid this money after one year. With the collected money, GB has generated disaster fund for the GB clients who might suffer from natural disasters.

The Vulnerable Groups Development programs evolved from the Vulnerable Group Feeding Program. Vulnerable Group Feeding started in 1975 became Vulnerable Group Development in 1986. The program targets destitute women in rural areas. It covers more than 500,000 women for 18 months from 1999. The government launched Vulnerable Group Feeding (VGF) to address a famine-like situation in greater Rangpur and Dinajpur regions where thousands of poor people are starving because of severe scarcity of job and food. However, there have been allegations in distribution of VGF cards and corruptions in relief distribution. Currently, the programs run under three sub-projects Income Generation; Women's Training Centers; and Group Leader Extension Workers sub-projects administered in Bangladesh by BRAC.

Bangladesh has a program calls ``Rural Maintenance Scheme``, which is launched in 1983 using Canada Food Aid. The Phase-1 and Phase-11 of the program are implemented by the Ministry of Relief and Rehabilitation Bangladesh in collaboration with CARE, an international NGO. In 1997-98, 41000 destitute women participated in the program from 4100 unions in 435 thanas in 61 districts in Bangladesh.

13.3. Income Generation for Vulnerable Group Development (IGVGD) program in Bangladesh

The Income Generation for Vulnerable Group Development (IGVGD) program is a collaborative food security intervention jointly led by the Government of Bangladesh, the World Food Program (WFP) and the Bangladesh Rural advancement Committee (BRAC). The IGVGD program targeted towards destitute rural Bangladeshi women who have little or no income earning opportunities. IGVGD program has provided food grain assistance and savings and credit services to nearly a million participants over a 10-year period. Two-thirds of these women have graduated from absolute poverty to becoming microfinance clients, and have not slipped back into requiring government handouts.

BRAC's Income Generation for Vulnerable Group Development (IGVGD) program seeks to combine some assurance of household food security with assistance in enterprise development over a longer-than-usual time frame. It targets the poorest poor women: members of asset less households, women with irregular or no household income, women who work as casual wage Bangladesh labor and female households' heads. They are expected to form savings group and to participate in training on income generating activities (poultry, livestock and sericulture). Credit is provided to help them setup these activities. Relief, credit and training are thus combined in this attempt to address the exclusion of the very poor. BRAC is providing training to IGVGD recipients on Employment and Enterprise Development Training to the poorest sections. The aims of this scheme are to provide skills, development and confidence-building and prepare participants to initiate an enterprise of their choice.

The IGVGD scheme is built on a governmental safety net program that provides free food grain for an 18-month period to destitute, female-headed households that are at the highest risk of hunger. Through its experience, BRAC has discovered that it is difficult to include the poorest in its conventional microfinance operations and it is looking for another "entry point" to involve the destitute in its development activities. BRAC's food grain donations provided a strong incentive for the hardcore poor to participate in programs. BRAC adds skills training and savings and credit services to build their development capacity. Hence, when the cycle of free food grain ends, participants are able to engage in income-generating activities and become clients of regular microfinance programs, earning at least the same money equivalent of the wheat they received by way of their newly acquired skills. Although

IGVGD program was a pilot scheme in 1985, it becomes a national program covering more than a million women in Bangladesh.

The IGVGD program is jointly administered by the Government and BRAC (through microfinance program). There are three essential elements to the program: a food grain safety net, skills training and financial services in the form of savings and credit. Women entering the program as recipients of free food grain are selected by local elected representatives (Councillors). These elements targeting costs for BRAC as well as protecting it from the politics of selecting food grain recipients. The selection of households is based on three criteria: Headed by widows or abandoned women; own less than half an acre of land; and earn less than 300 Tk. per month. BRAC also selects 90% of the women who are receiving food relief for its program. BRAC provides them training on poultry, livestock raising, vegetable gardening etc. The IGVGD clients required to save Tk. 25 per month with BRAC. IGVGD members can receive microloans with 15% flat rate interest in one year after their completion of the training from BRAC and they repay their loans on weekly basis.

Thirty kg food grain is distributed monthly to IGVGD participants plus BRAC provides training to grain receivers that are liked and chosen by the participants. BRAC provides training for six months and disbursed the first loan to them. The IGVGD members can withdraw their saving after 18 months. At 18 months, BRAC halts the wheat grain distribution to the IGVGD members, but BRAC encouraged its IGVGD members to continue their membership in BRAC as regular micro credit recipients. Jagoroni Chakra also has used a similar model to its destitute clients and it is successful. Moreover, CARE-Bangladesh has successfully linked microfinance to government-guaranteed employment schemes.

BRAC has achieved a successful graduation of two-thirds of the women of the IGVGD to regular microfinance programs. More than one million women have been enrolled in the IGVGD program since its beginning, two-thirds of them have entered microfinance program. However, BRAC excludes about 10 percent of the women receiving food grain from IGVGD for being too old or disabled (Hashemi & Maya 2001). Therefore, the program does not represent a panacea for all those in safety net programs. They need for other more continuous social services for the poorest remains. Moreover, IGVGD relays on limited set of economic activities which is their vulnerability to macro and external socks. Poultry diseases take on epidemic proportions and wipe out poultry holdings, leaving large number of clients in debt. Floods and disease death a heavy blow to the sericulture and silk-worm based IGVGD component. To face these crises, contingency plans are essential that is absent in IGVGD scheme. Anyway, there are more examples can be found in Bangladesh that are successful social safety net programs that are dedicated to deepening their outreach program narrating below.

14. Food-based programs in Bangladesh

Food-for- work (FFW) is a cluster of different food assisted public works programs in Banghladesh. Together these programs aim to provide immediate relief to rural poor people and also help to build and maintain rural infrastructure mainly maintenance and construction of rural roads, river embankments and irrigation channels. Wages are usually given in wheat rather than cash. Food-for-Work programs are usually referred to as 'self-targeting'; targeting is achieved by the requirement to participate in manual labor at low enough rates of remuneration (ideally close to the prevailing market wage for unskilled labor) to exclude the non-poor. FFW in Bangladesh is started in 1975 in the wake of the famine. At that time, as with other similar programs, its focus is on relief rather than 'development' as Aids the case now. It runs mainly over the dry session between November –April every year when earthworks are possible.

14.1. Economic rationale for Food for Work

Using food as a wage is appropriate when the market for food is disrupted or fails due to conflict or famine or when increased local demand results in higher prices rather than an inflow of food from outside the area. Payment in the firm of food can also have nutritional benefits if food that enters the household falls under women's control. However, providing food as a wage to households that are in absolute poverty should not affect market prices since the bulk of the food that they receive is an addition rather than a substitution for food that they would otherwise have purchased. However, Food-for Works Programs' food is available from international donors whereas equivalent amounts of cash would need to come from the government's own budget.

14.2. Food-for Work programs

Food-for Work (FFW) programs have long been used to protect households against the decline in purchasing power that often accompanies seasonal unemployment, climate-induced famine or other periodic disruptions by providing them with employment. In situations where FFW provides a guaranteed source of employment, it is truly a 'safety net,' assuring a minimum level of income for households with members who can work. It is not an income transfer but an opportunity for employment. However, one goal of FFW is to allow household members to work for their benefits rather than receive them as handouts. FFW is used to promote household food security as well as contribute to create or improving infrastructure, such as roads, wells or irrigation systems, that is constructed using FFW labour. However, only physically capable people can work in this FFW program.

14.3. School feeding programs in Bangladesh

School feeding programs use school as the distribution points for providing a ration to school-age children. School feeding programs often aim to reduce the prevalence of malnutrition among school age children by providing nutrient-dense meals or snacks, but they also can address short term hunger, which may interfere with children's attention span and learning ability. The school feeding has been criticized as a poor nutrition intervention because school-age children have passed the period of the greatest development vulnerability to the effects of malnutrition. The School feeding programs are often designed with academic as much as nutritional goals in mind-to increase school attendance and enrollment and to improve academic performance and cognitive development. The author himself enjoyed his launch made of wheat-milk mixed soup supplied by the School when he was a student of Dabidower High School in 1961. However, this school feeding service did not continue for long.

14.4. Food for Education

Food for education is launched in 1993, in what are seen 460 'backward unions in 460 thanas, to address the problem of poor children not attending school because their families could not afford either the direct schooling costs or the opportunity costs of children's help in the home or outside the home. Participating children receive monthly rations of wheat or rice if they attend at least 85% of their primary school classes. It is rapidly growing program that accounts for half of the primary education budget Tk. 4.05 billion in fiscal 1998-99.

14.5. Social Safety Net services for the elderly in Bangladesh

Government Bayashkas Bhata Scheme: Although about 80% of the population in Bangladesh live in rural areas, only a small fraction of the elderly are covered by formal pensions. Here is no public safety net for poor aged people living in poor families, particularly in rural areas. In 1998, the government introduced a new pension program for the elderly population. The scheme is called "Bayashka Bhata". It provides Tk. 100 per month to the 10 poorest and most vulnerable aged persons in each ward of a union. There is a condition of ten people; at least five must be women. This pension program reaches to 44,500 out of the million of older people who live in extreme poverty. Now Bayashka Bhata has been increased from Tk. 100 to Tk. 500.

Bayashka Bhata Scheme, distribution system, leakage and barriers: A study conducted by Center for Policy Dialogue (CPD) finds 18% of the Bayashka Bhata recipients faced difficulty while receiving the money; however, their main problem they are facing is the waiting time. Therefore, since certain percentage of elderly population is disabled and physically weak, the procedure of receiving the Bhata should be simplified. Many find some benefit is lost to transportation costs to collect payment. Many seniors ask for free food, cloth, treatment, shelter and medicine. Moreover, they asked for increasing the allowances. There is another point raised by seniors that NGOs, MFIs are not providing micro-credit to them to do business from home, but MFIs excluded older persons from providing credit to them because their age limits to 60 years. CPD provides suggestions to the Bayashka Bhata Scheme in Bangladesh. NGOs should include elderly into health program, forestation program, women functional literacy program etc. Expand this program from district level to Upzila level and then to the union level gradually. Avoid leakage in selecting seniors for the Bayashka Bhata. This program is popular in Bangladesh, so the local government should have included this program in their schemes. CPD also recommends for motivate religious institutions for the welfare of the elderly people.

14.6. Bayashka Punarbashan Kendra

Bayashka Punarbashan Kendra is a rehabilitation centre for the elderly population. It has been working in Gazipur since 1987. It is a full-fledged old home where elderly people 60+ from any religious faith can live. Moreover, a number of other organizations have a limited number of programs with older people, including the Elderly Initiative for Development; Bangladesh Retired Government Employees Welfare Association has been working since 1976 as registered organization. It provides medical services to the elderly population. Bangladesh Girls

Guides Association, Bangladesh Education Board Retired Employee's Welfare Association and Bangladesh Society of Gerontology are also working for the welfare of the elderly population.

There is a pilot project called "Resource Integration Center" (RIC) scheme in two locations in Bangladesh: Moheskhali and Norshindi where it provides micro loans to grandson with a condition that grandson uses his/her loans along grandfather or grandmother (disabled elderly) for running businesses jointly on poultry raising, handicraft and agriculture etc. This RIC projects attained at sustainable level being managed by the income of the projects. This project encourages intra-generational skills use. RIC now realizes that the money should be given to the elderly people by visiting their houses.

NGOs support to Elderly Population: Although many NGOs are working in Bangladesh, a very few of them have programs directed towards elderly population. Programs for the elderly population by the NGOs include: Bangladesh Association for the Aged and Institute of Geriatric Medicine (BAAIGM) popularly known as "Probin Hitioishi Sangha" whose activities include healthcare, recreation, rehabilitation, seminars, workshops, research and publications. Currently, it provides services at 34 locations. It has a plan to gradually extend its program to all the 64 districts.

Resources Integration Centre (RIC) provides community level assistance to poor and disabled elderly people with a primary focus on older women, as well as coordinating the celebrations of International Older Pensions' Day.

Bangladesh Women's Health Coalition (BWHC): Older women are increasingly included in education services for women and children through clinic based in urban and rural areas by taking a "life cycle approach" to healthcare.

Grameen Bank, BRAC, ASA, Proshikaa and many other MFIs in Bangladesh all require compulsory regular savings from their members as contributions to a de-facto 'lump-sum' pension, which members could only claim when they left the organization. This has limited a to potentially important source of consumption-smoothing, an important aspect of the demand by the poor for financial services. Recognition of the failure of micro credit programs to reach the extreme poor has elicited a number of different responses. On the one hand, there are those who argue that 'micro-credit is not relevant for the poorest of the poor and the most illiterate of the illiterate. For them wage employment is necessary for poverty reduction'. As poor people has no skills, their paid job market is limited.

Nijera Kori Bangladesh has cottage industries vocational training and micro-credit loans services for poor people in Northern Bangladesh. However, there are still argues that the problems does not lie with the provision of microfinance per se, but with the objectives for which it is provided and the terms on which it is provided. Researchers have traced failures of outreach to the shift to the 'promotional model of poverty alleviation through micro credit financed enterprise expansion' over the past decade or so. Such a model may benefit moderately poor households who may have the capacity for enterprise and the willingness to take risks, but it excludes the poorer sections of the poor whose livelihoods are extremely insecure and who are in need of preventive and productive rather than promotional support. However, this means moving beyond the 'micro credit template' promoted by Grameen Bank and institutionalized around the world to the adoption of a much wider, and more flexible range of financial services, which include savings and insurance (Dowla & Barua, 2006). A number of NGOs in Bangladesh have sought to redesign their interventions on account to their failure to reach the extreme poor.

15. Components of Canada's social safety net programs

The social safety nets/welfare programs are planned initiatives that provide financial assistance and or direct services to Canadian individuals, families and groups (Ralphel, 2007). It has income-security programs and personal social services taken together known as Canada's social safety net (Chappell, 2006; Hick, 2004; Ralphel, 2007). Income-security benefits are tangible basic goods like money, food, shelter, clothing and utilities. Although the income-security system is often criticized for failing to meet the basic needs of Canadians, but it intended to ensure all citizens live above a social minimum (Neysmith, 1991). The social income security program has four components: First selective cash transfer-individual income or asset fall below a certain level (Guaranteed income supplement, social assistance and income programs for people with severe disabilities). The second component is social insurance program that has forced savings plans that are required working individuals to contribute to a program that then compensates them when they are not working, it is called employment insurance (EI), social insurance; third element is Tax credits are reductions in the amount of income tax paid by low or moderate income earners. Examples are the Canada Child Tax Benefit, and the Goods and Services Tax/Harmonized Sales Tax Credit, Provincial Security Tax etc. The fourth component is the compensation benefits. These benefits are awarded to individuals who have suffered a loss as a result of an accident or another person's actions. Workers' compensation awarded to victims of crime or child sexual abuse fit in this category. Canada uses the needs tests and means tests for eligibility of applicants in order to determine their eligibility of social security safety nets services described above.

In Canada, there are 13 different social assistance programs across Canada. For example, Ontario Works, BC Benefits, Supports for Independence (Alberta) etc. are social assistance public agencies in Canada that are providing publicly financial assistance to people who are in transitionally unemployment, children, people with disabilities and seniors (age over 65). They constitute a process which enables the widening and deepening of people's access to basic needs as a precondition for sustainable human development over time. Moreover, in Canada, personal social services sub-divided into four broad categories: socialization program, personal development programs, therapy and rehabilitation and information, referral and advocacy services. In addition, the Canada Welfare system has two broad categories: selective program and universal program. Selective programs are normally targeted at certain population like children, people with disabilities who meet some predetermined criteria of being in 'need'. Universal programs are available to all Canadians as a right regardless of economic status or need of Canadian residential citizens. Canada Child benefits, health care services, crisis interventions, referral services etc. are universal programs of Canada social safety nets.

15.1. History of Canadian social safety net measures

Sister Marguerite Bourgeoys is the first Canadian social worker founded the *Sisters of the Congregation of Notre Dame* in Montreal in 1653. By the late 18th century, French-speaking colonists in Lower Canada are raising funds through voluntary organizations to support the charity functions of the Catholic Church (Chappell, 2006). The British introduced the English Poor Laws in Halifax in 1749 by Queen Elizabeth 1. Many aspects of the English Poor Laws influenced the way early British settlers treated the poor. The Poor Laws classified the poor as being either 'worthy' or 'unworthy' of relief. The worthy poor included poor children, aged, sick or disabled people who are to receive relief who are put into large poorhouse, separated on the basis of gender. Unworthy poor are able-bodied unemployed persons, who are often banished to workhouse where they learn good work habits and pay for their keep through labour (Guest, 1969). The Poor Law legislation assigned the responsibility for managing the poor to local governments or parishes which financed relief programs through property tax revenue. Nova Scotia and New Brunswick enacted Poor Law legislation in 1763 and 1786 respectively. The residual approach is assigned to churches in French Canada is discouraged handouts, treated it like personal failures. A highly residual approach to social welfare predominated into the 19th century; the bulk of responsibility for social welfare is assigned to the provincial level of government, many of the provinces delegated social welfare functions to municipal governments or local charities.

The early British settlers find that many Aboriginal groups relied on family/clan systems to maintain order and provide mutual aid. These systems utilized for local supports specialization like spiritual healers, elders, teachers, law keepers, medicine, people and hunters. During the 1800s, certain Aboriginal groups in Upper Canada are placed in designated areas called reserves-isolate them from their homes and lands in the name of civilizing and normalizing for adapting British rules. The period from 1870 to the 1920s is the time of experimentation for Canadian government's social policy and the establishment of a wider range of programs for the poor and the needy. However, the British Poor Law tradition is highly discriminating and stigmatizing, toward a more equitable, nonjudgmental and responsive approach to social welfare. However, during the early years of industrialization, the use of primitive and dangerous machines increased the incidence of work-related accidents and injuries in Canada.

In the late 1800s and early 1900s, workers could sue their employers for injuries that happened on the job. In 1914, Canada's first comprehensive and compulsory social insurance plan is established in Ontario. Moreover, the federal government setup a variety of charities to aid Canadian solders overseas and to provide relief to solders' families at home after World War 1. Additionally, by World War 1, social and political forces have stimulated the mothers' pension movement, which called for legislated income security for mothers and abandoned wives and their children. In 1916, Manitoba has introduced the first mother's allowance that provides income to all women with dependents (Evans, 2001). Canada's child welfare Act (protections and reformation of neglected children in Ontario legislated in 1887 initiated by John Joseph Kelso, a reporter for the Toronto Globe. The pace of social welfare development quickened during the 1960s with the introduction of major programs such as the Canada Assistance Plan, the Canada/Quebec Pension Plans and Medicare. However, in the early 1970s, Canada faces decline of economic growth and failing government revenues and the attitudes towards social welfare began to change, extensive restructuring happens, severe cuts in spending on social programs and services (Hick, 2004).

The Old Age Pensions Act enacted in 1927, marked the federal government's commitment to social security on an ongoing basis and established pensions as a right to which all older Canadians are entitled. To collect pension benefits, Canadians has to be 70 years or older, but now 65 year's old people are eligible for old age income pension. In 1929, Canadian economy is drastically declined because of Great Depression. Consequently, the unemployment rates soared this period particularly 1929-1933. 19%-27% of Canadians are unemployed in 1933 (Chappell, 2006). High unemployment created additional social and health problems. Canada is unprepared to meet the widespread need created by the Great Depression. No unemployment insurance is existed, but public relief aid available. 15% of Canadians received public relief in 1933; by 1934, the figure has risen to 2 million (Chappell, 20006). Direct relief is available in three forms: cash, vouchers for groceries and clothing or fuel and relief 'in kind' (actual food, coal, clothing or other commodities). Indirect relief is provided through government-funded work project (road and bridge construction) designed to get the unemployed back to work. However, these public works projects poorly planned, uncoordinated, and unable to meet the demand.

During the Depression, private charitable organizations, such as the Federation of Jewish Philanthropies in Montreal and Toronto and the Canadian Welfare Council are involved in fundraising campaigns to help people in need. In addition, municipal governments continued to provide relief services, but these avenues of help have little impact on the problem of mass unemployment and widespread need. In July 1940, British Parliament gives the Canadian government for passing the Unemployment Insurance Act. This Act is the Canada's first large-scale income-security program. Almost 4.6 million Canadians draw unemployment insurance benefits during the plans first year (Chappell, 2006; Guest, 1980). However, currently ten percent (approx) Canadians (unemployed people, people with disabilities, low income single mothers, and seniors) are receiving social safety net services in Canada (Statistics Canada 2017).

Family Allowance Act is approved in 1944 to ensure a minimum income level for Canadian families and to address the poverty although the family income is small for a large family. The aim of this Family Allowance Act is to solve the growing problems of poor nutrition and high infant mortality. Because the allowance is universal, recipients do not have to prove need or submit to a means test. The Old Age Security Act amended in 1951 by replacing with two new pension plans: Old Age Security, which provided universal benefits and it is fully funded and administered by the federal government, and Old Age Assistance is paid by the provincial and federal governments and administered by the provinces (Chappell, 2006).

Canada Assistance Plan (CAP) is enacted in 1966 where all provinces are constitutionally responsible for establishing social welfare program. However, the poorer provinces usually Northern provinces could not always afford to carry out this obligation. Under CAP, the provinces are required to meet certain standards, but they have to design and administer social assistance and personal social services. However, the federal government pay only 50% of their costs. Social assistance recipients received financial aid to meet basic living needs including food, clothing, shelter, utilities and personal needs, in some cases, assistance is also available for transportation, day care and uninsured health need such as dental and eye care. Welfare services included protection services for children, rehabilitation programs, and home support for seniors and people with disabilities, employment and community development services and child care.

In 1974, Ontario introduced the Guaranteed Annual Income System (GAINS) to ensure a basic income for residents aged 65 and older; however, Canada Legislation has accepted the minimum Guaranteed Annual Income (GIA) implies to all citizens who have the right to a minimum income either as the result of paid work or government subsidies (Canadian Council on Social Development, 1969). Social Security Review of 1973 led to changes in social welfare programs, but did little to help the working poor. By the end-1970s, Canadians support for the welfare state is waning as a result of its expenses and perceived ineffectiveness.

Harmonization of social programs is governed by the Federal Government of Canada. Canadian governments have traditionally subsidized many social and regional development programs across the country. The provision of grants considered unfair trade practices under North American Free Trade Association (NAFTA). To create a 'level playing field' among trading partners, NAFTA requires participating countries to harmonize or otherwise bring their policies and programs in the line with those of their trading partners. This means that Canada must reduce government subsidies so that its business and regions can compete in similar environments in the USA and Mexico (Drover, 1992; Dillon (1996) notes the changes made to Unemployment Insurance (UI) between 1989 and 1996 as the result of harmonization efforts. Further privatization of social welfare programs shifts of responsibility of governments for meeting human needs to individuals and private market are either non-profit or profit-making.

15.2. How Canadian social safety net is functioning

Many Canadians fear of free trade because it encourages more privatization of welfare programs and services. The term privatization describes a process in which a government withdraws from the regulation, funding and delivery of services. In a 1994 report, Improving Social Security in Canada mentions the key to dealing with social security is 'helping people get and keep jobs'. Here Governments across Canada have introduced initiatives that focus on improving people economic lives and thereby reducing the need for social security programs.

The federal and provincial governments have relinquished many of their separate social welfare responsibilities to each other. The two levels of government have assumed or relinquished certain responsibilities in order to achieve social objectives. Result of this intergovernmental exchange of power and responsibility is what Banting (1987) refers to as an increasingly 'bifurcated welfare state' means making social welfare a shared responsibility between the two levels of government. Canada's Social Union policy 1996 aim is to renew and modernize health and social policy (Ralphel, 2007).

Neoliberal policies in the 1990s downsize government and cut public spending. They support pro-market economic policies (Pal, 1998; Chappell, 2006). However, the Canadian public contributes to the development of social policy through citizen participation (NGOs). Interest groups try to benefit their own members or the public by influencing government. The values and ideology of welfare state play an important role in the social security safety net measures although 1990s has swung toward a neoliberal agenda that supports the downsizing of government and cutbacks in public spending. During this period, Canada faces fiscal crisis and budget deficits and growing debt means over time, the ability of governments to finance social programs is diminished. Then liberal government cutbacks in social and other public spending that are needed to reduce government deficits. Canadian governments at all levels have continued to curb public spending; for example, freeze or redirect funds from many existing social welfare programs to other priorities and initiatives (Chappell, 2006, p. 83). In 1989, the Progressive Conservative Government announced that benefits from Old Age Security (OAS) pension would be *clawed back* from high-income earning seniors. That gives sign to a virtual dismantling of Canada's welfare system (Hick, 2004; Ralphel, 2007). However, government simplifying and improving the income tax system that assist Canada to keep and continue its welfare state services to its citizens, but several citizens' movement push government to retain Canada's welfare system.

In 1990, Parliament severely altered the Unemployment Insurance Act-the termination of support by the federal government: UI became fully funded by employer and worker contributions. The amendments resulted to restrictive eligibility criteria, shortened benefit periods, and higher premiums. The amendment clause also includes severe penalties for pensions who quit their jobs without 'just cause'.

In 1996, Canada adopted the policy that replaces the Canada Assistance Plan (CAP) by the 'Canada Health and Social Transfer' (CHST), a new funding arrangement and altered the way the federal government supports and governs the social programs and transfer of funds from the federal to the provincial and territorial governments (Chappell, 206; Hick, 2004; Steinhauer, 1995). The CHST allows the federal government to provide the provincial and territorial governments with a lump sum or block fund. Under CHST, standards in Canada's social welfare programs do not remain same (Rice &Michael; 2000). For example, CAP probation of workfare programs is ended. CHST provides many restrictive eligibility rules regarding receipt of unemployment insurance benefits reduced the number of Canadians eligible for benefits (Raphael, 2007). The federal government appears to be reducing its central role in setting national standards. CHST provides *block fund*. As a result in response to funding cuts under the CHST, many regional governments have cut welfare benefits, decreased social services, and embraced devolution, privatization, contracting out, and purchase-of-service contracts as strategies for reducing program costs (Chappell, 2006).

Since Canada's social welfare programs have developed at different times, under different administration to response to different needs across the country, there is no single administrative or funding body for all social welfare services. Rather, there is a mix of service delivery system, funding sources, and methods for managing SSNs programs. The social welfare system composes two broad service sectors: the public sector and the private sector. The private sector further splits in the commercial and volunteer sectors. Thus, there are three general service sectors exist in administering CAP. (1) The public sector includes all programs and agencies that are funded fully by tax revenue, administered by government departments and delivered by government employees; (2) the commercial sector is made up to private profit-making agencies that operate in the competitive business or market arena; and (3) the volunteer sector which is called the charitable, independent or third sector. It includes those NGOs, self-governing, and non-profit social welfare programs that do not neatly into public or commercial categories (Kazemipur & Halli, 2001).

Income security like Employment Insurance, Veteran's Pensions, the Old Age Security Pension, and the Canada/Quebec Pension Plans are administered by the Federal Government. The Federal Government also help Canada's personal social services such as family violence, job search, child care and programs for women. The regional governments (provincial and territories) are responsible for providing the services like mental health, child protection, foster care, and social assistance. Here there are three tiers of responsibility of social services finds at the regional level: (1) the central government ministry in each provincial capital has ultimate responsibility for programs, (2) district and branch offices that are set up across each province or territory to supervise the services provided in these areas, and (3) local government offices that deliver the services to the community.

15.3. Compare and contrast SSNs in Canada and Bangladesh

Social safety net services in Bangladesh	Social safety net services in Canada
Recently public funded social insurance few programs have started that are supported by the government agencies	Many social insurance programs exist for long and majority SSNS are supported by the public agencies; Public funding are available to income security programs, mental health programs and personal social services
SSNs few legislative acts and financial supports (Token) are available in Bangladesh	All SSNs are passed by the legislative acts
People with disability safety net legislative acts yet to passed; the government in collaboration with an international organization started to identify people with development disability and open training schools for the developmental children since 2015.	A special committee is formed on Disability People's issue, Disability Act declared in 1981 and the Rights and status of Disabled Persons Act is established. All people with disability (both physical and developmental) are receiving income support governed by public agency.

Social safety net services in Bangladesh	Social safety net services in Canada
Receive workers compensations by court claim decisions	Workers compensation Act passed in 1914 and enacted
No public funds are available to legally blinds for their income support, but the government is trying to provide logistic supports to blinds	The Canadian National Institute for the Blind (CNIB) is founded in 1918, the Blind Persons Act is passed in 1951 and provide support to all blinds Canadian citizens since then
Only one mental hospital is in Bangladesh, no mental patients receive benefits outside the mental hospital	The Canadian Mental Health Association is founded in 1918 and public hospitals and clinics have been supporting the mental patients following medical model
The Freedom fighters allowance passed in 1974. Registered freedom fighters are receiving monthly Tk. 10,000 allowances and health care supports from the government	The Solder Settlement Act is passed in 1919 and they are receiving benefits from the government. The War Veterans Allowance Act is passed in 1930
Nominal Boyaska Vatta (seniors allowance) has started in 2015, but it is not covered to all seniors of Bangladesh	The Old Age Pension Act is passed in 1927, the Old Age Assistance Act is passed in 1951 and the Old Age Security Act is passed in 1951
No Juvenile delinquents allowances available, but there is only one juvenile delinquents prevention center is in Tongi, Dhaka	The Juvenile Delinquents Act is passed in 1908
Employee Labour Acts available, but no unemployment assistance	The Employment Insurance Act is passed in 1940, the Unemployment assistance Act passed 1956, The Unemployment Insurance Act is amended (reduces benefits) in 1993 and Unemployment Insurance (UI) is converted to Employment Insurance (EI) in 1996; Employee Assistance programs (EAPs) available across Canada
Family public income support is unavailable	The Family Allowance Act is passed in 1945
No community housing services available to poor; however, only in Dhaka, Sarbahara Shelter Centers are available to acute poor at free of costs, but they are not sufficient	The National Housing Act is passed in 1944; Community Housing services are provided at discounted prices to low income people; however, its services contracted out to private agencies/community agencies

Social safety net services in Bangladesh	Social safety net services in Canada
No public health insurance to all Bangladeshi people; public hospitals are less supportive to poor although many public hospitals are equipped specialised doctors and modern equipments; many private clinics exist, but they are expensive	Canada's first health insurance program begins in Saskatchewan in 1947, now Canada Universal Health Care services free to all Canadians, community housing personal care services are available at free to all seniors
No immigrants services in Bangladesh, but recently Rohinghy refugees relief services exist since 2017	Federal Government implements settlement and integration programs for immigrants in 1948
The Tribal Acts made in 1976	The Indian Act is amended in 1951
No disability act passed in Bangladesh	Disabled Persons Act Passed in 1954; the Employability Assistance for People with Disabilities (EAPD) replaces the Vocational Rehabilitation of Disabled Persons Act in 1997
No hospital insurance Act	Hospital Insurance Act is passed in 1956
No Youth allowance	Youth Allowance Act is Passed in 1964
No universal public pension plans for all Bangladeshi	The Canada and Quebec Pension Plans are introduced in 1953, the Canada Pension Plan is universal and it initiated in 1966
Exist Medical Act, but less functional	Medical Care Act is passed in 1966
No spousal allowance	Spouse Allowance Act in introduced in 1975
Public housings are renting to government officials	The Non-profit Housing Program is established by the Federal Government in 1978
Employment equity law exist, but still gender employment discrimination exists in private sector	Employment Equity Act is passed in 1986. No gender employment discrimination exists in public and private sector
No child tax benefits and national child benefits	Refundable Child Tax Credit is converted to the Non-Refundable Child Tax Credit in 1988; Canada Child Tax Benefit (CCTB) is introduced in 1997; and National Child Benefit is introduced in 1998 (Ross, Katherine & Mark, 1996).
No multiculturalism Act, but Bangladesh is a secular country	The Canadian Multiculturalism Act is passed in 1988
No universal family allowances and old age security allowances	*Claw backs* are introduced into family allowances and Old Age Security in 1989

Social safety net services in Bangladesh	Social safety net services in Canada
Custom and excise duties are exists, but vats yet to implement	The Goods and Services Tax (GST) is introduced in 1992. Also governing Provincial Service Tax (PST) in many provinces in Canada
No Family Allowances	Family allowances are replaced by the Canada Child Tax Benefit in 1993
No tribal public child care program	The First Nations and Inuit Child Care Initiative is launched in 1995
No workfare services	Welfare to work program is termed *Ontario Works* in the Ontario province in 1997
No income support for the homeless, but occasional relief is available	The supporting Communities Partnership Initiative begins (aims to eliminate and prevent homelessness in 1999
Immigration and Refugee Protection Act exist	The Immigration and Refugee Protection Act is tabled in the House of Commons in 2000
Tribal child care public support services are not available	Aboriginal Child Care supported by the Territorial Government,; Aboriginal health and wellness program supported by different community services funded Aboriginal Foundation and Native Counsel of Canada
No universal income support services for the disables	Disability support services funded by the state agencies
No employment insurance supported by the employers or public agency	Employment insurance supported by the employers, public agency
No national child benefit services	National Child Benefit (previously Canada Child Tax Benefit) supported by the state; Child Care Centers are available at different locations and run/supported by public, private and community organizations
No free food banks, but the government has food security program	Food banks distribute food to low income people at free of cost
No community employment services, but print media, electronic media circulate employment notice for public	Human Resource Development supports and funds to the community employment services

Social safety net services in Bangladesh	Social safety net services in Canada
No commercial social services are working in Bangladesh	Foster Care Centers, Home Care Support Programs available at different locations and they are funded by the state. Moreover, many commercial social services are working in Canada
NO Guaranteed Annual Income (GAI) and Guaranteed Annual Supplements (GIS) are available in Bangladesh	Guaranteed Annual Income (GAI, Guaranteed Annual Supplements (GIS) supported by public agencies
No government Income Support Program for the Youth, but government provides training to youths to develop their various trade skills	Income Support Program for the Youths
Grameen Bank indentify landless people those have less than 40 decimals of land in the rural area or assets less than Tk.25000	Low income level is measured by the low income cut-offs (LICO) and need tests
Grameen Bank, BRAC and many other NGOs/MFIs are addressing poverty by providing loans to poor people	Low income people, unemployed people receive social assistance funded by the government
Retirement Income and Provident Funds are funded by both government and private and big national NGOs	Retirement Income and Provident Funds are funded by both government and private and big national NGOs
Boyakka Vatta (seniors allowance very minimum) have started from 2012	Seniors Independence Programs and Old Age Security services exist for long
Few social work agencies available, but maximum are religious and individual philanthropies	Huge social work agencies are working in Canada supported by public agencies and foundations
Few volunteers are working in SSNs programs	Huge volunteers (youths, adults and seniors) are working in SSN community organizations
Joinvile crime prevention centers are available only in major cities.	Child Development Centers are available everywhere in Canada

15.4. Canada Welfare State moving to the workfare model instead the residual approach

The term welfare refers to a country that is committed to correcting the problem of unequal distribution of wealth in a capitalist economy. According to Asa Briggs, (1961) the welfare state is a state that has three directions to modify market forces: Guarantying individuals and families a minimum income; second, to provide some social contingencies to address the crisis (e.g. sickness, old age and unemployment); and third ensure all citizens offered the best standards available to certain social services. Canada implements social security programs by using taxation to redistribute income from the rich to the poor. Its social welfare system has developed by the state as a formal mechanism to protect citizens against the economic and social hazards of modern society (Mishra, 1981). This system is introduced after the widespread economic and social disruption of the Great Depression in the 1930s to convince the Canadians of the need for government intervention during hard economic times.

Social agencies have a number of functions in common, such as securing funding, assessing clients' needs and ensuring the quality of services. The mix service agency offers is reflecting the community needs (Rice &Michael (2000). However, Canada's Welfare State has away from a residual approach to a more institutional approach to social welfare in mid 1960s (Davis, 2000). Central to this concept of the welfare state is the recognition of the governments has power to redistribute income in order to 'share the wealth' and prevent large segments of the population from living in poverty (Head, 1984). This redistributive approach is influenced by adopting the principles of Keynesian economics. However, Canada never abandoned its capitalist values or practices. So Canada's welfare state is the mixed capitalist system. However, Food Banks distribute dry and canned food at free (residual approach) to poor living in different neighbourhoods in Canada. These foods are donated by grocery buyers and food venders to food banks. However, food venders donate their unsold food items that have two-three expiry dates.

Canada has one of the highest poverty rates for individuals and families among wealthy industrialized nations (Innocenti Research Center, 2005). Here poverty means the inability to take advantage of all the opportunities provided by the state. Poverty is the strongest determinant of health (Hick, 2004; Ralphel, 2007). 16% Canadians are suffering from poverty (Raphael, 2007), unattached /children in female-led households poverty rate is very high (52.1%), (Statistics Canada, 2006), 15% Canadian children are living in poverty (Innocenti Research Center, 2005), social deprivation and social exclusion, developmental and ethical concerns. Canada's approach to public policy concerning the prevention of poverty, materials, social, mental and illness,- is quite underdeveloped as compared to most European nations (Chappell, 2006). However, Canada Universal Healthcare services address the health problem and it is world-famous. However, poverty has other concerns like safety, social cohesion, community solidarity, as well as general well being in addition to guaranteed income basics; these are measuring the quality of life for reaching Canadians full human and social potential. The public social safety net measures are trying to address these issues. In all these issues, Canadian government is very aware of them and it is constantly trying to address them through state interventions, contracting out to private agencies and community based organizations.

15.5. Canada welfare programs

The main goal of all social welfare programs is to change conditions that threaten personal or social functioning. The primary functions of social welfare is to fulfill human needs which are odds with people-the gap between or discrepancies between what is and what should be (OECD, 2005). Here the term social security refers to government programs and services that aim to assist people who have limited ability to earn income as a result of old age, disability, unemployment, sickness or other contingencies in order to solve their social and economic isolation, poverty, racism, unemployment and crime. Social programs are developed, implemented and administered in the areas of social welfare, health care and post-secondary student loans and stipends. Canada has unique student loans program for the post-secondary students. Researcher Kazi Rouf completed his undergraduate and graduate degrees by receiving Ontario Student Assistance Program (OSAP). Likewise Canadian many matured students receive public student loans to complete their diploma or other degrees in order to prepare them employable in the job market. Social programs developed many social work activities to help individuals, families, groups and communities to enhance their individuals and collective well-being to develop their skills and their ability to use their own resources and those of the community to resolve problems.

A variety of interventions are used to create change at the micro, mezzo, and macro levels in Canada. Micro-level change is directed at individuals, families and small groups. Social Case Worker uses a variety of techniques to help individuals address needs, issues and concerns. Family service workers help families' access resources and fulfill important roles. Social groups are often used to help people with similar goals and concerns work toward better social functioning. However, United Nations Human Development Index determines the income gap between the rich and poor in 17 countries. Canada is found to have the tenth-largest gap (Canada Council on Social Development, 1999b; Chappell, 2006, p. 198). Nevertheless, to reduce inequality, Canadian governments have established income-security programs designed to ensure that individuals and families receive a minimum income regardless of how much they make through earnings or how much property they own (Meklichercik, 1995). Canada's income security programs aim to achieve the following objectives:

- The sharing of Canadian resources provide an adequate income to people living in crisis;
- The maintenance of an appropriate degree of income security or stability;
- The equitable treatment of individuals and families in different situations;
- The encouragement of people to take responsibility for their own lives and livelihood when they are able to do so; and
- Respect for the personal dignity of the beneficiaries (Royal Commission on the Economic Union, 1985, p. 773).

Examples of income-security programs in Canada include: Employment Insurance, Old Age-Security, the Canada and Quebec Pension Plans, social assistance, veterans" pensions, the Guaranteed Income Supplement, and the Canada Child Tax Benefit etc. However, the Canadian Council on Social Development discovered that the poorest 20 percent of Canadians receive almost 40 percent of all government-sponsored income-security benefits. Within this low-income group, close to half are families headed by a senior; roughly one-third are single unattached people under age 65; and about one-tenth are single-parent families (Lochhead, 1998).

15.6. Canadian public SSN services' have shifted to private sector and third sector

The paper narrates earlier that Canadian Government SSN systems are being downsized, and many programs are being devolved from the public sector to the private sector. As the government shrinks its roles in social welfare, commercial enterprises step in to deliver services on a profit-making basis. Social Welfare programs that tend to be run by the commercial sector include nursing homes, residential homes for children, homemakers' services, and day-care centers. Commercial social welfare services are quickly gaining legitimacy through free trade agreements and other schemes that support free enterprises. As a result of competition, the commercial sector has the incentive to deliver services efficiently; however, commercial services are expensive and they are not massively accessible to low-income people.

Most third sector voluntary agencies can be classified as community service agencies, quasi-public agencies, or self-help groups. Voluntary agencies are usually governed independently and receive funds from government, foundations and or private sectors. The service delivery role of the voluntary sector is expanding in response to government downsizing. Voluntary agencies are compromising their goals as they compete with other agencies for funding (Neysmith, 1991). The cost sharing arrangements have blurred the boundaries between the voluntary and public sectors. The new partnership between the voluntary and public sectors evolve over three phases: Commitment, construction and consolidation. Rosalle Chappell (2006) comments that the 21st century is expected to bring further changes-at the macro, mezzo and micro levels-to the roles and responsibilities of Canada's public, commercial and voluntary sectors.

Since 1960s, many Canadians receive social welfare services in institutional settings are now being supported by community-based services. For example, residential social service centers provide round-the-clock care, while non-residential centers provide services on a drop-in, appointment, or outreach basis. Non-residential centers include drop-in centers, family services, work-place programs, on-line support, outreach services and multi-service centers (Ralphel, 2007). However, sometimes intake registration workers registered the clients to increase agencies registration numbers instead giving them proper services that the clients need. Direct services are social agency activities that involve face-to-face interactions with clients. The indirect social service agencies do not usually involving personal contact with clients rather they have indirect services, which include social administration, program development and social research etc. However, the accountability practices of social agencies have shifted from a bureaucratic or service focus to an outcome focus.

15.7. Unemployment in Canada and transition from UI to EI

Canada's unemployment insurance (UI) system is originally designed in 1940 to 'promote the economic and social security of Canadians by supporting workers from the time they leave one job until they another' (Hick, 2004). However, UI system has undergone several changes, the most dramatic change occurred in the 1990s. During that period, the federal government stopped funding UI, now this program is funded by joint contributions make by employers and workers and shortened the period workers can draw benefits. The overhaul of the UI system is promoted by recognition of the following flaws (Chappell, 2006):

1. UI does not help people who are unemployed for long periods in the labour market;
2. UI is easily abused by employers, who organized their hiring, work schedules and layoffs;
3. The continually rising premium that are necessary to maintain the system that has increasing burden for employers and workers; and
4. Coverage does not extend to a large segment of the workforce.

The unemployment Insurance Act in 1996 changed the name Employment Insurance (EI) (Chappell, 2006; Guest, 1999; and Hick, 2007). Here EI uses hours instead weeks worked to determine the amount of benefits received and reduce maximum insurable earnings and benefits. Although overall unemployment in Canada is declining in Canada, certain groups of people are underrepresented in the workforce. For example, researcher had layoff several times from his job and receive EI benefit, which is not enough to pay rent and cover daily basic needs. Anyway, unemployment has economic costs and it has been associated with social problems ranging from family breakdown to crime. The overhaul of the unemployment insurance system in 1996 resulted in a dramatic decline in the number of people who are eligible to receive benefits, but a greater emphasis on making employment program more active. The EI fund has accumulated a massive surplus because while more people are contributing to EI, fewer are collecting benefits.

15.8. Child benefits

One response of federal and regional governments to the problem of child poverty has been the introduction of child benefits (Ross et al., 1996). However, a number of child benefit schemes have been introduced, revised and scrapped over the years (Hick, 2006; Chappell, 2006 and Ross et al., 1996). The most recent child benefit scheme is called the *National Child Benefit* (NCB) introduced in 1998. Under the NCB, the federal government provides direct income support through the Canada Child Tax Benefits (CCTB); a tax-free monthly payment makes to low-income families with children below 18 years old. For example, in 2000, families received a maximum annual CCTB of CDN$2056 for the first child and CDN$1853 for each additional child (Ralphel, 2007). However, these amounts are not enough for children to fulfil their needs.

15.9. Canada affordable housing services

Canada has shelter and transition house schemes which are had been the primary resources for abused women, response to violence against women and children. Moreover, Canadian Government makes arrangements supportive housing for seniors and low income people. The Affordable housing for the seniors assist to have live independent life in their livelihoods. This scheme helps to low income people, single mothers, single parents and two income families as well as low income seniors to survive in their transitional modest life in Canada (Chappell, 2006; and Hick, 2004). Additionally, low-income family members can receive gym and pool facilities from the municipalities at a discounted price.

15.10. Services to Canadian aging population

Canada also responsive to aging population's safety and security issues priority basis related to elder abuse, crime against seniors and physical injury (Bryden, 1974). Seniors (Canada uses seniors instead older people) can use facilities like 'basic technologies such as automated teller machines, voice mail, and computerised library systems etc. The government ensures retirement income programs are adequate for them. Moreover, there are public transportation (Transit Wheels, care giver and health care) facilities are providing to the aging population. There are arrangements like foster care for seniors, personal support workers services, receive meals (mostly NGOs/churches) and housekeeping services for the seniors. Moreover, seniors are receiving many other kinesiology social services when they needed. They receive financial supports like pay for care, pensions options (CPP), RRSP, Tax credits; community-based supports services like referral services, advocacy, housing and home renovation, home help, nursing and therapies and

KAZI ABDUR ROUF

home support; informal net-works, working at home, on-site seniors day care, unpaid leave etc. (Chappell, 2006). There are many programs exist that culturally relevant for seniors in Canada. However, although Canada's retirement income system has contributed to a drop in the poverty rate for seniors, it has been criticized for keeping the incomes of many seniors below the poverty line.

15.11. First Nations communities' residential schools trauma counselling services

First Nations people accounted for about 3 percent of Canada's population (Hick, 2004). The Indian Act and enfranchisement policies put the federal government in control of people living on reserves. The First Nations movement began in the 1970s for their rights and needs. From 1883-1950s, the federal government attempted to assimilate First Nations into mainstream society by separating Aboriginal children from their parents and placing them in the residential schools (Lee, 1999) where they had been taught European languages, Christianity, European dresses, values and customs. However, they were suffered from sexual and physical abuse. To help First Nations people deal with the adverse effects of the residential school system, the Aboriginal Healing Strategy was established in 1997-98 in collaboration with First Nations Health Program and Northern Affairs Canada and Aboriginal Affairs of the Privy Council Office (Chappell, 2006). This strategy supported by the original Healing Foundation. The foundation funds to community based healing centers, which provide services on a holistic model and address the physical, emotional, mental and spiritual needs of individuals and families. Counseling and other services are also provided to address family violence, sexual abuse, alcohol and drug abuse, grief etc. (Hick, 2004; Raphel, 2007).

Moreover, in 1995, Human Resources Development Canada launched the First Nations and Inuit Child Care Initiative as part of a strategy to improve the economic situation for aboriginal families. The government supports more affordable quality child-care spaces;

484

increase opportunities for young children attend schools. Many child-care facilities have opened across Canada as a result of this initiative. Many Aboriginal communities are developing their own child welfare programs. The Native Friendship Centers are expanding services for urban youth (Hick, 2004; Raphel, 2004). To work with Aboriginal people for their well-being, Canada develops special trained Aboriginal Community Development Workers to improve the relationship between Aboriginal people and mainstream people.

Canada is a multicultural society. Over 100 ethnic groups live in Canada. Although Canada is promoting multiculturalism and a cultural mosaic idea; however, it supports among Canadians for a *melting pot approach* (Chappell, 2006; Hick, 2004). Canada's immigration policy has continued to evolve over the years for immigrants' integration and settlement in Canada. The federal government sponsors a wide range of settlement programs and funding supports that aim to help newcomers adjust to Canadian society. Millions of dollar spend to Immigrant Service Agencies (ISAs) like settlement counseling agencies, and ESL (English as Second Language) agencies, and employment counseling agencies etc. to support immigrants for their settlement, English/French Language learning and to be employable in Canada.

15.12. Canada disability support services

Canada disability support services excel in the world. More than 5 million Canadians or approximately 15.5 percent of the population, have a disability (Statistics Canada, 2015). The Canada Disability Support Services provides a greater public acceptance and government accommodation of people with physical and developmental disabilities. The disability income support system includes providing earnings income support and compensation. For example, the Ontario Disability Support Program (ODSP) introduces individualized funding and work incentives for people diagnosed with disability (Chappell, 2006). Rehabilitation programs for people with disabilities are inclusive. Government provide incentives to people with disabilities prepare for, find and keep jobs.

To address the needs of people with disabilities, barrier-free entrance buildings and special transportation system legislation Act passed for them. Many public agencies, volunteering organizations, community based-organizations are working for them (Hick, 2004; Ralphel, 2007). For example, the Canadian Association for Community Living, the Council of Canadians with Disabilities and community club house etc. are directly working for the people with disabilities. Moreover, Canadian National Institute for the Blinds (CNIB) provides many safety net services to visually impair or totally blind people of Canada. For example, in Toronto, visually impaired people can ride the TTC public transit by using CNIB-TTC travel passes at free of costs.

16. Prevent people from using social welfare services in Canada

There are a number of barriers that can prevent people from using social welfare services. Barriers are factors affecting relate to an agency's screening procedures, referral system, and environment; factors affecting availability include the number, distribution and coordination of services in a community (Chappell, 2006). The fear of being stigmatized is discouraging people from seeking help. For example, in Canada, Islamphobia hamper Muslim people to disclose their problems, needs to public institutions or community-based agencies. Many people are stigmatizing to welfare recipients or who are living in social housing or children living in foster care centers. The stigma attached to welfare can be traced to the English Poor Laws, which made distinctions between the 'worthy' poor and the 'unworthy' poor (Hick, 2004). Moreover, some services in a community are too fragmented and that hampers clients needs and delay receive services immediately if clients need to be refereed to several agencies or workers (Ralphel, 2007). Poor inter-agency coordination is also indicated when clients find too many agencies that provide the same service. Ironically, cutbacks in social security funding have motivated social agencies to improve inter-agency relations and coordination. MacLeod and Kinnon (1996) note, "It is (important) than ever to share information, to share experience, to avoid duplication and to stimulate courage for change". In order to stimulate and facilitate inter- agency coordination, some communities have established social planning councils, advisory committees, multidisciplinary teams, and inter-agency management committees (Hick, 2004).

The development of a global economy has implications for national welfare policies. It is argued in Globalization and the Welfare State that globalization limits the capacity of nation-states to act for social protection. Global trends have been associated with a strong neo-liberal ideology, promoting inequality and representing social protection as the source of 'rigidity' in the labour market (Mishra, 1999). World Bank and International Monetary Fund have been selling a particular brand of economic and social policy to developing countries. However, it is found there is an increased focus on selective social services to disadvantaged people in the world (Ibid, 1999).

17. Conclusions

Currently dominant scholars are away from the language of 'welfare', (Alderman, 2000; Bedard et al., 2000; Clarke, 1991; and Isabel, 2001, Yunus, 2008) with connotations of unsustainable relief, handouts and poor people's dependency and prefer the language of 'sustainable development'. In Bangladesh, health spending is not particularly redistributive (Davis, 2000). The bottom half of the population receives 57 percent of health expenditure compared to the bottom half of the population receiving only 38.4 percent of education expenditures (Hossain, 2000; Hossain & Ali 2012; and Mahmud, 2004). Bangladesh has a number of government-run safety net programs, funded largely by external food aid and international funding aid. The public supported food programs have significant contribution to safety net services in Bangladesh. For example, Food for Work Program provides wheat in exchange for work in rural infrastructure projects. This is the largest of the programs in Bangladesh to address safety nets started from 1974 famine. Moreover, Food for Education (FFF) provides wheat and rice to poor children in return for regular primary school attendance. This began in 1993-4 in selected villages and is the fastest growing of programs in Bangladesh. Additionally, Vulnerable Group Development (VGD) provides food grain and training to disadvantaged women. Although their benefits are difficult to compare, all three programs appear to be cost-effective, with FFW and VGD somewhat better targeted (Hossain & Ali 2012; Kabir, 2004).

There are other government administered programs exist in Bangladesh. For example, Test Relief supports activities like cleaning ponds and bushes and making minor repairs to rural roads, schools, mosques and madrasahs during raining seasons. The Rural Maintenance Program employs destitute women in labour-intensive rural road maintenance work. Compared to the state social safety programs, NGOs play a much more significant role in the field of poverty reduction and social protection in Bangladesh than they do in India (Hossain & Ali 2012; Newsnetwork, 2004). The NGOs have built up an international reputation based on their size, effectiveness and influence in policy matters (Mahmud, 2004). Grameen Bank, BRAC and many other NGOs/ MFIs in Bangladesh have reached a size that puts their poverty reduction programs on a same level of the government (Hossain & Ali, 2012). However, there are many myths around the relationship between government and NGOs in Bangladesh. The government expressed concern about NGO cost-effectiveness, accountability and heavy reliance on foreign funds, while NGOs have accused the government of rigidity, failure to distinguish between different NGOs SSN performances and their very imperfect accountability (Hossain & Ali, 2012). However, recently there have been rise of partnerships between NGOs/MFIs and the government's executing agencies in the field of social safety net services in Bangladesh (Rahman & Hossain, 1995).

Although there are many challenges exist to meet safety net rest on state, family, society, local agencies, and NGOs/MFIs; the coverage of all the existing programs should be widened. They should not limit by name and numbers. Moreover, Hosain Zillur Rahman and Liquat Ali (2012) suggest Bangladesh state and non-state agencies should go for more effective programs like Tiffin-feeding in schools because school-feeding service has proved quite successful in many developing countries including Bangladesh (Kabir, 2004). Contrarily in Canada, the safety net basic income measures have made by Fraser Institute in 1996 and its LICO calculation has continued till today (Chappell, 2006); however, housing rents, other necessities of life expenditures have skydived. The Simon Fraser Institute calculated money is not sufficient for low income people or people with social assistance to support their daily necessities like food, clothing, housing, health and education; therefore, there are huge protests against the basic income calculations on safety net basic incomes for many years in Canada.

In response to the movement, the Ontario Liberal Government has initiated a pilot scheme named 'Ontario basic income projects' in Hamilton-Brant, Thunder Bay and Lindsay cities in 2016 to find whether unconditional cash support could boost health, education and housing for people on social assistance or living on low incomes who have been receiving up to $14,000 a year or $24,000 for couples under the Ontario Liberal Government. However, critics find increasing social assistance money to people on social assistance have enabled participants to move into apartment and go back to school or other training programs to lift themselves off social assistance (NDP Leader and Green Leader weigh in at the star.com/gta, August, 2, 2018, p. 5). Nevertheless, the future of poverty in Canada primarily depends upon the policy influence of political parties in federal and provincial parliaments (Star Metro Toronto, August 2, 2018).

18. References

Alderman, H. (2000). *Multi-tier targeting of social assistance: The role of inter-governmental transfer*, Washington: World Bank.

Alderman H. (2000). *Do local officials know something we don't? Decentralization of targeted transfer in Albania*, World Bank

APEC (2001). *A proposal for revitalization of APEC social safety net activities by the Republic of Korea and Thailand*, Twelfth APEC Ministerial Meeting, 2000/ANM/019

Banting, Keith G. (1987). *The Welfare State and Canadian Federalism*, Second Edition, MacGill-Queen's University Press

Bark Sooni, Kim Meegon and Hwang Deoksoon (2006). *Social safety net in the Republic of Korea: analysis and prospect*, ESCAP

Battle, K. and Michael Mendelson (1997). *Child benefits reform in Canada: An evaluative framework and future directions.* Ottawa: Caledon Institute. Retrieved from http://www.caaledonnist.orgg/cbr-toc.htm on *August 15, 2018*

Beatrice Lorge Rogers and Jennifer Coates (2002). *Food based safety nets and related programs.* Tufts University School of Nutrition Science and Policy, Medford, Massachusetts.

Bedard, Marcel, Lean-Francoes Bertrand and Louise Grignon (2000). *The unemployed without recent employment*, Ottawa: HRDC

Blackstock, Sarah (1999). Bandaid Banwaghon. *New Internationalist*, Issue 314

Briggs, A. (2006). The welfare state in historical perspective. European *Journal of Sociology*, Vol. 2, pp. 251-259

Bryden, Kenneth (1974). *Old age pensions and policy making in Canada*, Montreal: McGill-Queens University Press

Chaabane, M. (2002). *Towards the universalization of social security: The experience of Tunisia.* ILO, Extension of Social Security, ESS paper #4

Chappell, Rosalie (2006). *Social welfare in Canadian society*, Toronto: Nelson

Clarke, M. (1991). *Fighting poverty through programs: Social and Health programs for Canada's poor children and youth*, Ottawa: Children* Enfants* Jeunesse*Youth

Conning, Jonathan and Kevin, Michael (2000). *Community based targeting mechanisms for social safety nets*, Boston University and Santa Clara University

Cook, S. (2000). Beyond the iron rice bowl. *IDS Discussion Paper 377 Brighton*, UK: Institute of Development Studies, University of Sussex.

Coudouel, A., Marine, S. and Macklewright (1999). *Targeting social assistance in a transition economy: The Mahallas in Uzbekistan.* Discussion Paper # 2064, CRPR

Davis, Peter (2000). *Rethinking the welfare regime approach: The case of Bangladesh.* IFIPA, University of Bath, Paper presented at the European Network of Bangladesh Studies Sixth Workshop, University of Oslo, Norway

Dowla, Asif and Dipal Barua (2006). *The poor always pay back: The Grameen 11 story,* Bloomfield, CT: Kumarian Press, Inc.

Eichler, M. (1987). Social policy concerning women. In Shankar A. Yelaja (Ed.), *Canada Social Policy* (rev, ed., pp 139-156). Waterloo: Wilfred Laurier University Press

Epstein, L. (1988). *Helping people: The task-centered approach* (2nd ed.). Columbus: Merrill Publishing

Evans, Patricia (2001). Women and social welfare: Exploring the connections. In Joanne Turner and Francis Turner, eds., *Canadian social welfare,* Toronto: Pearson Education

Feit, M. D. & Feit, N. C. (1996). An overview of social work practice with the elderly. In M.J. Holosko and M. D. Feit (eds.), *Social work practice with the elderly* (2nd ed.), pp. 3-20. Toronto Scholar Press

Findlay, P. (1983). Social welfare in Canada: The case for universality, *Canada Social Work Review'* 83, pp. 17-24

Fultz, E. (2003). *Recent trends in pension reform and implementation in the EU accession countries,* ILO

Grameen Kalyan (2017). *Grameen Kalyan Annual Report, 2017.* Dhaka: Grameen Kalyan

Guest, Denis (1999). *The emergence of social security in Canada,* 3rd ed. Vancouver: University of British Columbia (BC) Press

Hashemi, Syed and Tudor, Maya (2001). *Linking microfinance and safety net programs to include the poorest: The case of IGVGD in Bangladesh.* The World Bank Focus note 21

Hick, Steven (2004). *Social welfare in Canada: Understanding income security,* Toronto: Thomson

Hossain, Mirza Altaf (2000). *Food security and nutritional wellbeing in Bangladesh-lessons learnt and tasks ahead,* Dhaka: FAO

Hossain Zillur Rahman and Liaquit Ali Chowdhury ((2012). *A social safety nets in Bangladesh. Volume- 2. Ground realities and policy challenges,* APPRC-UNDP Research Initiative. Dhaka: Power and Participation Research Center

Ife, Jim (2001). *Human rights and social work towards right-based practice,* Cambridge, UK: Cambridge University Press

Innocenti Research Center (2005). *Child poverty in rich nations, 2005.* Report card no. 6. Florence: Innocenti Research Center

Irawan, Puguh ((2001). *Analysis and recommendations on social safety nets: prospects in Indonesia,* Presented in Regional Seminar on strengthening policies and programs on social safety nets, 1-3 May2001, ERSCAP SD/SS.INF

Isabel, Ortiz (2001). *Reforming social protection systems in Asia and the Pacific: A perspective from the ADB,* paper presented in OECD workshop 9-10 April, COM/DEELSA/CD (2002)20, Paris

Kabeer, Naila (2002). *Safety nets and opportunity ladders: Addressing vulnerability and enhancing productivity in South Asia.* Institute of Development Studies, University of Sussex

Kabir, Ekram (2004). *Strengthening social safety nets in Bangladesh.* Dhaka: Newsnetwork,

Kazemipur, A. and Halli, S. (2001). The changing colour of poverty in Canada. *Review of Sociology and Anthropology,* Vol. 38(2), pp. 217-238

Khandker, Shahid (1998). *Fighting poverty with microcredit: Experience in Bangladesh,* New York; Oxford University Press

Laliberte, P. (1998). Setting new priorities for Canada's employment insurance program. *Perception,* Vol. 23(2), pp. 9-12.

Lee, K. (1999). Measuring poverty among Canada's Aboriginal people, *Perception,* Vol. 23(2), pp. 9-12

Mahabub Hossain, (1988). *Credit for alleviation of rural poverty: The Grameen Bank in Bangladesh,* Washington DC: IFPRI

Mahmud, Wahidudin (2004). *Attacking poverty with microcredit,* New Age. Introductory remarks made at the inaugural session of the International Seminar on 'attacking Poverty with Microcredit

Miller, Victoria (2000). Central bank reactions to banking crises in fixed exchange rate regimes. *Journal of Development Economics*, Vol. 63 (2), pp. 451–472

Mishra, Ramesh (1999). *Globalization and the welfare state*, UK: Edward Elgar Publishing Inc.

Moscovitch, Allan and Andrew Webster (1995). Aboriginal School Assistance Expenditures. In Susan Philips, eds., *How Ottawa spends 1995-1996; Mid-life crisis*. Ottawa: Carleton University Press

National Council of Welfare (1999). *A Pension Primer*, Ottawa: National Council of Welfare

Neysmith, Sheila (1991). *From community care to a social model of care, in women's caring: Feminist perspectives on social welfare*, Carol Baines, Patricia Evans and Sheila Neysmith, eds., Toronto: McClelland & Stewart Ltd.

Organization for Economic Co-operation and Development (2005). *Society at a glance: OECD social indicators* (2005, ed.), Paris: OECD

Pal, L. A. (1998). *How Ottawa spends, 1998-1999-Balancing Act: The post-deficit mandate* (pp. 1-30). Toronto: Oxford University Press

Rahman, Hossain Zillur and Hossain, Mahabub (1995). (Eds) *Rethinking rural poverty: Bangladesh as a case study*, New Delhi: SAGE Publications

Raphael, Dennis (2007). *Poverty and policy in Canada*, Toronto: Canadian Scholars' Press Inc.

Raphael, Dennis. (2004). *Social determinants of health: Canadian perspectives*. Toronto: Canadian Scholars' Press

Rice, James and Michael, Prince (2000). *Changing politics of Canadian social policy*, Toronto: University of Toronto

Ross, David, Katherine Scott, and Mark Kelly (1996). *Child poverty: What are the consequences*, Ottawa; Canadian Council on Social Development

Rouf, K. A. (2018). *Compare and contrast NGO/MFIs developed social safety net services (SSNs) in Bangladesh and state-managed SSNs measures in Canada,* T-space, University of Toronto, https://tspace.library.utoronto.ca/handle/1807/90254

Rouf, K. A. (2018). *Grameen social business services in Bangladesh,* T-space, University of Toronto, https://tspace.library.u*toronto.ca/handle/1807/90254*

Sayed Hashemi and Sinney Schuler (1996). Rural credit programs and women's empowerment in Bangladesh, *World Development,* Vol. 24(4), pp. 635-653

Schleberger, E. (2002). *Namibia's universal pension scheme: Trends and challenges,* ILO, Extension of social security, ESS paper #6

Schwarzer, H. and Querino, A. (2002). *Non-contributory pensions in Brazil: Assessing the impac*t *of poverty reduction.* ILO, Extension of social security, ESS paper #11

StarMetro Toronto (August 2, 2018). *Ontario basic income projects participants feel fear, betrayal.* Thestart.com/gta

Statistics Canada (2006). *Low income in Canada., pre-tax LICOs, CANSM tables*, Ottawa, Statistics Canada.

Statistics Canada (2015). *A portrait of persons with Disabilities*, Ottawa: Ministry of Industry, Science and Technology

Statistics Canada (2017). *Social safety net services in Canada.* Ottawa: Ministry of Industry, Science and Technology

Steinhauer, P. (1995). *The Canada Health and Social Transfer: A threat to the health development and future productivity* of *Canada's Children and Youth.* Ottawa: Caledon Institute of Social Policy

Townsend, P. (1993). *The international analysis of poverty.* Milton Keynes, UK: Harvester Wheatsheaf

World Bank (2018). *Social safety nets context.* http://www.worldbank.org/en/topic/safetynets

Yunus, Muhammed (2008). *Creating a world without poverty*, Dhaka: Subarna

Zhiqin, Shao (2002). *Social safety net in Thailand: the role government.* Retrieved from kumlai.free.fr/.../Thailande/Social%20Safety%20Net%20in%20Thailand%20the%20R dated 11 July, 2018.

Organizing, Designing, Building and Forming of Groups and Centers and Grameen Bank Service Strategies in Bangladesh

Abstract

The objective of the paper is to narrate the Grameen Bank (GB) group and center organizing, designing, forming, and building tools in Bangladesh and to identify what mistakes the author and his colleagues have made during their journey in GB. It explores how they could do better jobs in organizing, designing, building and forming groups and centers and other activities if they are skilled in the community work ahead of their jobs in GB. The paper discusses different concepts, thoughts and ideas of community organizing, community designing, community building, and different mechanisms of GB loans and savings services for poor in Bangladesh. GB is continuously changes its center organizing and building tools; and developing innovative loans, savings products those are suitable to its borrowers to overcome their poverty.

The paper narrates the author and his colleagues' personal working experience in GB during late 1970s and 1980s. Moreover, the paper incorporates different challenges GB faces like social and economic barriers at the macro and micro level in implementing its services to poor people in Bangladesh at different times; and how GB overcomes these challenges and developed different innovative products and services in its Phase-1 and Phase-11. The narrated history of forming groups and organizing centers of GB and its different loan and savings products evolution process generates new knowledge and evidence in the field of group-based micro-credit. The process of evolution of GB would be a learning lesson for the readers, micro-finance practitioners, researchers and different community organizers in Bangladesh and elsewhere.

Keywords: Center and group management of Grameen Bank, community, civic engagement, social capital, community organizing, community building, community social planning, and Grameen Bank.

1. Introduction

This paper is about the experience of participatory decision-making process of group forming; center organizing, center designing and building of groups and centers of Grameen Bank; and implementing strategies of different savings and loan products of it in Bangladesh. The primary objective of the paper is to narrate the Grameen Bank group formation, center organizing, designing and planning experience in the villages of Bangladesh. Moreover, the paper identifies what mistakes I have made; but how I could do better jobs in group forming, center designing, organizing, planning and other activities if I had knowledge and skills on community organizing and planning ahead of my jobs in Grameen Bank in late 1970s and 1980s. Because through my working experience and research in community-based organizations in many countries, I have realized that I could do better jobs in my group forming, community (center) organizing, designing, building and center planning assignments in Grameen Bank the 1970s and 1980s. However, the good thing is that I have learnt lots from mistakes and improve my jobs from there. Even Grameen Bank learns and changes many of its loans and savings products from its field experience. The GB center structure and operation system was not developed by outside experts rather its center organizing, designing, group forming, planning and implementation strategies have been developing by the inputs come from the field staff of GB since 1976.

2. Objectives

The purposes of this paper are:

- To discuss community, civic engagement of the community, community organizing, and community social capital development and their relationships to GB center organizing and group formation
- To explore different approaches to community organizing, designing and building and applying them to Grameen Bank specific circumstances and issues, and
- To discuss different savings and credit products of GB both in Grameen Bank Phase-1 and Grameen Bank Phase-11 and their implementation strategies in Bangladesh.

3. Community synonym terms

The word "community" can mean different things to different people at different places. Community refers to communities of association based on religion, gender, race, or geography. Cohen (1985) defines community as a system of norms, values, and moral codes that provide a sense of identity for members. Fellin (2001) describes a community as a group of people who form a social unit based on common location (e.g., city or neighborhood), interest and identification (e.g., ethnicity, culture, social class, occupation, or age) or some combination of these characteristics.

In Bangladesh, NGOs are not using the term 'community' rather they are using village organizations, group, neighbourhood, center, association, or society. For example, Grameen Bank uses the term 'Center', BRAC uses 'Village Organization', ASA uses 'Association', Nejara Kari uses 'Group', Society. However, in North America, Europe and in many other countries use the term "community'. Below the paper first discusses community participatory decision-making process, community organizing, community building, community, community building and planning different thoughts and approaches;

secondly the paper narrates author's community working experience in Canada and compares his working experience with Bangladesh; thirdly, how Grameen Bank is organizing, designing, forming, building and planning its groups and centers; and how GB is managing its centers, groups; and its different loans and savings products in Bangladesh. Fourthly, the paper also discusses GB operational policies and strategies in Bangladesh at different periods.

4. Community participatory decision making process

Community organizing has implications for those who express opinions about how their intended community is shaped: participatory planning and decisions means exchanging information, ideas, opinions, and process and positions with those people who live near the neighbourhood. However, citizen participation, community people participation is necessary for every community people voice and choice. Because the concept of participatory decision-making that people should deliberate together over issues that affect their future and make decisions accordingly. It helps community members, group members and individuals understand one another's point of view, and it facilitates decisions making for the common good (Rouf, 2016). In professional terms, participatory decision-making means that the professional or the source of political power is not the sole decision maker, rather someone who works with the people to help them reach decisions. In community planning terms, participatory decision-making means that community planner works with people, helps them reach decisions about community designing, planning issues, and translate these decisions into planning language throughout the decision-making process. However, the problem is if the community worker is not within the community, or he/she does not know the community's background and its different the issues behind.

Therefore, in the community meeting, community organising and planning, community worker would be a facilitator, is not a decision maker. Rather, he should identify what community voices and choices are. If the community people spontaneously participate and express their choices that are needed for them, the community worker tries to accommodate their voices and choices into community building and planning documents. However, to reach common understanding among all community people, it is sometimes difficult. In the community participation decision-making meeting, there might many opposition views. In that situation, community organizing and planning worker might think the community is not a homogeneous or a heterogeneous or conflicting notion. There should be different opinions among the community peoples, but the community organizing worker should have skills and capacity to translate opposite views are also community views, but in the decision-making process, only include majority's demand into community design, building and action plan as a priority basis. It is important to remember that community organizing, designing, building, and planning process is inherently democratic. Umut Toker (2012) thinks the participatory decision-making community organizing, designing and planning have been developed to achieve the following benefits:

- To let professionals become facilitators in the community decision making process of different issues and demands of the community people
- To efficiently design, manage, and analyse community design events
- To move toward consensus building
- To help reach design decisions collaboratively, and
- To guide parties that will contribute to and manage implementation so that the decisions made are implemented as desired by the community

5. Community organizing

Community organizing is the coordination of cooperative efforts and campaigning carried out by local residents to promote the interests of their community. Community organizing is a process where people who live in proximity to each other come together into an organization that acts in their shared self-interest. It refers to the entire process of organizing relationships, identifying issues, mobilizing around those issues, and maintaining an enduring organization. This process of building and mobilizing community is called "community organizing." It involves "the craft" of building and enduring network of center people, who identify with common ideals, and who can engage in social action on the basis of those ideals in the context of Grameen Bank (Rouf, 2016). In practice, it is much more than micro-mobilization or framing strategy (Snow et al., 1986.). According to Saul Alinsky if the community already exists, someone has to help transform it to support political action. Sometimes that requires reorganizing the community by identifying individuals who can move the community to action.

According to Elizia Pan (2012) and Perticipedia community organizing is a process where people who live in proximity to each other come together into an organization that acts in their shared self-interest. Unlike those who promote more-consensual community building, community organizers generally assume that social change necessarily involves conflict and social struggle in order to generate collective power for the powerless. A core goal of community organizing is to generate durable power for an organization representing the community, allowing it to influence key decision-makers on a range of issues over time. Community organizers work with and develop new local leaders, facilitating coalitions and assisting in the development of campaigns. Its organizers generally seek to build groups that are democratic in governance, open and accessible to community members, and concerned with the general health of a specific interest group, rather than the community as a whole. Community organizing seeks to broadly equally empower community members.

Community organizing is the process of building power that includes people with a problem in defining their community, defining the problems that they wish to address, the solutions they wish to pursue. The organization will identify the people and structures that need to be part of these solutions, and, by persuasion or confrontation, negotiate with them to accomplish the goals of the community. In the process, organizations will build a democratically controlled community institution that can take on further problems and embody the will and power of that community over time." (Beckwith et al., 1997).

In general, community organizing is the work that occurs in local settings to empower individuals, build relationships, and create action for social change (Bobo et al, 1991; Kahn, 1991, Beckwith and Lopez, 1997). Community organization is the process that builds a constituency that can go on to create a movement, and it occurs at a level between the micro-mobilization of individuals (Snow et al., 1986). Within the Alinsky model the organizing process, centers on identifying and confronting public issues to be addressed in the public sphere. In the Alinsky model, the organizer isn't there just to win a few issues, but to build an enduring organization that can continue to claim power and resources for the community--to represent the community in a public sphere pluralist polity. The organizer shouldn't start from scratch but from the community's pre-existing organizational base of churches, service organizations, clubs, etc. This model uses the small group to establish trust, and build "informality, respect, [and] tolerance of spontaneity" (Hamilton l991, 44). However, in many cases, new type of community work done by community workers from scratch.

6. What is community design?

Community design is the act of design the physical attributes of a community. Community design is the art of making sustainable living places that both thrive and adapt to people's needs for shelter, livelihood, commerce, recreation and social order (Hall and Porterfielld 2001, p. 3). Physical attributes of the community are location, and structure of the community organizing, building and planning. The physical structure of the community settings may affect people's ways of doing things (Lennertz, 1991). The community design approach includes (1) a community planner or designer makes decisions with people's interests and community planning worker's own professional background in mind, (2) people occupy the social positions and social capital and products, and (3) people adapt to the social positions and community settings while the community settings adapt to people's needs.

Community design is a process working with people, not for people (Hester, 1990). Therefore, a community worker works with people and facilitates a process during which people and community workers learn from each other; the community worker translates the wishes and aspirations of the people gathered during the process into community design and uses community workers' experience. Moreover, the social capital products like social network, solidarity are the outcome of those community designs and plans, is adapted to the people. Therefore, community design is the process of organizing community and making design decisions in collaboration with the community people who stand to be impacted by those decisions. As a community worker, we GB field workers in Bangladesh learn from center members about their day-to-day relationships with their physical settings of their neighbourhood. Community design also is the documents, legal structure of the community plan. Therefore, GB center organizing, designing and planning is the participatory decision- making process with the center members of GB. Grameen Bank field workers advocate for participatory decision-making principles like understanding center members' needs, adopting their situations and learning from them.

Key components of community organizing are developing a timeline, identifying tasks and instruments, tools, specifying goals, identify participatory activities of the community people, and develop outreach plan and activities.

The community design and advocacy model materialized in the US in Saul Alinsky's work (Sanoff, 2000). As a community organizer, Allinsky went beyond planning and design issues and got involved in the social and organizational aspects of community building. He focused mainly on lower income communities and worked with them for social change. His well-known *Rules for Radicals* (1971) provides guidelines for proponents of this approach.

According to Umut Tokker (2012) the community design has the following stages:

- What does the community want to get out of the process?
- When and by what step does the community achieve the outcomes (time line development)?
- What types of activities and tools is helpful for achieving the desired outcomes.
- How will community people be informed about the process and invite too provide input (identification of outreach techniques)
- Interact with the community outreach and receive inputs from them and record them
- The community design process is a nonlinear, and
- Collect feedback from community people before finalize community design and translate the community design into tangible products.

Outcomes of community design: Community designers go through systematic idea generation processes with group of people and translate these ideas into action for the wellbeing of community members. Such process requires a good amount off coordination, organization and collaboration. However the question is what are the outcomes of community design processes? Following are the possible outcomes may arise from the community design. (1) Learning from each other. (2) Community people become empowered by close interactions among community people and by providing inputs to community decision making process. (3) Fulfil community intended goals. (4) Develop unique solutions for each community projects. In the community organizing process, it acknowledges and embraces the multiple ideas of people and it develops an approach that includes multifaceted input.

7. Community building

Another model of community organizing is community building, which encompasses elements of both locality development and social planning approaches. Community building focuses on strengthening the social and economic fabric of communities by connecting them to internal and outside resources (Smock, 2004). The goal of community building is to build the internal capacity of communities by focusing on their assets/strengths, and engaging a broad range of community stakeholders to develop high-quality and technically sound comprehensive plans (Smock, 2004). Moreover, community building facilitates developing bridging and bonding of social capital in the community by creating social networks among community people and large numbers of agencies and institutions based on normative ties (i.e., a shared vision of the common good of the community). The focus is on the identifying the common interests of the community members and agencies who have a stake in the neighborhood. The field staff of Grammen Bank lets group members interact among them to develop their social networks and solidarity among them as well as let them identify their own problems, and solve their problems by them through their mutual interactions, dialogues and cooperation. To develop their bridging and bonding social capital in the group and center, field workers of GB are only the facilitators and mentors of their social capital and economic capital development in their life in Bangladesh.

Building a community involves real participation with people actively engaged, creating options and making decisions about them; it is a practice of genuine democracy (Alperovitz, 2009). Community governance is about practicing that mutually agreed by the worker and the community people. Community workers develop strategies, work with strategies for stabilizing local economics, and building community include small independent firms, cooperatives, worker owned companies, neighbourhood corporations, municipal utilities and new approaches to community banking and social investing.

There is an approach called self-help and self-built approaches. It is contrast to the community organizing model. This self-help approach focuses on empowering community people by helping them develop their means and skills to effect their incremental change. John F. C. Turner (1972) endorsed individuals and families' rights to self-build. John Lucien and J. Kroll turned their attention more to the physical implications of self-building. Habraken, MIT community organiser, thinks develop 'support structure' would provide the infrastructure needed the community based on their needs. However, there is a question what happens when there are conflicting interests exist among community people? If the conflicting interests are not solved immediately, it would turn to community crisis situation.

Role players in the community design process: The leading group of people in the community are community members, community leaders, members of the local governments and members of the NGOs. Key informant is someone who can provide the community designer with 'insider' information, but he should not be spaying to community worker. Participant is an individual who is likely to be affected by the outcomes of the community design process and the project. Project champion is a person who is particularly interested in the success of the community organizing and believes in the advantage of community collective well-beings. Through this process, the community designer starts translating community-based ideas into planning and design language. Muhammed Yunus is the champion of designing and streamlining the Grameen Bank centers in Bangladesh.

8. Community social planning

In terms of community social planning, it is a form of community organizing that focuses a technical process of problem solving regarding substantive social problems that utilizes the expertise of professionals (Rothman, 2001). The goals of community social planning include the design of community formal plans and policy frameworks for delivering goods and services to community people who need them

(Rothman, 2001). The Community social planning facilitates bridging the social capital, economic capital and civic capital based on normative ties among community people. However, the focus is on the interests of participating agencies and the community at large, rather than the individual self-interest of neighbours. In case of Grameen Bank Center organizing and group formation planning, we field workers keep the center area within a half kilometer of the neighbourhood of the members; we form a group with five members and form a center with thirty members with six groups. Conduct the center meeting within the middle location (house) of the neighbours of the members.

9. Grameen Bank group formation and center design structures in Bangladesh

Grameen Bank Project is a project of Bangladesh Bank, a Central Bank of Bangladesh, in 1976-1983. The Grameen Bank Project is attempted to serve those rural people in a group who are not covered by the traditional banking system. In order to provide loans to poor landless people in Bangladesh, the Grameen Bank project formulated the following rules and regulations, center, group and village association structures etc.

Center is the village landless association (Landless community association) of GB is organized and build by the field workers of Grameen Bank Bangladesh. The village landless association of Gramreen Bank is the center of GB which is the grassroots organizational structure of landless people in GB; it is the primary and vital unit center structure of GB. In the Center, the landless micro-borrowers of GB conduct their weekly meetings, annual general meeting; discuss their different issues and plans, deposit their savings, propose for loans and receive loans, and develop their future plans. A General Assembly (Shadharan Parishhad) of the Village Landless Association is constituted with the Chairman of all the landless groups of GB.

9.1. Grameen Bank Group of formation design

Only the village landless poor are eligible to form a group. Any member from a family (i.e. a household unit) owning less than 0.4 acre of cultivable land is considered to be a landless poor person and he can form a group (five people together form a group). A group can be formed with a minimum of five members. All the members of the group are the inhabitants of the same village or neighbourhood. Group shall be formed with persons who are like minded, are in similar economic condition and enjoy mutual trust and confidence. There shall not be more than one member from the same household in any one group. If more than one person from the same household intended to become members of the landless groups, they do so by becoming members of different groups. It is not desirable to form a group with close relatives (e.g. father, brother, uncle, father-in-law etc.). There are a Chairman and a Secretary in each group. They are elected by the group members. Election is held at the time when a group is formed and subsequently in the month of Chaitra (last month of Bengal calendar year) every year. Chairmen and Secretaries assume their offices from the first of Baishak, the first day of the Bengal year. As of June 2018, GB has 2,568 branches in Bangladesh, its total numbers of groups are 1,384,180 and total numbers centers are 139,314 and it is working in 81,675 villages.

9.2. Grameen bank center design, savings and loans transactions policies and their implementing instructions

Below is describing the Grameen bank center design, savings and loans transactions policies and their implementing instructions.

The Biddimalla of Grameen Bank has an article (article 10) that designs center meeting structure, rules and regulations. Meeting center of the GB borrowers is a place where borrowers organize and conduct their weekly group meetings in their neighbours. Each meeting-center shall have a 'Center-Chief'. The group Chairmen of all the groups in the center elects a Center-Chief and a Co-Center Chief' from among themselves. The Center Chief' and the Co-Center Chief' is elected in the month of Asharh (June) every year. They assume their offices on the first day of Shraban (July). The overall responsibility of conducting weekly meeting shall rest on the 'Centre-Chief'. In his absence, the Co-Center-Chief', performs this responsibility.

The savings, insurance and loan products of GB and their repayment systems designed at different times to address GB borrowers' different needs and situations. Grameen Bank executives particularly Muhammed Yunus always looks at the center organizing, group forming, and their management dynamics, clients' socio-economic dynamics and the chain of command of GB management dynamics. For example, Grameen Bank has developed the disaster loan products at different times to address the borrowers' disasters situations, but they are different from normal loan transaction systems. Grameen Bank group formation and center management experience is not always linear. There have been huge conflicts among group members, facing breakdowns of groups, and violation of disciplines of bad debt defaulters since inception. Many abnormal situations created by the disaster that consequences borrowers' suffering. However, bank workers are used to such breaking and reorganizing the group and center situation since GB inceptions.

9.3. Bylaws (*Biddimalla*) of Grameen Bank

The Bylaws of Grammen Bank are called Bidimalla that is drafted in 1978 and is finalised in 1981. Group and Center of Grameen Bank and their designs, structures, functions; conducting group meetings, GB loans and savings products etc, describes in the Biddimalla. As part of conducting the meeting, the Center Chief ensures attendance of the group members at the meetings, payment of installments and overall discipline and order. He helps the bank worker present at the meeting in receiving installments and deposits and explaining bank rules. If any Center Chief absents him from half or more of the weekly meetings held during any three consecutive months, the post of the Center Chief shall be deemed to have fallen vacant and a new Center Chief shall be elected in his place. In the Article 10.6 the Biddimalla also mentions if the Center Chief becomes a 'difficult loanee' at any time i.e. if he does not pay his installments for ten consecutive weeks or remains absent from the weekly meetings for ten consecutive weeks or if he has not fully repaid his loan in 52 weeks), he is disqualified for the post of Center Chief and the post of the Center Chief is deemed to have fallen vacant. In such cases, a new Center Chief is elected to replace him.

9.4. Duties and responsibilities of the group members of Grameen Bank

The Chairman and the Secretary of a group maintains constant contact with the Landless Association and the loan-giving Bank (borrowers of GB receive loans from different national commercial banks during 1978-1983; however, the borrowers directly receive loans from Grameen Bank when GB become an independent Bank). The Chairmen and the Secretaries of the groups is responsible for recommending credit requirement of the individual members, ensuring proper utilization of the credit and repayment of loans. All members of the group should remain present in the weekly meetings of the group. The weekly center meeting, each member of the group must deposit at least one taka (One taka until 2000, five taka since then) as his regular savings. This amount which is collected is as his/her weekly savings deposit in the group's own account with the Bank. In the weekly meeting, the Chairman of the group maintains discipline, collect weekly dues from the individual members and deposit it to the representative of the Bank.

Here most important strategy of the bank is the bank officials goes to the door-step of the borrowers and collect the money from the borrowers' neighbourhood whereas in Canada micro-credit borrowers have to deposit their installments and savings in the office. Every member of the group must be fully aware of his responsibilities as a member and of the rules and regulations governing the activities of the group. All members keep vigilance over each other regarding the proper use of bank credit and regular payment of installment. They also make sure that every member attends the weekly meetings regularly. Any person qualified as per provisions of these regulations, may become a member of a particular group at any time subject to the consent of all the members of that group. At the beginning (1978-1985) maximum ten people could form a group, but after 1986, only five people can form a group. Moreover, if the group has defaulter borrowers or any one decline to continue to be members of the group, there may be less than five people (at least three) in a group. However, if there are less than three members in an existing group, the members of less than three people should merge to the nearest another group (1990). This process of group formation and credit delivery is called GB group-based collateral free microcredit.

If a member of group is found indulging in activity subversive of discipline (such as absence from weekly meetings, irregularity in payment of installments, etc.) the remaining members can impose fine on him. The money so received deposits in the Group Fund; however, currently group fund dismantled. Group Fund structure and its functions discuss later in the paper.

There is a rule for member for leaving the group. A member who has no outstanding liability with the bank may leave the group voluntarily at any time. While leaving the group, he/she is allowed to take back the entire amount of his personal savings. If a member who has no outstanding liability with the bank may leave the group voluntarily at any time. While leaving the group, he shall be allowed to take back the entire amount of his personal savings. If a member, who has outstanding bank loans, desires to leave the group, he must repay the entire bank loan before he leaves the group. If any member leaves the group without paying off his bank loans, the group is responsible for repayment of the loan of the member concerned. If the members dissolve the group without repaying bank loans, the Center (Association) is liable to pay off all the outstanding loans. This rule has been usually functional to all non-defaulter and disciplined centers.

However, defaulter groups or bad debt undisciplined centers unable to collect the pay off the outstanding loans from all the members of the center, rather create chaos in the center. In such situation, GB has provision for write-off the bad debt loan since 1990.

Here is a rule in the Biddimalla section 7.4 mentions that if the membership of any group is reduced to less than five members due to desertion by one or more of its members, the group concerned must fulfill the condition of minimum membership i.e. five) within 3 months by enrolling new members. It is okay in the disciplined group. However, after 1990 many group members are absent in the group for long time and center is unable to fill the gap meaning take new members in the group to fulfill five members in a group. Therefore, many groups have been running in GB less the required number of members centers for long (mostly after 1991). If the required number of new members cannot be enrolled within the prescribed time-limit, the incomplete group has to merge with some other group.

Alternatively, two or more incomplete groups may unite to form a complete group. This practice is continuing now to fill up the gaps of the group membership where needed. However, it is a very complex job to merge one incomplete group with other groups to make five group memberships in a group in a center because it required lots of paper works, change bookkeeping and share transfer jobs etc. Please note that members can buy one share of GB started in 1983, but the Bidimalla was written in 1978. This new rule buying share of GB is included, but it is not in the Bidimalla. Buying GB share certificates and their instructions prepare separately in 1983. Huge paper works needed for maintaining the members' share buying and selling transactions.

There is another Article in section 9.0 of the Biddimalla that states if the total quantity of land owned by the family of any member during the tenure of his membership of the Landless Association exceeds 0 .4 acre or the value of the assets owned by his family exceeds the amount prefixed by the bank, he or she shall be compelled to resign from his membership of the Association. Field workers are trying to find out the real information from the respective members, screened by cross checking with other members of the center and or with their neighbours about the assets or land owned by the members; however, many members hide their actual assets and liability information to the field workers. Now many GB borrowers are receiving loans by hiding information to GB from multiple agencies are those working in their areas.

Therefore, many borrowers of GB who have huge loan burden. Many scholars termed it feminization of indebtedness and feminization of financialization; many of them become defaulters and they are noising in the center if expel them or forced them resign from membership from GB. These default borrowers influence other members to breach the discipline of the group or center until GB accept him to provide further loans to him. To face such defunct situation of the center or group is challenging for many field staff. Even I have faced many challenges to deal with the indiscipline group members in the centers. GB field offices cannot sue to against aggressive borrowers. Only motivation and negation has been the tools for tackling such defunct borrowers. Therefore, it is difficult to follow the Bylaws of the Center/group legal design and structure of GB, because field workers sometimes need to negotiate with the demand and request of members. However, field workers of GB have faced the audit for departing their job from the written instructions.

10. Working experience in the field of GB

At the beginning in 1976-1982, GB employees work in the Grameen Bank Project without community work experience and without manuals. For example, there are no guidelines, knowledge and idea how we field workers can organize the centers in order to develop the center structures and functions. After working three years from scratch in 1981, a Biddimala (bylaw) draft is streamlined from field experience and then the Bidimalla is supplied to the field officials. The improved version of the Biddimala was circulated in 1982. We follow the bylaws of group formation, center organizing, designing, center structure and center management of GB. The written bylaws of GB center legal structure and functions assist us to do our jobs in a better way by following Biddimala. This Biddimla has been a training manual for the trainees and the field staffs of Grameen Bank since 1981.

In 1980s and onwards, GB has developed written guidelines and instructions for loan transactions and savings collections rules and regulations for the field workers to follow them uniformly in Bangladesh. It was hectic for us (the field workers) to face the disaster situations at different times and uniformly follow and apply the instructions to borrowers. However, the good thing is if we field workers inform our problems and disaster situations as well as about the departing situations for addressing the disaster of the borrowers to the head office, then head office is flexible to immediately change the instructions. We adapt and respond to the ongoing situations to face and to solve the problems through interactive center meetings management process. In this way, we field staff follow the center participatory decision making process under the framework of the GB bylaws and other instructions, *Nitimallas*. We find center and group decisions are more effective to members if it is quickly response to their knowledge and inputs from them.

However, at the pilot stage of Grameen Bank project, we field officials including Muhammed Yunus work without any guideline. Whatever daily working experience we have with micro-borrowers, we field workers discuss our daily experience in person with Muhammed Yunus. The venues of discussions are in different school fields, under trees or other public places. When the loan demand increased more than one village, it is requested by field staffs to make a guideline that can help all field workers work uniformly specially center organizing, group forming, loan disbursing, and savings is collections etc. The *Biddimaala* streamlines all the field experience of staff, and rules and regulations of forming groups and centers of GB. The different loan products and savings invention of GB have developed at different times to address the changing environment of the borrowers of GB.

Each loan products operation instructions (*Nitimala*) and their implementation guidelines are also changed at different time to address borrowers' different situations. Borrower's weekly savings, Group Funds and Center Emergency Disaster Funds, Grameen Pension Scheme (GPS) and other participatory innovative financial safety net savings products (weekly regular savings, individual voluntary savings, and insurance etc.) have changed at different time their book keeping and accounting jobs. However, the *Bidimala*, (the Bylaw) of group forming, center organizing, designing and building of GB remain unchanged (1979-2018).

However, there are chaotic situations have existed in the center with other members of the center which the bank workers need to solve them immediately. Because many anti-GB elites and the center chief become influential in the center and diverts the members towards biased them. They does not listen or follow bylaw of the bank rather claim for undue demands like provide more loans to defaulters although defaulters are not regularly paying loans and breach the center discipline. Many center chiefs have linked with political giants and they give us hard time by asking for undue loans or claim for undue demands from the Bank.

11. Grameen Bank Phase 1

11.1. Group Fund savings products (currently not exists)

Group fund savings dissolve in Grameen Bank Phase-2 in 2001. However, Group Fund savings had been running from 1978-2000. In group fund account, five percent of the loan amount shall be deducted as contribution to the Group Fund. This amount of money is known as 'group tax' or 'group saving'. This money shall be deposited in the group's own account and the member has no personal right or claims over it. All members have equal rights to this fund. Withdrawals from this fund shall be made under joint signatures of the group Chairman and the Branch Manager. While withdrawing money from this account, the group Chairman and the Secretary have to be present in person at the bank.

If any member of the group intends to leave the group voluntarily or is expelled at any time, he shall not get back any share of his money. The combined fund of group savings and weekly individual savings shall be known as 'Group Fund'. Up to a maximum of 50% of the total amount accumulated in the Group Fund may be borrowed and invested by the group members' jointly in partnership with another group and or taken by individual group members as loans for any purpose with the approval of all the members. In taking individual loans from the Group Fund, a special meeting of the group members in the presence of the bank worker shall be necessary. Money from the Group Fund may be withdrawn only on the basis of unanimous decision of that meeting. This meeting decides the term, repayment procedures etc. of the loan.

Moreover, five percent of the loan money shall be deducted as 'Group Tax' at the time of disbursement of loans from the Group Fund. Each group fixes its own rate of interest on loans from the Group Fund (the group may also advance loans without charging any interest, if it so desires). The rate so fixed applies to all loans. The group is fully responsible for the recovery of the loans given from the Group Fund. However, if this loan money is not repaid in due time according to its terms and conditions, it is considered by the bank as breach of discipline of the group. When a member leaves the group, he is entitled to a refund of the entire amount of his personal savings deposited in the Group Fund at the rate of one taka per week. This compulsory weekly personal savings, however, cannot be withdrawn for any other reason except leaving the group.

If any member of the group does not repay bank loans willingly or unwillingly, the loan has to be repaid in full from the Group

Fund deposits. If any loan taken from the Group Fund remains unpaid even after the expiry of the agreed time limit, no new loan shall be advanced from the Fund. If all the members of any group leave the group willingly or if the members do not keep the group in operation, the group savings of that particular group shall be deposited in the Emergency Fund of the Center/ association. All the loonies shall pay interest on all loans taken from the bank at the rate fixed by the bank. However, many anti-propaganda, campaign against the group fund savings had raised by the borrowers of GB. In 2001, group fund savings rules erased from Grammen Bank bylaws. However, Group Fund system was a economic social safety nets for borrowers to face their economic crisis of the borrowers by using the group fund savings.

11.2. Emergency Fund

The center emergency fund is one of the safety net services to the members of Grameen Bank in Bangladesh. This emergency fund generates from borrowers contribution. After payment of the total interest accrued on bank loan, an amount equal to half that amount is deposited in a special fund of the Center/Association which is called 'Emergency Fund'. This fund creates through compulsory contributions of all the members of the center deposited in the Emergency Fund. Money accumulates in the Emergency Fund of the center/association can spend for the following purposes: To repay the bank loan of any member who becomes unable to repay the loan due to any accident (e. g. the death of a cow purchased with the loan money, damage of a rickshaw in accident etc.). This emergency fund can extend grants for repayment of the outstanding amount of loans in case a member of any group fails to repay his/he loan for any other reason where the total saving of the particular group is not sufficient repayment of the same.

Moreover, the emergency fund utilises for other activities making arrangement for veterinary services, adoption of health care programmes for the members etc.). However, the expenses for such programmes shall not exceed 50% of the total savings in the Emergency Fund. Moreover, arrangement of insurances of different types for the members e.g. cattle insurance, crop insurance, life insurance etc pay from the emergency fund. The money from the Emergency Fund can be spent in such programs only on the basis of decisions taken by the General Assembly of the Center/Association.

The Emergency Fund operates under the joint signatures of the Center Chief and Associated Center Chief and the field Manager. The Emergency Fund system of GB was a social safety nets for borrowers to meet their emergency crisis; however, many borrowers misunderstood this concept and they thoughts GB is doing business with them by taking money from them and deposited these money in GB Emergency Funds.

Loan taken from the bank repays generally in weekly installments according to the terms and conditions of the loan. However, the loan money must be utilized within one week of the receipt of the loan in activities for which it has been taken. Those who fail to utilize the money within one week, they must keep it deposited in the bank until opportunity for its proper utilization comes. Any sort of deviation from this shall be considered as serious breach of discipline.

11.3. Loan disbursement and repayment procedures

Credit facilities offered by the bank to the members shall primarily depend on the regular attendance of all group members in the weekly meetings, their sense of discipline and regularity in payment of loan installments. Failure of members to attend weekly meetings in time, absence from meetings, underpayment of loan installments, non-payment etc., disqualify the group for receiving the bank facilities.

Loans are given to borrowers only after Grameen Bank recognizes group members. The bank considers loan applications from the registered members (receivers of the loans) of the groups, for different economic activities. Group membership alone is not entitled a member to get back loans. The members are considered qualified for loans from the bank only if they abide the rules and regulations of the bank. Receiving loans by the remaining members in subsequent turns demand on regular payment of installments by the members who already received loans, and strict observance of rules and regulations by all group members.

In the article section 4.4 of the Biddimalla mentions that all loans are taken from the Bank is generally repayable in weekly installments in the weekly center meetings of the center. In cases where the utilization of a loan generates opportunity for daily or weekly incomes, the loans have to be paid off in weekly installments. However, in cases where utilization of a loan does not create opportunity for daily or weekly incomes, but generates a large income in a lump after the expiry of a certain period of time, a "token installment" can be paid every week. The remaining amount should be paid in one single installment immediately after the receipt of the lump income. Failure to pay this token weekly installment is considered as a breach of discipline as in cases of non-repayment of 'regular' instalments.

12. Functions of the members of Grameen Bank

The Biddimalla (Bylaws) of Grameen Bank mentions that it is the responsibility of the center/association to motivate its members to create among them a proper attitude, a sense of discipline and a spirit of cooperation among each other and with the bank, to take full advantage of the opportunities created by the Grameen Bank in order to change their social and economic conditions. The Center/association takes special care to create a sense of responsibility among the members and the groups who are callous and prone to violate rules and regulations of the bank. The center/association considers it as its responsibility to ensure proper utilization and timely repayment of all loans given by the bank to its members.

The center takes steps to create opportunities of training for, and take new initiatives in, helping increases the efficiency and skill of the members in different trades with a view to ensuring gradual improvement of their economic condition through the financial cooperation of the bank. The Center/association evolves and develops within itself a permanent and effective institutional mechanism for mediation, and settlement of all disputes and removal of misunderstanding among its members.

The Center takes special care to create and maintain a cordial and cooperative atmosphere among its members. All center members meet once in at least two months and after reviewing its program, take practical steps to keep the center/association moving forward. The Center Chief of the center maintains regular contact with the bank and extends all help and cooperation to the bank authorities for smooth operation of this special credit program. In practice, usually center itself do not call meetings for reviewing their performance and defaults rather sometime they sit together for conspire against repayment, stop savings, increase loan size or blame bank reduce interest rates, and waive interest rates. Sometimes center leaders call for meeting for voting to their favourite leaders etc. Although these deviant type meetings are not frequent, but general borrowers suffer for following center disciplines and repaying their loans. In such situation, bank managers, and area managers visit together and talk about the negative effects of negative propaganda for refreshing and motivating borrowers. Sometimes several meetings need to reorganize and to revive the center discipline.

13. How I survey and organize members of Grameen Bank in 1980.

I joint Grameen Bank in GB Project Office in Dhaka in April 1980. After one day briefing, I am sent to Narandia Tangail Branch which is 250 km from my home village Comilla and 150 KM away from Dhaka Capital City. The Bank of Narandia Project office is situated in the Narandia Bazar and all the branch staffs live in a Tin Sheet house beside the branch. There is no latrine in the branch or near the branch. However, luckily there is a tube well that water we use for cooking, washing, baths, and drinking.

I am shadowed under an existing bank manager of the branch. I go to a village called Palima with him by walking on my second day in the branch. We talk together on the way; the manager describes me his working experience how he has organized the landless associations, centers and form groups; and what are the challenges he has faced to conduct meetings, form groups, organize centers and deal with the village elites. Before we arrive at the center meeting at 7.30 am, all center male members sit together in an open space under a tree. The center chief starts the meeting and then the bank worker collects the loan installments and savings from borrowers. At the end of the meeting, three members proposed for their loans, the respective group chairman, and center chief endorsed their loan proposals and then bank worker receive the loan proposals; we visit the second center meeting in another village Pusna Pallima at 9:00 am the same day. I am amazed to see the discipline of the members of centers and loan repayment and savings collection system and their recordings and bookkeeping.

We walk to a new village adjacent to the meeting centers. There I observe, twenty women are waiting for us in a house. The manager and a bank worker talk with them about how to form groups, centers; how to maintain center disciplines, conduct meetings; how to propose loans and get loans for them and deposit savings in the bank. They talk with us for 45 minutes. We ask them to choose five women together to form a group and attend for seven consecutive days for group training in the same place at the same time. Afterward, we returned to the office. The bank worker completes his bookkeeping jobs and other paper works related to loans collection and savings deposits. It takes him about one hour. Then we go for lunch for one hour in the dormitory where we live. We again go to another village for group training at 2:30 pm, return to the office at 5:30 pm and debrief our whole day jobs with other branch staffs.

The manager tells me next day I should work independently; know myself about the branch geography, village names; land leasing system, sharecropping system, big trees in villages, loan borrowing formal and informal agencies exist in villages and their loan borrowing mechanisms and conditions. Moreover, I should know about different classes of people, and their occupations and social locations. Map out different physical infrastructures in the area like roads, bridges, rivers, canals, big ponds, hospitals/clinics, schools (when they established, how many students, (male and female students)), droop out student numbers in each grade. Moreover, I visit different clubs, government offices; as well as visit religious institutions like Mosques, churches, temples to find out the Purdah system, religious rituals, customs, people's local traditions, values, and believes etc. of the local people within the branch area.

Moreover, I collect local market products and their prices; visit cooperatives and commercial banks, NGOs, private and public institutions that are working in the area. I explore local transportation facilities, means of agriculture, irrigation facilities for agriculture, pure drinking water facilities and cultivable lands and their frequency of annual crop productions in the area. My job also includes knowing about the demographics and literacy rates of each village, main manufacturing products, and their processing centers. Moreover, I discern money lenders economy, share economy practices in the villages, wages of different occupants, and laborers both male and women; poor people's household economy, different economic opportunities available for the poor people, and other loan proving institutions in the villages. I collect data on food habits of the poor people, women status in the family and in the society; and village arbitration system. In addition to these, find out people's citizenship participation status in public decision-making practices. Moreover, I collected floods, cyclones, hurricanes, draughts and other natural disasters events and their records in the area and their effects on public life.

In addition, my job is to survey what are social, economic, political and environmental different sufferings of the people that they are suffering from in the area? The branch manager also advises me to find out where and how many poor associations/centers can be formed for Grameen

Bank. He also asks me to collect detail two case histories of two poor women from two villages. I draw a map with all information in a paper and submit it to the office after two months.

In addition to all these jobs, the manager also ask me organizes open house meetings, conduct group training, and attend special meetings with other branch staffs where they would be.

In order to collect all this information, I go out every day in the villages to find out and to talk with money lenders, farmers, labours, fishermen, carpenters, blacksmiths, formal and informal elites, village Punchayets. Moreover, I visit backyard poultry, homesteads gardening, identify food intake behaviors of people like what they are eating and how many meals they take per day; what they are buying. Besides, I attend different Punchayet meetings in the villages and observe their arbitration system.

I map out the geographical boundary of the branch. At the same time, I visit and attend the existing centers' meetings of Grameen Bank and observed members' attitudes, behaviors and disciplines. Simultaneously, I learn office documentation jobs. It is very labor intensive and hard working jobs, but I enjoy my apprenticeship in the branch. Although I born and raise in a village of Bangladesh; however, I do not know about the miserable life of the poor people particularly poor women in villages, but I have realized poor people's suffering by working in Grameen Bank. Usually, all GB field workers do the same survey jobs that I have done.

14. My first experience of organizing groups and center schools in Grameen Bank

On the third day morning (7:30 am) of my posting in the branch, Narandia Kalihati, I go to Luhuria village by walking, which is four miles away from the branch that is within the boundary of the branch. The purpose is to know about the physical geography of the village and peoples' occupations, socio-economic conditions, their dress code, house patterns, irrigation system, crops processing mechanisms, and to know what children are doing in the morning, noon, evening and in the night. I observe many day labours and farmers are working the fields, plowing lands with cows/buffalos; many children age (6-14) are assisting their parents in the crop field; many women are manually processing their crops in their houses. Poor women are working in the rich and upper middle farmers houses.

At 10:00 am, I sit under a tree for taking rest and to eat the biscuits that I carried with me. Many labours come to the tree for taking rest and for smoking. I informally talk with them; know about their life, about their socio-economic conditions as well as know what their wives and children are doing at home, and what they do in lean session etc. After one hour, I visit a school to know about the school and its students. At 2:00 pm, I again sit under another tree where many cottages that are made of straw are located and many women do bamboo works in their houses. Some women ask me why I, a literate person, am sitting in this place. According to them, none in their life have seen a literate person sit and talk with poor women.

I introduce myself to them and tell them about Grameen Bank micro-credit program service opportunity for the poor people in their area. If they are interested, I could provide them with more information about the bank. One senior lady tells me that the village poor ladies are not smart enough to understand my discussing topics. She offers me come to this neighborhood next night and discuss services of GB with people. I agree. However, when I am returning to the office around 3:00 pm of the day, on the way I observed many naked malnourished children are playing marble game besides the street. I ask them why they are not going to school.

I again went to Luhuria village by walking next day and talked with people those are sitting, resting at street corners, Madras, and school playgrounds and offer them to attend the open house meeting at the North West Luhuria neighbourhood about my open house meeting in the evening. At 5:00 pm, I find many poor children are sitting under a tree and gossiping there. As a fun, I show my fingers one by one to teach them numbers. Some children quickly learn numbers by displaying fingers and enjoy. I tell them if they could come here every evening to learn literacy and numeracy skills, I can teach them voluntarily. There is a lady seated beside us; she invites me to teach the poor kits there. She can assist me to open a school here. She tells me, in school, teachers are not allowing poor children to be in the classes without having clothing. I started pity and parrot exercise with the children in open spaces in their neighbourhood. Twenty-five children started to learn basic literacy classes and do the exercise here with joy. I continue teaching in this center school and named it the Luhuria Center School.

At one moon night, I and other staff of the branch visit another neighbourhood located at the South West Luhuria to conduct another open house meeting to inform them about the mission, vision, objectives of Grameen Bank. About fifty people (male and female) attend this open house meeting. Men sit in front of us; women sit behind of us and they listen to our speech. I observe many middle-class men also attended the open house meeting. We talk there for one hour that night. Many people express their interest in receiving loans from GB.

I collect people names and tell them I would come to this place for providing training on the GB group formation mechanism, center structure, members/borrowers responsibilities, loan transaction system; savings deposit collections and repaying rules and regulations. They request me to conduct training in this place at early night. I tell them they (loan receiving interested people) should provide me all information on their assets and liabilities during the training period. Those poor people properly completed the training are able to register with GB and qualify for the loans.

In order to provide training to the poor people, I go to the agreed scheduled place every night at 7: 00 pm. We sit together on a mat in an open space under a tree. There I teach them GB manual for ten days. At the beginning of the training, twelve men attend the training sessions, but only five people continue to complete the training. These five trained people agree to abide by the rules and regulation of the bank. They chose their own group chair and group secretary and filled the GB Form-1. Form-1 is a form for collecting socio-economic demographic data from the successful passed trained members. The trained five member (men) deposit their seven days savings (each one taka for one day) Tk. 35.00 in the bank at the end of the training. With this savings money, they opened their group fund account in the bank. However, although after 2001, Group Fund savings erased, borrowers deposit their weekly savings in their accounts with Grameen Bank.

Although the training starts at night, I go to the center school every day at 4:30 pm to teach basic literacy and numerical skills to the children. The total numbers of children (both sex different ages) increase to forty-five in the center school. I accept them whatever their dress codes are. In the center school, children first play for half an hour and then sit under the tree for learning the basic literacy skills.

One day, it is raining during the lessons period in the school. It affects children learning. I discuss this situation with their parents; they agree to build a house with bamboo and straw within three days. The house is built and children learn in this house. The house named "Center House "; the members propose this house could be used for educating the children religious education and basic literacy education as well as conducting the weekly center mettings. This house also uses for group training at night.

After two weeks of membership registration of the trainees, firstly two members of the group receive loans, then another two members and lastly the Chairman of the group receive loan. The loan size varies from $100-$125. I start to collect savings and installment from them every Monday morning. However, every day I go to this neighbourhood by walking for teaching poor children. On my way to this village, I talk with other villagers whoever I meet. It is my tremendous exciting job that I have enjoyed working with Grameen Bank. I utilize my this working experience to organize community schools in other countries like Afghanistan, Namibia, Lesotho, and Botswana when I work there.

On one day noon, I meet with a moneylender under a Bansai tree. He is looking at me in an angry mood and asks me why I have giving loans to poor people in this village. I answer him with honor that the bank has mandated to provide loans to poor people here. He again utters at me and tells me I should not again come to this village. The borrowers come to me and tell me that this man also cautious them do not borrow money from the bank. They are scary. I talk to the office about this situation. Next day we all office staff go to the village and make clear that it is their liberty and rights to receive loans from banks wherever they like. We also request rural elites do not threat the borrowers who received loans from GB. However, the money lender is not cool, but he keeps silent.

I have another open house meeting with poor people in other parts of the village. We (I and the manager) are talking with women in a house near their location. Three people (the moneylender, Immam, and a Mattabarr (village leader)), meet us in the open house meeting and challenge us why we are talking with women that break the Purdah in the village. We make a dialogue with them and confirm them poor women are not destroying their Purdah by attending the meeting rather we are helping them to involve in income generation activities to alleviate their poverty. After a long conversation with them, the Mattabarr tells us women field workers can do jobs with women borrowers. However, the moneylender cautious me I should not come to the village for giving loans to poor people. I ask him why? He replays to me that the bank loan receivers are not labouring in his lands. I find it is his conflict of interest with GB loan borrowers.

I tell the Immam that the women attendees are maintain their veiling and Purdah in the meeting; and I am respectful to their Purdah. I am also a Muslim. Women attendees and I am not breaching the Purdah here. It is a hectic situation for me to work in this village.

I immediately report to the Union Councillor of the village; and I narrate him about my mission, vision and activities in the village, but the protest against my work from the elites are disturbing my job. I explain him about GB project which is recognized by the Government of Bangladesh. If rich people of this village can receive loans from commercial loans; poor people (both men and women) have rights to receive loans from Grameen Bank

After forty years, now I understand people who are working in the community in a more sustainable way, who are community change agents. This work requires understanding the environmental, economic, political and social system and their interconnectedness and the ability to think of multiple scales in the face of very big issues. However, the community organizing work needs courage, patient, and ability to love and interact with all classes of people outside of job descriptions, understand disciplines and engage in big thinking. Community workers require the ability to communicate clearly, listen and collaborate with the community; it demands humility, authentic appreciation for diverse ways of serving community people and thinks; recognize all peoples mistakes and efforts in together for their integrative positive development. It is important because of the majority of people in the community struggle with issues of everyday life and economic survival in the capitalistic society.

People are willing to make change if the changes are very easy to do or if they took solutions that lead to better life both at collective and individual labels. In order to have effective social diffusion, community workers must be trust worthy of the beneficiaries, meaning community workers thinking, services and deal with the community people in such a way they realize the community worker is working for their wellbeing. Therefore, it is important to contact people in person at their door steps which is very effective in spreading the innovative work messages and influence community beneficiaries for their sustainable development. Community workers' simple language communication is appreciating and important for understandable to community people.

Moreover, community workers should have the willingness to form partnerships among community people, particularly who do not cooperate for whom he/she is working for in the community. Community sustainability work is not a single pathway rather sustainability has many goals; issues are many and varied, but each of us has our own sets of skills and understanding. But these skills and understanding should open; because openness to accept or deal with all issues and tries to satisfy all peoples need and demand. The more we are open to alternative voices, the stronger our social community design and community build that could enhance our richer choice of potential sustainable community collective futures. These all skills can develop among community workers through hard work and love community people. It is more likely to generate novel responses to changing conditions, and some of the innovation leads to solutions with good fit to new conditions (Worldwatch Institute, 2013).

I tell the local councilor of the village that if women members of GB do business and earn extra money in the family, they can use this money for their children's education, food and for a better life etc. The councilor attentively listens, but he does not give me the answer. However, I challenge myself and continue my group training job with women in the neighbourhood. However, the women who are interested to take loans from GB, they decline to receive group training and to receive loans from the bank. I ask them why they have declined to receive training and receive loans from GB. They report to me that the money lender, Immam, and Mattabbar threat them; they shall be ousted from the village by the elites if they receive loans from GB. I talk with the poor people of the village and explained them there is a conflict of interest of the elites against their loan receiving. To destroy their vicious cycle of poverty, it is necessary to take the challenge with these unethical elites. They should challenge this threat. I am also the part of their challenge. They inspired. Although my group training job is disturbed, I continue my group training and loan collection jobs in addition to my the center school volunteering teaching job there. All classes of people in the village support me to do my volunteer schooling job there.

I am always looking for alternatives and dialogue with the people where I am obstructed to do my center organizing jobs. My jobs have not been linear there. I always adapt the situation with alternatives and following Biddimalla, the bylaws of GB.

There are three groups (fifteen members) form in this Luhuria Center in three months. I get support from the poor people of the neighbourhood. It is a hard work and it needs a lot of talk with the elites and with the poor people to understand my job in the village. In the fifth month, six poor widowed, three single poor mothers come to me for providing them with training and loans. They tell me that their children have been suffering from food, housing, clothing, education and healthcare for long. Rural elites exploit their labours. They want to do their own business by taking loans from the bank.

At the seventh months, one female group is registered in Luhuria and received loans from the bank. It is hurrah for these people and for me. The message spreads all over the village even neighbouring villages. The situation is favorable to me for working with poor women in the village and the neighbouring villages. The center members are the spokesmen of my work in the villages. After one year, I am able to form four male groups in one center and six women groups in another center in the West North of Luhuria village and two center schools in the village. One female field worker is recruited in the branch who takes over the charge of the female center from me. I have seen the socio-economic change of the members of Grameen Bank while I am working with them. For example, their weekly income has increased, their family members eat three meals a day, and members buy new clothes for their children. They are happy with their business and income; I am excited to see the immediate positive change in the members' life.

I also start to organize another women group and male group separately in the neighbouring village, Kurua, in the seventh month of my posting in the branch. The male group meeting is in the South East part of the Kurua village and women group in the middle of the village. In the open house meeting in this village, I talk to people about my working experience in the neighbouring village Luhuria like organizing a center school there. They get the reference point of my work. When I collect installments and savings in Luhuria village centers, three women come from Kurua to visit the center activities and to talk with the members of the Luhuria who provided them (the visitors from Kuria) positive experience of income generations, center disciplines and their solidarity in the center. The visitors of Kurua village encourage them to join GB and do business with the borrowing loan. I am inspired to start group training in Kuria village. Ten poor women and five men are trained to register with GB there in two months.

However, one day noon, three boys come to the branch and blame me I am involved with a love affair with one divorced young lady, a member of a group, although it is false. I am surprised even the lady is ousted from the group by their neighbours. This woman is chosen as a chair of one group. However, thereafter she declined herself to be a group chair with frustration. The other group members also declined to form groups. I find three young boys from rich families of the village are observing my activities in the village; their fathers are elites of the village. I continued to conduct training for male members. After one-day training session with male members, I do not find my bicycle; it is stolen. I am nervous, but I suspect these young boys who are the thieves of my bicycle. These boys who blamed me about love affairs with the divorced young lady. I report to a teacher in the neighbourhood who is an influential person in the village.

Next day morning, one center school boy of the Kurua village secretly tell me he has seen my bicycle under the water of a pond. I give this information to the teacher to whom I seek help rescue my cycle. He calls a meeting near the ponds with three other Mattabbars. They asked a boy for searching the cycle. After searching, the boy brings the cycle from a pond to the arbitration place. The teacher calls the three young boys (who blamed me with the love affairs with the young divorced lady). After cross-talking with the divorced young lady, the boys and with me; the teacher found it is a false conspiracy against me for stopping me center organizing training in this Kurua village. These boys steel my cycle. It is a conspiracy instructed by the money lender, the Mattabbar, and the Imam. The teacher advises the villagers including these elites and the boys they should cooperate with me to do my jobs in the village. The teacher also warns them do not make false blamed against me rather cooperate me to work in the village.

Next day, I visited each of the poor women in the neighbourhood and invited them for receiving group training in their own neighbourhood. The blamed divorced lady is happy and she agrees to continue her group chair responsibility with GB. Later she became the Center Chief of the center when there were fifteen members registered in the center. However, it takes me two months to revive and to reorganize the groups and the center. Many poor males assist me to form male groups in this Kurua neighbourhood.

Moreover, I again face a serious sensitive religious problem when start to organize another female group and center training in other parts of the village. Muslim people decline to be in one center if Hindu people are in the same center although all Hindu people and Muslim people are in separate groups. I already completed bookkeeping jobs of this center and included both religious people in one center. It was a serious sensitive issue raised by Muslim religious leaders in the village even it spread to neighbouring villages. Thereafter, I split the center into two centers with homogenous religious faith people, but I was in tension if any uncomfortable situation and issue arise among the people. However, my alternative steps of separating two centers by religion have assisted me to avoid the faith-based tension among members. I talk about this problem to the manager, and solve the problem.

Here in the paper, I describe the above two villages' group formation challenging job experience to inform the readers that community organising, designing, building, and planning needs to tailor and adapt to the local situation although there might have job guidelines and instructions that are assigned for community workers. The Grameen Bank microcredit program in the village is not welcomed by money lenders, elites and rich people in 1970s and 1980s because the Grameen Bank group-based micro-financing is threatening to money lenders' businesses. The reason is Grameen Bank microcredit services hamper money lenders money lending business in the villages.

The Grameen Bank micro-credit lending program liberates and relives poor people from money lenders bondage, exploitation, and injustice. The borrowers' incomes have increased by using loans received from GB. The elites felt uneasy and jealous for poor children schooling. The rich people cannot use poor children as cheap labour working for them. Rather poor women do the business of their own instead of doing jobs in rich peoples' houses. Poor women are saved from false blame by Mullahs' Purdah domination. Grameen bank activities in these two villages spread to other neighbouring villages. Later, I receive a support from the group members if I had faced any difficulty in organizing, forming, designing, groups and centers in villages. After one year, it is easy for me to form groups in other villages.

As male group members and borrowers are working in the outside of their homes, I conduct the male center meetings and their loan collection sessions at night (6:00 pm-8:00 pm), but women center meeting conduct in the morning (7:30 pm-9:30 am). I am respectful of the borrowers' customs, cultures, traditions, proposals, and time. I solve their problems with politely. Within one year, the general public of the village finds us (GB staffs) honest, sincere and hardworking with our jobs. Now all kinds of villagers welcome our loan service jobs although there are politics involved regarding GB at the national level in Bangladesh. Even though, there are many critics and false propaganda exists in Bangladesh against Muhammed Yunus until now;

however, the current Government of Bangladesh supports Grameen Bank activities in Bangladesh.

If I look back to my center organizing work strategies and Grameen Bank bylaws, I find there are huge change happened now. It is because to adapt and to adjust to the changing situation of borrowers, time and context. Grameen Bank introduces many new loan products, design new savings' policies and strategies to face and to address the borrowers' contemporary issues and situations. Muhammed Yunus accept mistakes and admit workers decisions if it is not breaching the basic discipline of Biddimalla and the framework for organising the groups and centers of Grameen Bank Bangladesh.

15. Community organizing work experience in Canada

If it is compared to Toronto community development different works, I find various types of community agencies are working in Toronto. They are very efficient in dealing with problems although they are very formal. Here communities are more structured. People have fewer interactions with their neighbours. Toronto communities are more multicultural nationalistic-based, faith-based, racial-based, class-based, aged-based, and gender-sexuality based society. In Canada, disadvantaged people particularly, single mothers and newly immigrant poor women are isolated and away from different community participation decision-making process. They are very busy to earn income for their surviving in this individualistic and capitalist expensive society. There is no 'sharing economies' among people here in Toronto. I have involved with many community-based agencies, social economic institutions in Toronto even in the US since 1993. Here community workers usually are not walking in the community; they do not visit clients at their doorsteps; they are not individually talking with community people and invite people for community meeting rather they are referring displaying written information in the notice boards in community centers, churches, street corners and other public places like community houses; community newspapers, community radios, weekly/monthly newspapers etc.

Food/light refreshment usually serves in the community meeting for the attendees. However, few people are attending community meetings. In Toronto, community meeting schedules are tied meaning start and finish meeting at a particular time. Topics of community meetings are community health education, nutrition education, drug prevention education, religious education, community gardening, English as Second Language education etc. Immigration community agencies are briefing on different resources and their locations in Toronto, familiarise them with Canadian economic, social and multicultural education, community dance festivals and community street festivals etc. Here community gardens and community kitchens are available for public where people do their gardening and cook foods in these community kitchens facilities

Community Street festivals are usually organized by ethnic community people in summer. Open concerts, music, dances, arts and other cultural activities are popular in these street festivals. Food Vendors displayed and served their ethnic foods and do business in these festivals. Ethnic dresses are displaying and selling in the street festivals. Vendors are promoting their business products at the festivals. These vendors are promoting consumerism in the festivals. I have observed in the street festivals food and clothes, costumes, jewelry, and toys are expensive than usual shops and restaurants; poor people cannot afford them. However, free food samples deliver from vendors to the festival visitors for their food business promotion.

The City of Toronto organizes many meetings in the City Hall and support many community events. However, in these community meetings and events, the City of Toronto tries to disseminate its own different agenda like multiculturalism, community gardening, historic arts, promoting cultural heritage, public health education, community peace education etc. Surprisingly, none of the agencies are involved in micro-financing activities for low-income people in Toronto, but many agencies are involved in providing small business training to people. Maximum of these training agencies are receiving SME training funds from City of Toronto, Provincial Government, and Foundations even from private donors.

If we look at Grameen America, it is a 501 nonprofit microfinance organization and its head office based in New York City, which is founded in 2008. It follows the group-based micro-credit model in the USA. There are eight Grameen Bank officials seconded to Grameen America. It is working in 12 US cities of USA. The branches are in New York City, Harlem, Omaha NE, Los Angles, Indianapolis, Boston, Oakland, San Jose, Union City, San Juan, Charlotte NC, Austin TX, and Miami Florida. Its repayment rate is 99% and its borrower's average credit scores are 640. As of 2016, Grameen America passed an incredible milestone of investing more than half a billion dollars in more than 86,000 women entrepreneurs around the country. Grameen America's members have saved $USD 5.9 million deposited in different US Chartered banks. Its total income is $USD 17.4 million and expenses are total $USD15.7 million (Grameen America, July 2018).

Likewise, Canada could initiate group-based microcredit scheme lessons learned from Grameen America. However, the important thing is the credit workers should be hard working and field oriented (80% of their work in the field), physically and intensively visit clients' business sites. The field worker should not feel that they are superior to their clients; they do not be panic and hypocrites to clients, do not hide true information with the public and do not show rude face to clients rather respect and love clients, trust clients; learn from them and happy to see clients success.

In Canada, the community meetings are usually done in monthly, bi-annual and annual basis; few agencies do have weekly meetings. All type of meeting agencies are serving light refreshments, hot lunch or dinner to attract people to join meetings. However, after the meetings, few people interact with each other. Here in Toronto, people are busy to do paid jobs or searching for paid employment. However, people enjoy eating food and talk to each other in the meetings, in the parks and recreational centers too.

The professional associations' meetings are highly sophisticated. Their meetings are usually conducting in the private hotels and they have strong social network among them.

The Government of Canada is attentive to seniors' services like meditation exercises, community swimming, senior health care and safety services, drug prevention education etc. Senior homes in Toronto organize many events like indoor game competitions, music, dance, food, selling second-hand clothing, antiques etc. Here churches are organizing many faith lectures and community dinners in the community. Seniors are enjoying these events; they do enjoy potluck food events where they prepare food and bring food to the events and eat together with other seniors. Many senior service agencies and disability agencies are arranging tripe to different historical places cost shared by the seniors or by the agencies.

There are many employment resource centers and immigration service are available in Toronto. The Government of Canada emphasis on Youth Employment Services; the government agencies are supporting these employment resource centers. These employment centers are fully equipped with computers, printers, internets and other employment information. These employment resource agencies are offering employment development services to youths even open their services to all other unemployed people at free of costs. Employment resource centers like COSTI, South Asian Community Support Services, YMCA, YWCA, Career Foundation Center, ACCESS Community Support Services, and Cross-cultural Community Services, Storefront Community centers, Community Police etc. are organizing different lectures related to employment, community safety, community gardening and workplace safety. All ages of people join these employment resource centers and browse computers/internets searching for jobs, read newspapers and other inquiries. However, very few people find professional jobs in Toronto through employment resource counseling services.

Many youth centers are providing anti-drug campaigns, health hygiene education, public health education, safe sex education, and peace education. Moreover, here community agencies are organizing seminars on public health and nutrition education, environmental basics education. However, here client-worker relationships are very formal and structured. Disadvantaged poor people shall be very happy if they have cordial relationships with their community workers.

It is found in Toronto, many community centers are working with people for providing Basic English Language training at free of costs for those who have English as a Second Language (ESL), but such language training at free of costs is absent in Bangladesh. Moreover, junior schools, secondary high schools have social workers who are organizing parental meetings in the schools where they discuss on parental relations with parents and children; discuss how parents could deal better with their children and educate their children better in Canada.

Here many rich and middle-class families have the personal support workers who are taking care of the seniors like bathing them, change bedclothes and dress seniors, clean clothes and houses, prepare food and assist them to eat food and medicines etc. Personal support workers also bring disabled people (all ages of people) to child care centers, senior centers, schools, community centers and other recreational centers. Red Cross Canada has food services for the seniors called 'Meals on Wheels'. This program delivers healthy food to seniors at minimum costs. Many churches have such services for their old age members too. Toronto Transit Commission (TTC) has Trans wheel vehicles that are providing transportation services to the seniors and physically disabled people where they need to go. These are great facilities and services available in Toronto. Unfortunately, these services are unavailable in Bangladesh. Here universal health care facilities provide great services to all citizens of Canada that are absent in Bangladesh. Here community agencies, hospitals, and clinics are very popular for their efficient services to people in Canada.

Table 1: Compare and contrast community working experience in Bangladesh and Canada

Community organizing experience in Bangladesh	Community organizing experience in Canada
Bangladesh uses the terms group, center (Kendra), society (Samitty) and village organization synonym to community.	Canada uses the terms community, association and society
Maximum community organizations are in the rural area	Almost all community agencies are working in the urban areas
Micro-financing institutions are more in Bangladesh both in rural and unban	Few microcredit agencies are working in Canada although huge demand for micro credit among low income Canadians
NGOs are depend on outside funding sources or MFIs are covering their costs from loan investments and savings refinancing	Receive funding from local government, regional /national government and or from foundations
Field workers are not involved in fundraising events	Every community organizations have fund raising program through community dinners or fund raising campaigns throughout the year
Community field workers have flexible to implement agencies guidelines to serve clients	Community field workers strictly follow the manual of work, they are not tailoring their jobs to clients' needs
Field workers are flexible to discuss various topics in community meeting and flexible to the schedule their meetings	Very tied rigid meeting topics and meeting schedule
Usually bottom- up approach	Usually top-down approach

Community organizing experience in Bangladesh	Community organizing experience in Canada
NGOs are focusing on people's need and request	Strictly follow job assignment and follow the manual of the job.
Field workers are less critical	Field workers are more critical and analytical
Executives are connecting their activities to progress reports for the donors or future plan and design outcomes	Community organisers able to connect their activities and thinking to organizational future planning and design outcomes
Maximum workers are do their job manually and documents their jobs by hand writing	All documentations are done electronically, very few jobs are done manually
Few anti-drug education, mental issue services, disability services, and seniors' services in Bangladesh	More anti-drug services, basic English language education, mental services, disability services and seniors' services are available to people
Maximum beneficiaries are micro-borrowers	Beneficiaries are usually non-micro borrowers, new immigrants and non-mainstream low income people
No small business training available to micro-borrowers	Small business training available to the interested people by community organizations both at free of costs and at costs
MFIs or NGOs can collect savings from micro-borrowers	MFIs or NGOs are not permissible to collect savings from their clients
Field workers are usually stay within their working area	Field workers are not necessarily staying within the community
Community workers visit group, centers by walking and by cycles	Community workers visit or attend their meetings by driving cars or riding public transits
People can talk/contact the worker any time	People can only talk during the meeting particularly at the end of the session as declared by the worker
Workers have primary relationships with low income people	Community people has secondary or formal relationships with their workers

Community organizing experience in Bangladesh	Community organizing experience in Canada
Maximum woks done through mutual discussion	Work done pre- written instructions
Usually poor people are beneficiaries of NGOs	Lower middle class youths, low income unemployed, part-time worker are the beneficiaries of community organizations
Learning by doing, improve services from mistakes	Do job with pre-instructions; zero tolerance for mistakes
Field worker usually do their job manually	Use computers, cell phones, power points or other electronics in meetings
Field workers provide loans and services to low income people	Mostly educational and training services to community people
Few outreach program can be seen organized by colleges and universities	Every community college, university has community outreach programs and community outreach research centers
No food supply for attendees in the meeting	Usually every community meeting delivers food for the attendances
Dialogue based informal discussions in meetings	Very prescribed formal discussions in meeting
Very few social safety net services available for the clients	Social safety net services available for beneficiaries from both public agencies and community based agencies

Civics is important as people re-learn skills for participating in democratic governance (Toker, 2012). The Grameen Bank has bylaws of changing Group Chair, Group, Secretary, Center Chief and Associate Center Chief in a democratic way elect in every year in order to develop all its members' leadership and to maintain center disciplines. This system of changing leadership is not only a process of leadership development, rather it is a process to empower all members of the center. Moreover, communities will become more decentralized and more resilient, with greater control over many aspects of their lives if they could build networks among them. In Canada, community members' connect with other community members using information technology in order to continue to build collective learning both at the community micro level, mezzo level, and national level. Many young people in Bangladesh connect with each other by email, Facebook and Linkedin. World Watch Institute (2013) mentions community workers find a place to stand for working for the wellbeing of the community people. Its community building slogan is chosen what you love. Start from there, do what you can, and connect with others.

16. Grammen Bank loans products and their implementation strategies during Phase 1

Grameen Bank starts providing general business loans individually to its group members and it still continues. However, in the early 1980s, GB experiments with the collective loan, a bigger loan given to a group and center instead of to the individual. The motivation of these larger loans was that they would enable members to fund more profitable activities that required greater capital, such as the installation of rice mill, oil and weaving mills and leasing of markets, orchards, Jamahal (ponds) etc. However, some members felt that they were doing most of the work while others enjoyed the benefits. Conflict among the group members in the centers resulted the limited success of these loans, and then the bank eventually abandoned them.

In Grameen Bank Phase-1 (Classical phase (1978-2000)), Grameen Bank has initiated the housing loans for the members for constructing their houses. This loan is introduced on small scale in 1984, but it is expanded rapidly after the devastating flood of 1987. I first disburse this housing loan for the flood victims in my branch called Gobindashi Vhuapur branch during my Area Managership in Vhuapur area. Grameen Bank thinks that better housing for the poor should be categorised as an investment rather than as consumption, as the borrower can use a good house both as factory space and as protection from natural calamities detrimental to health. The housing loan provides to borrowers for a longer-period to be repaid by weekly installments over several years, with an annual interest rate of 8% per year. Initially, a sum of TK. 7000 is given to housing loan borrowers as the "Moderate Housing" loan.

However, the amount of housing loan was raised to TK. 25,000 taka to account for the rising cost of building materials. The houses built with the loans to purchase four concrete pillars, a sanitary latrine, and corrugated iron roofing sheets. This type of houses provides protection against floods, cyclones, and rain.

This housing loan was exclusively given to poor women borrowers. The land on which the house is built has to be in the woman's name. Grameen included this condition to make sure that the women would not be evicted from her home in case of dissolution of the marriage. Owning a piece of land through a housing loan from Grameen Bank may be the only way for a woman to have "a house of her own." GB also introduced "Basic Housing Loan" to rebuild homes of the borrowers that were damaged by the flood of 1987. The loan size was Tk.7000-Tk.12.000. The maximum period for repayment of a housing loan is five years (Dowla & Barua, 2006). However, the repayment rate of housing loan is not satisfactory. As the loan repayment rate is for more than one year, borrowers are relaxed to pay the loans regularly. However, they could complete repaying their housing loan in their lifetime. GB introduces to awards to those Grameen Bank field workers who provide more housing loans to borrowers and recovers the loans regularly. As of June 2018, GB provides housing loans to 721,306 borrowers of GB in Bangladesh.

During the 1980s, Grameen Bank promoted children's education by helping to establish schools in the centers that I discuss in the paper earlier. Majority of borrowers hope that their children will become educated and successful to find respectable occupations like medical doctors, engineers, lawyers or join government services. However, the cost of higher education is high that results the drop in higher education enrolment of borrowers' children. In 1997, the higher education student loans are introduced with easy terms and conditions for the children of GB borrowers. By receiving this loan, many children of GB borrowers completed their education and become doctors, lawyers, engineers, chemists, biologists, physicist, and social scientists in Bangladesh.

Loan receiving graduated students are regularly repaying their loans. As of June 2018, GB disburses higher education loans $USD 52. 25 million (female loans $USD 13. 89 million and male students $USD 38. 36 million) to 53, 933 students (male student 40,970, and female students 12,963) in Bangladesh.

I am assigned to draft the Grameen Bank higher education student loan manual in 1997. Grameen Bank decides to provide this student loan to finance higher education to the children of GB members. Currently, all children of borrowers who are on a basic loan or flexible loan and have been members of the bank for at least a year are eligible to receive student higher education loans. Grammen Bank introduces scholarships for the children of GB borrowers in 2001. Scholarships are given with priority to girls every year to encourage them to get better grades in schools. On an average 3,000 children, at various levels of school education, receive these scholarships every year (Yunus, 2002). Now I am voluntarily conducting a research on Grameen Bank higher education student loan services in Bangladesh attached with the Center for the Learning Social Economy and Workplace, University of Toronto and School of Education, Indiana University Bloomington, USA.

Grameen Bank Phase-1 has proved that the poor are creditworthy. Poor become self-employed and overcome their poverty by using loans from GB. Below the paper precisely describes the Grameen Bank Phase-1 activities and policies of micro-lending to poor people in Bangladesh (Extract from Dowla & Barua, 2006).

- Grameen Bank targets poor, particularly poor women, as identified by land ownership
- It offers micro-loans to its borrowers for starting income-generating activities
- GB is providing loans to poor without collaterals, it is based on trust
- All loans must be paid back in installments (weekly or bi-weekly)

- To receive loans, poor people must form groups and belongs to centers
- A borrower can receive a new loan, often larger size, if the previous loan is repaid
- Borrowers must paid to the Group Funds, weekly savings and the Emergency funds
- The borrowers need to memorise and follow the 'Sixteen decisions", the social development charter developed by GB in 1984. I was involved to draft the sixteen decisions that time.

Some of these key features of GB have changed in course of time and cope with borrowers' needs and situations; however, some of the aspects of the classical Grammen Bank loan products changed and center structured improved. However, the bank management structure like the branch office, Area office, Zonal office and Head Office has remained same except the field workers designation. Previously, it is called "Bank Workers", now it has been designating them as "Center Manager" since 2000.

The Grameen Bank worker is likely to find himself multi-rules performers like the roles of marriage counselors, conflict negotiators, group trainers, civic leaders, community organisers and center managers etc. Every day they are working either in the office or in the field for organizing and forming groups, mitigate conflicts, revive center disciplines, advice defaulter borrowers, collect loan proposals and loan installments, and savings etc. They work from 6:00 am until 10:00 pm at night. They spend 65% of their time in the field for organizing centers, maintaining group disciplines, collect installments and savings. Now Center Managers are collecting a huge amount of cash money from the borrowers and carrying these cash money from centers to the office every day. It is a risky job. They are like emergency room doctor (Woolcock, 1999). However, because now it is very risky for carrying cash in Bangladesh. Therefore, GB should develop alternative strategies for carrying cash from the center to the branch.

GB uses the following ten indicators to assess whether members are moving out of poverty:

1. The members and their families are living in a tin-roofed house or in a house worth at least Tk. 25,000; the family members sleep on quilts or a bed instead of the floor
2. Drink pure water from tube-wells, boiled water or arsenic-free water or purified by the use of alum, purifying tables or pitcher filters
3. All children of members attending schools or finished at least primary school GB education
4. The members' can repay minimum weekly installment is Tk.200
5. All family members are using sanitary latrine
6. All family members have sufficient clothing to meet daily needs
7. Members have vegetable garden, fruit bearing trees etc.
8. Members maintains an average annual balance e of Tk. 5000 in their savings accounts
9. The members are able to feed their family members three meals a day throughout the year
10. All family members are conscious about their health; they are able to treatment if they are suffering from illness.

Source: Grameen Bank Training Institute poverty reduction survey parameters

By using these poverty free indicators, the internal survey of GB shows the following data of borrowers free from the poverty line.

Table 2: Year wise poverty declining rates of Grameen Bank borrowers

Year	% above the poverty line
1997	15.1
1998	20.4
1999	24.1

2000	40.0
2001	42.0
2002	46.5
2003	51.1
2004	55.0
2005	58.4

Source: Monitoring and Evaluation Department, Grameen Bank

I find in my survey (2011) credit program participation leads to women borrowers taking a greater role in the household and public space decision making (87%), it is because borrowers having greater access to financial and economic resources. They have developed their social capital with their neighbours, increased their choices and voices in the community. The study finds borrowers have developed their bargaining power with their husbands, family members and with their neighbours. I also find they have increased their social, physical and psychological mobility. Moreover, they increase and develop their capacity to think about their children education.

Halen Todd (1996) found that bargaining position of Grameen Bank borrowers in her sample improved as a result of participation in the bank, join in the center and attendance in the weekly center meetings. Borrowers of GB maintain their center disciplines, regularly deposit savings; receive bigger loans, increased their business and repay their loans regularly although it is mismatched during 1996-2000.

17. Evolution of Grammen Bank Phase 11; its products and implementation strategies

The Grameen Bank repayments rates fall to 65% during 1996-2000. The New York Times published news in its front page about Grameen Bank borrowers' default status with statistics in 2001. The reasons for increasing loan default rates are several consecutive disasters like floods, cyclones, droughts, and hurricanes and political turmoil from 1996 to 2001. In order to resolve the problem, Grameen Bank has developed a Samassha (Problematic) Cell headed by Muhammed Yunus in Dhaka. The Samassaha Cell executives analyze centers' problems, identifies 'borrowers sufferings and looking for possible solutions for the struggling members those are victims of natural disasters. The solutions make case by case to revive credit discipline among defaulters and struggling members of Grameen Bank, but it is like window dressing; however, there is necessary to overhaul the whole Grameen bank credit and savings design as well as reenergize the field workers of GB.

In 2001-2002, Muhammed Yunus himself has visited many problematic centers, areas offices and meet with the field staffs of different zones; even he stays in the fields and heard the field problems directly from field staff and collect information, ideas from them to design Phase 11. He redesigns the loan products, savings products and introduces an attractive pension scheme for the borrowers in Grameen Bank Phase-11. The redesign of loan and savings products and implement them contributes to an extremely important role in the rebuilding of the centers and revive center discipline and regularize borrowers' creditworthy behaviours. The discussion with field staffs creates an open floor for good ideas generation. Through deliberation, debate and extended discussion, dialogues with field staffs and executives of Grameen Bank, the winning ideas are incorporated into Grameen Bank Phase -11.

Throughout Yunus's visit to the branches, give him to find out cause and effects of the defaulting behaviours of the borrowers. Moreover, he finds the cause of problems is not only of natural disasters, but also bad rumors by other agencies against GB. The rumors are anti-GB propaganda. Muhammed Yunus also realizes the problems that are caused by structural faults with the system of Grameen Bank (Dawla & Barua, 2006). These problems also have crystallized from the organized protest by religious leaders in Bangladesh. He finds their causes also included too much on loan disbursement and mismanagement by the field staffs.

The borrowers' lack of interaction with the bank is also revealed as the major cause of problems at the branches. When members stopped coming to the regular weekly meetings, the centers become mismanaged. Moreover, Muhammed Yunus explores lack of attendance at weekly meetings is a major reason for the crisis. Another flaw identifies the inappropriate use of loan money. After an exhaustive study of the causes of the crisis of 1996-2000, the various task forces started working on steps to rebuild their respective branches. Through consultation, debate, and discussions, Muhammed Yunus with other executives is able to learn from each other. They realize that loan disbursement and installment collection systems are rigid under Grammen classical Phase-1. Then they think to redesign the whole Grammen loan products, savings, and insurance products.

However, Muhammed Yunus emphasizes and requests to field staffs to reorganize and rebuild the centers, give hopes to members and tell them Grameen Bank is for them; any crisis they face, GB is with them. Grameen Bank provides the loan to borrowers in certain standard rules that benefit members of GB in Bangladesh. Moreover, Yunus (2001) instructs to field staffs for developing trust and rehabilitate borrowers for rehabilitating their businesses as a joint partner of the borrowers. He advises them for continuous motivation and hopes to borrowers with face-to-face dialogue in center meetings and center special meetings.

However, field staff reports to Muhammed Yunus only verbal motivation alone would not work. Borrowers need something tangible new loan products and system to motivate borrowers to restart repaying their loans and to revive borrowers businesses. Muhammed Yunus also finds to ensure effective participation and execution of necessary changes, there needs special attention to improving staff morale and performance. Through the process of trial and errors and small-scale pilot testing during the field study periods in two years 2000-2001, the main elements of Grammen Bank

Phase-11 have begun to take shape. There are many new loan products tested with the new loan repayment system; however, not all tested products are included in the regularised new products in the Phase-2. However, through deliberation, debate and open process of dissemination and critical evaluation of results, only the winning ideas survived and incorporated into the new system of Grameen Bank Phase- 11 (Dawla & Barua, 2006). Now GB has 8.9 million borrowers in Bangladesh. The paper below shortly narrates Grameen Bank Phase-2 system.

The massive succeeded tested experiences are written down and circulated to all branches of Grameen Bank across Bangladesh as a recreation process formalized in the written documents called Nittimala: Written instructions are how to work and implement sustainable record documents and monitor the performances. After intensive visiting and collecting information from fields, Muhammed Yunus has given importance on increasing center attendance, savings collections and building social capitals among borrowers. He also instructs them to share each other work experience with new products and new system and learn from each other. Grammen Bank Phase-11 grows out of the collective efforts of staffs and borrowers led by Muhammed Yunus.

18. Grameen Bank Phase-11 rules and procedures

Grameen Bank Phase-11 come up with a number of fundamental changes in the elements of Grameen Bank loan transactions including the flexible loan, the basic loan and the six-month repayment schedule and six-month quality control check. The flexible loan has a limit in that whatever amount a borrower repays, he or she can borrow twice the amount back at a six-month interval, and then every six months thereafter an amount equivalent to the amount repaid (Dawla & Barua, 2006). However, there is a credit limit of the flexible loan where borrowers (defaulters) have to pay off half of the loan in six months in order to stay current.

At the beginning of initiation of the Grameen Bank Phase-11, field staff has faced difficulty tracing borrowers, and even if they could not find them. Borrowers do not come forward to reorganize them because they think there is no incentive to repay the loan. On other hand, borrowers felt that because they had defaulted, the bank would not give them another loan even they repay their old loans. In order to reach out to these borrowers, the field staff establishes contact with many of the defaulters and urge them to restart their installment payments. However, it is found distrust among default borrowers and field workers. Moreover, field workers find that while many borrowers would promise to come back and repay, they would not keep the promise. Then grameen bank introduces the written contract (a Chukti) for the borrowers with the bank. Then come to the idea of 'Chukti Rin', a contractual loan called 'flexible loan'.

Another outcome of development has reached is the dismantling of the group fund and emergency funds that are essential elements of Grameen Phase- 1. In 1996-2000, there were huge problems in the centers of GB on the Group Funds and Emergency Funds across Bangladesh. Savings are decreased, default rates had increased; centers had disorganized even many borrowers of GB refrain from repaying their loans and deposit their savings in their accounts. Many centers conducted meetings and provide motivational speeches in the centers, but these are less effective. The overall repayment rate declined to 65% and members' attendance in the center meetings drastically declined.

Then after in 2000-2002, GB develops the new loan products (mentioned earlier in the paper) and an attractive insurance policy (Grameen Pension Scheme) that motivates default borrowers of GB to revive the center disciplines and receive new loans (flexible loan and easy loan) for reviving their business capital. Borrowers start to deposit their weekly savings, voluntary savings and premiums of their pensions (Grameen Pension Schemes (GPS)). The Group Fund and Emergency Fund are abolished in Grameen Bank Phase-11. Although Emergency Fund safety net stopped, each year families of deceased borrowers of

GB receive a total of TK. 8 to 10 million in life insurance benefits. Each family receives up to a maximum of TK. 2,000. A total of 54,469 borrowers died so far in Grameen Bank. Their families collectively received a total amount of Tk. 114.0 million (Dawla & Barua, 2006). Borrowers are not required to pay any premium for this life insurance. Borrowers come under this insurance coverage by being a shareholder of the bank (Yunus, 2002). As of June 2018, GB life insurance accumulated $USD 194. 039 million and total amount paid out from life insurance to borrowers of GB $USD5.91 million in Bangladesh.

Field staffs reenergize them through new financial incentives and promotional incentives designed for them in 2001. Now GB repayment rate regains to 97%. The premium deposits of Grameen Pension Scheme (GPS) are 100% although all members of the center are not present on time in their weekly center meetings. Even now members are not coming at one time; some come early and others wait for the late comers which are wastage of time for the early attendees and disturb their business and urgent jobs. However, bank workers go to the weekly center meeting in the morning and start loan and savings collection whoever is repaying their loans and savings. Now GB is flexible to the attendance of the borrowers in the weekly meetings than before. If any reason all members need to sit together or need to resolve any problem, they organize special meetings at their own convenient places at nights.

Table 3: Grammen Bank different loan items and savings products developed at different times

Name of the loan products and savings products	Date of commencement	Status
Unwritten piloted general loan	August 1976	Discontinued in Grammen Bank Phase 11
Collective enterprise loan	November 1982	Do
Housing loan	May 1984	Continue
Basic housing loan	Sept. 1987	Continue
Capital recovery loan	Sept. 1990	Discontinue after Grammen 11

Name of the loan products and savings products	Date of commencement	Status
Family loan	July 1992	Discontinued
Food stock loan	March 1992	Discontinued
Installation of Tube-well loan	November 1992	Discontinued
Building sanitary loan	February 1993	Discontinued
Leasing	October 1993	Continues
Supplementary loan	October 1994	Discontinued
Cattle rearing	December 12994	Continues
Loan for homestead purchase	March 1996	Continues
Pre-basic housing loan	October 1996	Continues
Special general loan (scaling up)	June 1997	Discontinued
Seasonal loan 2	September 1997	Discontinued
Seasonal loan 3	September 1997	Discontinued
Intermediate loan	October 1997	Discontinued
Higher education loan for member's children	October 1997	Continues
New flexible loan	December 29, 1999 for Jamalpur Special project	Continues with improvement
New Flexible loan	April 24, 2000, for three projects (Jamal pur, Habijong and Nilphamari)	Continues with improvement
Flexible loan(September 2000 edition)	May 22, 2000, for all zones	February 13, 2001, for all zones and projects
Flexible loan(September 2000 edition)		Continues
Basic loan for golden members	May 24, 2000, for all zones and projects	XX
Basic loan for regular members	May 31, 2000, for all zones and projects	Xx
Basic loan for golden members	May 31, 2000, for all zones and projects	Xx
Basic loan for regular members (September 2000 edition)	September 14, 2000, for all zones and projects	Continues
Basic loan for regular members (February 2001 edition)	February 13, 2001, for all zones and projects	Continues
Group Fund	1980	Discontinued
Center Emergency Fund	1980	Discontinued

Name of the loan products and savings products	Date of commencement	Status
Individual savings	1978	Continued but saving amount increase to Tk. 5 from Tk. 1
Individual voluntary savings	2001	Continues
Central Emergency Fund	2001	Continues
Grammen Pension Scheme	2000	Continues
Buy Grammen Share	1983	Continues
Beggars loan	2003	Discontinued
Beggars voluntary savings	2003	Continued
Beggars join to GB group members	2005	Continued
Housing accessories buying loan	1999	Continued
Center School savings	1982	Discontinued
Central Emergency fund	2001	Continued
Deposits/savings for "double in seven years."	2001	Continued
General public deposit savings	2003	Continued
Monthly income Plan (usually staffs retired pension money), but borrowers can save more than Tk. 20, 000 under this plan at least for five years and receive the monthly benefits	2002	Continued

Source: Dawla & Barua, 2006).

The newly designed contractual savings plans have enabled the poor to break free from the trap of low savings in Grameen Bank Phase-11. Savings in large amounts by group members have promoted others in the group and even non-members to save more money in Grameen Bank. Now in many Grameen Bank branches, savings exceed loans by a wide margin. Borrowers used their savings to withstand the flood and other crisis in 2004 situation. Grameen Bank also used the cushion of large amounts of internal members' savings to deal with the two stages of the flood- the first in July and second in September 2004 (Dawla & Barua, 2006). GB cumulative loan disbursed as of June 2018 $USD25 billion dollars and members' savings deposited $UD1.6 billion dollars and non-members savings deposited $USD 751 million in Bangladesh.

Savings mobilization among members and non-members is the most important change instituted under Grameen Bank Phase-11. Now center managers are needed to explain all these new products in their group training and center meetings as well as in general meetings in order to inform borrowers about Grameen Bank Phase-11 products and services that are for them. Although now Muhammed Yunus is out of Grameen Bank; the Grameen Bank Phase-11 is running very well because the design of Grameen Bank Phase-11 is more suitable for borrowers than before; they feel more comfortable with the present loan operation system and savings deposit collection procedures. The bank has developed trust with its borrowers through the new loan operation and savings collections system.

Grameen Bank takes a long preparation to develop a new flexible system and field-tested it over months. Grameen Bank finally introduced the new system in September of 2000. It is a simplified and generalized Grameen bank loan transaction system. Now this works equally well both in normal and disaster situations. It allows the enterprising borrowers to move ahead faster. Muhammed Yunus comments everybody has fallen in love with it. Borrowers love it, staffs love it because it is so simple because it offers tailor-made loans rather than previous single-size-fits all type of loans. The new system basically has introduced two types of loans-(a) Basic loan and (b) Flexible loan. A borrower can take a basic loan for any income-generating purpose with mutual agreement between the borrower and the bank, unlike the old system where all loans are for one year. Basic loans can be for only 6 months (Yunus, 2002).

19. Grameen Bank Phase-11 operation incentives to field staff

Both regular borrowers and defaulter borrowers are happy with these new products and procedures. However, field workers paid more attention to the flexible loan in order to regularize defaulters into basic loans where they can receive more loans then flexible loan limits. Those branches who achieve into Grameen Bank Phase- 11, the respective field workers, branch managers receive awards from Muhammed Yunus and got a quick promotion, incentives from the bank. Through this process, Grameen Bank default borrowers become regularised, revived, and reorganized center disciplines within two years.

The new system has brought excitement and inter-branch competition in Grameen Bank to reorganize the centers, to revive the disciplines among the borrowers and the centers (Dawla & Barua, 2006). This system has introduced a grading system for branches. This grading system creates competitions among field staff and the centers. This grading system awards color-coded "Stars" to indicate the quality of performance of a branch and the centers. If a branch has 100 percent repayment and 100 percent center discipline record for two consecutive years it is awarded a "green star". If the repayment falls below it during any two successive years, the star is lost. Likewise, GB introduces different colored stars like 'blue star' 'violet star' and 'red star' on the various performance of the branch. Branch staff can wear the stars as a badge of honor and display their stars in the branch stationary to show their achievement (Dawla & Barua, 2006).

20. Conclusions

Grameen Bank group forming, center organizing and designing of different types of loans and savings products are based on Grameen Bank members need and their feedback on Grameen products and services. GB has streamlined its bylaw and its different products after testing in centers at different places in Bangladesh. At the beginning, we Grameen Bank field workers do our jobs from scratches, without guidelines, but we improve our jobs from learning by doing and from mistakes. We make lots of mistakes in our jobs. Muhammed Yunus, the employer of us, accept our mistakes and give us an opportunity to correct mistakes with innovation. He gives us liberty to experiment with new ideas and let it shapes a program for the wellbeing of poor people in Bangladesh. Now the rules of group formations, center organizing and designing structures of GB are streamlined. However, we had faced huge difficulty from the money lenders, rural elites, and community agencies during the 1970s and 1980s. However, our persistent persuasions, sincerity, and cooperation of borrowers and proper leadership of Muhammed Yunus lead to our job success in Grameen Bank Bangladesh. This bank is continuously flexible to accept new ideas from the field and develop suitable services for its borrowers. Grameen Bank builds its structure and develops its different loans and savings' products throughout its internal innovations.

21. References

Alinsky, Saul (1971). *Rules for radicals.* New York: Vintage Books

Alperovitz, Gar (2009). *What then must we do?* White River Junction, VT: Chelsea Green

Beckwith, David with Cristina Lopez. (1997). *Community organizing: People power from the grassroots.* COMM-ORG: The On-Line Conference on Community Organizing and Development. http://sasweb.utoledo.edu/comm-org/papers.htm

Bobo, K., J. Kendall, and S. Max. (1991). *Organizing for social change: A manual for activists in the 1990s.* Cabin John, MD: Seven Locks Press

Cohen, A. P. (1985). *The symbolic construction of community.* New York: Tavistock Publications and Ellis Horwood Limited

Dowla, Asif and Barua, Dipal (2006). *The poor always pay back-the Grameen-11 story,* Bloomfield, CT, Kumarian Press Inc.

Fellin, P. (2001). *The community and the social worker* (3rd ed.). Itasca, IL: F. E. Peacock Publishers

Grameen Bank (2018). *Grameen Bank monthly statement*, Dhaka, June, 2018.

Grameen America (2016). *Grameen America Upd*ates, New York City.

Hamilton, Cynthia (1991). Women, home, and community. *Women of Power* (Spring): pp. 42-45

https://participedia.net/en/methods/community-organizing

Kahn, Si. (l991). *Organizing: A guide for grassroots leaders.* Silver Springs: MD: NASW Press.

Pan, Elizia (2012). Community Organizing, *Participipidia*: https://participedia.net/en/methods/community-organizing

Rahma, Rushidan Islam (1998b). *The hard core poor and NGO intervention*, Dhaka: Bangladesh Institute of Development Studies

Rothman, J., (2001). Approaches to community intervention. In J. Rothman, J. Erlich, & J. Tropman (Eds.), *Strategies of community intervention: Macro practice,* pp. 27-64 (6th ed.). Itasca, IL: F. E. Peacock Publishers, Inc.

Rouf, A. (2018). Organizing*, designing, building and forming of groups and centers of Grameen Bank and its services implementation strategies in Bangladesh*, Toronto: Center for Learning Social Economy and Workplace, T-Space, University of Toronto, http://hdl.handle.net/1807/89322

Rouf, K. A. (2011). Grameen bank women borrowers' family space and community space development in patriarchal Bangladesh, *International Journals of Research Studies in Psychology.* Vol.1 (1), pp. 17-26. ISSN 2243-7681.

Rouf, K. A. (2016). Eradication of Poverty through Community Economic Development using Micro Financing: Lessons Learned from Grameen Bank Bangladesh. *International Journal of Research Studies in Management,* Vol. 5(2), pp. 1-10

Rutherford, Stuart (2002). *Money talks: Conversions with poor households in Bangladesh about managing money,* Finance and Development Policy and Management, University of Manchester

Smock, K. (2004). *Democracy in action: Community organizing and urban change.* New York: Columbia University Press.

Snow, David A., E. Burke Rochford, Jr., Steven K. Worden, and Robert D. Benford (1986). Frame alignment processes, micro-mobilization, and movement participation. *American Sociological Review*, Vol. 51, pp. 464-481

Sobhan, Rahman (2005). *A macro policy for poverty eradication through structural change*. Discussion paper no. 2005/3, World Institute for Development Economics Research

Todd, Helen (1996*). Women at the center: Grameen Bank borrowers after one decade*, Boulder, CO: Westview Press

Umut Toker (2012). *Making Community Design Work*, Chicago: Planners Press

Tietjen, Karen (2003). *The Bangladesh primary education stipend project: A descriptive analysis. Partnership for sustainable strategies on girl's education,* Dhaka: Education Watch

Wahid, Abu (1993). *The Grameen Bank: Poverty relief in Bangladesh*, Boulder Co: Westview Press

Worldwatch, Institute (2013). *State of the World: Is sustainability still possible*? Washington, DC: Island Press

Woolcock, Michael (1999). *Social theory, development policy and poverty alleviation: a comparative-historical analysis of group-based banking in developing economics.* Department of Sociology, Brown University

Yunus, Muhammed, (1998). *Alleviating Poverty through technology,* Science 2282, No. 5388, pp. 409-410

Yunus, Muhammed (2002). *Grameen Bank 11: Designed to open New Possibilities*, Dhaka: Grameen Bank

Yunus, Muhammed (2002). *Revisiting: The Wall Street Journal, Financial Times and Grameen Bank*. Dhaka: Grameen Bank

Yunus, Muhammed (2003a). Expanding microcredit outreach to reach the Millennium Development Goal: Some Issues for Attention. Paper presented at the *International Seminar on Attacking Poverty with Microcredit* organized by PKSF in Dhaka, January 8-9

Yunus, Muhammed (1978). *Bidmalla*, Dhaka: Oslo Printers.

Index

Micro credit plus programs 192
micro-enterprise loans 226, 305
microfinance Institutions
    (MFIs) 204
micro-finance marketing 291
Millennium Development Goals
    (MDGs) 2, 7, 103, 216, 237,
    246, 345
mission growth 205, 227
Mohila Samilty 338
Mullah 351, 359
multinational corporations (MNCs)
    290, 374
Muslim customary laws 328
Muslim Family property laws
    ordinance 1961 359

N

natural capital 1, 3, 183, 192, 261,
    321, 371
Natural capitalism 321
Nejara Korri 360
networking Café 19
Networking Café-Mentors Circle
    program 20
NGO Bureau of Affairs 229
Nimgashi Fisheries Project
    (NFP) 269
non-governmental organizations
    (NGOs) 205, 233, 237
Nuclear family 33

O

OECD 410
one stop shop 198

P

Pancha Chakra model 14

participatory development 347,
    352, 353
participatory rural appraisal (PRA)
    237, 343
participatory rural development
    approach 351
Patnaik 35
patriarchal values 328
Patriarchy 328, 332, 338, 358
Pauperization 46
peasant culture 29, 45
peasant economy 29, 32, 37, 40, 41,
    43, 48
peasant society 31, 33, 34, 35, 36,
    37, 38, 39, 40, 41, 42, 44,
    45, 48
Peasants Subsistence Production
    Economy 38
peasant subsistence economy 29
Permanent Land Settlement
    Act 336
perverse subsidies 190, 191
petty bourgeoisies 336
PKSF 343, 348
planet 116, 188, 193, 196, 292,
    366, 368, 369, 375, 377
plantation economy 31
Polarization of Peasants in
    Bangladesh 46
political mobilization 235, 351,
    352, 353, 354, 356
poverty 1, 2, 4, 5, 7, 10, 11, 14, 17,
    21, 28, 29, 30, 84, 85, 90,
    102, 103, 104, 105, 106, 107,
    108, 114, 177, 178, 180, 181,
    191, 197, 198, 199, 200, 204,
    205, 208, 211, 212, 213, 214,
    216, 217, 218, 219, 221, 225,
    226, 228, 231, 232, 236,

www.ingramcontent.com/pod-product-compliance
Lightning Source LLC
Chambersburg PA
CBHW020718180526
45163CB00001B/19